THE MOTORCYLE YEARBOOK
2008

CHRONOSPORTS
EDITEUR

ISBN 978-2-84707-155-9
Also available in French **ISBN 978-84707-148-1** and in German **ISBN 978-2-84707-160-3**

© **NOVEMBER 2008, CHRONOSPORTS S.A** - Vergnolet Parc, CH-1070 Puidoux, Suisse.
Tél: +41 (0) 21 694 24 44 - Fax: +41 (0) 21 694 24 46 - Email: info@chronosports.com - www.chronosports.com

COORDINATION & PAGE LAYOUT - Loraine Lequint Elsig **CONCEPTION** - Patricia Soler

PRINTED BY IMPRIMERIE CLERC - 18206 St-Amand Montrond, France.

BOUND BY RELIURES BRUN - 45331 Malesherbes Cedex, France.

THE MOTORCYLE YEARBOOK

2008

PHOTOS Stan Perec Lukasz Swiderek
THANKS TO Nello Zoppe (Nikon France) for his valued
TEXTS Jean-Claude Schertenleib
TRANSLATION Stuart Sykes

CONTENTS

CALENDAR 2009

April 12	Qatar	Losail-Doha	**August 16**	Czech Republic	Brno
April 26	Japan	Motegi	**August 30**	Indianapolis	Indianapolis
May 3	Spain	Jerez de la Frontera	**September 9**	San Marino & Riviera di Rimini	Misano
May 17	France	Le Mans	**September 20**	Hungary	Balaton
May 31	Italy	Mugello	**October 3**	Portugal	Estoril
June 14	Catalunya	Catalunya	**October 18**	Australia	Phillip Island
June 27	Netherlands	Assen	**October 25**	Malaysia	Sepang
July 5	United States (*)	Laguna Seca	**November 8**	Valencia	Cheste-Valencia
July 19	Germany	Sachsenring			
July 26	Great Britain	Donington Park	(*): MotoGP only.		

Lukas Swiderek and Stan Perec,
the photographers of the
Motorcycle Yearbook

BARONS - RED AND BLUE

Dateline Jerez de la Frontera, early Spring 2008 : the IRTA tests, dress rehearsal for the World Championship, the time when they all come out thinking, « Yep, this will be my year... I've never been in better shape... and we've made so many technical improvements this winter... just wait and see ! »

Every year the same script, the same scenario - the same wilful blindness. And the same responsibility to the people who put up the money - and not just so they can listen to their bloke telling them his main aim this year is not to finish last. Some would have their work cut out in that regard, and some big names among them, but that's another story...

So where were we ? Dateline Jerez de la Frontera, early Spring 2008 : the IRTA tests. Just a few hours from now the hype will really start as motorcycle racing's premier class gets going again. What will be the trigger - a great shot, the first lap record, some other on-track sensation ? No, not yet. There's another reason why the world's media are about to discover a sudden passion for the little world we live in. Two major dailies, Switzerland's Le Matin and France's L'Equipe, have both dropped a Sunday bombshell : « Michael Schumacher to go bike racing! »

The red baron, the prince of modern F1 : on two wheels ? Not just hot air, either, it was absolutely true : the man who won everything there is to win, the man whose future is set in financial stone, was off looking for new challenges just to keep himself amused. It's a scoop that goes down well in the paddock, though instantly pooh-poohed in F1 circles : why would the superstar of the world's biggest show go paddling about in the mud and smelly oil that still seems to stick to motorcycle racing ?

But there you have it : Schumi thumbed his nose at all the nay-sayers, took up the challenge, liked life in the paddock, and was a quick learner, often to be seen in the German Superbike series - sometimes on the deck, but always smiling just the same. He even put in an appearance in a World Endurance Championship event, 'just for fun'.

So the retired Red Baron still had it in him. And at the same time the Blue Baron, the one we were so afraid was about to give up two wheels for four in F1, came back to remind us that you need to be having fun if you want to stay at the top.

This was the year when Valentino Rossi started winning again - because he was having fun. Mike Di Meglio opened up a bit - and became 125cc World Champion. And Marco Simoncelli was uncatchable in the 250s because his was the style of a man with nothing to lose.

What Schumi, Vale, Mike and Marco-the-Mane were telling us was this : all those millions, all the star treatment in the world don't mean a thing if you're just not enjoying what you do.

JEAN-CLAUDE SCHERTENLEIB

2008 MotoGP Worl

TEAMS | MOTO GP

OUT WENT SMALL-SCALE PROJECTS ILMOR AND KR AS THE GRID CONTINUED TO SHRINK IN QUANTITY DESPITE AN IMPROVEMENT IN QUALITY. MAJOR CHANGE : ROSSI'S SWITCH TO BRIDGESTONE AND ITS AFTERMATH, WHICH SAW THE FIAT YAMAHA TEAM SPLIT IN TWO. THE CLASS WELCOMED SOME BATTLE-HARDENED ROOKIES : THE TOP THREE IN THE 2007 250 CHAMPIONSHIP ALL MADE THE MOVE UP.

T he Desmosedici GP8 was an evolution of the 2007 Championship-winning machine, the Italian engineers having worked on every aspect of the bike. The new chassis was lighter and a lot of effort had gone into making it as rigid as possible, to counter problems with flexing. Also new was the rear suspension geometry. On the engine side the aim was to gain a bit more horsepower without adversely affecting consumption. The most significant change was quite an historic one : for the first time since the Desmosedici MotoGP campaign began, Loris Capirossi was no longer working with the Borgo Panigale team, replaced by Marco Melandri. As in 2007, *Luis D'Antin's team also had GP8 bikes, Bridgestone-shod, for Toni Elias and Sylvain Guintoli to work with.

DUCATI MARLBORO TEAM

Via Cavalieri Ducati 3, 40132 Bologne (Italia).
www.ducati.com

ORGANISATION CHART
General Director Ducati Corsica: Claudio Domenicali.
MotoGP Director: Livio Suppo.
Technical Director: Filippo Preziosi.
Technical Managers: Cristian Gabarrini (Casey Stoner)
and Cristhian Pupulin (Marco Melandri).

1 CASEY STONER

33 MARCO MELANDRI

RIDERS
Casey Stoner
Date of birth: 16th october 1985.
Place of birth: Kurri-Kurri/Gold Coast (Australia).
First race: 1989.
First GP: Great Britain, 2001 (125).
Number of GP victories: 23 (2/125; 5/250; 16/MotoGP).
First GP victory: Valencia, 2003 (125).
- Challenge Aprilia 125 RS Champion of Ausralia (2000).
- MotoGP World Champion (2007).

Marco Melandri
Date of birth: 7th August 1982 in Ravenna (Italia).
First race: 1989.
First GP: Czech Republic, 1997 (125).
Number of GP victories: 22 (7/125; 10/250; 5/MotoGP).
First GP victory: Netherlands, 1998 (125).
- BMX Italian Champion (1988).
- Minibike Junior A Italian Champion (1992).
- Minibike Junior B Italian Champion (1994).
- Italian Champion 125 (1997).
- Honda Trophy Champion Italia (1997).
- 250cc World Champion (2002).

ALICE TEAM

Poligono Industrial Gitesa, c/Ramon y Cajal 25, 28814 Algete, Madrid (Spain).
www.aliceteam.com

ORGANISATION CHART
General Director: Luis D'Antin (*).
Team manager: Paulo Campinotti.
Coordinator: Felix Rodriguez.
Chiefs mechanics: Fabiano Sterlacchini (Elias) and Sergio Verbena (Guintoli).

24 ANTONIO "TONI" ELIAS

50 SYLVAIN GUINTOLI

RIDERS
Antonio «Toni» Elias
Date of birth: 26th March 1983.
Place of birth: Manresa (Spain).
First race: 1997.
First GP: Spain, 1999 (125).
Number of GP victories: 10 (2/125; 7/250; 1/MotoGP).
First GP victory: Netherlands, 2001 (125).

Sylvain Guintoli
Date of birth: 24th June 1982.
Place of birth:: Montélimar (France).
First race: 1995.
First GP: France, 2000 (250).
- Scooter French Champion (1995).
- 250cc French Champion (2000).

(*): Luis D'Antin, who set up his own team back in 1999 while still an active 250cc rider, withdrew after the Dutch GP, officially for 'personal' reasons - which in fact masked enormous financial difficulties.

DUCATI MARLBORO TEAM

ALICE TEAM

Outclassed by European technology in 2007, the first year of the 800cc era, motorcycle big guns Honda had to hit back hard. From the first winter tests they brought out a new pneumatic valve engine for works riders Dani Pedrosa and Nicky Hayden. The Spaniard injured his hand badly and spent most of the close season carping about team-mate Hayden's development work. Honda picked up Randy De Puniet, with Lucio Cecchinello, added one from its own nursery in Andrea Dovizioso and hung on to Shinya Nakano, joining Fausto Gresini's team aongside another rookie in the shape of Alex De Angelis, that team staying loyal to Bridgestone.

REPSOL HONDA TEAM

European Office, Industriezone Noord V, Wijngaardveld 1c, 9300 Aalst (Belgium).
www.world.honda.com

ORGANISATION CHART
Team manager: Makoto Tanaka.
Coordinator: Roger Van der Borght.
Technical Chiefs: Mike Leitner (Daniel Pedrosa) and Pete Benson (Nicky Hayden).

2
DANIEL PEDROSA

69
NICKY HAYDEN

RIDERS
Daniel Pedrosa
Date of birth: 29th September 1985.
Place of birth: Castellar del Vallés (Spain).
First race: 1993.
First GP: Japan, 2001 (125).
Number of GP victories: 29 (8/125; 15/250; 6/MotoGP).
First GP victory: Netherlands, 2002 (125).
- Minibike Spanish Champion (1998).
- 125cc World Champion (2003).
- 250cc World Champion (2004).
- 250cc World Champion (2005).

Nicky Hayden
Date of birth: 30th July 1981.
Place of birth: Owensboro/Kentucky (USA).
First race: 1986.
First GP: Japan, 2003 (MotoGP).
Number of GP victories: 3 (MotoGP).
First GP victory: USA, 2005 (MotoGP).
- Supersport 600 American Champion (1999).
- Superbike America Champion (2002).
- MotoGP World Champion (2006).

JIR SCOT TEAM

JiR Scs Company, Place des Moulins, Le Continental B, 98000 Principauté de Monaco.
www.jir.it

ORGANISATION CHART
Team manager: Cirano Mularoni.
Director: Gianluca Montiron.
Technical Director: Gianni Berti.
Chief mechanic: Pietro Caprara.

4
ANDREA DOVIZIO

RIDER
Andrea Dovizioso
Date of birth: 23rd March 1986.
Place of birth: Forlimpopoli (Italia).
First race: 1994.
First GP: Italie, 2001 (125).
Number of GP victories: 9 (5/125; 4/250).
First GP victory: South Africa, 2004 (125).
- Pocket Bike Junior B Italian Champion (1997 and 1998).
- Vainqueur du Challenge Aprilia Italie (2000).
- 125cc European Champion (2001).
- 125cc World Champion (2004).

REPSOL HONDA TEAM

JIR SCOT TEAM

LCR HONDA MOTOGP

LCR-X Racing, S.A. M., Gildo Pastor Center, 7 rue du Gabian, 98000 Monaco.
www.hondalcr.com

ORGANISATION CHART
Team manager: Lucio Cecchinello
Technical Chief: Christophe Bourguignon.

14
RANDY DE PUNIET

RIDER
Randy De Puniet
Date of birth: 14th February 1981.
Place of birth: Andrésy (France).
First race: 1987.
First GP: France, 1998 (125).
Number of GP victories: 5 (250).
First GP victory: Catalunya, 2003 (250).
- Typhoon Cup French Winner (1995).
- Promosport 125cc French Champion (1997).
- 125cc French "national" Champion (1997).
- 125cc French Champion (1998).

SAN CARLO HONDA GRESINI

Gresini Racing S.R.L., via Mengolina 18, 48018 Faenza (Italia).
www.gresiniracing.com

ORGANISATION CHART
Team manager: Fausto Gresini.
Technical Director: Fabrizio Cecchini
Chiefs mechanics: Fabrizio Cecchini (Alex De Angelis) and
Antonio Jimenez (Shinya Nakano).

15
ALEX DE ANGELIS

56
SHINYA NAKANO

RIDERS
Alex De Angelis
Date of birth: 26th February 1984.
Place of birth: Rimini (Italia).
First race: 1995.
First GP: Imola, 1999 (125).
Number of GP victories: 1 (250).
First GP victory: Valencia, 2006 (250).

Shinya Nakano
Date of birth: 10th October 1977.
Place of birth: Chiba Prefecture (Japan).
First race: 1982.
First GP: Japan, 1998 (250).
Number of GP victories: 6 (250).
First GP victory: Japan, 1999 (250).
- 250cc Japanese Champion (1998).

LCR HONDA MOTOGP

SAN CARLO HONDA GRESINI

« The best Yamaha ever built, » said the smiling faces in the two teams putting M1s on the grid, even before the season got under way. The Japanese engineers rose to the challenge of a trying 2007 by reducing the power gap to the Ducatis and making theirs perhaps the best-balanced bike out there in the early part of the year. Not only that, but to drive development Yamaha now had a satellite team in Tech 3, whose performances no longer hinged on their tyre supplier as Colin Edwards and new arrival James Toseland were now on Michelins. Tyres, in fact, were the big news of the close season, with Rossi demanding - successfully - a move to Bridgestone, which meant the works Fiat team was now one of two distinct halves. One of them welcomed a gifted rookie, the man who had taken the 250cc title for the past two years, Jorge Lorenzo, who was to provide one of the major talking-points as the season got going.

FIAT YAMAHA TEAM

Yamaha Motor Racing SRL, Via Tinelli 67/69, 20050 Gerno di Lesmo (Italia).
www.yamahamotogp.com

ORGANISATION CHART
Team managers: Davide Brivio (Valentino Rossi) and Daniele Romagnoli (Jorge Lorenzo).
Director: Masahiko Nakajima.
Technical Managers: Jeremy Burgess (Valentino Rossi) and Ramon Forcada (Jorge Lorenzo).

46 VALENTINO ROSSI   48 JORGE LORENZO

RIDERS
Valentino Rossi
Date of birth: 16th February 1979.
Place of birth: Urbino/Pesaro (Italia).
First race: 1992.
First GP: Malaysia, 1996 (125).
Number of GP victories: 97 (12/125; 14/250; 13/500; 58/MotoGP).
First GP victory: Czech Republic, 1996 (125).
- Endurance Minibike Italian Champion (1992).
- 125cc Sport-Production Italian Champion (1994).
- 125cc GP Italian Champion (1995).
- 125cc World Champion (1997).
- 250cc World Champion (1999).
- 500cc World Champion (2001).
- MotoGP World Champion (2002)
- MotoGP World Champion (2003)
- MotoGP World Champion (2004)
- MotoGP World Champion (2005)
- MotoGP World Champion (2008)

Jorge Lorenzo
Date of birth: 4th May 1987.
Place of birth: Palma de Mallorca (Spain).
First race: 1990.
First GP: Spain, 2002 (125).
Number of GP victories: 22 (4/125; 17/250; 1/MotoGP).
First GP victory: Rio, 2003 (125).
- 250cc World Champion (2006).
- 250cc World Champion (2007).

YAMAHA TECH 3

635, chemin du Niel, 83230 Bormes-les-Mimosas (France).
www.yamaha-racing.com

ORGANISATION CHART
Team manager: Hervé Poncharal.
Coordinator: Gérard Vallée.
Chiefs mechanics: Guy Coulon (James Toseland) and Gary Reynders (Colin Edwards).

5 COLIN EDWARDS   52 JAMES TOSELAND

RIDERS
Colin Edwards
Date of birth: 27th February 1974.
Place of birth: Conroe/Texas (USA).
First race: 1990.
First GP: Japan, 2003 (MotoGP).
- 250cc American Champion (1992).
- Superbike World Champion (2000).
- Superbike World Champion (2002).

James Toseland
Date of birth: 5th October 1980.
Place of birth: Doncaster (Great Britain).
First race: 1988.
First GP: Qatar, 2008 (MotoGP).
- Superbike World Champion (2004).
- Superbike World Champion (2007).

FIAT YAMAHA TEAM

YAMAHA TECH 3

RIZLA SUZUKI MOTOGP

Pneumatic distribution, fuel injection… in the first season of the 800cc era Suzuki were already using cutting-edge technology. Honda themselves would not give Nicky Hayden a pneumatic distribution system to try out until after the Catalunya race. The major change to Paul Denning's outfit was the arrival of class veteran Loris Capirossi in place of John Hopkins. The American had been seduced by the siren song from Kawasaki, the green team whose colours match the dollar's…

Crescent Suzuki Performance Centre, 23 Black Moor Road, Ebblake Ind. Est.,
BH31 6AX Verwood (Great Britain).
www.suzuki-motogp.com

ORGANISATION CHART
Team manager: Paul Denning.
Technical Director: Shinichi Sahara,
Engineers: Stuart Shenton (John Hopkins)
and Tom O'Kane (Chris Vermeulen).

7
CHRIS VERMEULEN

65
LORIS CAPIROSSI

RIDERS
Geoffrey «Chris» Vermeulen
Date of birth: 19th June 1982.
Place of birth: Brisbane (Australia).
First race: 1994.
First GP: Australia, 2005 (MotoGP).
Number of GP victories: 1 (MotoGP).
First GP victory: France, 2007 (MotoGP).
- Supersport World Champion (2003).

Loris Capirossi
Date of birth: 4th April 1973
Place of birth: Bologna (Italia).
First race: 1987.
First GP: Japan, 1990 (125).
Number of GP victories: 29 (8/125; 12/250; 2/500; 7/MotoGP).
First GP victory: Great Britain, 1990 (125).
- 125cc World Champion (1990).
- 125cc World Champion (1991).
- 250cc World Champion (1998).

KAWASAKI RACING TEAM

Continuity is not Kawasaki's long suit : a year after the shake-up that ended their collaboration with Harald Eckl, boss of the MotoGP program from the outset, they had now changed their number one rider. Randy De Puniet had been politely shown the door, to be replaced by John Hopkins. After spending his career to date with Suzuki, the American quickly found out that the Ninja was no easy beast to master. Anthony West, recruited midway through 2007, was kept on. His place in the team would come under question several times before the halfway stage, though he managed to avoid the axe.

Kawasaki Racing Team
Sourethweg 10, 6422 PC Heerlen (Netherlands).
www.kawasaki-motogp.com

ORGANISATION CHART
General Director: Yoshio Kanamura.
Motorsport Director: Ichiro Yoda.
Team manager: Michael Bartholemy
Technical Chiefs: Juan Martinez (Anthony West) and
Fiorenzo Fanali (John Hopkins).

13
ANTHONY WEST

21
JOHN HOPKINS

RIDERS
Anthony West
Date of birth: 17th July 1981.
Place of birth: Mayborough (Australia).
First race: 1997.
First GP: Australia, 1998 /125).
Number of GP victories: 1 (250).
First GP victory: Netherlands, 2003 (250).
- 125cc Australian Champion (1998),
- 250cc Production Australian Champion (1998).

John Hopkins
Date of birth: 22nd May 1983.
Place of birth: Ramona/California (USA).
First race: 1987.
First GP: Japan, 2002 (MotoGP).
- 250cc Challenge Aprilia RS American Champion (1999).
- Supersport 750 American Champion (2000).
- Formule Xtreme American Champion (2001).

RIZLA SUZUKI MOTOGP

KAWASAKI RACING TEAM

2008 MotoGP World Champ

onship

TEAMS | 250cc

WITH TWO-STROKE TECHNOLOGY DUE TO BE LAID TO REST IN LATE 2010, THE JAPANESE HAVE TURNED THEIR BACK ON THE CLASS. HONDA HAD A HALF-HEARTED PRESENCE, WITH YUKI TAKAHASHI, OTHERWISE IT WAS AN ALL-EUROPEAN AFFAIR, NOT JUST WITH BIG GUNS PIAGGIO (APRILIA AND GILERA), BUT ALSO KTM, WHO SUPPLIED A SATELLITE TEAM FOR THE FIRST TIME IN THE CLASS. AND LET'S NOT FORGET THERE WAS ONE YAMAHA THERE FOR THE WHOLE SEASON…

ate-season success in 2007 had sharpened KTM's appetite, and just as well. With Honda neglecting both two-stroke classes, Alberto Puig's Repsol team had also opted to go with the Austrian brand. That meant Julian Simon would be on the same 250FRR as works KTM riders Kallio and Aoyama. The bike had undergone further improvement : during winter testing Kallio in particular showed superior speed to the best of the Piaggio (i.e. Aprilia and Gilera) riders.

RED BULL KTM 250

Stallhofnerstrasse 3, 5230 Mattighofen (Austria).
www.ktm.at

ORGANISATION CHART
Technical Director: Harald Bartol.
Coordinator: Francesco Guidotti.
Technical Manager: Mario Galeotti.

RIDERS

Hiroshi Aoyama
Date of birth: 25th October 1981.
Place of birth: Chiba (Japan).
First race: 1999.
First GP: Pacific, 2000 (250).
Number of GP victories: 5 (250).
First GP victory: Japan, 2005 (250).

Mika Kallio
Date of birth: 8th November 1982.
Place of birth: Valkeakoski (Finland).
First race: 1997.
First GP: Germany, 2001 (125).
Number of GP victories: 12 (7/125; 5/250).
First GP victory: Portugal, 2005 (125).

4 | 36
HIROSHI AOYAMA | MIKA KALLIO

REPSOL KTM 250

Repsol KTM 250
Ctra. D'Engolasters 53, Edif. 3, àtic 2, AS700 Escaldes Engordany
(Principality of Andorra).
www.repsolmedia.com

ORGANISATION CHART
Team manager: Jaume Colom.
Technical Director: Raul Jarà.
Chief mechanics: Guido Cecchini (Julian Simón).

RIDER

Julian Simón
Date of birth: 3rd April 1987.
Place of birth: Villacañas (Spain).
First race: 1993.
First GP: Spain, 2002 (125).
Number of GP victories: 1 (125).
First GP victory: Great Britain, 2005 (125).
- Motocross 50 Spanish Champion (1997).

60
JULIAN SIMÓN

RED BULL KTM 250

REPSOL KTM 250

With factory RSA's for Alex Debon, who had swapped his test rider role for a place with Jorge Lorenzo's double title-winning team, and for Barbera, Bautista and Luthi, as well as new arrival in the category Pasini, Aprilia had plenty of strings to its bow. The Italian factory also made some useful LE models (the works RSW of the previous year) available to the likes of Czech duo Abraham and Pesek and 125cc runner-up Hector Faubel. Brand engineer Gigi Dall'Igna pressed on with the development of a top-class bike, coming up with an electronic anti-wheelspin control system at the French GP, where Debon got to grips with the new technology best.

LOTUS APRILIA

Motorsport 48, La Barca 5-7, 08107 Martorelles/Barcelona (Spain).
www.belsonderbi.com

ORGANISATION CHART
Team manager: Dani Amatriain.
Technical Director: Massimo Capanna.
Chiefs mechanics: Massimo Capanna (Alex Debón) and
Quique Quijal (Aleix Espargaró).

6
ALEX DEBÓN

41
ALEIX ESPARGARÓ

RIDERS

Alex Debón
Date of birth: 1st March 1976.
Place of birth: Vall d'Uixó (Spain).
First race: 1992.
First GP: Madrid, 1998 (250).
Number of GP victories: 2.(250).
First GP victory: France, 2008 (250).
- 250cc Spanish Champion (2001).

Aleix Espargaró
Date of birth: 30th July 1989.
Place of birth: Barcelone (Spain).
First race: 2001.
First GP: Valencia, 2004 (125).
- 125cc Catalunyian Champion (2003).
- 125cc Spanish Champion (2004).

EMMI - CAFFÈ LATTE

Paddock, s.r.o , Pucova 691/11, 15800 Praha 5 (Czech Republic).
www.paddock-gp-racing.com

ORGANISATION CHART
Team manager Daniel M. Epp.
Coordinator: Thien Terrell.
Chief mechanics: Mauro Noccioli (Thomas Lüthi).

12
THOMAS LÜTHI

RIDER

Thomas Lüthi
Date of birth: 6th September 1986.
Place of birth: Linden (Switzerland).
First race: 1997.
First GP: Germany, 2002 (125).
Number of GP victories: 5 (125).
First GP victory: France, 2005 (125).
- Pocket-Bike Junior A Swiss Champion (1999).
- Pocket-Bike Junior B Swiss Champion (2000).
- 125cc World Champion (2005).

LOTUS APRILIA

EMMI - CAFFÈ LATTE

BLUSENS APRILIA

c/Mestre Nicolau 6, Nave 3 Poligono Industrial Sud, 08440 Cardedeu/Barcelona (Spain).
www.teambqr.com

ORGANISATION CHART
Team manager: Raúl Romero.
Technical Director: Ricard Jové.
Chiefs mechanics: Andreu Viudez (Russel Gomez) and Christian Lundberg (Eugene Laverty).

7
RUSSEL GOMEZ

50
EUGENE LAVERTY

RIDERS
Russel Gomez
Date of birth: 17th November 1987.
Place of birth: Barcelona (Spain).
First race: 2003.
First GP: Portugal, 2008 (250).
- Supersport Catalunyian Champion (2006).

Eugene Laverty
Date of birth: 3rd June 1986.
Place of birth: Ballymena (Ireland).
First race: 2001.
First GP: Great Britain, 2004 (125).

TEAM TOTH

Foti ùt 055 Hrsz, 2120 Dunakeszi (Hungary).
www.teamtoth.com

ORGANISATION CHART
Team manager: Imre Toth Senior.
Technical Director: Rossano Brazzi.
Chiefs mechanics: Giuseppe Galante (Imre Toth) and Rossano Brazzi (Hector Barberá).

10
IMRE TOTH

21
HECTOR BARBERÁ

RIDERS
Imre Toth
Date of birth: 6th September 1985.
Place of birth: Budapest (Hungary).
First race: 2000.
First GP: Japan, 2002 (125).

Hector Barberá
Date of birth: 2nd November 1986.
Place of birth: Dos Aguas/Valencia (Spain).
First race: 1995.
First GP: Japan, 2002 (125).
Number of GP victories: 7 (6/125; 1/250).
First GP victory: Great Britain, 2003 (125).
- Aprilia Cup 125cc Spanish Champion (2001).
- 125cc Spanish Champion (2002).

MATTEONI RACING

Moto Racing Team Matteoni, Via Bandi 5, 47814 Bellaria (Italia).

ORGANISATION CHART
Team manager: Massimo Matteoni.

25
ALEX BALDOLINI

RIDER
Alex Baldolini
Date of birth: 24tg January 1985.
Place of birth: Cesena (Italia).
First race: 1994.
First GP: Italia, 2000 (125).

BLUSENS APRILIA

TEAM TOTH

MATTEONI RACING

MAPFRE ASPAR

Plaza Sociedad Musical no 8, 46600 Alzira (Valencia), Spain.
www.teamaspar.com

ORGANISATION CHART
Team manager: Jorge «Aspar» Martinez.
Sporting Director: Gino Borsoi.
Chiefs mechanics: Andrea Orlandi (Alvaro Bautistá) and
Enrique Peris (Hector Faubel).

RIDERS
Alvaro Bautistá
Date of birth: 21st November 1984.
Place of birth: Talavera de la Reina (Spain).
First race: 1993.
First GP: Spain, 2002 (125).
Number of victories: 14 (8/125; 6/250).
First GP victory: Spain, 2006 (125).
- 125cc Spanish Champion (2003).
- 125cc World Champion (2006).

Hector Faubel
Date of birth: 10th August 1983.
Place of birth: Lliria (Spain).
First race: 1993.
First GP: Spain, 2000 (125).
Number of victories: 7 (125).
First GP victory: Turkey, 2006 (125).
- Aprilia Cup 125cc Winner, Spain (1998).
- 250cc Spanish Champion (2002).

19 ALVARO BAUTISTÁ

55 HECTOR FAUBEL

CARDION AB MOTORACING

Joukalova 13, Brno GB5 00 (Czech Republic).
www.abmotoracing.com

ORGANISATION CHART
Owner: Karel Abraham Senior.
Team manager: Zuzana Ulmanova.
Chief mechanics: Didier Langouët.

RIDER
Karel Abraham
Date of birth: 2nd January 1990.
Place of birth: Brno (Czech Republic).
First race: 2001.
First GP: Spain, 2005 (125).

17 KAREL ABRAHAM

MAPFRE ASPAR

CARDION AB MOTORACING

AUTO KELLY CP

Paddock, s.r.o , Pucova 691/11, 15800 Praha 5 (Czech Republic).
www.paddock-gp-racing.com

ORGANISATION CHART
Team manager: Daniel-M. Epp.
Coordinator: Terrell Thien.
Chief mechanics: Tommaso Loreto Raponi (Lukas Pesek).

RIDER
Lukas Pesek
Date of birth: 22nd November 1985.
Place of birth: Praha (Czech Republic).
First race: 2000.
First GP: Czech Republic, 2002 (125).
Number of GP victories: 2 (125).
First GP victory: China, 2007 (125).

52
LUKAS PESEK

POLARIS WORLD

Parque Empresarial Polaris World, Autovia Murcia-San Javier, Km 18, 30591
Balsicas-Murcia (Spain).
www.polarisworld.com

ORGANISATION CHART
General Director: Jose Maria De la Puerta.
Team manager: Roger Marcaccini.
Chief mechanics: Giovanni Sandi (Mattia Pasini).

RIDER
Mattia Pasini
Date of birth: 13th August 1985.
Place of birth: Rimini (Italia).
First race: 1994.
First GP: South Africa, 2004 (125).
Number of GP victories: 9 (8/125; 1/250).
- Minibike Junior B Italian Champion (1996).

75
MATTIA PASINI

AUTO KELLY CP

POLARIS WORLD

Honda had called a halt to its two-stroke development in response to an ever-shrinking market, particularly for 250cc machines. That left the representatives of the world's biggest manufacturer looking like absolute dinosaurs ; even Alberto Puig got the message and took himself elsewhere, i.e. to KTM. So there were just two Honda RS250RW's there at the start of the season, in the hands of Japan's Yuki Takahashi for Gianluca Montiron, and Thai rider Ratthapark Wilairot.

JIR SCOT TEAM

JiR Scs Company, Place des Moulins, Le Continental B,
98000 Principality of Monaco.
www.jir.it

ORGANISATION CHART
Team manager: Cirano Mularoni.
Director: Gianluca Montiron.
Technical Director: Gianni Berti.
Chief mechanics: Yutaka Hirano.

RIDER
Yuki Takahashi
Date of birth: 12th July 1984.
Place of birth: Saitama (Japan).
First race: 1991.
First GP: Pacific, 2001 (125).
Number of GP victories: 2 (250).
First GP victory: France, 2006 (250).
- 250cc Japanese Champion (2004).

72
YUKI TAKAHASHI

THAI HONDA PTT SAG

Calle Cadi 6, 08272 Sant Fruitos de Bages, Barcelona (Spain).
www.thaihondapttsag.com

ORGANISATION CHART
Owner: Eduardo Perales.
Coordinator: Père Flores.
Chief mechanics: Arnau Vidal (Ratthapark Wilairot).

RIDER
Ratthapark Wilairot
Date of birth: 14th April 1988.
Place of birth: Chonburi (Thailand).
First race: 2003.
First GP: Japan, 2006 (250).

14
RATTHAPARK WILAIROT

Yamaha were back on the 250cc scene by way of their Indonesian distributors, who had been supporting Doni Tata Pradita for several seasons after finding him on a 125 in Malaysia in 2005. In charge was German Dieter Stappert, but sadly the legendary guiding-hand behind Bradl Senior, Roth and Waldmann suffered serious health problems on the eve of practice for the British GP.

YAMAHA PERTAMINA INDONESIA

www.yamahapertaminaindonesia.com

ORGANISATION CHART
Team manager: Dieter Stappert.

RIDER
Doni Tata Pradita
Date of birth: 21st January 1990.
Place of birth: Jogjakarta (Indonesia).
First race: 2003.
First GP: Malaysia, 2005 (125).

45
DONI TATA PRADITA

JIR SCOT TEAM

THAI HONDA PTT SAG

YAMAHA PERTAMINA INDONESIA

METIS GILERA

Corso Sempione 43, 20145 Milano (Italia).

ORGANISATION CHART
Sporting Director: Giampiero Sacchi.
Technical Director: Luigi Dall'Igna.
Team manager: Luca Boscoscuro.
Technical Chief: Aligi Deganello.

15
ROBERTO LOCATELLI

58
MARCO SIMONCELLI

RIDERS
Roberto Locatelli
Date of birth: 5th July 1974
Place of birth: Bergamo (Italia).
First race: 1989.
First GP: Italia, 1994 (125).
Number of GP victories: 9 (125).
First GP victory: France, 1999 (125).
- Enduro Novice 50 Italian Champion (1990).
- Enduro Novice 80 Italian Champion (1991).
- 125 Sport-Production Italian Champion (1993).
- 125cc World Champion (2000).

Marco Simoncelli
Date of birth: 20th January 1987.
Place of birth: Cattolica (Italia).
First race: 1996.
First GP: Czech Republic, 2002 (125).
Number of GP victories: 8 (2/125; 6/250).
First GP victory: Spain, 2004 (125).
- Minimoto Italian Champion (1999 et 2000).
- 125cc European Champion (2002).
- 250cc World Champion (2008).

CAMPETELLA RACING

Via de Gasperi n. 74, 62010 Montecassiano (Italia).
www.campetella.it

ORGANISATION CHART
Team manager: Eros Braconi.
Technical Director: Eros Braconi.

32
FABRIZIO LAI

54
MANUEL POGGIALI

RIDERS
Fabrizio Lai
Date of birth: 14th December 1978.
Place of birth: Rho (Italia).
First race: 1994.
First GP: Valencia, 2001 (125).
- Minibike European Champion (1996 et 1997).
- Honda Trophy Italian Champion (1999).
- 125cc Italian Champion (2002).

Manuel Poggiali
Date of birth: 14th February 1983.
Place of birth: Chiesa Nuova (Republic of San Marino).
First race: 1994.
First GP: Imola, 1998 (125).
Number of GP victories: 12 (7/125; 5/250).
First GP victory: France, 2001 (125).
- Minibike Italian Champion (1997).
- 125cc Italian Champion (1998).
- Honda Trophy Italian Champion125 (1998).
- 125cc World Champion (2001).
- 250cc World Champion (2003).

METIS GILERA

CAMPETELLA RACING

2008 MotoGP World Champion

TEAMS | 125cc

ANOTHER ALL-EUROPEAN DOMAIN, CENTRED ON THE PIAGGIO GROUP, WHICH WAS STREETS AHEAD THANKS TO ITS TWO MAKES, DERBI - TITLE-WINNERS WITH MIKE DI MEGLIO - AND, OF COURSE, APRILIA. AS THE RIDERS' AGES CONTINUED THEIR DOWNWARD SPIRAL, SOME PROMISING 'BABYFACES' STEPPED UP, NOTABLY SCOTT REDDING AND MARC MARQUEZ.

Piaggio's Spanish arm had doubled its quota with four riders on Derbi-branded RSA's and RSW's. Most notable among them was the experienced Mike Di Meglio, much more at ease in the team run by Finn Aki Ajo, the man who discovered Mika Kallio. The move came about thanks to financial backing from carfashion.ch, a brand belonging to Swiss group Métraux, set up by IRTA's much-missed first president. Swiss rider Dominique Aegerter was also drafted in alongside Di Meglio. Belson also backed experience in the shape of Olive in tandem with youth - Pol Espargaro, the latest diamond to be polished by Dani Amatriain.

BELSON DERBI

Motorsport 48, La Barca 5-7, 08107 Martorelles/Barcelona (Spain).
www.belsonderbi.com

ORGANISATION CHART
Team manager: Dani Amatriain.
Technical Director: Stefano Riminucci.
Chiefs mechanics: Fabio Protti (Joan Olivé) and Alfio Tosi (Pol Espargaró).

RIDERS
Joan Olivé
Date of birth: 22nd November 1984.
Place of birth: Tarragona (Spain).
First race: 1992.
First GP: Japan, 2001 (125).
- 50cc Spanish Champion (1998).
- Joven Cup 125 Spanish Champion (1999).
- 125cc Spanish Champion (2000).

Pol Espargaró
Date of birth: 10th June 1991.
Place of birth: Granollers (Spain).
First race: 2000.
First GP: Catalunya, 2006 (125).
- 125cc Catalunyian Champion (2004).
- 125cc Spanish Champion (2006).

6 JOAN OLIVÉ

44 POL ESPARGARÓ

AJO MOTORSPORT

Hämeentie 20, 37800 Toijala (Finland).
www.ajo.fi

ORGANISATION CHART
Team manager: Aki Ajo.
Telemetry: Stefan Kurfis.
Chiefs mechanics: Aki Ajo (Mike Di Meglio)
and Stefan Fuhrer (Dominique Aegerter).

RIDERS
Mike Di Meglio
Date of birth: 17th January 1988.
Place of birth: Toulouse (France).
First race: 2001.
First GP: Japan, 2003 (125).
Number of GP victories: 5 (125).
First GP victory: Turkey, 2005 (125).
- 50cc French Champion (2000).
- Conti Cup 50 French Champion (2001).
- 125cc World Champion (2008).

Dominique Aegerter
Date of birth: 30th September 1990.
Place of birth: Rohrbach (Switzerland).
First race: 1995.
First GP: Portugal, 2006 (125).
- Motocross Kid 60 Swiss Champion (1999).

63 MIKE DI MEGLIO

77 DOMINIQUE AEGERTER

BELSON DERBI

AJO MOTORSPORT

Was there all that much difference, performance-wise, between the RSA - the 2008 model - and the RSW, the two options the Piaggio group had on offer for teams in the class ? Everyone will have their own view, and some gave theirs with a smile : « The big difference, » they said, « is 100,000 Euros - the price gap between the two. » The truth of it is that while the RSA did seem to work better, some teams did pretty well with the RSW. Among the top riders outgoing champion Gabor Talmacsi stuck with the class for another year as we welcomed a new generation of young Turks out to make a name for themselves, such as Britain's Scott Redding and German Stefan Bradl.

BANCAJA ASPAR

Plaza Sociedad Musical no 8, 46600 Alzira (Valencia), Spain.
www.teamaspar.com

ORGANISATION CHART
Team manager: Jorge «Aspar» Martinez.
Sporting Director: Gino Borsoi.
Technical Directors: Mauricio Soli (Gabor Talmacsi), Jose Manuel Ruiz (Sergio Gadea) and Alberto Bernardi (Pere Tutusaus, then Adrián Martin).

RIDERS
Gabor Talmacsi
Date of birth: 28th May 1981.
Place of birth: Budapest (Hungary).
First race: 1986.
First GP: Czech Republic, 1997 (125).
Number of GP victories: 9 (125).
First GP victory: Italia, 2005 (125).
- 125cc Hungarian Champion (1999).
- 125cc World Champion (2007).

Pere Tutusaus
Date of birth: 19th October 1990.
Place of birth: Igualada (Spain).
First race: 1998.
First GP: Valencia, 2005 (125).

Sergio Gadea
Date of birth: 30th December 1984.
Place of birth: Puzol (Spain).
First race: 2001.
First GP: Spain, 2003 (125).
Number of GP victories: 2 (125).

1
GABOR TALMACSI

30
PERE TUTUSAUS

33
SERGIO GADEA

BLUSENS APRILIA JUNIOR

c/Mestre Nicolau 6, Nave 3 Poligono Industrial Sud, 08440 Cardedeu/Barcelona (Spain).
www.teambqr.com

ORGANISATION CHART
Team manager: Raúl Romero.
Technica Director: Ricard Jové.
Chiefs mechanics: Andreu Viudez (Efrén Vazquez) and Christian Lundberg (Scott Redding).

RIDERS
Efrén Vazquez Rodriguez
Date of birth: 2nd August 1986.
Place of birth: Bilbao (Spain).
First race: 1994.
First GP: Great Britain, 2007 (125).
- 125cc Criterium Spanish Champion (2001).

Scott Redding
Date of birth: 15th January 1993.
Place of birth: Quedgeley/Gloucestershire (Great Britain).
First race: 2005.
First GP: Qatar, 2008 (125).
Number of GP victories: 1 (125).
First GP victory: Great Britain, 2008 (125).
- Metrakit Cup Winner (2005).

7
EFRÉN VAZQUEZ RODRIGUEZ

45
SCOTT REDDING

EMMI-CAFFÈ LATTE

Paddock, s.r.o , Pucova 691/11, 15800 Praha 5 (Czech Republic).
www.paddock-gp-racing.com

ORGANISATION CHART
Team manager: Daniel-M. Epp.
Coordinator: Thien Terrell.
Chief mechanics: Mario Martini (Sandro Cortese).

RIDER
Sandro Cortese
Date of birth: 6th January 1990.
Place of birth: Ochsenhausen (Germany).
First race: 1997.
First GP: Spain, 2005 (125).
- Pocket Bike Junior A European Champion (1999).
- Minibike German Champion (2002).

11
SANDRO CORTESE

BANCAJA ASPAR

BLUSENS APRILIA JUNIOR

EMMI-CAFFÈ LATTE

GRIZZLY GAS KIEFER RACING

Kiefer Racing GmbH & Co. KG, Zur Rothheck 12, 55743 Idar Oberstein (Germany).
www.kiefer-racing.com

ORGANISATION CHART
Team managers: Stefan et Jochen Kiefer.
Technical Director: Jürgen Lingg.
Technical Managers: Jürgen Lingg (Stefan Bradl), Luciani Calosi (Robin Lässer)
and Ralf Waldmann (Robert Muresan).

RIDERS
Stefan Bradl
Date of birth: 22nd November 1989.
Place of birth: Zahling (Germany).
First race: 2003.
First GP: Catalunya, 2005 (125).
Number of GP victories: 2 (125).
First GP victory: Czech Republic, 2008 (125).
- 125cc German Champion (2005).
- 125cc Spanish Champion (2007).

Robin Lässer
Date of birth: 12th January 199.
Place of birth: Isny (Germany).
First race: 1998.
First GP: Germany, 2006 (125).
- Pocket Bike Junior German Champion (2000).
- Pocket Bike German Champion (2002).
- Minibike German Champion (2004).
- 125cc German Champion (2006).

Robert Muresan
Date of birth: 22nd March 1991
Place of birth: Arad (Romania).
First race: 1998.
First GP: Turkey, 2006 (125).
- Pocket Bike Classe III Romanian Champion (2001).
- 125cc Romanian Champion (2003).
- 125cc Champion of the Baltic (2004).

17 STEFAN BRADL **21** ROBIN LÄSSER **95** ROBERT MURESAN

JACK & JONES WRB

Calle Acústica 16, Poligono Industrial Santa Rita, ES08755 Castellbisbal (Spain).

ORGANISATION CHART
Team manager: Manuel Burillo.
Sporting Director: Josep Crivillé.
Chiefs mechanics: Santiago Mulero (Nicolas Terol)
and Italo Fontana (Simone Corsi).

RIDERS
Nicolás Terol
Date of birth: 27th September 1988.
Place of birth: Alcoy/Alicante (Spain).
First race: 2000.
First GP: Valencia, 2004 (125).
Number of GP victories: 1 (125).
First GP victory: Indianapolis, 2008 (125).

Simone Corsi
Date of birth: 24th April 1987.
Place of birth: Roma (Italia).
First race: 1994.
First GP: Italia, 2002 (125).
Number of GP victories: 5 (125).
First GP victory: Turkey, 2007 (125).

18 NICOLÁS TEROL **24** SIMONE CORSI

GRIZZLY GAS KIEFER RACING

JACK & JONES WRB

WTR SAN MARINO TEAM

Piazza E. Enriquez 12, 47891 Dogana (San Marino).
www.wtr-team.com
ORGANISATION CHART
Owner: Loris Castellucci.
Team manager: Matteo Napolitano.

27 STEFANO BIANCO

48 BASTIEN CHESAUX

RIDERS
Stefano Bianco
Date of birth: 27th October 1985.
Place of birth: Chivasso (Italia).
First race: 1997.
First GP: Australia, 2000 (125).

Bastien Chesaux
Date of birth: 2nd November 1991.
Place of birth: Belmont-sur-Lausanne (Switzerland).
First race: 2006.
First GP: Germany, 2008 (125).

I.C. TEAM

Worldwide Communication sàrl, 43 route d'Arlon, 8009 Strassen (Luxemburg).
www.worldwidegroup.net

ORGANISATION CHART
General Director: Fiorenzo Caponera.
Technical Director: Alessandro Tognelli.

29 ANDREA IANNONE

60 MICHAEL RANSEDER

73 TAKAAKI NAKAGAMI

RIDERS
Andrea Iannone
Date of birth: 9th August 1989.
Place of birth: Vasto (Italia).
First race: 1996.
First GP: Spain, 2005 (125).
Number of GP victories: 1 (125).
First GP victory: China, 2008 .

Michael Ranseder
Date of birth: 7th April 1986.
Place of birth: Schärding (Austria).
First race: 1993.
First GP: Czech Rep., 2004 (125).
- 125cc German Champion (2004).

Takaaki Nakagami
Date of birth: 9th February 1992.
Place of birth: Chiba (Japan).
First race: 1996.
First GP: Valencia, 2007 (125).

POLARIS WORLD

Parque Empresarial Polaris World, Autovia Murcia-San Javier, Km 18, 30591
Balsicas-Murcia (Spain). www.polarisworld.com

ORGANISATION CHART
General Director: Jose Maria De la Puerta.
Team manager: Roger Marcaccini.
Technician Manager: Daniele Cecchini (Bradley Smith).

38 BRADLEY SMITH

RIDER
Bradley Smith
Date of birth: 28th November 1990.
Place of birth: Garsington/Oxford (Great Britain).
First race: 1997.
First GP: Spain, 2006 (125).
- Supercross Kids British Champion (2001).
- «Future West» Supercross Champion (2003).

DE GRAAF GRAND PRIX

Panoven 20. 3401 RA Ijsselstein (Netherlands).
www.molenaarracinf.com

ORGANISATION CHART
Team manager: Jarno Janssen.
Technical Director: Arie Molenaar.
Chief mechanics: Hans Spaan (Steve Bonsey, Hugo Van Den Berg and Daniel Webb).

51 STEVE BONSEY

56 HUGO VAN DEN BERG

99 DANIEL WEBB

RIDERS
Steve Bonsey
Date of birth: 18th January 1990.
Place of birth: Salinas (USA).
First race: 2003.
First GP: Qatar, 2007 (125).
- Dirt-Track Amateur 450
American Champion (2005).
- Dirt-Track Pro Sport American Champion (2006).

Daniel Webb
Date of birth: 22nd March 1991
Place of birth: Pembury (Great Britain).
First race: 1997.
First GP: Catalunya, 2006 (125).

Hugo Van Den Berg
Date of birth: 23rd May 1990.
Place of birth: Hulshort (Netherlands).
First race: 2000.
First GP: Catalunya, 2005 (125).

WTR SAN MARINO TEAM

I.C. TEAM

POLARIS WORLD

DE GRAAF GRAND PRIX

With their 125 RRR at its peak, the Austrian factory felt able to supply bikes to satellite teams. Four of them, seven riders in all, had the same equipment for the season, as director Harold Bartol was quick to point out : « From a technical point of view the four teams are all on the same level : they have the same equipment, the same degree of support. The fact that Randy Krummenacher is on a KTM in Red Bull colours doesn't mean he has any works rider advantages. » The big move in the close season, of course, was Repsol Honda's switch from Honda to KTM in both the 125 and 250 categories.

ISPA KTM ARAN

Racing World srl, Via Ventotto Luglio 218, Borgo Maggiore (Republic of San Marino). www.ispaktmaran.com

ORGANISATION CHART
Team manager: Stefano Bedon. Director: Marco Tresoldi.
Technical Director: Roberto Bava.
Chiefs mechanics: Romano Fusaro (Lorenzo Zanetti) and Alex Battistini (Koyama).

8 LORENZO ZANETTI

71 TOMOYOSHI KOYAMA

RIDERS
Lorenzo Zanetti
Date of birth: 10th August 1987.
Place of birth: Lumezzane/Brescia (Italia).
First race: 1996.
First GP: Italia, 2004 (125).

Tomoyoshi Koyama
Date of birth: 19th March 1983.
Place of birth: Kanagawa (Japan).
First race: 1999.
First GP: Pacific, 2000 (125).
- 125cc Japanese Champion (2000).
Number of GP victories: 1 (125).
First GP victory: Catalunya, 2007 (125)

REPSOL KTM 125

Ctra. D'Engolasters 53, Edif. 3, àtic 2, AS700 Escaldes Engordany (Principality of Andorra). www.repsolmedia.com

ORGANISATION CHART
Team manager: Jaume Colom. Technical Director: Raul Jarà.
Chief mechanics: Paolo Cordioli (Esteve Rabat and Marc Marquez).

12 ESTEVE RABAT

93 MARC MARQUEZ

RIDERS
Esteve Rabat
Date of birth: 25th May 1989.
Place of birth: Barcelona (Spain).
First race: 2002.
First GP: Valencia, 2005 (125).

Marc Marquez
Date of birth: 17th February 1993.
Place of birth: Lleida (Spain).
First race: 1998.
First GP: Portugal, 2008 (125).
- 50cc Catalunyian Champion (2003).
- 125cc Catalunyian Champion (2005 et 2006).

ONDE 2000 KTM

C/Valle del Tormes, 2. Local 106. Ciudad Comercial Las Lomas. 28660 Boadilla del Monte, Madrid (Spain). www.onde2000-media.com

ORGANISATION CHART
Team manager: Angel Junior «Gelete» Nieto.
Technical Director: Giancarlo Cecchini.
Chiefs mechanics: Angel Perurena (Pablo Nieto) and Gigi Perotti (Raffaele De Rosa).

22 PABLO NIETO

35 RAFFAELE DE ROSA

RIDERS
Pablo Nieto
Date of birth: 4th June 1980.
Place of birth: Madrid (Spain).
First race: 1995.
First GP: Catalunya, 1998 (125).
Number of GP victories: 1 (125).
First GP victory: Portugal, 2003 (125)

Raffaele De Rosa
Date of birth: 25th March 1987.
Place of birth: Napoli (Italia).
First race: 2003.
First GP: Spain, 2005 (125).

RED BULL KTM 125

Stallhofnerstrasse 3, 5230 Mattighofen (Austria). www.ktm.com

ORGANISATION CHART
Technical Director: Harald Bartol. Coordinator: Francesco Guidotti.
Team manager 125: Konrad Haefele.
Chiefs mechanics: Santi Hernandez (Randy Krummenacher).

34 RANDY KRUMMENACHER

RIDER
Randy Krummenacher
Date of birth: 24th February 1990.
Place of birth: Wetzikon (Switzerland).
First race: 1995.
First GP: Great Britain, 2006 (125).
- Pocket-Bike Junior A Swiss Champion (2001).
- Pro Junior Cup German Champion (2003).

ISPA KTM ARAN

REPSOL KTM 125

ONDE 2000 KTM

RED BULL KTM 125

'Chinese' brand Loncin made their GP debut in 2008. Created in 1993, the company now numbers over 10,000 employees ; in 2007, they produced 3 million engines and 2 million motorcycles. A private group, Loncin's 2007 exports were worth 200 million euros ; as BMW's Chinese partners they produce the engines for the 650 series. Behind them : the Bologna company Engines Engineering set up by Alberto Strazzari in 1979 which has worked for a number of bike-makers including Malaguti, who took up the 2002 prototype at the start of 2003 and, with Fabrizio Lai aboard, took the Engines group to the Italian 125cc title in 2002.

LONCIN RACING

Engines Engineering S.p.a., Via Pasquali 6, 40055 Castenaso (Italia).
www.enginesengineering.com

ORGANISATION CHART
Team manager: Nicola Casadei.
Technical Director: Olivier Liégeois.
Project Manager: Antonello Maino.
Technical Responsable: Tiziano Altabella.

RIDERS
Alexis Masbou
Date of birth: 2nd June 1987.
Place of birth: Nîmes (France).
First race: 2001.
First GP: France, 2003 (125).
- 125cc French Champion (2004).

Jules Cluzel
Date of birth: 12 octobre 1988.
Place of birth: Montluçon (France).
First race: 2001.
First GP: France, 2005 (125).

5
ALEXIS MASBOU

16
JULES CLUZEL

2005 World Champion Thomas Luthi will go down in history as the last man to take a two-stroke title on a Honda. Outclassed for the last two seasons, the Japanese giants had lost interest : one solitary rider was a 2008 Championship regular, and that was Frenchman Louis Rossi (no relation…), on a Japanese machine which had had no development work done on it for two years.

FFM HONDA GP 125

Fédération française de motocyclisme, 74 Avenue Parmentier, 75011 Paris (France).
www.teamffmgp125.com

ORGANISATION CHART
Team manager: Daniel Barthelemy.
Sporting Director: Alain Bronec.
Technical Director: Gilles Bigot.

RIDER
Louis Rossi
Date of birth: 23 juin 1989.
Place of birth: Le Mans (France).
First race: 2004.
First GP: Portugal, 2007 (125).
- Winner of the Challenge de l'Avenir FFM (2007).

69
LOUIS ROSSI

LONCIN RACING

FFM HONDA GP 125

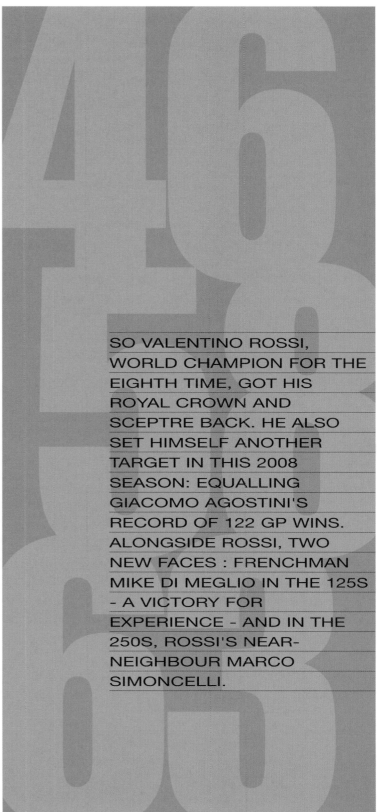

SO VALENTINO ROSSI, WORLD CHAMPION FOR THE EIGHT TIME, GOT HIS ROYAL CROWN AND SCEPTRE BACK. HE ALSO SET HIMSELF ANOTHER TARGET IN THIS 2008 SEASON: EQUALLING GIACOMO AGOSTINI'S RECORD OF 122 GP WINS. ALONGSIDE ROSSI, TWO NEW FACES : FRENCHMAN MIKE DI MEGLIO IN THE 125S - A VICTORY FOR EXPERIENCE - AND IN THE 250S, ROSSI'S NEAR-NEIGHBOUR MARCO SIMONCELLI.

ROSSI:
RETURN OF THE 'REAL' VALE

46

Maybe he had just won too often, too well, too easily : whatever the reason, the critics had their knives out for him. Over the last couple of years, badly advised, keeping the wrong company, he had certainly got a few things wrong. But 2008 saw the return of the 'real' Vale, lord of the MotoGP rings, the man who sends the figures skywards - not only in the finance and social pages, either. All year long, not a sniff of any new scandal, no hint of the London-based Rossi having no more interest in Italy. Instead, we got the 'real' Vale back, the man and his own brand of humour. Asked who was looking after his affairs these days, he answered with a laugh : « Me, of course - I'm the one who knows Valentino Rossi's strengths best. And I can tell you one thing : that Rossi fellow may be greedy, but he's not hard to sell ! »

Half as rich, twice as happy

The transformation was down to an important change in his life. Valentino Rossi had paid his dues to the past. He was less rich - but a lot more happy. And a happy rider, a rider at peace with himself, is also a winning rider. To those who expressed concern about his bachelor state, he retorted : « I have absolutely no desire to have a steady fiancee, and certainly not one who's in the paddock all the time, because she would make it impossible for me to concentrate. And to tell you the truth I don't think a fiancee could make my life any better than it is right now. »

Happy, then, to have put that turbulent time behind him ? « Yes, of course, it's hard to come to terms with what happened last year. The trouble with the taxman made me realise I had a lot of enemies - people who gave me sideways looks, wanted to know what I was doing, who I was. And that meant I couldn't just be myself, I had to hide, lock myself away. It was just awful. »

So what - apart from the fact that you really should pay your taxes - is the moral of the tale ?

« When you are a top-flight sportsman you need to be spared all those other worries. You know, I'm a sensitive guy : I've always accepted that some fans might support other riders, but I hate it when people are against me. »

And in 2007 it seemed that the whole world was against him…

Big gamble

So Valentino Rssi took his fate in his own hands by insisting on a change of tyre supplier, so he could see where he really stood in relation to Casey Stoner. Meanwhile Yamaha was developing its best GP bike yet. And Valentino, back to himself as Vale the Great, did the rest. He never lost his cool early in the season when things weren't going quite right, he took stock of his opponents and then dished out the kind of treatment only the Doctor knows how to dish out. Casey Stoner's confidence took a big knock at Laguna Seca and it took him a while to get it back. By then, Rossi was already World Champion for the eighth time…

INTERVIEW

« LAGUNA SECA WAS THE RACE THAT EVERYTHING HINGED ON - AND I WON IT »

Valentino, you have taken back what's rightfully yours : the world title ?
- Yes, it was a great year for me, a fantastic Championship. But it was also very difficult, very hard - and very important.

Perhaps the most important of all, after all the troubles of the last two years ?
- Every title has its own story, or stories even. So every one is important in its own way. But I think this is the one that took most out of me. I was focussed from the first day to the last, I worked harder than I've ever worked. Yes, I deserved this title.

Better even than 2004, your first title with Yamaha ?
- Absolutely. In 2004, while I had changed bikes (from Honda to Yamaha), I had just enjoyed a very fortunate period, with three straight world titles. But this year I didn't start as favourite. What's worse, I was coming off two difficult seasons - two difficult years all round, since I had trouble off track as well as on it. In 2006 I made some uncharacteristic mistakes, but I also had my share of bad luck. But in 2007 I was beaten fair and square : Stoner was much faster than we were.

So is it fair to say that 2008 was a mature man's title ?
- It was a particularly important Championship because we put in a lot of work ahead of it, from last winter on. My team and I took a big decision to go with Bridgestone, but that wasn't the only change : we also decided to review the technical staff thoroughly, especially the engine group, and the men who look after the electronic systems.

You make it sound as if you built a whole new bike.
- Well, it has to be said that the first version of the 800cc Yamaha wasn't all that good. I started talking to Furusawa, the head of the race department, right after the 2007 Valencia GP. That's when we started working - and that's when we started being winners again.

So Valentino Rossi was in control, but it was a team effort this year ?
- Absolutely, and if I tried to thank everyone who played a big part in this title, it would take quite some time. My biggest thank you goes to Yamaha, of course, and especially Masao Furusawa for believing in our project. Thanks, too, to Bridgestone and of course to all my team, and Jeremy Burgess.

Okay, that's fine - but all those people must owe a big 'Thank you' to Valentino Rossi too, don't they ?
- It's fair to say that I've grown up. By the end of 2005 I had achieved all my goals, I was practically unbeatable. And that was my first mistake, because after the problems we had that winter, I just thought that by the start of the 2006 season we'd have got it all right, there was no reason to think things wouldn't go on as they were. And as I said earlier, last year we were beaten by a better team. Looking at it a little more closely, I think we can say that defeat had a very positive outcome for us.

Any doubts as the season went on ?
- As soon as we went testing in winter I knew I had the right bike and tyres, and I knew then that we were ready to do great things again. The first race in Qatar was our worst of the season, but depite that lapse (5th) I knew we had solved the previous year's problems and that we would soon be back at the front.

Fifth but not too unhappy : that doesn't sound like Valentino Rossi !
- So much so that after the race - i.e. in the wee small hours, since it was a night race - my team were all a bit down in the dumps and I was the one telling them not to worry, we'd made the right choice !

A quick impression of the 2008 season ?
- There were different phases : a Michelin period to start with, as Lorenzo and Pedrosa were on song. On our side, at that stage we just got on with our work, building up a handy advantage over Stoner. From Barcelona on, the Ducati got a lot better and Stoner came on very strong, often impossible to beat. Then we came to the US

Grand Prix at Laguna Seca.

And you said that with a smile on your face...
- In California I didn't just win a race, I won the race on which the whole Championship turned. We never gave up : while Ducati was on a high we fought Stoner, then we started beating him.

Three titles with Yamaha in MotoGP, three with Honda : time to try something else ?
- For me the Yamaha titles mean more. I feel much more of a Yamaha rider than I ever felt I was with Honda, and that's an important point. Yes, I've had offers from Ducati, and I could have gone back to Honda, but I decided to stay right where I am. There have already been some major changes during my career. Now I want to stay in an environment where I feel good, that's what gives me my motivation.

A lot of criticism has come your way these last two years. Werer there any comments that particularly got to you ?
- In 2006 people started having a go at me just because I had thought about Formula 1. But for goodness' sake, I was given the chance to test, I couldn't pass that up ! Everyone must know that my decision to stay in bikes had been made before the Championship started. But then we had technical problems that same year ; everybody thought we would be able to overcome that handicap, and they were all wrong. That being the case, it was easy for people to think my heart wasn't in it any more.

Note: the interviews in the MotoGP Yearbook are a selection of quotable quotes made during the year.

VISITING CARD	CAREER HIGHLIGHTS			
Name Rossi	1989	First kart races	1997	125cc World Champion (Aprilia)
First name Valentino	1990	Regional kart champion	1998	Runner-up, 250cc World Championship (Aprilia)
Date of birth 16th February 1979	1991	5th, Italian Junior kart championship ;	1999	250cc World Champion (Aprilia)
Place of birth Urbino/Pesaro (Italia)		first minibike race win	2000	Runner-up, 500cc World Championship (Honda)
Marital status Single	1992	Italian minibike enduro champion	2001	500cc World Champion (Honda)
First race 1992	1993	12th, Italian Sports Production 125cc	2002	MotoGP World Champion (Honda)
First GP Malaysia, 1996 (125)		championship (Cagiva)	2003	MotoGP World Champion (Honda)
Number of GP victories 97	1994	Italian Sports Production 125cc	2004	MotoGP World Champion (Yamaha)
(12/125; 14/250; 13/500; 58/MotoGP)		champion (Cagiva)	2005	MotoGP World Champion (Yamaha)
First GP victory Czech Republic, 1996 (125)	1995	3rd, European 125 ; 11th, Spanish Open	2006	Runner-up MotoGP World Championship (Yamaha)
		125 ; Italian 125 champion (Aprilia)	2007	3rd, MotoGP World Championship (Yamaha)
	1996	9th, 125cc World Championship ; 10th,	2008	MotoGP World Champion (Yamaha)
		European Open 125 championship		

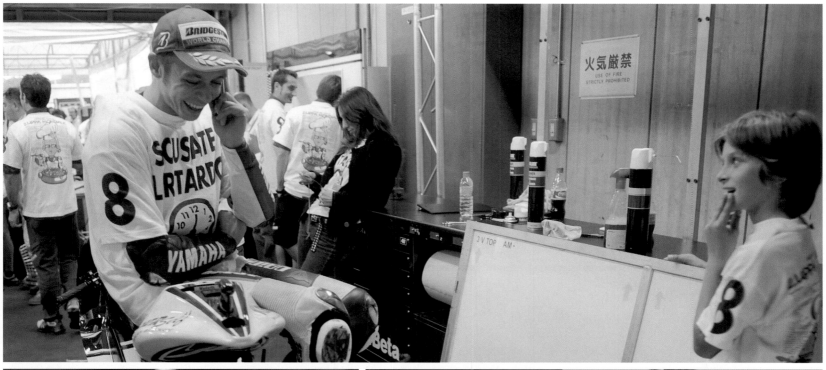

Another date with glory at Motegi, where Valentino Rossi became World Champion for the eighth time, with his half-brother Luca (top), learning the ropes as a rider himself, looking on. Rossi stressed that the 2008 title was a team effort; a change of tyre supplier (right) restored the King to his throne.

SIMONCELLI: OLD HEAD ON YOUNG SHOULDERS

58

When you're born in Cattolica, on the Rimini Riviera which now has its own Grand Prix, you grow up surrounded by kart tracks - which means minibikes. It's a passionate environment to come into, one in which local heroes have gone on to be champions ever since the dawn of motor sport at the very end of the 19th century.

No, the land where Marco Simoncelli saw the light of day isn't all about beaches, it's also about motor sport. Small wonder, then, that young Marco - not yet the man with the big hair we know today - should badger his Dad into taking him along to tracks where a certain Valentino Rossi was already plying his trade.

What happened next seems inevitable, looking back. Marco had found his idol ; he was to become his friend as well, his buddy and his training sidekick. And the king would be generous with his advice. European 125cc champion at a very young age in 2002, Simoncelli was already being hailed as the new Rossi. « The only problem with that, » he says, « is that there's only one Valentino Rossi. At the time a lot of people seemed to forget that. » His character already well established, the Aprilia novice set about practising his scales - with a few false notes along the way. « Oh yes, he's quick all right, that Simoncelli, but he'll never win a world title, he's just not consistent enough, » people said.

2005 : a first GP win, fifth in the Championship : it seemed Simoncelli was already well on his way, but no, the youngster with the growing pains wasn't going to hang around in 125s. He was promoted to a Gilera works 250 bike ; now we would see what he was made of.

And we did : there was tremendous pressure on those young shoulders, he was still mistake-prone, but he hung in there, he paid heed to what his mate Rossi was telling him, and he learned the value of patience. Last year he was shuffled back to second rider status - and promptly blossomed. With a new technical crew, we got a new Simoncelli as well. Sure, he was still 'only' 10th overall, but it had been plain for all to see that the errors were fewer and a lot farther between in the second half of the season.

And he was impressive in winter testing, putting the LE, the Piaggio group's model from the previous year in among the quickest RSA bikes ridden by Bautista and Luthi. « Simoncelli ? Oh, he's only an outside shot, you can't go with him for a whole season, » was the refrain. « Nope, Bautista's the hot favourite, he'll have it all sewn up pretty quickly. » The only one not listening as the curtain rose on the 2008 season was… Marco Simoncelli.

Yes, he kicked off his season with two no-scores, but he and the people around him were already sure he'd laid the demons of the past to rest. Simoncelli was hardly making a mistake these days, even though there were some doughty fighters among the opposition. He got a bit hot under the collar at Misano as Barbera kept at him, but it didn't stop him becoming the irresistible force in the latter part of the season. After a Malaysian race that left him dehydrated and on the brink of collapse, third place made Marco Simoncelli World Champion.

And Valentino Rossi could come and say 'Well done' any time he liked !

INTERVIEW

« ROSSI IS MY HERO, THE ONE I WANT TO EMULATE »

No more Marco mistakes : how do you explain the transformation in 2008 ?
- Any improvement in my performance at the end of last season and during the winter is down to my team. Don't forget I also won races early in the season, when I only had the LE, a bike that was 10-12 km/h slower than the RSA my main rivals were on. Life got easier once I got my hands on the works Gilera.

But Simoncelli the rider has also come on a great deal - witness that perfect race you rode in Motegi.
- It's fair to say that success owed something to a new maturity. When I needed to I was able to lift the pace, and when Bautista got back on terms with me I kept calm and took him on. Isn't that how you define the perfect race ?

And you needed to be perfect, because Bautista was a serious contender right to the end. It looks as if you have a lot of respect for each other, would we be wrong in saying that ?
- No. Alvara is a rider who never gives up. If I'm in the lead I never have to look very far, it's usually him right behind me. All the time, everywhere we go, he's always very quick. He's not one of those guys that will do anything out there, taking every possible risk just to run three seconds off the pace. That's not Bautista's style, and his performances made the 2008 Championship one that really was worth winning.

What about Kallio ?
- Yes, he's quick everywhere as well, but perhaps not as quick as we are.

Can you see room for further improvement in your own riding ?
- This is one of those jobs where you can never afford to sit back. Now that I'm World Champion, I will have to keep improving… my English, because I'm fed up with everyone laughing when I'm at the microphone in the press conferences !

Valentino Rossi was one of the first to congratulate you. A real friend of yours ?
- Absolutely. I have a lot of time for Valentino as a rider, but also as a man. Whenever I need advice I go to him for it and he always gives me the answers. People talk about tactics, but what does his example tell us ? Easy : he starts every race intending to win it,

that's the only strategy you get from a one-off like him.

Does he offer any other advice ?
- We've got into the habit of watching each other's races on TV. When he sees me making a mistake, he puts me right.

More and more people are drawing comparisons between you, seeing you as the natural heir to Valentino. How do you cope with that ?
- The problem is that we're quite similar in character. When I came into Grand Prix racing, too many people thought I would win as much as he has. There's just one problem, and it's an easy one : there is only one Valentino. And that's him.

Valentino is your mate, Bautista's an opponent you respect - but what about Barbera ? There were one or two little moments between the two of you this year…
- Since Misano I've pretty well ignored him, I don't want to talk to him any more. After the race I went up to Race Control to complain about his riding, but the officials decided there was no need to issue a reprimand. I couldn't work out why.

Especially as you were the one that got the warning after Mugello, when you touched on the main straight and the Spaniard went down.
- There you have it ! In Italy I was very aggressive, it's true, and I got a warning. Barbera has used the same riding style all year long and never had any problem. People will have to make up their own minds.

Let's talk about other things. Your hair gives you the Jimi Hendrix look : are you a fan ?
- Not especially, I'm too young to have known him. I've seen pictures of him, of course, and naturally I like the way he looked.

More than his music ?
- I'm very Italian in that regard, I love Vasco Rossi and Giovanotti.

Still, the look is part of your make-up now. And people all around the world like Marco Simoncelli now, not just in Italy, are you aware of that ?
- Not really. I'm not here to play some kind of part, I am what I am, I live naturally. If the public like it, so much the better. And if not, too bad, I'm not about to change.

You sound just like Valentino Rossi !
- Vale has always been my hero. When I was still on a pocket-bike he was already a GP rider - and a winner. I'm his biggest fan, I claim that title. He's won so

much, he's been at the top for so long. Valentino is a one-off, the greatest there's ever been.

OK, we get the picture, you're Rossi's number one fan. Anyone else ?
- Before Valentino, I liked Schwantz and Lawson. Kevin, because he had such a unique riding style, Eddie because he was just so consistent. You'll laugh, but I have to come back to Rossi - because he combines those two great champions in one !

Your Dad is always in your pit box, your Mum and your kid sister made the trip to Malaysia for the deciding race - what about your girl-friend ?
- Kate ? We've been together for a year now and she tries to come to races as often as she can.

So how does a World Champion spend his spare time ?
- I train every day : gym, running, motocross. I love it. In the evenings, usual stuff : meet friends, go out.

You often do motocross training with Rossi. Do you ever beat him ?
- Forget it : it's not realistic to think you can bet him. I'm happy not to lose more than three seconds a lap on the courses where we go riding for fun !

Marco, it seems strange to have a 250cc World Champion who's not moving up to MotoGP.
- I love this class : the mixture of power and agility sutis me down to the ground and I get a lot of fun out of it. Why change ?

Despite other offers ?
- I had three : one from Honda Gresini, one from the satellite Ducati team and a third one from Yamaha.

Yamaha ?
- Yes, Hervé Poncharal was looking at me, but that was very early on this season. And when Colin Edwards extended his contract, that was that.

Note: the interviews in the MotoGP Yearbook are a selection of quotable quotes made during the year.

VISITING CARD		CAREER HIGHLIGHTS		
Name Simoncelli	1996	Runner-up, Italian minibike championship	2004	11th, 125cc World Championship (Aprilia)
First name Marco	1997	5th, Italian minibike championship	2005	5th, 125cc World Championship (Aprilia)
Date of birth 20th January 1987	1998	Runner-up, Italian minibike championship	2006	10th, 250cc World Championship (Gilera)
Place of birth Cattolica (Italy)	1999	Italian minibike champion	2007	10th, 250cc World Championship (Gilera)
Marital status Engaged to Kate	2000	Runner-up, European minibike	2008	250cc World Champion (Gilera)
First race 1996		championship ; Italian minibike champion		
First GP Czech Republic, 2002 (125)	2001	26th, Spanish 125 championship (Honda)		
Number of GP victories 8 (2/125; 6/250)	2002	33rd, 125cc World Championship ;		
First GP victory Spain, 2004 (125)		European 125 champion (Aprilia)		
	2003	21st, 125cc World Championship (Aprilia)		

Bautista, Simoncelli et Kallio, the top three in the class. Not only is Simoncelli a good mate of Valentino Rossi's, he is actually quite like him. Which means a big burn-out was a foregone conclusion. And that hair's been everywhere, man - Jimi Hendrix would love it.

DI MEGLIO:

THE DAY MIKE SMILED AGAIN

63

Japan 2003 : a 15-year-old French kid exploring the world. Thick black eyebrows give him a serious look, in total contrast to the guy's character. He is painfully shy, an introvert. When he meets someone he hardly exchanges a glance ; a handshake from this backward youngster is little more than a quick caress.

And when it comes to talking, well, that's the supreme sacrifice where Mike Di Meglio is concerned. There really isn't much sign of his distant Sicilian background, in fact the way he behaves, you'd think he must have had a difficult upbringing. Not one of those sons of famous fathers, not one of those kids born in the paddock, not one the old-timers laugh about as they recall his first pranks on trike or minibike. None of that : Mike's a bit different, but the talent is there, hidden deep inside his complex make-up. It will just take time to come out.

Hampered by being French

For while Mike Di Meglio dreams of being a champion, he has one major handicap right from the start, and that's his passport. In a country where the major channels and dailies don't give much space to motorcycle racing (Olivier Jacque was the last popular GP guy in France, where even Arnaud Vincent's 2002 125cc world title went largely unnoticed), it's hard to find financial backing, which means decent equipment.

So Mike works, and works - and makes some progress. In fact we thought he was on the road to fame and fortune back in 2005, when he won the first-ever Turkish GP, riding for an Italian team that had faith in him. But once again he got it wrong. Maybe he had no option, but he

accepted an offer to join the French Federation's own team, running a Honda whose competitive days were long gone. One step forward, two back : it seemed a promising career had been nipped in the bud.

A parting of the ways pays off

How to get things back on track ? Take a look at the big wide world ; go, get away - time to make the break, sometimes not an easy thing to do, but in this case absolutely the right one. Alain Bronec, the FFM's man on the ground, a man who keeps his ear to the ground, felt he could do a good deal by offering a well-backed team a number one and a good apprentice. In fact it was a master-stroke.

He knew Finn Aki Ajo as a sound team boss, an old-fashioned one even: solid technical work was more important to him than the size of the motorhome or the menus on offer. He also knew that young Swiss rider Dominique Aegerter, with some serious backing from CarFashion.ch, part of the Métraux Services group built by the late former IRTA president, was looking to move on.

All the pieces of the puzzle came together nicely, and Mike Di Meglio and Dominique Aegerter found themselves together with Derbi, the former on a works RSA that would make him leader of the pack, the latter one of the finds of the season. Well played.

And that's how Mike got his smile back…

INTERVIEW

« I SEEM TO HAVE A LOT MORE FRIENDS IN THE PADDOCK NOW ! »

Mike Di Meglio, tell us what it's like to be World Champion.
- It's great, really great ! And it's the reward for a lot of hard work. Mind you, I still haven't really come to terms with what I've achieved this year. In my mind, it was just one stage among many - at least I hope so, because I really want to go on from here.

What do you mean by that ?
- Valentino Rossi's career has been really magnificent, but I doubt if I can do what he's done. But if I can stay up there among the front-runners, I think that will be good enough for me. I mean, look at Rossi : he never drops the ball, he's always analysing what he does, and that's the sign of the really great riders. I'm going to try and do the same, then we'll see if I've got the talent to do great things.

How did you feel once tht title was yours : proud, relieved, or a bit of both ?
- Very happy, first of all, because it was a difficult year, I had to stay focussed, not let up, not make mistakes. I did make one (Misano), but that's the way it goes. It really was a very tough year.

What was going through your mind as you crossed the line at Phillip Island ?
- I didn't know I was World Champion ! I was really happy, because I'd just ridden a terrific race, winning by 10 seconds on a track where it's usually hard to break away, and that was fantastic. It was only when I collected a flag from a fan that I saw the words 'World Champion' on one of the big screens, I couldn't take it all in.

Is there one particular moment you'd hang on to from the season ?
- That win in Australia. Winning my home race in France was magnificent, but there was something special about that perfect weekend in Australia, on a track I love, setting some super times from qualifying on. I honestly never thought it could be possible.

This year you also became the first French rider to win a GP in France for 26 years. That must have given you a great deal of pleasure ?
- I knew before that Le Mans weekend it was a long time since a Frenchman had won, so I gave it my best shot. When you're racing at home, in front of your own fans, it's a very special thing. Every time I came out of corner I could see everyone shouting for me and I'd never felt such a lift. Yes, it was another great moment in the season.

You're also the first French World Champion in six years. Was there extra pressure, with the hopes of an entire nation riding on your shoulders ?
- Not at all. I go my own way, and it's going well, so I'm enjoying it while I can.

Like a number of riders of your age, you started your career quite early - a bit too early, perhaps ?
- I rode in my first GP when I was 15 and no, that wasn't too soon. It was my choice. Although I did have some difficult times after that, I was really down sometimes. Now I'm on top of the ladder and I can tell you it's a pretty good feeling !

Tell us about those times : did you ever get disheartened ?
- Oh yes, there were times when I was really down. I really didn't know if it was me or the bike. At times like that you look at everything, but you don't know where to find the answers to all your questions. You can't find the way out, and it's very difficult.

Yes, but you did find it, didn't you ?
- Yes, because things changed from one track to the next. There were some races where things just didn't go right at all, but there were others where the conditions suited my bike a bit better and that gave me a lift. This year there was none of that : I had the best bike and the best team, I was up there no matter what the circumstances, and that's how you win titles.

What did those tough times teach you ?
- That when the going gets tough, you need to stay focussed. But I also think it's a whole raft of things that helps you do better ; personally, I've always tried to look closely at myself and see how I could improve. Last year, when I couldn't work out why things were going so badly, I found out who was who in the paddock. Now I've got a lot more people around me - and a lot more friends.

Note:the interviews in the MotoGP Yearbook are a selection of quotable quotes made during the year.

VISITING CARD		CAREER HIGHLIGHTS		
Name Di Meglio	2000	French 50cc champion	2006	25th, 125cc World Championship (Honda)
First name Mickaël «Mike»	2001	Winner, French 50cc Conti Cup	2007	17th, 125cc World Championship (Honda)
Date of birth 17th January 1988	2002	17th Spanish 125 championship,	2008	125cc World Champion (Derbi)
Place of birth Toulouse (France)		3rd French 125 championship		
Marital status Single	2003	28th, 125cc World Championship (Aprilia)		
First race 2001	2004	18th, 125cc World Championship (Aprilia)		
First GP Japan, 2003 (125)	2005	11th, 125cc World Championship (Honda)		
Number of GP victories 5 (125)				
First GP victory Turkey, 2005 (125)				

AUSTRALIAN GRAND PRIX

In the Phillip Island press conference after winning the title (above), Mike Di Megio is just coming to terms with what has happened. He knows this title is also down to a terrific team effort from Finnish outfit Ajo (left). Two weeks later, Di Meglio received Shark champion's helmet with gold letters on a white background. And (below), victory champagne and a close moment with team-mate Dominique Aegerter.

A flamboyant red bike pierces the Doha night as history is made.

The souk in the old town compared to the styles at the end of the road: Qatar is a country of contrasts.

STONER,
THE NIGHT BIRD

FOR THE FIRST TIME EVER, A WORLD
CHAMPIONSHIP MOTORCYCLE GRAND PRIX IS
HELD AT NIGHT. A CRAZY GAMBLE? NOT AT ALL,
A GREAT MARKETING SUCCESS IN FACT AND A
TRIUMPH FOR THE REIGNING CHAMPION.

THE RACE

MOTOGP AS GROUP THERAPY

Jorge Lorenzo took pole position at his first attempt and Andrea Dovizioso carved up no less than Valentino Rossi on the last lap: the youngsters were scared of no one.

The motorcycle has done it, secured a place in the history books, as this is the first ever grand prix to be run at night. What was it like? Good…at least for the advertisers who had invested in plastering the side of the track with their slogans, lit by millions of Watts, making them more visible than ever before. And the sport? In all three categories, the records tumbled: pole position, fastest race lap, winner's average speed. Night time, or more accurately, the difference in track temperature, had no effect on performance. Putting aside this unusual element, the first GP of the season confirmed that the blue riband category is an excellent experiment in group therapy. If in 2007, the general feeling was that Stoner's influence and dominance could only be an exception that proves the rule, then this time, the performance of Lorenzo, Dovizioso and Toseland proved beyond doubt that the category no longer holds any fears for newcomers.

For a long time, those who had dared

defy the established order were quickly put in their place. And if they happened to win - remember Alex Criville up against Mick Doohan - then there was all hell to pay for their audacity and their fall was soon to follow.

The icon of this new movement is undoubtedly Jorge Lorenzo. Not yet 21 years old, the double 250 cc world champion immediately got his bravura noticed right from his first moments in GP racing. In the 125 class at Donington, he once tried to go through the downhill chicane without braking and he had literally cut the pack in two. On moving up to the 250s, the hot-head was less unpredictable, but still as merciless towards his rivals. How would he deal with his move to the big school, and cohabitation with the giant that is Valentino Rossi? Still there were no signs of nerves. Proof of that came on the morning of this first GP, when he told a Spanish journalist: "the bosses at Yamaha know that in me they have a

credible number 1."

At 22 years of age, Andrea Dovizioso is less flamboyant. But he possesses another quality in that he hardly ever makes a mistake. And when he decides to turn up the wick, he too can be unbeatable. The Master, Valentino Rossi will happily confirm that fact, having had to bend to his compatriot's will at the end of the race.

That leaves the 27 year old James Toseland, who did not do his schooling in the two-stroke classes, choosing instead supersports and then superbikes. He too is not overawed by it all and brought up on the hand to hand combat that is part of the charm of superbikes, he will have no second thoughts about using his elbows, or even knees, and all with a genuinely relaxed attitude. Toseland is happy to be a professional racer and happier still to now be doing his job in the brightest of spotlights and not just those that light up the Losail circuit, but also those that bring fame and glory!

A perfect race from Stoner (above) and Herve Poncharal (opposite) has something to smile about again with James Toseland at the end of qualifying. It was easy to forget the race took place at night, as can be seen with this shot of a blue Suzuki (above) apparently flying in the desert.

STONER WORTHY OF HIS NUMBER 1 AND THE ROOKIES SUCH AS JORGE LORENZO ARE SENSATIONAL.

RUNNERS AND RIDERS

There are now just eighteen riders in the category, as Kenny Roberts Senior has shut down his KR team, but the quality is higher than ever with the promotion of the two men who dominated the previous year's 250 class; Jorge Lorenzo, with Rossi at Yamaha and Dovizioso. In addition, we have the reigning world superbike champion, James Toseland, with Tech 3. There was a lot of talk about tyres the previous year and 2008 gets underway with the same theme: Dunlop has pulled out (Tech 3 switches to Michelin) and most importantly, Rossi has demanded and got Bridgestones on his M1, while Lorenzo who finally gets to share a garage with the great man, is on Michelin.

QUALIFYING

Three Yamahas on the front row…but Rossi only seventh: it's a nice taster of how the tyre war will pan out. At the top of the tree are two rookies, with Jorge Lorenzo taking pole, showing he is not at all fazed by the complexities of MotoGP, just as was the case over the previous two seasons in the 250s.

START

Pedrosa storms off the third row to lead from Edwards, Toseland, Lorenzo and Stoner, who is about to be jumped by Rossi. At the end of the opening lap, Pedrosa leads Edwards by 646 thousandths.

LAP 3

Still Pedrosa. Rossi is second at 857 thousandths, ahead of Lorenzo, Stoner, Toseland and Dovizioso. Edwards is struggling to match the pace.

LAP 5

Rossi, who seemed to be struggling, pulls a superb move on Pedrosa. Lorenzo, Stoner and Dovizioso are in touch, but not Toseland, who now trails by a second.

LAP 7

Lorenzo passes Pedrosa and Stoner takes the opportunity to follow through as the bikes touch.

LAP 8

Stoner has just taken the lead as they cross the line.

LAP 9

Overawed Mr. Lorenzo? Not at all, as the Spaniard passes Rossi in an impossible spot.

LAP 10

Vermeulen pulls into his pit.

HALF-DISTANCE (11 LAPS)

Stoner and Lorenzo have broken away, with the Spaniard trailing the world champion by 231 thousandths. Pedrosa and Rossi are a further 1.4 seconds behind. Vermeulen gets going again.

LAP 14

Stoner has stepped up the pace, Lorenzo dropping to 923 thousandths behind. But the real interest is behind this duo, as Pedrosa, Rossi, Dovizioso and Toseland are all wheel to wheel.

LAP 16

Pedrosa makes the break in the scrap for third as Rossi is 8 tenths down.

LAP 17

Alex de Angelis falls.

LAP 20

Dovizioso passes Rossi who then counter attacks.

FINISH (22 LAPS)

With the first three places sorted, the excitement switches to the battle for fourth, where incredibly, Dovizioso has taught Rossi a lesson.

GP QATAR | 9th March 2008 | Losail | 5.380 m

STARTING GRID

1	48	J. Lorenzo	Yamaha	1'53.927
2	52	J. Toseland	Yamaha	1'54.182
3	5	C. Edwards	Yamaha	1'54.499
4	1	C. Stoner	Ducati	1'54.733
5	14	R. De Puniet	Honda	1'54.818
6	69	N. Hayden	Honda	1'54.880
7	46	V. Rossi	Yamaha	1'55.133
8	2	D. Pedrosa	Honda	1'55.170
9	4	A. Dovizioso	Honda	1'55.185
10	21	J. Hopkins	Kawasaki	1'55.263
11	7	C. Vermeulen	Suzuki	1'55.540
12	15	A. De Angelis	Honda	1'55.692
13	65	L. Capirossi	Suzuki	1'56.070
14	24	T. Elias	Ducati	1'56.251
15	56	S. Nakano	Honda	1'56.434
16	33	M. Melandri	Ducati	1'56.730
17	50	S. Guintoli	Ducati	1'57.198
18	13	A. West	Kawasaki	1'57.445

RACE: 22 laps = 118.360 km

1	Casey Stoner	42'36.587 (166.665 km/h)
2	Jorge Lorenzo	+ 5.323
3	Dani Pedrosa	+ 10.600
4	Andrea Dovizioso	+ 13.288
5	Valentino Rossi	+ 13.305
6	James Toseland	+ 14.040
7	Colin Edwards	+ 15.150
8	Loris Capirossi	+ 32.505
9	Randy De Puniet	+ 38.354
10	Nicky Hayden	+ 38.354
11	Marco Melandri	+ 44.284
12	John Hopkins	+ 49.857
13	Shinya Nakano	+ 49.871
14	Toni Elias	+ 58.532
15	Sylvain Guintoli	+ 58.930
16	Anthony West	+ 1'05.643
17	Chris Vermeulen	+ 1 lap

Fastest lap

S: Stoner, in 1'55.153 (168.193 km/h). New record.
Previous: Stoner, in 1'56.528 (166.208 km/h/2007).

Outright fastest lap

Lorenzo, in 1'53.927 (170.003 km/h/2008).

CHAMPIONSHIP

1	C. Stoner	25 (1 win)
2	J. Lorenzo	20
3	D. Pedrosa	16
4	A. Dovizioso	13
5	V. Rossi	11
6	J. Toseland	10
7	C. Edwards	9
8	L. Capirossi	8
9	R. De Puniet	7
10	N. Hayden	6

MATTIA PASINI ALSO WANTED TO BE PART OF THE DEBUTANTS BALL IN THE STYLE OF THE 2008 QATAR GP.

RUNNERS AND RIDERS

The top three from the previous year's championship - Lorenzo, Dovizioso and De Angelis - have moved up to MotoGP. There are two clear favourites, the boys who had won from their very first year in the category, Bautista and Kallio. The Piaggio group is ambitious, as Luthi, Barbera, Simoncelli and Locatelli are also armed with the "RSA." For the first time since its 250 cc debut, KTM also fields a second crew, the Repsol team, with Julian Simon, who has turned his back on Honda. Another novelty is that Yamaha is back in the 250 GP class, through its Indonesian importer. Pasini and Faubel have moved up from the 125 class and the former world champion, Manuel Poggiali has come out of retirement. One absentee: Spain's Russel Gomez sustained an injury a few days before the start of the season.

QUALIFYING

Lorenzo might have gone, but Debon is the perfect replacement, as he takes his first pole position, ahead of two of his compatriots, Barbera and Bautista. Kallio completes the front row ahead of Pasini, Simoncelli and Luthi.

START

A super start from Luthi off the second row. The Swiss rider completes the opening lap 168 thousandths ahead of Kallio, who is followed by Bautista. Barbera is 8 tenths behind.

LAP 2
Bautista takes the lead just as it's declared that Luthi jumped the start.

LAP 3
Bautista has disappeared into the distance. Barbera overtakes Luthi.

LAP 4
Luthi comes in for his penalty and rejoins twentieth, his rear tyre already destroyed.

LAP 6
Bautista leads Barbera by 368 thousandths. Debon is third, but over three seconds down, with Kallio and Pasini on his back wheel.

LAP 8
Simoncelli falls.

HALF-DISTANCE (10 LAPS)
Barbera has just gone in front, with Bautista 446 thousandths behind. The third place scrap is a further 2.6 seconds adrift and features Pasini, Debon, Kallio and Takahashi.

LAP 12
Bautista has suddenly lost a second because of his rear tyre.

LAP 14
Bautista appears to be in big trouble and has dropped to fourth, having been passed first by Debon and then by Pasini. Kallio is also about to get by.

LAP 15
Luthi is back in the points after Baldolini is a faller.

LAP 17
Barbera, Debon, Pasini and Kallio: the top four are all within a mere 1.422. Bautista is only sixth.

LAP 19
Pasini ambushes Barbera and Debon in one move.

FINISH (20 LAPS)
Pasini leads by 2 tenths going into the final lap and makes no mistake in winning his maiden 250 race.

Thomas Luthi is the first leader of 2008, but the Swiss rider was a bit too eager and would have to take a penalty for a jumped start. Newcomer Pasini (75) and Hector Barbera (above) at his hundredth GP, could not ask for more.

GP QATAR | 9th March 2008 | Losail | 5.380 m

STARTING GRID

1	6	A. Debón	Aprilia	1'59.470
2	21	H. Barberá	Aprilia	1'59.629
3	19	A. Bautistá	Aprilia	1'59.694
4	36	M. Kallio	KTM	1'59.814
5	75	M. Pasini	Aprilia	1'59.863
6	58	M. Simoncelli	Gilera	1'59.911
7	12	T. Lüthi	Aprilia	2'00.108
8	72	Y. Takahashi	Honda	2'00.326
9	41	A. Espargaro	Aprilia	2'00.365
10	15	R. Locatelli	Gilera	2'00.403
11	17	K. Abraham	Aprilia	2'00.517
12	4	H. Aoyama	KTM	2'00.609
13	32	F. Lai	Gilera	2'00.854
14	60	J. Simón	KTM	2'00.975
15	55	H. Faubel	Aprilia	2'00.998
16	52	L. Pesek	Aprilia	2'01.000
17	25	A. Baldolini	Aprilia	2'01.149
18	54	M. Poggiali	Gilera	2'01.391
19	14	R. Wilairot	Honda	2'01.487
20	50	E. Laverty	Aprilia	2'02.482
21	10	I. Toth	Aprilia	2'03.538
22	43	M. Hernandez	Aprilia	2'03.703
23	45	D.-T. Pradita	Yamaha	2'05.343

RACE: 20 laps = 107.600 km

1	Mattia Pasini	40'16.202 (160.317 km/h)
2	Hector Barberá	+ 0.557
3	Mika Kallio	+ 1.029
4	Alex Debón	+ 1.418
5	Yuki Takahashi	+ 12.944
6	Alvaro Bautistá	+ 14.480
7	Karel Abraham	+ 16.721
8	Roberto Locatelli	+ 18.987
9	Aleix Espargaro	+ 32.232
10	Hector Faubel	+ 41.102
11	Julian Simón	+ 41.457
12	Fabrizio Lai	+ 41.694
13	Ratthapark Wilairot	+ 43.192
14	Manuel Poggiali	+ 44.228
15	Thomas Lüthi	+ 48.760
16	Hiroshi Aoyama	+ 1'11.031
17	Doni Tata Pradita	+ 2'05.461

Fastest lap

Debón, in 1'59.379 (162.239 km/h). New record.
Previous: De Angelis, in 2'00.121 (161.237 km/h/2007).

Outright fastest lap

Debón, in 1'59.379 (162.239 km/h/2008).

CHAMPIONSHIP

1	M. Pasini	25 (1 win)
2	H. Barberá	20
3	A. Debón	13
5	Y. Takahashi	11
6	A. Bautistá	10
7	K. Abraham	9
8	R. Locatelli	8
9	A. Espargaro	7
10	H. Faubel	6

SERGIO GADEA HAS GONE FROM FFERING TO TRIUMPH, BUT HERE TOO THE LITTLE 'UNS WERE MUCH IN EVIDENCE.

RUNNERS AND RIDERS

34 entries have been attributed, which is two more than the previous year. There's a notable KTM presence (7,) whereas Honda has all but disappeared, (just one, the French team for Louis Rossi) and the Chinese have arrived in the shape of Loncin. Hidden behind this name is the Italian Engines Engineering team, which had run the Malaguti programme. The bikes for French riders Cluzel and Masbou are evolutions on a Honda theme, run by Belgian technical director, Olivier Liegeois. One rider is already missing from this first roll call: Spain's Marc Marquez broke his left arm in the IRTA test at Jerez.

QUALIFYING

"Do you speak English," A new season and surprises in the shape of three British riders - Bradley Smith on pole, Scott Redding, only 15 years and 2 months old, fourth at his first grand prix and Danny Web, fifth, cause a sensation. The reigning champion Talmacsi, secures a spot on the front row with Mike Di Meglio.

START

It is 20h 01 and 59 seconds as the first night time GP gets underway on 9th March 2008. Smith charges into the lead ahead of Talmacsi and Di Meglio.

Rabat falls a bit later.

LAP 2

Smith is in trouble, just like Pasini, when he ran the same colours last year, and drops to eighth. Talmacsi heads the field.

LAP 5

De Rosa has snatched second place off Di Meglio, who is joined by Olive. Four of them are now in 371 thousandths. Gadea trails by half a second in fifth.

HALF-DISTANCE (9 LAPS)

After Olive and Gadea take their turn, it's the number 1, Talmacsi, who is back in charge. Seven of them - Talmacsi, Gadea, De Rosa, Olive, Webb, Redding and Di Meglio - are scrapping for the three podium places. Smith is still running, but out of the points.

LAP 13

A superb Redding is now third in his first GP!

LAP 15

It's Talmacsi's turn to have engine problems, leaving Di Meglio out in front.

LAP 16

De Rosa falls and impales Olive. Gadea leads the dance.

FINISH (18 LAPS)

Gadea has built himself a lead of 8 tenths going into the last lap and he bursts into tears as he wins, falling into the arms of Doctor Claudio Costa. The Spaniard had cracked his right collar bone, just a week earlier in the pre-GP test! Olive is second, Di Meglio is battling Redding and Bradl and it's the young German who takes his maiden podium. Talmacsi has salvaged four points for twelfth place. Sign of the times, or maybe the passing of time, but the best Italian, Simone Corsi is down in seventh.

A week before this first GP, Sergio Gadea snapped his right collarbone and then in qualifying(above) worse was to come with another fall. But he still made it to the top step of the podium. On the right, the new Swiss hope, Dominique Aegerter.

GP QATAR | 9th March 2008 | Losail | 5.380 m

STARTING GRID

1	38	B. Smith	Aprilia	2'05.242
2	1	G. Talmacsi	Aprilia	2'05.308
3	63	M. Di Meglio	Derbi	2'05.351
4	45	S. Redding	Aprilia	2'05.545
5	99	D. Webb	Aprilia	2'05.593
6	35	R. De Rosa	KTM	2'05.618
7	18	N. Terol	Aprilia	2'05.833
8	33	S. Gadea	Aprilia	2'05.953
9	6	J. Olivé	Derbi	2'06.074
10	24	S. Corsi	Aprilia	2'06.096
11	12	E. Rabat	KTM	2'06.132
12	27	S. Bianco	Aprilia	2'06.205
13	11	S. Cortese	Aprilia	2'06.218
14	51	S. Bonsey	Aprilia	2'06.329
15	17	S. Bradl	Aprilia	2'06.347
16	22	P. Nieto	KTM	2'06.380
17	29	A. Iannone	Aprilia	2'06.388
18	44	P. Espargaro	Derbi	2'06.402
19	7	E. Vazquez	Aprilia	2'06.477
20	77	D. Aegerter	Derbi	2'06.585
21	71	T. Koyama	KTM	2'06.702
22	60	M. Ranseder	Aprilia	2'06.787
23	74	T. Nakagami	Aprilia	2'07.016
24	8	L. Zanetti	KTM	2'07.338
25	34	R. Krummenacher	KTM	2'07.603
26	30	P. Tutusaus	Aprilia	2'07.605
27	21	R. Lasser	Aprilia	2'08.000
28	5	A. Masbou	Loncin	2'08.381
29	56	H. Van Den Berg	Aprilia	2'08.502
30	16	J. Cluzel	Loncin	2'08.769
31	95	R. Muresan	Aprilia	2'09.257
32	13	D. Lombardi	Aprilia	2'09.632
33	19	R. Lacalendola	Aprilia	2'09.827
34	69	L. Rossi	Honda	2'10.153

RACE: 18 laps = 96.840 km

1	Sergio Gadea	38'09.444 (152.274 km/h)
2	Joan Olivé	+ 0.932
3	Stefan Bradl	+ 1.660
4	Mike Di Meglio	+ 1.771
5	Scott Redding	+ 1.819
6	Danny Webb	+ 7.689
7	Simone Corsi	+ 8.684
8	Pol Espargaro	+ 8.693
9	Efren Vazquez	+ 9.054
10	Nicolas Terol	+ 10.902
11	Sandro Cortese	+ 10.945
12	Gabor Talmacsi	+ 12.618
13	Stefano Bianco	+ 12.709
14	Andrea Iannone	+ 20.086
15	Michael Ranseder	+ 23.575
16	Bradley Smith	+ 23.890
17	Dominique Aegerter	+ 29.406
18	Pablo Nieto	+ 32.891
19	Takaaki Nakagami	+ 33.346
20	Pere Tutusaus	+ 33.649
21	Lorenzo Zanetti	+ 36.696
22	Randy Krummenacher	+ 36.754
23	Robin Lasser	+ 45.317
24	Esteve Rabat	+ 56.440
25	Louis Rossi	+ 1'14.502

Fastest lap
Redding, in 2'05.695 (154.087 km/h). New record.
Previous: Talmacsi, in 2'06.267 (153.389 km/h/2007).

Outright fastest lap
Smith, in 2'05.242 (154.644 km/h/2008).

CHAMPIONSHIP

1	S. Gadea	25 (1 win)
2	J. Olivé	20
3	S. Bradl	16
4	M. Di Meglio	13
5	S. Redding	11
6	D. Webb	10
7	S. Corsi	9
8	P. Espargaro	8
9	E. Vazquez	7
10	N. Terol	6

Only the second GP of the season and, already in qualifying Colin Edwards provides the best image of the season. Super!

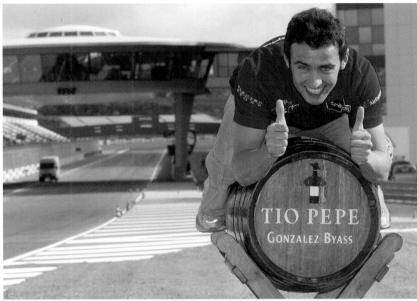

Jerez, with its lunar module-like main viewing box, its shapely girls…and its fine wines. Hector Barbera seems to like it!

DANI PEDROSA,
THE FAITHFUL VALET

A SERIOUS, DEDICATED AND EDUCATED STUDENT: DANIEL PEDROSA IS THE COMPLETE OPPOSITE TO THE WHIRLWIND THAT IS JORGE LORENZO, WHO HAS JUST ARRIVED IN THE BLUE RIBAND CATEGORY. THE KING HIMSELF HAD TO STEP IN TO CALM THEM DOWN.

THE RACE

THE KING, THE PAGE BOY AND THE KNIGHT

Since 1975, Spain has been a monarchy with a democratically elected parliament. Its sovereign, His Majesty Juan Carlos I, is an accomplished sportsman. He is also a huge fan of motor and motorcycle racing and if he has not put in many trackside appearances recently it does not mean he has lost interest. However, since the terrorist attacks of 2001 in the United States and of 2002 in Madrid, public appearances by the king had been voluntarily limited for the obvious security reasons.

But this time, the King had insisted on travelling to Andalusia, as he had an important mission to accomplish, namely to dampen down the verbal duel for control of the world of motorcycle racing, which raged between two of his subjects. The little page boy Daniel Pedrosa and the knight, Jorge Lorenzo.

Was it a simple conflict between two riders with the same ambition? No, because as the history books relate, decisive duels are always preceded by intrigue, the spice that has brought glory and sometimes decadence to royal households over the centuries.

So, behind Pedrosa, we have his mentor, Alberto Puig who likes no one, especially not himself! He always tries to break the thread of ambition of those who dare challenge him. And it all came together for this little tale, as in the other camp is a certain Dani Amatrian, a former track rival of Puig, who plays perfectly the role of counter insurgent

ever since he discovered, on the island of Majorca, the precocious talent of a young lad by the name of Jorge Lorenzo. So we have the little prince with the stately backing, both financial and sports-politic of Repsol, against the knight with nothing, not even any self-doubt. It looks like being a good joust and it has already split Spain into two camps, as the fascinating duel is not only played out on the race track, with two podiums for the two protagonists this year, two poles for rookie Lorenzo, but also behind the scenes. And it is in this area that the weapons are always more treacherous, in the form of murderous asides and small gestures of cruelty.

Therefore, while it is clear that Pedrosa and Lorenzo will never take a holiday together, the atmosphere has become so tense that they refuse to shake hands on Saturday after qualifying. It was too much for Spain to handle. And on Sunday, underneath the podium, the King of Spain demanded that his two subjects exchange the friendliest of handshakes. The two men accepted of course, as respect for the king is a duty. But this ceasefire would not last long. Making the most of a weekend without the Stoner-Bridgestone tandem, Pedrosa, the impressive winner and Lorenzo, took the opportunity to move to the top of the world championship scoreboard. The rest of the fight would be fantastic, according to the man best placed to judge the outcome of the duel, a certain Valentino Rossi!

Total opposites: up against the up front Jorge Lorenzo (above,) Dani Pedrosa is total discretion, until he gets on the track where, if he can get away in front, he is unbeatable.

A PEDROSA PARADE, WITH STONER PLAYING IN THE SAND AND LORENZO ONCE AGAIN ON THE PODIUM.

RUNNERS AND RIDERS

Everyone is on parade…and especially Lorenzo, who is now dominating the headlines in Spain. There's already a sense of panic in the Kawasaki camp and rumour has it that Mario Illien, the father of Ilmor could be appointed their saviour.

QUALIFYING

For the second consecutive time, Lorenzo takes an amazing pole, ahead of Pedrosa, which promises a fantastic duel. Edwards is again on the front row, having saved an almost certain tumble with his elbow. The Ducatis are struggling, as Stoner is only seventh. Elias, Guintoli and Melandri, who fell, are on the back row.

START

His Majesty King Juan Carlos of Spain is at the circuit from the morning. Of course, he steps out on track to support his two loyal subjects, Lorenzo and Pedrosa. Dani gets the best start, ahead of Lorenzo, Hayden, Stoner, Edwards and Capirossi. Dovizioso had gone off at the first corner and is down in sixteenth place.

LAP 2

Pedrosa has a lead of 6 tenths over Lorenzo.

LAP 3

Stoner gets it wrong and plays in the sand, ending up 17th and last. Randy de Puniet is a faller.

LAP 4

Rossi is back and swallows up Lorenzo to lie 1.499 behind Pedrosa.

LAP 5

Edwards falls from sixth place. He picks up his bike, restarts, but stops shortly afterwards. At the front, Pedrosa increases his lead over the two Yamaha-Fiats (2.074 on Rossi.)

HALF-DISTANCE (13 LAPS)

Pedrosa is a polite young man and as he's been told to pay homage to his king, he continues to dominate, lapping in the 1'40.8 bracket with metronomic regularity. No surprise then that his lead over his pursuer - Rossi - has now climbed to 3.734. Lorenzo is a further 6 tenths behind.

LAP 20

Dovizioso has passed the old man and is just behind the two Italians.

Toseland gets past Vermeulen in spectacular style. At the front the Pedrosa to Rossi gap is now 4.463.

LAP 24

Stoner, in attempting to pass Nakano and Vermeulen in one fell swoop, goes off again.

FINISH (27 LAPS)

Pedrosa controls the situation. Rossi suddenly loses 9 tenths to Lorenzo, as he thought the race was over! But he gets back to work. There was no time to get bored in the battle for fifth and it's the old stager, Capirossi, who has the last word up against Toseland, Hopkins and Dovizioso.

CHAMPIONSHIP

The king of Spain is a happy man as his two countrymen dominate the world championship after two races: 41 points for little page boy Pedrosa and 36 for Lorenzo the knight.

Hayden and Rossi beaten once again. On right, Stoner fights for…eleventh place with West and Melandri.

GP SPAIN | 30th March 2008 | Jerez | 4.423 m

STARTING GRID

1	48	J. Lorenzo	Yamaha	1'38.189
2	2	D. Pedrosa	Honda	1'38.789
3	5	C. Edwards	Yamaha	1'38.954
4	69	N. Hayden	Honda	1'39.061
5	46	V. Rossi	Yamaha	1'39.064
6	14	R. De Puniet	Honda	1'39.122
7	1	C. Stoner	Ducati	1'39.286
8	52	J. Toseland	Yamaha	1'39.334
9	21	J. Hopkins	Kawasaki	1'39.439
10	65	L. Capirossi	Suzuki	1'39.484
11	56	S. Nakano	Honda	1'39.559
12	7	C. Vermeulen	Suzuki	1'39.704
13	4	A. Dovizioso	Honda	1'39.767
14	15	A. De Angelis	Honda	1'40.037
15	13	A. West	Kawasaki	1'40.088
16	24	T. Elias	Ducati	1'40.286
17	50	S. Guintoli	Ducati	1'40.939
18	33	M. Melandri	Ducati	1'41.027

RACE: 27 laps = 119.421 km

1	Dani Pedrosa	45'35.121 (157.183 km/h)
2	Valentino Rossi	+ 2.883
3	Jorge Lorenzo	+ 4.339
4	Nicky Hayden	+ 10.142
5	Loris Capirossi	+ 27.524
6	James Toseland	+ 27.808
7	John Hopkins	+ 28.296
8	Andrea Dovizioso	+ 28.449
9	Shinya Nakano	+ 32.569
10	Chris Vermeulen	+ 35.091
11	Casey Stoner	+ 42.223
12	Marco Melandri	+ 44.498
13	Anthony West	+ 45.807
14	Alex De Angelis	+ 45.871
15	Toni Elias	+ 1'09.558
16	Sylvain Guintoli	+ 1'14.442

Fastest lap

Pedrosa, in 1'40.116 (159.943 km/h). New record.
Previous: Rossi, in 1'40.596 (158.284 km/h/2005).

Outright fastest lap

Lorenzo, in 1'38.189 (162.164 km/h/2008).

CHAMPIONSHIP

1	D	Pedrosa	41 (1 win)
2	J	Lorenzo	36
3	V	Rossi	31
4	C	Stoner	30 (1 win)
5	A	Dovizioso	21
6	J	Toseland	20
7	N	Hayden	19
8	L	Capirossi	19
9	J	Hopkins	13
10	S	Nakano	10

BAUTISTA'S APRILIA BREAKS ON THE LAST LAP, CAUSING THE SPANIARD TO FALL, TAKING SIMONCELLI WITH HIM. KALLIO LAUGHS.

RUNNERS AND RIDERS

As in Doha, Manuel Hernandez (Junior) replaces Gomez, who is still injured. There are no wild cards in the class and that tells a tale, as the days of 250 cc two-stroke technology are numbered, with no national championships and a weak field in the European series.

QUALIFYING

While the KTMs set the tone on Friday with three in the top four, Bautista takes pole on Saturday, ahead of Kallio, Debon, who injured himself in a place that makes men's eyes water and Luthi. The top twelve are all within less than a second and, as is often the case at Jerez, the lap times seen at the IRTA test are out of reach.

START

Kallio takes off ahead of Luthi, while Debon botches his start. First time across the line and the Finn has 131 thousandths in hand over the Swiss, who leads Bautista. Simon has dropped two spots at the hairpin after a vigorous double attack from Bautista and Simoncelli.

LAP 2

Bautista has taken the lead, Simoncelli has got past Luthi to take third place. Faubel falls.

He who laughs last laughs longest: actors in a thrilling duel, Bautista and Simoncelli (above) will not see the finish, much to the delight of Pasini, Kallio and Takahashi, who end up on the podium. Below, Luthi meets the King of Spain on the grid.

LAP 4

Simoncelli is now second at 166 thousandths. Behind him, locked in combat are Kallio, Barbera and Luthi.

HALF-DISTANCE (13 LAPS)

Bautista and Simoncelli are inseparable (218 thousandths.) Kallio is third, but over 6 seconds behind. Having saved his tyres in the early stages is Luthi, 1.159 off the KTM rider. Behind them, a great scrap between Takahashi, Barbera and Simon.

LAP 17

Luthi took two goes to surprise Kallio and take third place, 8.456 down.

LAP 19

Simoncelli and Bautista trade places several times. Kallio and Takahashi latch onto Luthi.

LAP 21

Kallio retakes third spot.

LAP 23

Luthi is thrown off his mount and has a terrible fall. Simoncelli has just taken the lead.

LAP 24

Bautista is back in charge and there's an amazing battle for the win.

FINISH (26 LAPS)

Going into the last lap, the two leaders are split by 131 thousandths. Simoncelli attacks like a mad thing and cannot avoid Bautista at the precise moment that the Spaniard's Aprilia has a mechanical problem which sees him slow very suddenly. Kallio gets it ahead of Pasini, who has come from nowhere, followed by Takahashi.

CHAMPIONSHIP

Two races, two podiums: it's looking good for Pasini and Kallio and much less so for two other big favourites for the world title. After this opening European round, Bautista is only eleventh in the championship (6 points) with Luthi last on 1.

GP SPAIN | 30th March 2008 | Jerez | 4.423 m

STARTING GRID

1	19	A. Bautistá	Aprilia	1'43.071
2	36	M. Kallio	KTM	1'43.111
3	6	A. Debón	Aprilia	1'43.286
4	12	T. Lüthi	Aprilia	1'43.596
5	60	J. Simón	KTM	1'43.629
6	4	H. Aoyama	KTM	1'43.640
7	21	H. Barberá	Aprilia	1'43.748
8	15	R. Locatelli	Gilera	1'43.823
9	58	M. Simoncelli	Gilera	1'43.921
10	75	M. Pasini	Aprilia	1'43.935
11	72	Y. Takahashi	Honda	1'44.022
12	32	F. Lai	Gilera	1'44.032
13	55	H. Faubel	Aprilia	1'44.166
14	52	L. Pesek	Aprilia	1'44.228
15	17	K. Abraham	Aprilia	1'44.249
16	41	A. Espargaro	Aprilia	1'44.335
17	25	A. Baldolini	Aprilia	1'44.754
18	54	M. Poggiali	Gilera	1'44.754
19	14	R. Wilairot	Honda	1'45.753
20	50	E. Laverty	Aprilia	1'46.034
21	10	I. Toth	Aprilia	1'46.710
22	43	M. Hernandez	Aprilia	1'46.835
23	45	D.-T. Pradita	Yamaha	1'47.989

RACE: 26 laps = 114.998 km

1	Mika Kallio	45'27.908
2	Mattia Pasini	+ 4.277
3	Yuki Takahashi	+ 4.287
4	Hiroshi Aoyama	+ 4.876
5	Hector Barberá	+ 5.968
6	Alex Debón	+ 13.633
7	Julian Simón	+ 16.372
8	Roberto Locatelli	+ 22.571
9	Aleix Espargaro	+ 28.606
10	Lukas Pesek	+ 32.726
11	Alex Baldolini	+ 38.602
12	Ratthapark Wilairot	+ 43.371
13	Karel Abraham	+ 54.159
14	Manuel Hernandez	+ 1'21.938
15	Imre Toth	+ 1 lap
16	Doni Tata Pradita	+ 1 lap

Fastest lap

Simoncelli, in 1'43.546 (153.775 km/h). New record.
Previous: De Angelis, in 1'44.295 (152.670 km/h/2007).

Outright fastest lap

Pedrosa, in 1'42.868 (154.788 km/h/2005).

CHAMPIONSHIP

1	M. Pasini	45 (1 win)
2	M. Kallio	41 (1 win)
3	H. Barberá	31
4	Y. Takahashi	27
5	A. Debón	23
6	R. Locatelli	16
7	J. Simón	14
8	A. Espargaro	14
9	H. Aoyama	13
10	K. Abraham	12

CORSI AND TEROL: WHEN TEAM-MATES GET ON LIKE A HOUSE ON FIRE.

RUNNERS AND RIDERS

Absent at Doha, after he was injured at the IRTA test, Marques hoped to make his comeback in front of his home crowd, but he had to give up on the idea. Things came close to disaster at KTM, as Swiss rider Randy Krummenacher had fallen while out mountain biking on the Monday before the GP. He travelled down to Andalusia by plane as planned, but on Friday morning he was in terrible pain so went to see the doctors, who sent him immediately to the hospital at San Lucar de Barrameda: he had a burst spleen and had already lost three litres of blood as he was rushed in for successful emergency surgery. Four riders have wild cards, including Axel, son of Sito, Pons, a double 250 world champion back in the Eighties.

QUALIFYING

Bradley Smith repeats his Qatar performance to take pole and he does it in style, as his closest pursuer, Terol, is over 4 tenths down, followed by the always excellent Stefan Bradl. Further back, the gaps are closer than ever, as seventeenth placed Pol Espargaro is only half a second off second placed Terol. A faller on Saturday morning, Germany's Robin Lasser is forced to pull out with a bruised twelfth vertebra.

START

Smith makes a perfect start ahead of Terol, Talmacsi and Bradl. Crossing the line for the first time, the Englishman heads Terol by 55 thousandths, but the second placed man is about to take matters in hand.

LAP 2

Terol lead Corsi by 236 thousandths, followed by Smith, Talmacsi and Bradl.

LAP 3

Talmacsi retires.

LAP 5

Terol, Smith and Corsi are glued together in 375 thousandths. Pablo Nieto is fourth, almost a second down.

LAP 7

Doha winner Gadea is a faller, as are Vasquez and then Bianco.

LAP 9

Webb and Joan Olive are fallers.

HALF-DISTANCE (12 LAPS)

Corsi, Terol, Smith, Nieto and Bradl: these five are fighting for the win, separated by 1.181. Behind them, Bonsey is a solitary sixth ahead of Di Meglio, Redding and the revelation of the weekend, the Swiss rider, Dominique Aegerter.

LAP 16

Corsi and Terol, sporting the same colours, have made the break, managing to pull out a lead of 1.406 over Bradl, who heads Smith and Nieto.

LAP 21

Corsi now has 1.245 over Terol.

FINISH (23 LAPS)

Corsi has a lead of almost 2 seconds going into the final lap. A superb duel for third place between Smith and Bradl.

CHAMPIONSHIP

The winner on the day moves into the lead, ahead of Stefan Bradl and Nicolas Terol; confirmation already that a wind of change is blowing through the category.

Terol and Corsi on the podium were more successful than Webb (99) and Olive. Opposite, Sito Pons double 250 world champion around 20 years ago, introduces his son, Axel.

GP SPAIN | 30th March 2008 | Jerez | 4.423 m

STARTING GRID

1	38	B. Smith	Aprilia	1'47.587
2	18	N. Terol	Aprilia	1'48.041
3	17	S. Bradl	Aprilia	1'48.070
4	1	G. Talmacsi	Aprilia	1'48.113
5	24	S. Corsi	Aprilia	1'48.128
6	51	S. Bonsey	Aprilia	1'48.146
7	63	M. Di Meglio	Derbi	1'48.165
8	45	S. Redding	Aprilia	1'48.315
9	99	D. Webb	Aprilia	1'48.333
10	35	R. De Rosa	KTM	1'48.345
11	77	D. Aegerter	Derbi	1'48.348
12	33	S. Gadea	Aprilia	1'48.437
13	22	P. Nieto	KTM	1'48.441
14	27	S. Bianco	Aprilia	1'48.481
15	11	S. Cortese	Aprilia	1'48.510
16	12	E. Rabat	KTM	1'48.520
17	44	P. Espargaro	Derbi	1'48.572
18	6	J. Olivé	Derbi	1'48.688
19	74	T. Nakagami	Aprilia	1'48.783
20	29	A. Iannone	Aprilia	1'48.791
21	71	T. Koyama	KTM	1'48.799
22	7	E. Vazquez	Aprilia	1'48.907
23	14	A. Pons	Aprilia	1'49.357
24	60	M. Ranseder	Aprilia	1'49.392
25	30	P. Tutusaus	Aprilia	1'49.446
26	5	A. Masbou	Loncin	1'49.720
27	16	J. Cluzel	Loncin	1'49.773
28	19	R. Lacalendola	Aprilia	1'49.879
29	95	R. Muresan	Aprilia	1'49.936
30	56	H. Van Den Berg	Aprilia	1'50.161
31	8	L. Zanetti	KTM	1'50.557
32	21	R. Lässer	Aprilia	1'50.942
33	78	D. Saez	Aprilia	1'51.362
34	69	L. Rossi	Honda	1'51.894
35	76	I. Maestro	Honda	1'52.070
36	79	A. Moncayo	Derbi	1'53.283

RACE: 23 laps = 101.729 km

1	Simone Corsi	41'46.100 (146.133 km/h)	
2	Nicolas Terol	+ 3.206	
3	Bradley Smith	+ 4.986	
4	Stefan Bradl	+ 5.022	
5	Pablo Nieto	+ 6.254	
6	Steve Bonsey	+ 20.563	
7	Scott Redding	+ 22.517	
8	Dominique Aegerter	+ 23.002	
9	Mike Di Meglio	+ 23.928	
10	Sandro Cortese	+ 33.541	
11	Raffaele De Rosa	+ 33.664	
12	Esteve Rabat	+ 33.987	
13	Tomoyoshi Koyama	+ 34.426	
14	Pol Espargaro	+ 40.038	
15	Takaaki Nakagami	+ 44.515	
16	Michael Ranseder	+ 45.498	
17	Jules Cluzel	+ 49.685	
18	Andrea Iannone	+ 53.186	
19	Pere Tutusaus	+ 58.037	
20	Roberto Lacalendola	+ 1'03.610	
21	Alexis Masbou	+ 1'04.732	
22	Ivan Maestro	+ 1'19.599	
23	Daniel Saez	+ 1'24.990	
24	Louis Rossi	+ 1'39.735	
25	Alberto Moncayo	+ 1'48.192	
26	Robert Muresan	+ 3 laps	

Fastest lap
Corsi, in 1'47.999 (147.434 km/h).
Record: Pesek, in 1'47.404 (148.251 km/h/2006).

Outright fastest lap
Pasini, in 1'46.937 (148.898 km/h/2006).

CHAMPIONSHIP

1	S. Corsi	34 (1 win)
2	S. Bradl	29
3	N. Terol	26
4	S. Gadea	25 (1 win)
5	J. Olivé	20
6	M. Di Meglio	20
7	S. Redding	20
8	B. Smith	16
9	P. Nieto	11
10	S. Cortese	11

A town centre race? Not quite yet, but development of the Estoril region is never ending and the buildings get ever closer to the circuit.

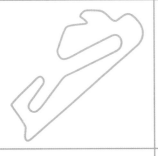

A star guest in the shape of Roger Federer who at the time, was still the tennis world number 1.

LORENZO,
THE GENIAL CRAZY GUY

WINNER AT HIS THIRD ATTEMPT IN
MOTOGP, JORGE LORENZO THUS JOINS
HIS COMPATRIOT DANIEL PEDROSA AT
THE HEAD OF THE CLASSIFICATION.

THE RACE

AH, IF ONLY THEY'D LISTENED…

Whether on track or from the top step of the podium, the show is omnipresent with Jorge Lorenzo, which is less and less amusing for reigning champion, Casey Stoner.

The not always infallible Enzo Ferrari was fond of saying: "It is important to know why one has lost a race, but even more important to understand why one has won." If only the Ducati MotoGP crew in their Borgo Panigale headquarters had listened to the late Commendatore, only a few miles down the road. While success certainly helps, even if at times it can make one blind, no one had been too convinced that the technical domination demonstrated in 2007 would yet again make the difference in 2008.

It is true that last year, the Stoner-Ducati-Bridgestone package was unbeatable over the course of the championship, but you would have to be really stupid to think the competition wouldn't react, especially when it consists of the two giants of the motorcycle world, Honda and Yamaha, not to mention the tyre giant, Michelin. You would also have to be somewhat naïve not to have realised that, given the way Loris Capirossi struggled

towards the end of 2007, that the Desmosedici GP7, while perfectly suited to the man who had become its star rider, still posed major problems to the man who had been the iconic figure in Ducati's MotoGP project. Looking at the last two races this year, it was clear at both Jerez de la Frontera and at Jerez, that Casey Stoner was a somewhat nervous world champion. Frustrated by these worries, the world champion was making some uncharacteristic errors.

If only Valentino Rossi had read the Enzo Ferrari biography. Would he have been so vehement about making the switch from Michelin to Bridgestone? Had he too been blinded by the almost total domination of the Japanese tyre company in 2007? With his obvious intelligence when it comes to racing, didn't he realise that Michelin would fight back? Didn't he know that the Clermont-Ferrand boys had the manpower and the means to match this challenge. The result,

where it matters, in the races is that within the works Yamaha team, Valentino is now having to follow the rules laid down by the good knight Jorge Lorenzo and his tyres supplied by Mr. Bibendum.

And what if Daniel Pedrosa's mentor, Alberto Puig had taken the time to flick through some motor racing history books. If he had been aware of Enzo Ferrari's golden rules, would he, having moulded the man in his image and turned him into a sad clone, realised that while Pedrosa held several key cards, namely his light weight and also, as was the case in the 125s and 250s, a made to measure bike from Honda, the opposition was going to fight back?

Yes, he should have understood all this. It might have stopped him from crying out that, "it's time to stop eulogising about Lorenzo as the level in the 250s has dropped ever since Dani left." In Portugal, on Sunday 13th April, he got his answer…

SPANISH WAS THE LANGUAGE AT THE PORTUGUESE GP WITH THE TOP TWO IN QUALIFYING, THE RACE AND THE LEAD OF THE CHAMPIONSHIP!

RUNNERS AND RIDERS

The biggest bluff of the weekend came on Thursday before first practice, as Rossi and Capirossi announce they are prepared to take the opportunity of the Chinese GP to demonstrate against the abuse of human rights, which causes plenty of consternation in this little world. The next day, Carmelo Ezpeleta reminds them of their responsibilities.

QUALIFYING

And for the third time in three races, his first three grands prix in the blue riband category - the fastest man is Jorge Lorenzo! More worries at Ducati, as Stoner, with one fall and several off track excursions throughout practice, is "only" ninth.

START

Yet again, it's Dani Pedrosa who is first off the mark, but first Rossi and then Lorenzo take charge, with Dovizioso tagging along. First time across the line and Rossi, Lorenzo, Dovizioso and Pedrosa have already pulled out almost a second on their pursuers, with Hopkins fifth and Stoner ninth.

LAP 7

Rossi has a lead of 351 thousandths over Lorenzo who is fighting off the attentions of Pedrosa and Dovizioso and Hopkins is not that far behind. Reigning champion Casey Stoner is still ninth, scrapping with Vermeulen and Toseland.

LAP 11

Pedrosa has got past Lorenzo at the end of the straight. Stoner has drifted to eleventh and Hayden has passed Hopkins.

LAP 13

Lorenzo is flying and has just shown Rossi how it's done in the uphill chicane at the Portuguese track.

HALF-DISTANCE (14 LAPS)

Lorenzo leads and, having produced a perfect lap, now leads Rossi by 438 thousandths, while Pedrosa follows like a shadow. Dovizioso is half a second behind in fourth.

LAP 15

Lorenzo goes quicker still, and Pedrosa, who has found a way past Rossi to go second, is 6 tenths down.

LAP 16

Dovizioso falls, having been a brilliant fourth up to that point.

LAP 18

Hayden falls. Lorenzo leads Pedrosa by a second and Rossi has been dropped.

LAP 21

Stoner has managed to get past Toseland and is now sixth.

LAP 27

De Puniet, who had just relieved Toseland of seventh place, hits the deck, but rejoins in fifteenth spot.

FINISH (28 LAPS)

With a 1.145 second safety net going into the final lap, Lorenzo takes his first victory in the big school. It's a giant moment and he picks up a pirate flag on the lap of honour to plant it further round the track.

CHAMPIONSHIP

Lorenzo has 61 points, so does Pedrosa: Spanish is the language of choice at the top of the tree. Rossi trails them in third by 14 points.

The first braking zone: Rossi has surprised Pedrosa (partly hidden) and Lorenzo who will fight back at half-distance. Just behind, number 4, Dovizioso will fall a bit further on. Above: Rossi and Capirossi wonder if they shouldn't make a human rights protest at the forthcoming Chinese GP, but they are soon brought into line.

GP PORTUGAL | 13th April 2008 | Estoril | 4.182 m

STARTING GRID

1	48	J. Lorenzo	Yamaha	1'35.715
2	2	D. Pedrosa	Honda	1'35.948
3	46	V. Rossi	Yamaha	1'36.199
4	69	N. Hayden	Honda	1'36.266
5	5	C. Edwards	Yamaha	1'36.289
6	52	J. Toseland	Yamaha	1'36.790
7	4	A. Dovizioso	Honda	1'36.998
8	14	R. De Puniet	Honda	1'37.223
9	1	C. Stoner	Ducati	1'37.253
10	21	J. Hopkins	Kawasaki	1'37.346
11	56	S. Nakano	Honda	1'37.664
12	65	L. Capirossi	Suzuki	1'37.786
13	7	C. Vermeulen	Suzuki	1'37.843
14	24	T. Elias	Ducati	1'38.561
15	13	A. West	Kawasaki	1'38.775
16	15	A. De Angelis	Honda	1'38.823
17	33	M. Melandri	Ducati	1'39.115
18	50	S. Guintoli	Ducati	1'39.355

RACE: 28 laps = 117.096 km

1	Jorge Lorenzo	45'53.089 (153.117 km/h)
2	Dani Pedrosa	+ 1.817
3	Valentino Rossi	+ 12.723
4	Colin Edwards	+ 17.223
5	John Hopkins	+ 23.752
6	Casey Stoner	+ 26.688
7	James Toseland	+ 32.631
8	Chris Vermeulen	+ 36.382
9	Loris Capirossi	+ 38.268
10	Shinya Nakano	+ 39.476
11	Alex De Angelis	+ 1'01.306
12	Toni Elias	+ 1'03.867
13	Marco Melandri	+ 1'09.525
14	Sylvain Guintoli	+ 1'09.634
15	Randy De Puniet	+ 1'11.542
16	Anthony West	+ 1'23.629

Fastest lap
Lorenzo, in 1'37.404 (154.564 km/h). New record.
Previous: Hayden, in 1'37.493 (154.423 km/h/2007)

Outright fastest lap
Lorenzo, in 1'35.715 (157.291 km/h/2008).

CHAMPIONSHIP

1	J. Lorenzo	61 (1 win)
2	D. Pedrosa	61 (1 win)
3	V. Rossi	47
4	C. Stoner	40 (1 win)
5	J. Toseland	29
6	L. Capirossi	26
7	J. Hopkins	24
8	C. Edwards	22
9	A. Dovizioso	21
10	N. Hayden	19

IT HAD SEEMED LIKELY AND IT WAS CONFIRMED IN PORTUGAL AT ESTORIL: ALVARO BAUTISTA IS UNBEATABLE.

RUNNERS AND RIDERS

No change among the regular riders, but three wild cards: China's Chow and Italy's Sandi, as well as Portugal's Sergio Batista, who has just turned sixteen, taking part in his first GP.

QUALIFYING:

Alvaro Bautista has a reputation for being strong here and the Spaniard confirms that from the very first qualifying session, even if he cannot shake off Simoncelli, as it's the Italian who takes pole position. Pasini and Kallio complete the front row. "Local boy" Batista misses the qualifying cut by a long way.

START

The World Tennis Number 1, Switzerland's Roger Federer, has come to cheer on his compatriot Thomas Luthi. Simoncelli dashes into the lead from Bautista, Kallio and Debon. Bautista takes charge to lead the first lap by 667 thousandths from Simoncelli.

LAP 2

A first break has been made in the pack. At the front there's Bautista, Simoncelli, Debon, Pasini, Takahashi and Aoyama, all within three seconds. Pesek leads the second group, over three seconds down.

LAP 4

Third placed Debon is a faller, while

The Pesek-Barbera duel was played out to the nearest centimetre. Above, Marco Simoncelli tried everything but Bautista was definitely the strongest.

Bautista and Simoncelli have charged off into the distance.

LAP 7

Bautista racks up the fastest laps and leads Simoncelli by 2.204. Kallio, Pasini, Takahashi and Aoyama are all scrapping for third.

HALF-DISTANCE (13 LAPS)

As expected, it's a case of Bautista and then the rest. His lead over Simoncelli is 7.251 seconds. Kallio in third trails by 12.243, still tussling with Pasini, Aoyama and Takahashi. Luthi is seventh and trying to catch the pack.

LAP 15

Kallio has built a 2 second cushion between himself and Pasini and the rest. Luthi and Simon, glued to the Swiss rider's back wheel, have got back in touch.

LAP 18

Luthi passes Pasini, then Aoyama and finally Takahashi to go fourth. At this point, he is the quickest man on track, as the cameras show a proud Federer supporting his countryman.

LAP 21

Pasini was sixth, but falls. The Italian gets going but falls again.

FINISH (26 LAPS)

Bautista has the race in his pocket, but Kallio has closed to 8 tenths of Simoncelli for second spot going into the final lap. Kallio tries to make the most of the slipstream and the two riders touch within sight of the finish, with the Gilera rider securing second place by a mere 13 thousandths of a second.

CHAMPIONSHIP

Kallio is the most consistent rider so far this season and leads Pasini by 12 points. This GP sees a return to form for Bautista, Simoncelli and to a lesser extent for Luthi.

GP PORTUGAL | 13th April 2008 | Estoril | 4.182 m

STARTING GRID

1	58	M. Simoncelli	Gilera	1'40.257
2	19	A. Bautistá	Aprilia	1'40.554
3	75	M. Pasini	Aprilia	1'40.653
4	36	M. Kallio	KTM	1'40.772
5	72	Y. Takahashi	Honda	1'41.063
6	4	H. Aoyama	KTM	1'41.228
7	6	A. Debón	Aprilia	1'41.280
8	12	T. Lüthi	Aprilia	1'41.356
9	21	H. Barberá	Aprilia	1'41.370
10	55	H. Faubel	Aprilia	1'41.470
11	60	J. Simón	KTM	1'41.820
12	52	L. Pesek	Aprilia	1'41.841
13	41	A. Espargaro	Aprilia	1'42.080
14	25	A. Baldolini	Aprilia	1'42.179
15	54	M. Poggiali	Gilera	1'42.265
16	17	K. Abraham	Aprilia	1'42.360
17	14	R. Wilairot	Honda	1'42.472
18	32	F. Lai	Gilera	1'42.574
19	15	R. Locatelli	Gilera	1'42.813
20	90	F. Sandi	Aprilia	1'43.288
21	50	E. Laverty	Aprilia	1'43.297
22	10	I. Toth	Aprilia	1'44.853
23	45	D.-T. Pradita	Yamaha	1'45.402
24	7	R. Gomez	Aprilia	1'46.051
25	89	H. Chow	Aprilia	1'46.594

Not qualified:

91	S. Batista	Honda	1'57.196

RACE: 26 laps = 108.732 km

1	Alvaro Bautistá	44'34.257 (146.371 km/h)
2	Marco Simoncelli	+ 7''050
3	Mika Kallio	+ 7''063
4	Thomas Lüthi	+ 12.998
5	Hiroshi Aoyama	+ 14.666
6	Yuki Takahashi	+ 18.498
7	Julian Simón	+ 26.812
8	Hector Barberá	+ 28.012
9	Hector Faubel	+ 28.288
10	Lukas Pesek	+ 36.966
11	Aleix Espargaro	+ 38.296
12	Alex Baldolini	+ 52.070
13	Ratthapark Wilairot	+ 1'13.303
14	Federico Sandi	+ 1'17.592
15	Eugene Laverty	+ 1'21.363
16	Karel Abraham	+ 1'26.355
17	Manuel Poggiali	+ 1'27.438
18	Imre Toth	+ 1 lap
19	Doni Tata Pradita	+ 1 lap

Fastest lap

Bautistá, in 1'41.425 (148.436 km/h).
Record: Bautistá, in 1'40.521 (149.771 km/h/2007).

Outright fastest lap

Simoncelli, in 1'40.257 (150.166 km/h/2008).

CHAMPIONSHIP

1	M. Kallio	57 (1 win)
2	M. Pasini	45 (1 win)
3	H. Barberá	39
4	Y. Takahashi	37
5	A. Bautistá	35 (1 win)
6	H. Aoyama	24
7	A. Debón	23
8	J. Simón	23
9	M. Simoncelli	20
10	A. Espargaro	19

CORSI AGAIN AND TEROL STILL. BUT THIS TIME, JOAN OLIVE INSINUATED HIMSELF BETWEEN THE TWO MEN WHO DOMINATED THE EARLY PART OF THE CHAMPIONSHIP.

RUNNERS AND RIDERS

Injured at Jerez, Lasser is still absent, as is Randy Krummenacher, who underwent emergency surgery for a burst spleen, sustained four days earlier while mountain biking, on the Friday of the Spanish Grand Prix. He was sent home in a medical plane a week after the operation and had hopes of returning for the Chinese GP. Fifteen year old Marc Marquez, who had missed the first two grands prix after crashing at the IRTA test, was finally making his debut.

QUALIFYING

The WRB team, run by Manuel Burillo and Josep Criville, the brother of the former world champion, continues down the positive path of its Jerez debut, with Corsi on pole position and Terol third on the front row. The youngsters Bonsey and Webb are also well placed. Di Meglio, who looked particularly comfortable throughout practice, falls heavily on Saturday afternoon, but without injury. Fellow countryman Louis Rossi is not so lucky as he breaks his right tibia.

START

Terol has super reflexes, ahead of Webb, Corsi and Smith. The Spaniard has 4 tenths in hand over the Englishman at the end of the opening lap, which Van Den Berg fails to finish.

LAP 2

Corsi helps himself to second place and rejoins team-mate Terol: Olive and Smith are the only ones who can match the pace setters.

LAP 3

Olive has passed Corsi and takes the lead down the main straight.

LAP 4

Redding goes for a trip through the gravel.

LAP 6

The top four - Terol, Olive, Smith and Corsi are covered by 376 thousandths. Reigning champion Talmacsi, is a solitary fifth, at 1.6 seconds.

LAP 7

De Rosa has a heavy fall. Olive heads the field.

HALF-DISTANCE (12 LAPS)

Olive leads Corsi by 48 thousandths. Smith is 7 tenths down in third, with Terol on his back wheel.

LAP 13

Smith falls.

LAP 15

Olive and Corsi are still inseparable. Terol is a lonely third.

LAP 20

France's Mike di Meglio is in the thick of it, now fourth and battling with Bonsey.

FINISH (23 LAPS)

Olive is 3 tenths off Corsi going into the final lap, but the Italian is faultless to take his 2nd win in a row and consolidate his position at the top of the championship leaderboard.

CHAMPIONSHIP

59 points for Corsi, 42 for team-mate Terol: life is good in the Hispanic-Italian team. Olive is third, but already trailing by 19 points. KTM, who dreamed of the world title and had increased its numbers accordingly is having to swallow a bitter pill. The marque's best placed rider is Pablo Nieto in 15th spot.

The freestyle prize goes to Raffaele De Rosa. The one for concentration in the face of a beautiful girl goes to Dominique Aegerter. And finally, the disguise prize goes to Corsi the legionnaire.

GP PORTUGAL | 13th April 2008 | Estoril | 4.182 m

STARTING GRID

1	24	S. Corsi	Aprilia	1'45.367
2	51	S. Bonsey	Aprilia	1'45.621
3	18	N. Terol	Aprilia	1'45.622
4	99	D. Webb	Aprilia	1'45.782
5	33	S. Gadea	Aprilia	1'45.808
6	6	J. Olivé	Derbi	1'45.854
7	17	S. Bradl	Aprilia	1'46.026
8	63	M. Di Meglio	Derbi	1'46.144
9	1	G. Talmacsi	Aprilia	1'46.158
10	45	S. Redding	Aprilia	1'46.329
11	71	T. Koyama	KTM	1'46.448
12	29	A. Iannone	Aprilia	1'46.491
13	38	B. Smith	Aprilia	1'46.523
14	22	P. Nieto	KTM	1'46.622
15	7	E. Vazquez	Aprilia	1'46.679
16	35	R. De Rosa	KTM	1'46.736
17	27	S. Bianco	Aprilia	1'46.860
18	12	E. Rabat	KTM	1'47.016
19	77	D. Aegerter	Derbi	1'47.133
20	11	S. Cortese	Aprilia	1'47.292
21	44	P. Espargaro	Derbi	1'47.300
22	60	M. Ranseder	Aprilia	1'47.628
23	30	P. Tutusaus	Aprilia	1'47.717
24	74	T. Nakagami	Aprilia	1'47.724
25	5	A. Masbou	Loncin	1'47.734
26	93	M. Marquez	KTM	1'47.817
27	16	J. Cluzel	Loncin	1'47.953
28	8	L. Zanetti	KTM	1'47.971
29	56	H. Van Den Berg	Aprilia	1'48.495
30	95	R. Muresan	Aprilia	1'48.840
31	76	I. Maestro	Aprilia	1'49.355
32	14	A. Pons	Aprilia	1'49.669
33	13	D. Lombardi	Aprilia	1'49.690
34	36	C. Carillo	Honda	1'49.809
35	19	R. Lacalendola	Aprilia	1'50.539
36	37	K. Pesek	Aprilia	1'50.687

Not qualified:
	69	L. Rossi	Honda	---

RACE: 23 laps = 96.186 km

1	Simone Corsi	40'56.168 (140.979 km/h)
2	Joan Olivé	+ 0.299
3	Nicolas Terol	+ 6.355
4	Steve Bonsey	+ 14.973
5	Daniel Webb	+ 15.532
6	Gabor Talmacsi	+ 15.868
7	Mike Di Meglio	+ 15.875
8	Stefan Bradl	+ 17.887
9	Sergio Gadea	+ 18.123
10	Sandro Cortese	+ 22.613
11	Andrea Iannone	+ 27.490
12	Dominique Aegerter	+ 27.544
13	Pol Espargaro	+ 28.370
14	Michael Ranseder	+ 28.417
15	Efren Vasquez	+ 32.713
16	Tomoyoshi Koyama	+ 34.002
17	Stefano Bianco	+ 47.698
18	Marc Marquez	+ 51.637
19	Takaaki Nakagami	+ 51.679
20	Alexis Masbou	+ 51.717
21	Scott Redding	+ 1'07.908
22	Pere Tutusaus	+ 1'15.894
23	Dino Lombardi	+ 1'19.975
24	Robert Muresan	+ 1'39.194
25	Cyril Carrillo	+ 1'39.218
26	Axel Pons	+ 1'43.956
27	Ivan Maestro	+ 1 lap
28	Karel Pesek	+ 1 lap

Fastest lap
Corsi, in 1'45.557 (142.626 km/h).
Record: Talmacsi, in 1'45.027 (143.345 km/h/2007).

Outright fastest lap
Pasini, in 1'44.675 (143.828 km/h/2007).

CHAMPIONSHIP

1	S. Corsi	59 (2 wins)
2	N. Terol	42
3	J. Olivé	40
4	S. Bradl	37
5	S. Gadea	32 (1 win)
6	M. Di Meglio	29
7	S. Bonsey	23
8	D. Webb	21
9	S. Redding	20
10	S. Cortese	17

Valentino Rossi out on his own against the futuristic décor of the Shanghai circuit. First win of the season for the King…

Things are moving fast in the Empire of the east: after Loncin comes the news that Maxtra plan to enter GP soon.

LORENZO GETS
A FIRST WARNING

A SPECTACULAR FALL IN QUALIFYING AND A
RACE AGAINST TIME WITH THE DOCTORS:
THE SPANIARD DISCOVERS THE HARD
TRUTH OF THE BLUE RIBAND CATEGORY.

THE RACE

WELCOME TO SENIOR SCHOOL JORGE...

"Let them laugh, let them laugh, let's see how they feel the first time they're thrown off their bikes. They'll understand that the impact is nothing like anything they've experienced in the past in the little classes." Every time a newcomer shines in the early part of his time in the blue riband category, there's a certain glee in this kind of talk. And they are the same people who say that the MotoGP bikes are currently easy to ride thanks to all the various electronic aids and that these old boys would like to see how the current youngsters would have coped with the monsters that were the old 500 cc two strokes.

The old boys know however that we are not in some sort of "Jurassic Moto Park" created by some enthusiast on a desert island, on which he might have rebuilt the old time monsters. No, this is the present, a present moving evermore towards the future and these presents and futures are

represented by Jorge Lorenzo who turns 21 on the Sunday of the Chinese GP. A cool customer, the 250 double world champion? That's not the half of it. In three GPs, he has taken three pole positions, got three podium finishes and taken his first win in the "Big School." And now he has also been blooded: on the day after his win in Portugal, he underwent an operation for pump-up syndrome and in China, on Friday morning, at 10h37 to be precise, he was bucked off his thoroughbred. It looked frightening and the images were soon seen all over the world: Lorenzo flying through the air, crashing down on the tarmac, sliding into the gravel trap and immediately holding both his legs in pain. "His knees gone! His ankles have had it! His season's over!" Those watching the crash on television were convinced it was serious.

All that could be done was to wait, while listening to the usual litany in these situations: "Jorge has

been taken to the medical centre. After preliminary checks it has been decided to helicopter him to a Shanghai hospital for X-rays to both his ankles." Then, in the early afternoon, he returned to the track to watch qualifying on television and the verdict was "a broken left ankle and a badly bruised but unbroken right one. Lorenzo will try and ride tomorrow."

Tomorrow was Saturday. And there he was, hardly able to walk, needing to be lifted onto his bike, but he went on to set the fourth fastest time after yet another rodeo ride. He is still there on Sunday, smiling brightly on the grid, mollycoddled by Dr. Claudio Costa, who had known what to tell him (and what to get him to swallow?) in this type of situation. His race? It would be one of courage. Fourth at the flag and it was only when he got home to Spain that it was discovered his injuries were more serious than had been thought at the time.

Unseated by his Yamaha, Jorge Lorenzo is about to land painfully on his ankles. Concussed, he still takes part in qualifying on Saturday and the race on Sunday.

JORGE LORENZO'S COURAGEOUS DEMONSTRATION ALMOST ECLIPSES VALENTINO ROSSI'S FIRST WIN OF 2008.

RUNNERS AND RIDERS

The day after winning in Estoril, Lorenzo had an operation to deal with pump-up syndrome, carried out by Professor Mir in Barcelona, the procedure involving enlarging the muscle tendons in the forearms.

QUALIFYING

The first day features a fall for Lorenzo: thrown from his Yamaha in the Shanghai corkscrew, the championship leader flies two metres into the air before crashing down heavily. The result is a broken left ankle and extensive bruising to the right one. Lorenzo undergoes checks in a Shanghai hospital and returns to the track on Friday afternoon, before setting the fourth fastest time on Saturday! A fourth pole from four GPs for Yamaha, this time courtesy of Colin Edwards who heads Rossi and Stoner.

START

The race is declared "wet" but the track is dry. Edwards gets it right, as does Stoner, who squeezes past before having to give best to the Texan. Rossi is third, then comes Pedrosa ahead of the Lorenzo-Hayden duo.

LAP 2

Pedrosa takes the lead and immediately pulls out a 1.114 lead over Edwards, who is about to be passed by Rossi.

LAP 4

Rossi is the fastest man on track,

Lorenzo grits his teeth (top,) Rossi leads the parade (above.) Once again, Dr. Claudio Costa has been the magic healer.

closing to within 469 thousandths of Pedrosa.

LAP 5

Rossi finds a way past.

LAP 8

Rossi and Pedrosa are still inseparable (just 239 thousandths between them.) Stoner is over 4 seconds back and now it's Melandri in fourth: the Italian finally seems to have got the measure of the Desmosedici.

HALF-DISTANCE (11 LAPS)

The two leaders have got under the 2 minute mark for the lap. Rossi's lead remains stable at 241 thousandths. Stoner is now 8 seconds down, the world champion having a lonely race. Melandri is fourth, followed by Dovizioso and Edwards.

LAP 12

Lorenzo has passed Hayden for seventh place.

LAP 14

An incredible Lorenzo now takes Edwards and then Dovizioso to go fifth!

LAP 15

Lorenzo is fourth, as Melandri has also had to give best.

LAP 18

Rossi has just set a new lap record and he leads Pedrosa by 480 thousandths. One lap later, the king's advantage has tripled! It's all over.

LAP 20

Dovizioso is in trouble and is about to be passed by Capirossi and Elias.

FINISH (22 LAPS)

With 3.697 in hand, going into the final lap, Mr. Valentino Rossi takes his first win on Bridgestones. Hats off to Lorenzo who finishes fourth.

CHAMPIONSHIP

Pedrosa is now out on his own in the lead. Lorenzo is 7 points down, Rossi 9. The rest of the season looks very promising.

GP CHINA | 4th May 2008 | Shanghai | 5.281 m

STARTING GRID

1	5	C. Edwards	Yamaha	1'58.139
2	46	V. Rossi	Yamaha	1'58.494
3	1	C. Stoner	Ducati	1'58.591
4	48	J. Lorenzo	Yamaha	1'58.711
5	2	D. Pedrosa	Honda	1'58.855
6	65	L. Capirossi	Suzuki	1'58.941
7	52	J. Toseland	Yamaha	1'59.254
8	7	C. Vermeulen	Suzuki	1'59.325
9	14	R. De Puniet	Honda	1'59.357
10	69	N. Hayden	Honda	1'59.507
11	4	A. Dovizioso	Honda	1'59.559
12	33	M. Melandri	Ducati	1'59.678
13	56	S. Nakano	Honda	1'59.716
14	21	J. Hopkins	Kawasaki	1'59.740
15	24	T. Elias	Ducati	1'59.933
16	15	A. De Angelis	Honda	2'00.316
17	50	S. Guintoli	Ducati	2'00.760
18	13	A. West	Kawasaki	2'00.838

RACE: 22 laps = 116.182 km

1	Valentino Rossi	44'08.061 (157.947 km/h)
2	Dani Pedrosa	+ 3.890
3	Casey Stoner	+ 15.928
4	Jorge Lorenzo	+ 22.494
5	Marco Melandri	+ 26.957
6	Nicky Hayden	+ 28.369
7	Colin Edwards	+ 29.780
8	Toni Elias	+ 30.225
9	Loris Capirossi	+ 31.440
10	Shinya Nakano	+ 35.969
11	Andrea Dovizioso	+ 36.246
12	James Toseland	+ 43.191
13	Randy De Puniet	+ 43.442
14	John Hopkins	+ 45.855
15	Sylvain Guintoli	+ 46.330
16	Alex De Angelis	+ 50.593
17	Anthony West	+ 1'05.593

Fastest lap
Rossi, in 1'59.273 (159.395 km/h). New record.
Previous: Pedrosa, in 1'59.318 (159.335 km/h/2006).

Outright fastest lap
Edwards, in 1'58.139 (160.925 km/h/2008).

CHAMPIONSHIP

1	D. Pedrosa	81 (1 win)
2	J. Lorenzo	74 (1 win)
3	V. Rossi	72 (1 win)
4	C. Stoner	56 (1 win)
5	L. Capirossi	33
6	J. Toseland	33
7	C. Edwards	31
8	N. Hayden	29
9	A. Dovizioso	26
10	J. Hopkins	26

MIKA KALLIO AND KTM, TOTALLY DOMINANT IN DIFFICULT GRIP CONDITIONS.

RUNNERS AND RIDERS
No wild cards in the class, as even the Chinese Zonghsen team has pulled out of its home grand prix.

QUALIFYING
Bautista confirms he's the boss as the former 125 world champion dominates the two days of qualifying and eventually beats his closest pursuer, Barbera, by over 4 tenths. Kallio and Simon complete the front row, but the two KTM riders were not very consistent in qualifying, unlike Simoncelli and Luthi who are next up.

START
A dry line is beginning to emerge. Barbera gets the best start as Luthi remains glued to the grid. Simoncelli leads momentarily, but it's Barbera who heads the pack at the end of the lap. Futher back, Abraham, Baldolini, Poggiali and Laverty are fallers.

LAP 2
Bautista takes command, but Simoncelli, Barbera and Kallio hang on.

LAP 4
Barbera leads Bautista, Simoncelli, Kallio and Simon.

LAP 6
Simon goes off the track, Debon falls and collects Luthi as he rejoins the track, causing the Swiss rider to retire. At the front, Bautista has a lead of 658 thousandths over Barbera.

LAP 8
Kallio slips by Barbera to go second. The series leader is 1.335 off Bautista, who falls a bit further on. Lap 9: Kallio asked for nothing more: he finds himself leading by 1.182 from…his team-mate Aoyama, who has just passed Barbera and Simoncelli. Bautista finds himself in thirteenth place.

HALF-DISTANCE (11 LAPS)
Kallio leads Hiroshi Aoyama by 1.066. Takahashi is third at the mid-point, but he is about to be retaken by Simoncelli, while Barbera is struggling for pace on the drying track.

LAP 14
Takahashi has gapped Simoncelli, while Barbera continues to lose time and is passed by Pasini.

LAP 17
Takahashi is the fastest man on track and has closed to within 1.534 of Aoyama, who is still second, 1.804 off Kallio.

LAP 19
Pasini passes Simoncelli to go fourth and Debon has closed onto the back wheel of Barbera for sixth.

LAP 20
Debon has made the break. Kallio starts this lap with 3.550 in hand over Aoyama.

FINISH (21 LAPS)
A nice "orange" one-two and no Aprilias or sister Gileras on the podium…well, at least until the last braking point, when Takahashi went straight on. Suddenly, Pasini had made it to the third step.

CHAMPIONSHIP
It's a major coup for Mika Kallio, who already has a 21 point lead, equivalent to one win, after four rounds.

Kallio ahead of Aoyama. Bautista can't stop the mistake. Marco Simoncelli fourth, has not lost his smile and he will crop up again…

GP CHINA | **4th May 2008** | **Shanghai** | **5.281 m**

STARTING GRID					
1	19	A. Bautistá	Aprilia	2'04.882
2	21	H. Barberá	Aprilia	2'05.317
3	36	M. Kallio	KTM	2'05.402
4	60	J. Simón	KTM	2'05.651
5	58	M. Simoncelli	Gilera	2'05.724
6	12	T. Lüthi	Aprilia	2'05.853
7	75	M. Pasini	Aprilia	2'06.119
8	54	M. Poggiali	Gilera	2'06.192
9	15	R. Locatelli	Gilera	2'06.216
10	72	Y. Takahashi	Honda	2'06.245
11	4	H. Aoyama	KTM	2'06.276
12	6	A. Debón	Aprilia	2'06.279
13	55	H. Faubel	Aprilia	2'06.283
14	52	L. Pesek	Aprilia	2'06.428
15	41	A. Espargaro	Aprilia	2'06.559
16	32	F. Lai	Gilera	2'07.083
17	17	K. Abraham	Aprilia	2'07.101
18	14	R. Wilairot	Honda	2'07.114
19	50	E. Laverty	Aprilia	2'07.665
20	25	A. Baldolini	Aprilia	2'09.063
21	45	D.-T. Pradita	Yamaha	2'10.254
22	10	I. Toth	Aprilia	2'10.509
23	7	R. Gomez	Aprilia	2'11.624

RACE: 21 laps = 110.901 km		
1	Mika Kallio	48'12.217 (138.040 km/h)
2	Hiroshi Aoyama	+ 3.238
3	Mattia Pasini	+ 13.811
4	Marco Simoncelli	+ 18.474
5	Alex Debón	+ 21.066
6	Hector Barberá	+ 25.158
7	Yuki Takahashi	+ 29.990
8	Ratthapark Wilairot	+ 39.871
9	Aleix Espargaro	+ 48.344
10	Hector Faubel	+ 55.470
11	Roberto Locatelli	+ 55.832
12	Alvaro Bautistá	+ 1'00.442
13	Eugene Laverty	+ 1'00.732
14	Fabrizio Lai	+ 1'36.975
15	Doni Tata Pradita	+ 1'37.080
16	Imre Toth	+ 1'45.018
17	Russel Gomez	+ 2'13.718

Fastest lap
Kallio, in 2'15.834 (139.962 km/h).
Record: Lorenzo, in 2'05.738 (51.200 km/h/2007).

Outright fastest lap
Lorenzo, in 2'04.543 (152.650 km/h/2007).

CHAMPIONSHIP		
1	M. Kallio	82 (2 wins)
2	M. Pasini	61 (1 win)
3	H. Barberá	49
4	Y. Takahashi	46
5	H. Aoyama	44
6	A. Bautistá	39 (1 win)
7	A. Debón	34
8	M. Simoncelli	33
9	A. Espargaro	26
10	J. Simón	23

This time, Alexis Masbou has leaned just a bit too far. Opposite: Iannone takes his first GP win, watched by Sir John Surtees (above,) one of the partners in the Chinese Maxtra project.

A WET FIRST FOR ANDREA IANNONE. THE CONSISTENT MIKE DI MEGLIO IS BACK IN TOUCH.

RUNNERS AND RIDERS

34 days after having undergone emergency surgery for a burst spleen, Randy Krummenacher celebrates his comeback. Also back are Germany's Lasser, who had been injured at Jerez. The weekend is the occasion for an announcement that a second Chinese constructor, Maxtra, will join Loncin on the grid next year. Hidden behind this project are none other than John Surtees, the only man to be world champion on two and four wheels, seven times on bikes and once in Formula 1, Gary Taylor (former Suzuki team boss) and Jan Witteveen, the man who has 40 world titles in the two stroke classes.

QUALIFYING

Still very much on form, Terol misses out on pole by just 28 thousandths to Smith. Joining them on the front row are two experienced runners, Di Meglio and reigning world champion Talmacsi. Fallers on Saturday afternoon are Nieto (clavicle) and Cluzel (scaphoid) and both take no further part in proceedings.

START

The weather plays its part and even if the rain eases off ten minutes before the start, the track is soaked. Smith is promptest away, but its Iannone, off the second row who quickly veers into the lead. First time across the line, the Italian has a lead of 401 thousandths over Smith, who is followed by Talmacsi, Espargaro and Di Meglio.

LAP 2

Retirement for Gadea (engine.) Talmacsi takes the lead.

LAP 5

Series leader Simone Corsi falls, remounts and heads for the pits. Iannone has retaken the lead ahead of Talmacsi.

LAP 7

Smith falls, having been third.

HALF-DISTANCE (10 LAPS)

Ranseder is next to fall, having been sixth. At the front, Talmacsi has retaken the lead from Iannone by 41 thousandths. Di Meglio is third at 1"337.

LAP 11

Webb falls.

LAP 12

The victim on this lap is Cortese. Iannone has picked up the pace at the front and now leads Talmacsi by 1"095.

LAP 13

De Rosa falls and continues. Di Meglio relieves Talmacsi of second place.

LAP 14

Aegerter falls from tenth place and continues.

LAP 16

Redding falls.

LAP 17

Krummenacher retires (engine.)

FINISH (19 LAPS)

Iannone starts the final lap with 4.557 seconds in hand over Di Meglio, who is still fighting off Talmacsi. At the age of 19, the Italian takes his first GP win. Cortese falls after catching up with the fight for seventh.

CHAMPIONSHIP

Corsi maintains the lead, but Olive and Terol are now 9 points down, Di Meglio 10 and Bradl 11.

GP CHINA | 4th May 2008 | Shanghai | 5.281 m

STARTING GRID

1	38	B. Smith	Aprilia	2'12.364
2	18	N. Terol	Aprilia	2'12.392
3	63	M. Di Meglio	Derbi	2'12.905
4	1	G. Talmacsi	Aprilia	2'13.012
5	29	A. Iannone	Aprilia	2'13.147
6	6	J. Olivé	Derbi	2'13.149
7	44	P. Espargaro	Derbi	2'13.173
8	17	S. Bradl	Aprilia	2'13.184
9	33	S. Gadea	Aprilia	2'13.262
10	99	D. Webb	Aprilia	2'13.335
11	24	S. Corsi	Aprilia	2'13.404
12	11	S. Cortese	Aprilia	2'13.436
13	22	P. Nieto	KTM	2'13.744
14	77	D. Aegerter	Derbi	2'13.762
15	35	R. De Rosa	KTM	2'13.800
16	27	S. Bianco	Aprilia	2'13.845
17	51	S. Bonsey	Aprilia	2'13.947
18	74	T. Nakagami	Aprilia	2'14.031
19	60	M. Ranseder	Aprilia	2'14.180
20	7	E. Vazquez	Aprilia	2'14.561
21	30	P. Tutusaus	Aprilia	2'14.629
22	93	M. Marquez	KTM	2'14.796
23	12	E. Rabat	KTM	2'14.830
24	45	S. Redding	Aprilia	2'15.092
25	71	T. Koyama	KTM	2'15.122
26	5	A. Masbou	Loncin	2'15.325
27	8	L. Zanetti	KTM	2'15.721
28	16	J. Cluzel	Loncin	2'16.153
29	21	R. Lässer	Aprilia	2'16.362
30	19	R. Lacalendola	Aprilia	2'16.420
31	56	H. Van Den Berg	Aprilia	2'16.501
32	95	R. Muresan	Aprilia	2'16.693
33	34	R. Krummenacher	KTM	2'17.034
34	69	L. Rossi	Honda	2'18.440

RACE: 19 laps = 100.339 km

1	Andrea Iannone	46'02.275 (130.969 km/h)
2	Mike Di Meglio	+ 3.335
3	Gabor Talmacsi	+ 3.451
4	Pol Espargaro	+ 14.028
5	Stefan Bradl	+ 23.853
6	Joan Olivé	+ 31.962
7	Michael Ranseder	+ 33.758
8	Nicolas Terol	+ 34.696
9	Raffaele De Rosa	+ 34.838
10	Efren Vasquez	+ 41.011
11	Esteve Rabat	+ 41.139
12	Marc Marquez	+ 43.677
13	Tomoyoshi Koyama	+ 53.489
14	Steve Bonsey	+ 54.462
15	Pere Tutusaus	+ 58.706
16	Sandro Cortese	+ 59.454
17	Dominique Aegerter	+ 1'10.704
18	Louis Rossi	+ 1'47.918
19	Hugo Van Den Berg	+ 1'50.406

Fastest lap
Ranseder, in 2'23.432 (132.547 km/h).
Record: Bautistá, in 2'12.131 (143.884 km/h/2006).

Outright fsstest lap
Kallio, in 2'11.572 (144.495 km/h/2006).

CHAMPIONSHIP

1	S. Corsi	59 (2 wins)
2	J. Olivé	50
3	N. Terol	50
4	M. Di Meglio	49
5	S. Bradl	48
6	S. Gadea	32 (1 win)
7	A. Iannone	32 (1 win)
8	G. Talmacsi	30
9	P. Espargaro	26
10	S. Bonsey	25

Valentino Rossi is absolutely back in the title race: at Le Mans he again produced a perfect performance.

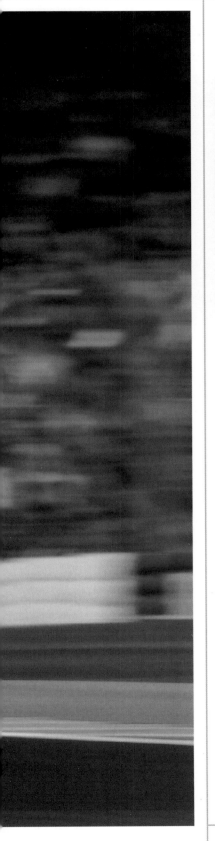

Two presidents - Vito Ippolito of the FIM and Herve Poncharal of IRTA on the start line, where this Caffe Latte team grid girl is turning a few heads.

ROSSI
EQUALS NIETO

IN WINNING HIS NINETIETH WORLD CHAMPIONSHIP WIN, VALENTINO ROSSI IS NOW LEVEL PEGGING WITH HIS MATE ANGEL NIETO. AHEAD OF HIM THERE IS NOW JUST ONE KING - GIACOMO AGOSTINI.

THE RACE

AIMING FOR KING AGO!

It had all been well organised as usual: on his lap of honour, Valentino Rossi stopped at the side of the track and Angel Nieto, in black leathers with "Bravo Valentino" on the back, took control of the winning Yamaha.

"We are back in business." We, the first person plural to underline that this latest win, the ninetieth in GP racing, is more than anything the result of teamwork.

Who won? Valentino Rossi of course, the rider who always has the last word, or the main role at least.

Who else won? Yamaha again, who last winter gave birth to its best ever M1. For the past few years, only Rossi and even then only with extreme difficulty, had managed to shine on the Yamaha, but now the Japanese bike is the one everyone wants and there's no better proof than this historic clean sweep of the top three spots at Le Mans. Three M1s at the top of the results sheet, but coming from two different teams and supplied by two competing tyre companies, proves its dominance.

Who else won? Bridgestone, or maybe it's more a case of the man who is the centre of interest for the Japanese manufacturer, Valentino Rossi. It always comes down to the rider, the key piece of the jigsaw in the world of motorcycle GPs.

What can one say about Valentino Rossi that hasn't been said or written before. He is a unique talent who has also mastered the art of communication. He is seen as motorcycling perfection made human and that's been the case for several years, even before it became clearer still in the early races of the 2008 season, as he seemed stronger than ever. He had grown in stature since having to tidy up his entourage and that had seem him become more confident within himself and almost a normal young man who needs his roots, his family and friends in order to feel good.

The great irony of the situation and this life that it was through losing the millions he had to hand over to the Italian tax authorities, that he found happiness again! And, at Le Mans, with its historic backdrop, Rossi very much part of that history, wrote another nice page of it, matching Angel Nieto's total of GP wins. When Rossi makes history, he does it in words and deeds and his innate sense of spectacle. On his lap of honour, he stopped as usual at a pre-arranged spot. His true fans were there, those who had been with him from the start and a little man squeezed into racing leathers with the number 90 on it. The writing on the leathers read "Bravo Valentino." The man in black held the handlebars of the Yamaha M1, while its usual rider got on the back of the seat, holding a flag specially made for the occasion. On this historic day, Angel Nieto (13 world titles or rather Angel 12 +1!) and Valentino Rossi were as one on the bike.

What's next? Sights set on Giacomo Agostini, Rossi's next target: "The 122 wins will be difficult. But the 68 in the blue riband category, who knows?" Rossi is already at number 64!

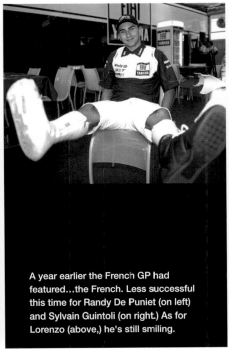

A year earlier the French GP had featured…the French. Less successful this time for Randy De Puniet (on left) and Sylvain Guintoli (on right.) As for Lorenzo (above,) he's still smiling.

ROSSI WITH PANACHE, LORENZO, WHO ASKED FOR A CHAIR TO SIT ON THE SECOND STEP OF THE PODIUM, WITH COURAGE!

RUNNERS AND RIDERS

"I couldn't have stood watching this race on television." On the Thursday before qualifying, Lorenzo confirms that his injuries are more serious than had been thought in China as he also has a fracture of the astragal bone and a torn ligament. But he wants to start this French GP.

QUALIFYING

With good reason, there is a lot more talk about Lorenzo than Pedrosa, who nevertheless takes pole. The double 250 world champion falls once on Friday and again on Saturday, after which he said "I thought I was going to kill myself" and he goes off the track twice more during qualifying.

START

Stoner, Pedrosa and Edwards lead as they go under the Dunlop bridge. Hayden, Rossi and Vermeulen are not far behind and De Puniet goes through the gravel trap.

LAP 2

Toseland touches Dovizioso and hits the deck.

LAP 7

As Stoner looked to be making a break, Rossi sounded the alarm and four of them, Stoner, Rossi, Pedrosa and Vermeulen are covered by 613 thousandths.

LAP 8

Rossi takes the lead.

LAP 10

Rossi leads Stoner by 1.128, with the Australian apparently holding up Pedrosa and Edwards. Lorenzo has passed Hayden for sixth.

LAP 11

Pedrosa passes Stoner with a stunning overtaking move.

HALF-DISTANCE (14 LAPS)

Rossi is untouchable, with a 3.116 lead over Pedrosa who still has Stoner and Edwards up his exhaust pipe. Just behind them, Lorenzo is about to overhaul Vermeulen for fifth place.

LAP 16

The rain is coming and the white flag is waved to indicate that, from this point on, riders can pit to change bikes.

LAP 17

Hopkins suffers a broken chain. Lorenzo closes on Edwards but has a moment.

LAP 20

It's raining over the pits, Lorenzo has just passed Edwards and Melandri who was last of all, is the first to come in and change bikes.

LAP 21

Stoner breaks down on the main straight as Lorenzo swallows up Pedrosa.

LAP 22

Edwards passes Pedrosa, so that there are three Yamahas in the top three slots!

LAP 23

Stoner restarts on his spare bike.

FINISH (28 LAPS)

Pedrosa has lost touch with Edwards on the penultimate lap. Rossi takes his 90th GP win to join Angel Nieto in the list of world championship winners. Lorenzo, who has to walk on crutches, pops an unbelievable wheelie. Edwards is third, completing an historic all-Yamaha podium.

CHAMPIONSHIP

Rossi moves into the lead, heading Lorenzo and Pedrosa by 3 points.

GP FRANCE | 18th May 2008 | Le Mans | 4.185 m

STARTING GRID

1	2	D. Pedrosa	Honda	1'32.647
2	5	C. Edwards	Yamaha	1'32.774
3	1	C. Stoner	Ducati	1'32.994
4	46	V. Rossi	Yamaha	1'33.157
5	48	J. Lorenzo	Yamaha	1'33.269
6	69	N. Hayden	Honda	1'33.286
7	52	J. Toseland	Yamaha	1'33.396
8	7	C. Vermeulen	Suzuki	1'33.440
9	21	J. Hopkins	Kawasaki	1'33.628
10	4	A. Dovizioso	Honda	1'33.689
11	65	L. Capirossi	Suzuki	1'33.707
12	14	R. De Puniet	Honda	1'33.723
13	56	S. Nakano	Honda	1'34.077
14	24	T. Elias	Ducati	1'34.561
15	15	A. De Angelis	Honda	1'34.670
16	50	S. Guintoli	Ducati	1'34.747
17	33	M. Melandri	Ducati	1'35.081
18	13	A. West	Kawasaki	1'35.349

RACE: 28 laps = 117.180 km

1	Valentino Rossi	44'30.799 (157.948 km/h)
2	Jorge Lorenzo	+ 4.997
3	Colin Edwards	+ 6.805
4	Dani Pedrosa	+ 10.157
5	Chris Vermeulen	+ 21.762
6	Andrea Dovizioso	+ 22.395
7	Loris Capirossi	+ 27.806
8	Nicky Hayden	+ 27.995
9	Randy De Puniet	+ 29.344
10	Shinya Nakano	+ 30.822
11	Toni Elias	+ 35.154
12	Alex De Angelis	+ 36.216
13	Sylvain Guintoli	+ 52.038
14	Anthony West	+ 1'29.307
15	Marco Melandri	+ 1 lap
16	Casey Stoner	+ 2 lap

Fastest lap

Rossi, in 1'34.215 (159.910 km/h). New record (new circuit layout).

Outright fastest lap

Pedrosa, in 1'32.647 (162.617 km/h/2008).

CHAMPIONSHIP

1	V. Rossi	97 (2 wins)
2	J. Lorenzo	94 (1 win)
3	D. Pedrosa	94 (1 win)
4	C. Stoner	56 (1 win)
5	C. Edwards	47
6	L. Capirossi	42
7	N. Hayden	37
8	A. Dovizioso	36
9	J. Toseland	33
10	S. Nakano	28

ALEX DEBON HAD TO WAIT UNTIL HIS 112TH GP TO FINALLY TAKE THE WIN.

RUNNERS AND RIDERS

The "Zonghsen Team Of China" did not take part in the Chinese GP…but it turned up at Le Mans with the same riders as in Portugal, namely Ho Wan Chow, who would fail to make the qualifying cut and Italy's Sandi. No other changes.

QUALIFYING

A thousandth! By a measly thousandth, Alex Debon stole the Tissot watch that goes with pole position from Alvaro Bautista. Simoncelli is not far off, neither is Luthi, with the top four all within 170 thousandths. Barbera is only eleventh, but he's back on the pace in the warm up. Pasini has a spectacular fall in qualifying, the Italian getting away with some bruises.

START

From pole, Debon starts on slicks, while most of the others have opted for cut tyres. Barbera is promptest away ahead of Simoncelli, Luthi and Debon. They're walking on eggshells in the descent after the Dunlop chicane. Crossing the line for the first time, Debon leads Kallio and Barbera.

LAP 3

Aoyama has come up to Debon's back wheel. Bautista has problems and is a long way back.

LAP 5

Debon is on form and now leads Aoyama by over 2 seconds, with

Takahashi closing on them.

LAP 8

Pesek is a faller.

LAP 10

Simon has passed Takahashi for second place. Out in front, Debon now has a 7 second lead.

HALF-DISTANCE (13 LAPS)

The skies have cleared again and, as the track dries, those who had taken the risks are rewarded. Debon still has a commanding lead, as Takahashi, who has re-passed Simon is 11.612 behind! Pasini and Kallio are duelling for fourth spot along with an excellent Poggiali and Simoncelli.

LAP 19:

The Kallio, Pasini, Poggiali trio is closing on the Takahashi-Simon duo, with Simoncelli not far behind.

LAP 22

Kallio and Pasini both go past Simon in one move. Poggiali also makes the most of the Spaniard's discomfort to move up a place. Their new target is now Yuki Takahashi.

LAP 23

Pasini is unstoppable and finds a way through.

FINISH (26 LAPS)

Debon sets off on his final lap with 9 seconds in hand over the Pasini-Simoncelli duo, who have also dealt with Takahashi. Simoncelli is scared of no one and passes his fellow countryman at the final braking point, to take a superb second place. Debon records his first GP win at his 112th attempt!

CHAMPIONSHIP

Kallio keeps the lead. Pasini is second, 16 points behind. Debon and Takahashi are third equal on 24. Two of the favourites, Bautista and Luthi, are a long way off.

Difficult conditions - what tyre to choose? Debon was brilliant on an Aprilia now fitted with electronic anti-spin and the race smiled on a Spaniard, but not the expected one, as Bautista, (on right) and Luthi, were losers in this lottery.

GP FRANCE | 18th May 2008 | Le Mans | 4.185 m

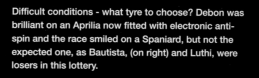

STARTING GRID

1	6	A. Debón	Aprilia	1'38.478
2	19	A. Bautistá	Aprilia	1'38.479
3	58	M. Simoncelli	Gilera	1'38.567
4	12	T. Lüthi	Aprilia	1'38.648
5	75	M. Pasini	Aprilia	1'38.788
6	36	M. Kallio	KTM	1'38.790
7	60	J. Simón	KTM	1'39.051
8	54	M. Poggiali	Gilera	1'39.064
9	41	A. Espargaro	Aprilia	1'39.184
10	4	H. Aoyama	KTM	1'39.197
11	21	H. Barberá	Aprilia	1'39.312
12	72	Y. Takahashi	Honda	1'39.446
13	55	H. Faubel	Aprilia	1'39.450
14	32	F. Lai	Gilera	1'39.724
15	52	L. Pesek	Aprilia	1'39.798
16	14	R. Wilairot	Honda	1'39.924
17	15	R. Locatelli	Gilera	1'40.171
18	50	E. Laverty	Aprilia	1'40.325
19	17	K. Abraham	Aprilia	1'40.455
20	90	F. Sandi	Aprilia	1'40.595
21	25	A. Baldolini	Aprilia	1'40.605
22	10	I. Toth	Aprilia	1'41.365
23	7	R. Gomez	Aprilia	1'42.820
24	45	D.-T. Pradita	Yamaha	1'42.847
Not qualified:				
	89	H. Chow	Aprilia	1'45.655

RACE: 26 laps = 108.810 km

1	Alex Debón		47'27.406 (137.569 km/h)
2	Marco Simoncelli		+ 4.816
3	Mattia Pasini		+ 4.998
4	Yuki Takahashi		+ 5.770
5	Mika Kallio		+ 6.197
6	Manuel Poggiali		+ 6.474
7	Hiroshi Aoyama		+ 14.909
8	Julian Simón		+ 17.526
9	Aleix Espargaro		+ 32.925
10	Hector Faubel		+ 36.719
11	Thomas Lüthi		+ 48.968
12	Hector Barberá		+ 56.837
13	Roberto Locatelli		+ 57.827
14	Alvaro Bautistá		+ 1'05.407
15	Ratthapark Wilairot		+ 1'24.336
16	Alex Baldolini		+ 1'24.577
17	Federico Sandi		+ 1 lap
18	Imre Toth		+ 1 lap
19	Russel Gomez		+ 1 lap

Fastest lap

Simoncelli, in 1'39.666 (151.164 km/h).
New record (new circuit layout).

Outright fastest lap

Debón, in 1'38.478 (152.988 km/h/2008).

CHAMPIONSHIP

1	M. Kallio	93 (2 wins)
2	M. Pasini	77 (1 win)
3	A. Debón	59 (1 win)
4	Y. Takahashi	59
5	M. Simoncelli	53
6	H. Aoyama	53
7	H. Barberá	53
8	A. Bautistá	41 (1 win)
9	A. Espargaro	33
10	J. Simón	31

Di Meglio heads the herd: from the top of the podium, the man from Toulouse savours his win, the first of the season. The French flag for one (Di Meglio) and a fall for the other, the world champion, Talmacsi. Maybe it was the handing over of power?

THE MARSEILLAISE PLAYS FOR MIKE DI MEGLIO IN THE SKIES ABOVE LA SARTHE, AS HE LEADS THE CHAMPIONSHIP.

RUNNERS AND RIDERS
Having got off the deck with a broken right scaphoid bone after falling in the Chinese GP, Frenchman Jules Cluzel pulls out and is replaced on his Chinese Loncin by Italy's Gioele Pellino.

QUALIFYING
Smith is the fastest man on Saturday, but he still misses out by 25 thousandths on beating Gadea's pole time from the previous day. Despite a harmless fall, Bradl is third ahead of series leader Corsi. KTM shows signs of fighting back with Rabat ninth, using one of last year's engines.

START
A super start from Gadea and Rabat too, who fires through from the third row. Crossing the line for the first time, Gadea leads his nearest pursuer, Bradl, by 290 thousandths.

LAP 3
Gadea is still out in front and now it is his world champion team-mate Talmacsi in second spot. Masbou, on the Chinese Loncin, is fourteenth.

LAP 5
A group of eight has made the break, led by Terol.

LAP 6
Marquez and Redding fall and Gadea is back in the lead.

LAP 8
Gadea, Talmacsi, Terol, Rabat, Bradl,

Di Meglio, Olive and Corsi are all within 1.238.

LAP 11
Bonsey falls at the chicane.

HALF-DISTANCE (12 LAPS)
Smith has rejoined the leaders, so there are now ten men fighting for the win, with Bradl leading Terol and Talmacsi. At the same time, the marshals indicate there are a few drops of rain at some points on the track.

LAP 14
Olive has taken matters in hand and immediately pulls out a one second lead, as rain falls at the chicane. One lap later, the red flag comes out and a quick look at the regulations shows that the order at the end of lap 14 decides the grid for the new start. There will be a five lap sprint to the flag to establish the final order.

SECOND START
Rabat, who had made the best start, falls at the chicane. Talmacsi completes the first lap in the lead, followed by Terol, Espargaro and Smith.

LAP 2
Talmacsi falls. Smith leads Terol and Di Meglio.

LAP 3
Di Meglio passes Smith and will soon move into the lead.

FINISH (5 LAPS)
Di Meglio wins the shortest race in history. It is his second world championship win and he becomes the first Frenchman, since Guy Bertin in 1979, to win his home GP. Masbou gives a Chinese bike its first ever world championship point.

CHAMPIONSHIP
Di Meglio does the double as he now leads the series. The GP Promoter, Claude Michy, is in seventh heaven.

GP FRANCE | 18th May 2008 | Le Mans | 4.185 m

STARTING GRID

1	33	S. Gadea	Aprilia	1'43.515
2	38	B. Smith	Aprilia	1'43.540
3	17	S. Bradl	Aprilia	1'43.710
4	24	S. Corsi	Aprilia	1'43.711
5	11	S. Cortese	Aprilia	1'43.811
6	63	M. Di Meglio	Derbi	1'43.956
7	18	N. Terol	Aprilia	1'44.116
8	1	G. Talmacsi	Aprilia	1'44.210
9	12	E. Rabat	KTM	1'44.344
10	44	P. Espargaro	Derbi	1'44.485
11	6	J. Olivé	Derbi	1'44.532
12	45	S. Redding	Aprilia	1'44.793
13	51	S. Bonsey	Aprilia	1'44.852
14	71	T. Koyama	KTM	1'44.864
15	99	D. Webb	Aprilia	1'44.874
16	60	M. Ranseder	Aprilia	1'44.893
17	35	R. De Rosa	KTM	1'44.945
18	29	A. Iannone	Aprilia	1'45.006
19	5	A. Masbou	Loncin	1'45.152
20	93	M. Marquez	KTM	1'45.250
21	27	S. Bianco	Aprilia	1'45.268
22	74	T. Nakagami	Aprilia	1'45.273
23	8	L. Zanetti	KTM	1'45.361
24	7	E. Vazquez	Aprilia	1'45.454
25	22	P. Nieto	KTM	1'45.541
26	56	H. Van Den Berg	Aprilia	1'45.864
27	77	D. Aegerter	Derbi	1'46.015
28	95	R. Muresan	Aprilia	1'46.140
29	30	P. Tutusaus	Aprilia	1'46.416
30	34	R. Krummenacher	KTM	1'46.569
31	52	S. Le Coquen	Honda	1'46.645
32	36	C. Carillo	Honda	1'47.185
33	21	R. Lässer	Aprilia	1'47.259
34	69	L. Rossi	Honda	1'47.330
35	61	G. Pellino	Loncin	1'47.371
36	19	R. Lacalendola	Aprilia	1'47.854
37	53	V. Debise	KTM	1'48.298
38	41	T. Siegert	Aprilia	1'50.021

COURSE: 5 tours = 20.925 km (*)

1	Mike Di Meglio	10'08.574 (123.781 km/h)	
2	Bradley Smith	+ 0.800	
3	Nicolas Terol	+ 3'.077	
4	Pol Espargaro	+ 10.407	
5	Andrea Iannone	+ 11.697	
6	Stefan Bradl	+ 11.881	
7	Lorenzo Zanetti	+ 16.372	
8	Joan Olivé	+ 16.545	
9	Raffaele De Rosa	+ 19.163	
10	Randy Krummenacher	+ 22.391	
11	Sandro Cortese	+ 22.847	
12	Pere Tutusaus	+ 23.195	
13	Simone Corsi	+ 23.553	
14	Gabor Talmacsi	+ 23.695	
15	Alexis Masbou	+ 24.240	
16	Takaaki Nakagami	+ 26.196	
17	Esteve Rabat	+ 26.411	
18	Roberto Lacalendola	+ 26.895	
19	Louis Rossi	+ 27.446	
20	Sergio Gadea	+ 31.829	
21	Daniel Webb	+ 34.810	
22	Robert Muresan	+ 35.190	
23	Dominique Aegerter	+ 47.840	

(*): The race was stopped on lap 15 by the arrival of rain. The classification was then taken from the previous lap (14) to establish the starting grid for a min race of 5 laps, the shortest in the history of the world championship.

Fastest lap
Espargaro, in 1'43.918 (144.979 km/h). New record (new circuit layout).

Outright fastest lap
Gadea, in 1'43.515 (145.544 km/h/2008).

CHAMPIONNAT

1	M. Di Meglio	74 (1 win)
2	N. Terol	66
3	S. Corsi	62 (2 wins)
4	J. Olivé	58
5	S. Bradl	58
6	A. Iannone	43 (1 win)
7	P. Espargaro	39
8	B. Smith	36
9	S. Gadea	32 (1 win)
10	G. Talmacsi	32

The Tuscan landscape is unique. So is race-winner Valentino Rossi.

06

Italy loves its racing. Naturally there are plenty of pro-Rossi fans, but there is plenty of room for a pretty smile from Alice…

ROSSI, KING
OF THE CASTLE

WIN NUMBER NINE FOR ROSSI ON THE
CIRCUIT HE HAS MADE HIS OWN,
MUGELLO. ON ONE OF THE SEASON'S
MOST DEMANDING TRACKS, THE KING
LEFT NOTHING BUT CRUMBS FOR HIS
UNDERLINGS - AND HIS LOYAL
SUBJECTS LOVED IT.

THE RACE

HE MAKES THE BANAL EXTRAORDINARY

In full cry, with his crazy crash-hat on, Vale was untouchable. And once he got onto the top step of the podium with a magnum of champagne in his hand, everyone got a spray.

What happened this stormy weekend in Tuscany is strange, very strange indeed. No, not the win for Rossi. Nor the friendly craziness of the crowd, as it is part of what makes this hilly region adorable, with its green forests and golden fields, with ancient villas tucked away in its folds and where every meal throws up more local treasures.

So, what was strange about this weekend? Quite simply an impression, a rare one in a world fought out to the nearest thousandth of a second, where riders rub shoulders at over 300 km/h as everyone is so close together and where the mechanical side and its occasional faults, can transform a given thing into a last minute sensation.

This unusual impression, come rain or shine is that nothing could affect Valentino Rossi. There was no question that here on his home turf of Mugello, anyone would be able to challenge his supremacy. Was it an impression? No, it was more

than an impression, much to the detriment of the gamblers who like to play it safe and who would have won nothing on betting on number 46 to win.

For the ninth time in his career and the seventh in the blue riband class, Rossi was untouchable. Right from qualifying, he wanted to remind everyone he is the one and only boss. So, he took his first ever Bridgestone-shod pole position, as well as helping a mate as he allowed Capirossi to hang on to his slipstream and take the third spot on the Suzuki. This was somewhat inconvenient for all those with plans of upsetting the king, as Stoner did the previous year.

But there was nothing to do about it. Neither Lorenzo, who ended up on the deck, nor Stoner, nor Pedrosa, who was suffering towards the end of the race, could worry Valentino, who is a much freer spirit now that he has found an element of calm within his entourage, now he has dropped

the hangers-on who had surrounded him, attracted by the amazing phenomenon that transformed excitement into dollars, a crowd that wanted him to believe it was helping him while in fact it was doing him so much harm. All that was now in the past. And even if past misdemeanours cost him a packet, he had few regrets, as he has rediscovered his true self.

Everything was now back on its regal course. And the special "Italian GP" helmet was an example of that, having thought it up with his pal Aldo Drudi, ending up with a more lifelike than real life version of Rossi, with his eyes in a wide open stare, a gob-smacked mouth, as though he'd just scared himself badly. Indeed, one of his first comments after the race referred to the helmet: "maybe instead of looking scared, I could be smiling, what do you think?" Everyone joined in the laughter. What's more to say? Nothing, just start the applause.

WHILE ROSSI WAS OUT OF SIGHT, LORENZO COULDN'T PUT PAID TO HIS DIFFICULT RUN OF FORM. ANGELIS REALLY CAUGHT THE EYE.

RUNNERS AND RIDERS

Lorenzo's pain is decreasing day by day and he no longer needs crutches. There's one guest with the return of Tadayuki Okada, Honda's development rider and HRC has entrusted him with the RC212V with pneumatic valves.

QUALIFYING

It's that man, Valentino Rossi, the king of Mugello and the rest of the world too, when on Saturday morning, he reveals his traditional Italian GP special helmet and it's definitely the most original of his nice collection, as Aldo Drudi has painted the boss's face on the boss's head, complete with wide open eyes and mouth. The boss? Rossi also proved that he is just that on the super fast track, which had been washed clean by two days of showers. He beats the best ever lap set on the Tuscan track, which dated back to the days of Sete.

START

Watched by Brad Pitt, yet again it's Pedrosa who gets the best start, ahead of Stoner, Capirossi and Rossi, who is about to move up.

LAP 2

Stoner moves ahead down the straight with Pedrosa, Rossi and Capirossi hanging on.

LAP 3

Dovizioso has passed Hayden and that allows Lorenzo to catch the American unawares. A bit later, Rossi gets ahead of Dani Pedrosa.

LAP 4

Rossi has passed Stoner in style on the vertiginous Mugello downhill section. He crosses the line with a lead of 150 thousandths.

LAP 6

Melandri and De Puniet fall. At the front, Rossi, Stoner and Pedrosa have pulled out a clear lead, as Capirossi cannot match their pace and is caught by Dovizioso and Lorenzo.

LAP 7

John Hopkins falls, followed a few seconds later by Lorenzo, just as he had overtaken Dovizioso.

LAP 8

Rossi has stepped up the pace. Result: 729 thousandths at the line. An incredible De Angelis is fourth, having set the fastest time in the warm-up.

HALF-DISTANCE (12 LAPS)

Still Rossi. Pedrosa is almost 2 seconds behind in second place, ahead of Stoner.

De Angelis is fourth and Toseland is now fifth.

LAP 13

Rossi continues his show run, while Stoner is on Pedrosa's back wheel and the Australian will get by shortly.

LAP 18

Rossi to Stoner is now 3.2 seconds and they have dropped Pedrosa.

FINISH (23 LAPS)

This is Rossi's seventh consecutive win in Tuscany, his third in a row this spring. The crowd is happy, as is the master, who thus provides Bridgestone with its first Mugello victory. Stoner is second, in front of Pedrosa, who watched De Angelis close on him over the last few laps.

CHAMPIONSHIP

With Lorenzo out of the running and Pedrosa finishing "only" third, Rossi assures his place at the top of the leader board.

Break-through time for Alex de Angelis as the San Marino rider (15) leads two Italians (left) in the shape of Capirossi and Dovizioso. Above: Edwards on the attack; opposite, Carlo Pernat hugs his protégé, Loris Capirossi, after the veteran planted his Suzuki on the front row.

GP ITALIA | **1st June 2008** | **Mugello** | **5.245 m**

STARTING GRID

1	46	V. Rossi	Yamaha	1'48.130
2	2	D. Pedrosa	Honda	1'48.297
3	65	L. Capirossi	Suzuki	1'48.313
4	1	C. Stoner	Ducati	1'48.375
5	5	C. Edwards	Yamaha	1'48.383
6	69	N. Hayden	Honda	1'48.666
7	48	J. Lorenzo	Yamaha	1'48.905
8	52	J. Toseland	Yamaha	1'49.025
9	56	S. Nakano	Honda	1'49.095
10	15	A. De Angelis	Honda	1'49.145
11	7	C. Vermeulen	Suzuki	1'49.220
12	14	R. De Puniet	Honda	1'49.246
13	4	A. Dovizioso	Honda	1'49.565
14	21	J. Hopkins	Kawasaki	1'49.601
15	8	T. Okada	Honda	1'49.829
16	24	T. Elias	Ducati	1'49.851
17	50	S. Guintoli	Ducati	1'50.275
18	33	M. Melandri	Ducati	1'50.465
19	13	A. West	Kawasaki	1'50.889

RACE: 23 laps = 120.635 km

1	Valentino Rossi	42'31.153 (170.231 km/h)
2	Casey Stoner	+ 2.201
3	Dani Pedrosa	+ 4.867
4	Alex De Angelis	+ 6.313
5	Colin Edwards	+ 12.530
6	James Toseland	+ 13.806
7	Loris Capirossi	+ 14.447
8	Andrea Dovizioso	+ 15.319
9	Shinya Nakano	+ 15.327
10	Chris Vermeulen	+ 30.785
11	Sylvain Guintoli	+ 39.621
12	Toni Elias	+ 50.021
13	Nicky Hayden	+ 50.440
14	Tadayuki Okada	+ 58.849
15	Anthony West	+ 1'00.736

Fastest lap

Stoner, in 1'50.003 (171.649 km/h). New record.
Previous: Biaggi, in 1'50.117 (171.472 km/h/2005).

Outright fastest lap

Rossi, in 1'48.130 (174.623 km/h/2008).

CHAMPIONSHIP

1	V. Rossi	122 (3 wins)
2	D. Pedrosa	110 (1 win)
3	J. Lorenzo	94 (1 win)
4	C. Stoner	76 (1 win)
5	C. Edwards	58
6	L. Capirossi	51
7	A. Dovizioso	44
8	J. Toseland	43
9	N. Hayden	40
10	S. Nakano	35

MUGELLO WAS GOOD FOR APRILIA AND BY THE SAME TOKEN FOR GILERA AS WELL, THANKS TO SIMONCELLI, DEBON AND LUTHI, WHO TOOK HIS FIRST PODIUM IN THE CLASS.

RUNNERS AND RIDERS

No absentees, no wild cards; there's definitely no great excitement in the intermediate category this year, on paper at least.

QUALIFYING

Everyone is fighting to the nearest hundredth in the second qualifying session on Saturday, as Friday's was held in the rain, Hector Barbera pulls off a more than perfect final lap, as he puts over 8 tenths in between himself and his closest pursuer, Bautista. Lorenzo's record lap is consigned to history at the end of a session characterised by a lot of fallers: Aoyama, Pasini twice and Luthi among others.

START

Bautista and Simoncelli show the quickest reflexes, ahead of Debon and Barbera. Crossing the line for the first time, Bautista and Simoncelli have already pulled out a gap of a few tenths over Barbera.

LAP 3

Barbera is back in touch, lowering the track record on the way. Pesek is a brilliant fourth.

LAP 5

Bautista, Simoncelli and Barbera are wheel to wheel. They have already made the break on the second group made up of Debon, Pesek, Luthi - the two team-mates having touched a bit earlier! - and Takahashi.

LAP 6

Barbera has dropped back as Bautista picks up the pace.

LAP 7

Bautista had been dominant but he falls. Simoncelli inherits the lead from Barbera and Luthi, who has finally managed to shake off Pesek and Debon.

HALF-DISTANCE (10 LAPS)

Having fallen back, Barbera is now on Simoncelli's back wheel, as the latter had chosen a softer front tyre than the rest: the Spaniard will move into the lead. There's a fight for third between Luthi and Debon. Faubel, Pesek and Poggiali are all fallers.

LAP 12

They're tripping one another up at the front, so Luthi and Debon close in, having taken 8 tenths off the leaders.

LAP 15

Debon has passed Luthi and indicates they should join forces. Takahashi is not far behind and the chasing group are again 4 seconds off the leader.

LAP 16

Barbera has moved to the front again, Takahashi has lost touch with the Debon-Luthi duel.

LAP 17

Takahashi is a faller.

FINISH (21 LAPS)

Simoncelli moves ahead as they start the final lap. Barbera falls on the straight, after colliding with the Spaniard, leaving Simoncelli out on his own, but Debon and Luthi are not far behind. The Swiss rider finally takes his first 250 podium. Kallio, whose KTM was off the pace all weekend, is a happy fourth, after Aoyamo nearly got him at the final turn.

CHAMPIONSHIP

Kallio is still in control of the situation, as Pasini, with an injured hand, finishes behind him.

Simoncelli wins, Bautista gets it wrong: not just a racing incident but a sign of the times.

GP ITALIA | 1st June 2008 | Mugello | 5.245 m

STARTING GRID				
1	21	H. Barberá	Aprilia	1'52.675
2	19	A. Bautistá	Aprilia	1'53.447
3	58	M. Simoncelli	Gilera	1'53.611
4	36	M. Kallio	KTM	1'53.635
5	52	L. Pesek	Aprilia	1'53.928
6	54	M. Poggiali	Gilera	1'54.144
7	6	A. Debón	Aprilia	1'54.271
8	12	T. Lüthi	Aprilia	1'54.376
9	75	M. Pasini	Aprilia	1'54.489
10	4	H. Aoyama	KTM	1'54.516
11	72	Y. Takahashi	Honda	1'54.546
12	55	H. Faubel	Aprilia	1'54.578
13	60	J. Simón	KTM	1'54.616
14	41	A. Espargaro	Aprilia	1'54.712
15	32	F. Lai	Gilera	1'54.735
16	17	K. Abraham	Aprilia	1'54.838
17	14	R. Wilairot	Honda	1'55.549
18	15	R. Locatelli	Gilera	1'55.888
19	10	I. Toth	Aprilia	1'56.325
20	50	E. Laverty	Aprilia	1'56.990
21	25	A. Baldolini	Aprilia	1'57.305
22	7	R. Gomez	Aprilia	1'58.069
23	45	D.-T. Pradita	Yamaha	1'58.731

RACE: 21 laps = 110.145 km		
1	Marco Simoncelli	40'19.910 (163.858 km/h)
2	Alex Debón	+ 0.499
3	Thomas Lüthi	+ 0.712
4	Mika Kallio	+ 7.403
5	Mattia Pasini	+ 12.542
6	Roberto Locatelli	+ 12.790
7	Karel Abraham	+ 16.114
8	Hiroshi Aoyama	+ 17.316
9	Aleix Espargaro	+ 19.642
10	Ratthapark Wilairot	+ 19.704
11	Julian Simón	+ 19.751
12	Alex Baldolini	+ 47.360
13	Eugene Laverty	+ 47.422
14	Fabrizio Lai	+ 1'13.423
15	Imre Toth	+ 1'25.891
16	Russel Gomez	+ 1'36.557
17	Doni Tata Pradita	+ 1'48.224

Fastest lap

Bautistá, in 1'53.669 (166.113 km/h). New record.
Previous: Barberá, in 1'54.061 (165.542 km/h/2007).

Outright fastest lap

Barberá, in 1'52.675 (167.579 km/h/2008).

CHAMPIONSHIP		
1	M. Kallio	106 (2 wins)
2	M. Pasini	88 (1 win)
3	A. Debón	79 (1 win)
4	M. Simoncelli	78 (1 win)
5	H. Aoyama	61
6	Y. Takahashi	59
7	H. Barberá	53
8	A. Bautistá	41 (1 win)
9	A. Espargaro	40
10	J. Simón	36

TYPICAL MUGELLO: JUST 36/1000THS COVERED THE TOP THREE. CORSI HAD DOUBLE CAUSE FOR CELEBRATION AS HE ALSO TOOK THE TITLE LEAD.

RUNNERS AND RIDERS

Having missed his home race, France's Cluzel (Loncin) is back. Five Italian riders have wild cards, including the promising Lorenzo Salvadori, who turned fifteen on 4th April. Also on duty is Luca Vitali, the son of a former racer in the 125 and 250 classes, Maurizio, who represents AGV helmets and works mainly with Rossi.

QUALIFYING

Once again, because of the weather, the starting grid was decided in just one session, on Saturday. Struggling since the start of the season, KTM, thanks to the efforts on a brilliant final lap from Raffaele De Rosa, takes its first pole for two years, ahead of series leader Talmacsi, Di Meglio and Pol Espargaro. Thirteen of them are all within a second.

START

Super Talmacsi charges into the lead ahead of Di Meglio and Iannone, the Chinese Grand Prix winner. Di Meglio snatches the lead on the opening lap, ahead of Talmacsi, Terol and Smith, who broke a finger in qualifying.

LAP 2

World Champion Talmacsi takes control, leading Terol, a very fiery Iannone and Di Meglio.

LAP 3

It's Terol's turn to lead. Bradl is the fastest man on track and has caught up to the leading group. Bianco falls.

LAP 4

Brilliant Bradl brakes later than anyone and leads. Twelve of them are nose to tail.

LAP 8

Series leader Di Meglio is back in charge, leading Talmacsi and Iannone.

HALF-DISTANCE (10 LAPS)

Di Meglio leads Talmacsi and Pol Espargaro. Terol, Corsi and the others are not far off, swapping places at every corner, as the Frenchman ends up fifth a few hundred metres further down the road.

LAP 12

The lead group is down to eight, as Bradl, Cortese and De Rosa have dropped off the back. Terol leads from Corsi.

LAP 13

Again Di Meglio, from Talmacsi and Espargaro. Olive has been dropped and now they are down to seven at the front.

LAP 15

Corsi is second behind Di Meglio with the top six within half a second.

LAP 18

It's Bradley Smith's turn to harass Di Meglio who still holds them off.

LAP 19

Smith goes by.

FINISH (20 LAPS)

Corsi has taken the lead going into the final lap, ahead of Gabor Talmacsi, Espargaro and Di Meglio. Corsi has the last word ahead of Talmacsi, Espargaro, Di Meglio and Smith. 158 thousandths separate first from fifth.

CHAMPIONSHIP

Simon Corsi joins Di Meglio at the top of the table. They have a twelve point advantage over Terol, but the Italian is officially the leader with three wins to one.

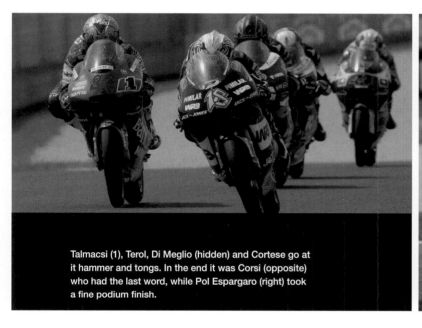

Talmacsi (1), Terol, Di Meglio (hidden) and Cortese go at it hammer and tongs. In the end it was Corsi (opposite) who had the last word, while Pol Espargaro (right) took a fine podium finish.

GP ITALIA | 1ST June 2008 | Mugello | 5.245 m

STARTING GRID

1	35	R. De Rosa	KTM	1'58.302
2	1	G. Talmacsi	Aprilia	1'58.467
3	63	M. Di Meglio	Derbi	1'58.490
4	44	P. Espargaro	Derbi	1'58.572
5	33	S. Gadea	Aprilia	1'58.631
6	11	S. Cortese	Aprilia	1'58.658
7	38	B. Smith	Aprilia	1'58.816
8	24	S. Corsi	Aprilia	1'58.895
9	18	N. Terol	Aprilia	1'59.065
10	71	T. Koyama	KTM	1'59.328
11	17	S. Bradl	Aprilia	1'59.351
12	29	A. Iannone	Aprilia	1'59.382
13	51	S. Bonsey	Aprilia	1'59.395
14	6	J. Olivé	Derbi	1'59.485
15	74	T. Nakagami	Aprilia	1'59.580
16	45	S. Redding	Aprilia	1'59.700
17	99	D. Webb	Aprilia	1'59.880
18	60	M. Ranseder	Aprilia	1'59.938
19	34	R. Krummenacher	KTM	2'00.341
20	12	E. Rabat	KTM	2'00.540
21	27	S. Bianco	Aprilia	2'00.562
22	40	L. Savadori	Aprilia	2'00.916
23	93	M. Marquez	KTM	2'01.384
24	16	J. Cluzel	Loncin	2'01.657
25	7	E. Vazquez	Aprilia	2'01.762
26	77	D. Aegerter	Derbi	2'01.799
27	22	P. Nieto	KTM	2'01.823
28	56	H. Van Den Berg	Aprilia	2'01.873
29	19	R. Lacalendola	Aprilia	2'01.900
30	95	R. Muresan	Aprilia	2'02.097
31	8	L. Zanetti	KTM	2'02.161
32	30	P. Tutusaus	Aprilia	2'02.195
33	21	R. Lässer	Aprilia	2'02.242
34	43	G. Ferro	Honda	2'02.344
35	47	R. Moretti	Honda	2'02.566
36	39	F. Lamborghini	Aprilia	2'02.779
37	69	L. Rossi	Honda	2'03.414
38	42	L. Vitali	Aprilia	2'04.221

Not qualified, but allowed to race:
	5	A. Masbou	Loncin	2'21.359

RACE: 20 laps = 104.900 km

1	Simone Corsi		39'59.020 (157.414 km/h)
2	Gabor Talmacsi		+ 0.019
3	Pol Espargaro		+ 0.036
4	Mike Di Meglio		+ 0.135
5	Bradley Smith		+ 0.178
6	Sergio Gadea		+ 0.490
7	Nicolas Terol		+ 0.832
8	Sandro Cortese		+ 3.865
9	Joan Olivé		+ 3.928
10	Stefan Bradl		+ 5.439
11	Steve Bonsey		+ 10.244
12	Andrea Iannone		+ 10.447
13	Raffaele De Rosa		+ 18.366
14	Scott Redding		+ 23.201
15	Michael Ranseder		+ 24.440
16	Takaaki Nakagami		+ 26.631
17	Randy Krummenacher		+ 30.629
18	Efren Vazquez		+ 30.730
19	Marc Marquez		+ 33.868
20	Lorenzo Zanetti		+ 36.928
21	Pere Tutusaus		+ 49.951
22	Lorenzo Savadori		+ 50.038
23	Jules Cluzel		+ 50.040
24	Dominique Aegerter		+ 50.052
25	Esteve Rabat		+ 56.360
26	Riccardo Moretti		+ 1'06.247
27	Alexis Masbou		+ 1'06.566
28	Robin Lässer		+ 1'06.982
29	Hugo Van Den Berg		+ 1'09.266
30	Luca Vitali		+ 1'10.551
31	Gabriele Ferro		+ 1'10.567
32	Louis Rossi		+ 1'36.451
33	Ferruccio Lamborghini		+ 1'39.883
34	Robert Muresan		+ 2 laps

Fastest lap
Di Meglio, in 1'58.570 (159.247 km/h). New record.
Previous: Gadea, in 1'58.636 (159.159 km/h/2007).

Outright fastest lap
Pesek, in 1'58.202 (159.743 km/h/2006).

CHAMPIONSHIP

1.	S. Corsi	87 (3 wins)
2.	M. Di Meglio	87 (1 win)
3.	N. Terol	75
4.	J. Olivé	65
5.	S. Bradl	64
6.	P. Espargaro	55
7.	G. Talmacsi	52
8.	A. Iannone	47 (1 win)
9.	B. Smith	47
10.	S. Gadea	42 (1 win)

One for the record books: a smile from Dani Pedrosa. And no wonder…

Calling all fans: the Catalunya GP took place on the weekend the European football championships kicked off.

PEDROSA BACK ON SONG

WITH NO LORENZO TO WORRY ABOUT – THE 250CC WORLD CHAMPION HAD SUFFERED ANOTHER SERIOUS INJURY – DANI PEDROSA LED THE RACE FROM START TO FINISH, JUST THE WAY HE LIKES IT.

THE RACE

WHEN DANI SMILES

It's often been said that he is nothing but a sad clone of his mentor, Alberto Puig, the king maker and character destroyer. Don't worry and the psychoanalysts all agree, Daniel Pedrosa has not changed overnight into a joyful prankster who dances on tables in the evening by the fireside. No, that would be too much, but one really gets the impression over the past few weeks, that this flower that was a closed bud has started to bloom.

The proof is there in the smile visible for the first time in a long time, as he stepped off the bike at the end of a perfect race: he lead from first to last, alone on his planet and far removed from the tussle in the pack.

There were even signs of this change on the day before first qualifying. In the sacrosanct environment of the pre-weekend press conference, he stared down one of the well known stirrers in the gaggle of press, who asked him: "Dani, where are we in the inter-Spanish war with Lorenzo? Does the fact he's said nice things about you, change your opinion of him?" Without hesitating and without seeking the protective approval of Alberto Puig, Pedrosa replied with a huge smile: "I've already given you an answer to that question in a one to one interview." Smack! The press room burst into spontaneous applause, not because a fellow hack had been put down, but because it signalled the birth of a new Pedrosa. What had happened to the mysterious little man? Let's start with the facts. Since the start of the season and despite a winter ruined by an injury sustained at the first test session, Pedrosa had destroyed his team-mate, former world champion Nicky Hayden, on the track. He is clearly the HRC Number One rider, just as he was during his apprenticeship in 125s and 250s. Second fact and a no less important one: since the Chinese GP and the first spectacular and damaging crash for Jorge Lorenzo, Pedrosa also realised that the man who had dared infiltrate his

world at the very start of the season had now discovered the harsh realities of what was to him a new category of racing. It therefore dawned on him that he was still the number 1 of Spanish motorcycling.

Strengthened by these revelations, all he had to do was get on with his work. Beaten to pole position by Stoner, Dani would manage, as always, to make the best start. Two laps later, he was already out on his own and could savour the moment.

But nothing lasts forever and anyone believing that doesn't know the man, nor indeed the harsh realities of this sport which is truly unique. On the day after his win, while trying the new pneumatic valved Honda engine, Pedrosa had an impressive highside, and was whisked off to the Dexeus hospital in Barcelona with serious lumbar bruising, where he stayed for 48 hours of observation, just as Lorenzo had been forced to do three days earlier!

He came, he saw, he conquered:
Pedrosa was untouchable in Catalunya.

Jorge Lorenzo took a terrible tumble (left), so much so that when he came to, he thought he was in China. When it comes to acrobatics, Randy de Puniet's no slouch either (opposite). Below, Valentino Rossi's 'Euro football' helmet.

LORENZO HAD A HORRIBLE CRASH IN QUALIFYING. WITH THE EARLY STAR OF THE SEASON OUT OF ACTION, COMPATRIOT PEDROSA CAME OUT ON TOP.

RUNNERS AND RIDERS

Lorenzo is getting better day by day - but it won't last...Honda has decided to wait for the following Monday's test following the GP to get its works riders to try the pneumatic valve engine. In the Ducati camp, it should also be the moment to see the 2009 prototype with its carbon fibre chassis.

QUALIFYING

Stoner takes pole ahead of six Michelin riders, but this wasn't the main story of the weekend so far, as the headlines were made on Friday when, yet again, Lorenzo had a terrible fall. Thrown into the air, he hit his head hard, before bouncing up again, using his already weakened ankles as suspension. Result: severe cranial bruising - when he arrived in the medical centre, he thought he was in China! - and open wounds on his right hand. Lorenzo was transferred to the Dexeus hospital in Barcelona where he stayed for 48 hours of enforced rest, as ordered by Doctor Mir, his trusted physician.

START

Pedrosa again, ahead of Stoner, Dovizioso, Edwards and De Puniet. Stoner makes a first mistake a few corners on, which allows Pedrosa to lead the first lap by 658 thousandths from Dovizioso. Rossi is eighth.

LAP 2

Stoner is back in second place. The stewards decide that Elias had a jumped start.

LAP 5

Rossi has passed Hayden and is sixth. At the front, Pedrosa leads Stoner by 3.304.

LAP 7

De Puniet is beaten and Rossi is fifth.

LAP 8

A second hiccough from Stoner sees Dovizioso go second and Rossi is fourth, having passed Edwards. Elias has failed to come in for his "drive through" and is shown the black flag.

LAP 9

Rossi is second, 6.618 down on Pedrosa.

LAP 11

Capirossi and De Angelis are fallers.

LAP 12

Randy de Puniet falls, having been sixth.

HALF-DISTANCE (12 LAPS)

Pedrosa is still in a class of his own, while Stoner can't do anything about second placed Rossi.

LAP 17

Stoner lets Ducati power do the talking.

LAP 24

Having stuck close to the world champion, Rossi now finds the gap and retakes second spot.

FINISH (25 LAPS)

Pedrosa begins the final lap leading Rossi by 4.376. Of course it's enough to win.

CHAMPIONSHIP

Pedrosa has taken five points off Rossi, so the two top men are now separated by seven points.

GP CATALUNYA | 8th June 2008 | Catalunya | 4.727 m

STARTING GRID

1	1	C. Stoner	Ducati	1'41.186
2	2	D. Pedrosa	Honda	1'41.269
3	69	N. Hayden	Honda	1'41.437
4	14	R. De Puniet	Honda	1'41.571
5	5	C. Edwards	Yamaha	1'41.609
6	52	J. Toseland	Yamaha	1'41.820
7	4	A. Dovizioso	Honda	1'42.053
8	7	C. Vermeulen	Suzuki	1'42.365
9	46	V. Rossi	Yamaha	1'42.427
10	15	A. De Angelis	Honda	1'42.580
11	56	S. Nakano	Honda	1'42.643
12	65	L. Capirossi	Suzuki	1'42.648
13	24	T. Elias	Ducati	1'42.808
14	21	J. Hopkins	Kawasaki	1'42.819
15	50	S. Guintoli	Ducati	1'43.204
16	33	M. Melandri	Ducati	1'43.719
17	13	A. West	Kawasaki	1'44.558

RACE: 25 laps = 118.175 km

1	Dani Pedrosa	43'02.175 (164.756 km/h)
2	Valentino Rossi	+ 2.806
3	Casey Stoner	+ 3.343
4	Andrea Dovizioso	+ 10.893
5	Colin Edwards	+ 16.426
6	James Toseland	+ 21.482
7	Chris Vermeulen	+ 21.548
8	Nicky Hayden	+ 22.280
9	Shinya Nakano	+ 22.375
10	John Hopkins	+ 46.835
11	Marco Melandri	+ 57.991
12	Anthony West	+ 59.168
13	Sylvain Guintoli	+ 1'00.779

Fastest lap
Pedrosa, in 1'42.358 (166.251 km/h). New record.
Previous: Hayden, in 1'43.048 (165.138 km/h/2006).

Outright fastest lap
Stoner, in 1'41.186 (168.177 km/h/2008).

CHAMPIONSHIP

1	V. Rossi	142 (3 wins)
2	D. Pedrosa	135 (2 wins)
3	J. Lorenzo	94 (1 win)
4	C. Stoner	92 (1 win)
5	C. Edwards	69
6	A. Dovizioso	57
7	J. Toseland	53
8	L. Capirossi	51
9	N. Hayden	48
10	S. Nakano	42

THE BIG BATTLE BETWEEN SIMONCELLI AND BAUTISTA WENT THE ITALIAN'S WAY.

RUNNERS AND RIDERS

On the eve of qualifying, news comes that the decision almost taken in China, to ban a second bike for riders in the 125 and 250 classes as from next year, has been dropped.

QUALIFYING

The Iberians are hot, which is nothing new. And it's Alvaro Bautista, despite a few scares including two Friday falls, who sets the fastest time, ahead of Debon, Hector Barbera and Marco Simoncelli. It's full house for Aprilia - the top six - with just one of its riders in difficulty, as Luthi has recurring traction problems and on top of that, on Saturday night news breaks he is having bother with his forearms suffering pump-up.

START

Bautista storms into the lead from Debon and a surprising Locatelli, who was eleventh on the grid! The former 125 world champion is a faller shortly after and Takahashi has to go off the track to avoid him. Out in front, Bautista completes Lap 1 with a lead of 632 thousandths over Debon, who is fighting off Simoncelli.

LAP 2

Simoncelli has closed on the leader and then passes him. The two men will soon be joined by Barbera.

LAP 3

The quickest men are Barbera and…Luthi, who has made it up to sixth place. Espargaro retires.

Kallio was nearly laughing on the other side of his face when he outbraked himself on the way into the pits during qualifying. Opposite: Tom Luthi explains that the pain in his forearm is still there. Below: Bautista (19) and Simoncelli fought out a fascinating duel.

LAP 5

Bautista, Simoncelli and Barbera can fit under a handkerchief measuring 281 thousandths. Debon heads Luthi for fourth, but the order is about to be reversed. Next up are Kallio and Pasini, but they already trail the leader by 3 seconds.

LAP 8

Abraham is a faller, while fighting his fellow countryman Pesek for eleventh place.

HALF-DISTANCE (12 LAPS)

The pace is frantic at the front. At the mid-point of the race, Bautista has precisely 7 hundredths in hand over Simoncelli, with Barbera half a second down. Seven seconds back in fourth, Debon has broken away from Luthi, who is being charged down by Pasini and Kallio.

LAP 13

Kallio passes Pasini.

LAP 16

Series leader Kallio has got the better of Luthi for fifth place.

LAP 17

Bautista and Simoncelli continue to turn up the wick, thus dropping Barbera behind.

LAP 19

High drama as Kallio retires with a broken engine (segment)

FINISH (23 LAPS)

248 thousandths between the two front runners going into the final lap. Bautista makes a mistake and runs wide, thus handing the win to Simoncelli, by just 39 thousandths.

CHAMPIONSHIP

For the first time, Kallio fails to score, so they all bunch up at the top of the leader board, with Simoncelli just 3 points behind, Pasini and Debon are 8 and 14 points down respectively. It's hot at the front!

GP CATALUNYA | 8th June 2008 | Catalunya | 4.727 m

STARTING GRID

1	19	A. Bautistá	Aprilia	1'45.636
2	6	A. Debón	Aprilia	1'45.767
3	21	H. Barberá	Aprilia	1'46.062
4	58	M. Simoncelli	Gilera	1'46.295
5	75	M. Pasini	Aprilia	1'46.363
6	55	H. Faubel	Aprilia	1'46.594
7	72	Y. Takahashi	Honda	1'46.668
8	4	H. Aoyama	KTM	1'46.856
9	36	M. Kallio	KTM	1'46.952
10	60	J. Simón	KTM	1'47.121
11	15	R. Locatelli	Gilera	1'47.190
12	12	T. Lüthi	Aprilia	1'47.207
13	41	A. Espargaró	Aprilia	1'47.422
14	14	R. Wilairot	Honda	1'47.510
15	17	K. Abraham	Aprilia	1'47.510
16	52	L. Pesek	Aprilia	1'47.666
17	54	M. Poggiali	Gilera	1'47.728
18	32	F. Lai	Gilera	1'47.818
19	25	A. Baldolini	Aprilia	1'49.272
20	50	E. Laverty	Aprilia	1'49.392
21	7	R. Gomez	Aprilia	1'49.618
22	10	I. Toth	Aprilia	1'49.776
23	92	D. Arcas	Honda	1'50.186
24	45	D.-T. Pradita	Yamaha	1'50.450

RACE: 23 laps = 108.721 km

1	Marco Simoncelli	41'01.859 (158.983 km/h)
2	Alvaro Bautistá	+ 0.039
3	Hector Barberá	+ 11.291
4	Alex Debón	+ 21.373
5	Thomas Lüthi	+ 26.621
6	Mattia Pasini	+ 26.720
7	Hiroshi Aoyama	+ 35.818
8	Hector Faubel	+ 36.321
9	Julian Simón	+ 36.964
10	Lukas Pesek	+ 41.237
11	Ratthapark Wilairot	+ 52.391
12	Yuki Takahashi	+ 56.656
13	Alex Baldolini	+ 59.282
14	Manuel Poggiali	+ 1'02.503
15	Fabrizio Lai	+ 1'02.656
16	Eugene Laverty	+ 1'07.418
17	Russel Gomez	+ 1 lap
18	Doni Tata Pradita	+ 1 lap

Fastest lap

Bautistá, in 1'46.143 (160.323 km/h).
Record: De Angelis, in 1'45.925 (160.653 km/h/2007).

Outright fastest lap

Lorenzo, in 1'45.098 (161.917 km/h/2007).

CHAMPIONSHIP

1	M. Kallio	106 (2 wins)
2	M. Simoncelli	103 (2 wins)
3	M. Pasini	98 (1 win)
4	A. Debón	92 (1 win)
5	H. Aoyama	70
6	H. Barberá	69
7	Y. Takahashi	63
8	A. Bautistá	61 (1 win)
9	T. Lüthi	46
10	J. Simón	43

Opposite: Bradley Smith showed how much he loved his bike by refusing to come off it until the very last minute. On the right, di Meglio - wrapped in the French flag - celebrates his second win of the season.

A NICE DOUBLE FOR MIKE DI MEGLIO: THE RACE WIN AND A FIRST USEFUL GAP IN THE CHAMPIONSHIP.

RUNNERS AND RIDERS

Five Spanish riders have wild cards, including a rookie, 19 year old Jordi Dalmau from Barcelona, Axel Pons, son of..., Ricard Cardus, nephew of..., with Maestro and Saez completing the list.

QUALIFYING

He was born in Granollers, just a few kilometres from the Catalunya circuit and so it was that he would record the first pole position of his career here at his track. Who is he? He is Pol Espargaro, a protégé of Dani Amatrian (Lorenzo's mentor,) who finally gets the better of another Derbi ridden by Di Meglio by 139 thousandths. Qualifying featured several fallers, including one that was more spectacular than serious for Bradley Smith and one more serious than spectacular for Esteve "Tito" Rabat, as the young Spaniard suffered a cerebral oedema and was kept in an artificial coma, which he came out of late on Saturday morning, only to ask at what time started the next practice session!

START

Espargaro, Nicolas Terol and Sergio Gadea are promptest off the line. Also showing quick reflexes was Stefan Bradl who was sixth first time round, having started from thirteenth. At the end of the opening lap, Terol has 325 thousandths in hand over Espargaro. Next up comes Gadea,

Iannone, Joan Olive and the rest of the pack.

LAP 2

Pablo Nieto retires. Gadea leads now followed by Terol, Espargaro, Iannone and Olive.

LAP 5

An on-form Di Meglio is the fastest man on track and has just taken the lead, with Terol and Gadea up his exhaust pipe.

LAP 8

Terol muscles Gadea across the gravel trap, from where he rejoins 24th. Di Meglio now leads Terol by 680 thousandths.

HALF-DISTANCE (11 LAPS)

Di Meglio and Terol are separated by 124 thousandths as they cross the line. Seven tenths behind, there's a scrap between Olive, Corsi, Espargaro, Talmacsi and Redding.

LAP 16

Redding has been dropped, while Mike Di Meglio is still in control.

LAP 18

Andrea Iannone is a faller and De Rosa goes off the track.

LAP 20

The leaders have bunched up (Di Meglio, Terol, Espargaro, Talmacsi and Olive) although the last mentioned is a faller, so that six of them are separated by 6 tenths.

LAP 21

Terol falls.

FINISH (22 LAPS)

Di Meglio sets off for his final lap 610 thousandths ahead of Espargaro and Talmacsi. The Frenchman makes no mistake to record his second win in the discipline, after the shortened Le Mans race. Gadea has come from nowhere to finish ninth.

CHAMPIONSHIP

Di Meglio comes out of it really well, as Corsi, having fallen heavily in the warm-up, finishes only fifth and is now 14 points adrift.

GP CATALUNYA | 8th June 2008 | Catalunya | 4.727 m

STARTING GRID

1	44	P. Espargaro	Derbi	1'50.557
2	63	M. Di Meglio	Derbi	1'50.696
3	18	N. Terol	Aprilia	1'50.740
4	45	S. Redding	Aprilia	1'51.101
5	24	S. Corsi	Aprilia	1'51.365
6	33	S. Gadea	Aprilia	1'51.399
7	1	G. Talmacsi	Aprilia	1'51.436
8	38	B. Smith	Aprilia	1'51.439
9	29	A. Iannone	Aprilia	1'51.500
10	6	J. Olivé	Derbi	1'51.518
11	11	S. Cortese	Aprilia	1'51.564
12	35	R. De Rosa	KTM	1'51.566
13	17	S. Bradl	Aprilia	1'51.593
14	93	M. Marquez	KTM	1'51.650
15	7	E. Vazquez	Aprilia	1'51.780
16	51	S. Bonsey	Aprilia	1'51.932
17	77	D. Aegerter	Derbi	1'51.976
18	34	R. Krummenacher	KTM	1'52.074
19	74	T. Nakagami	Aprilia	1'52.076
20	22	P. Nieto	KTM	1'52.080
21	99	D. Webb	Aprilia	1'52.161
22	71	T. Koyama	KTM	1'52.250
23	5	A. Masbou	Loncin	1'52.428
24	8	L. Zanetti	KTM	1'52.428
25	21	R. Lässer	Aprilia	1'52.474
26	27	S. Bianco	Aprilia	1'52.593
27	12	E. Rabat	KTM	1'52.752 (*)
28	60	M. Ranseder	Aprilia	1'52.769
29	30	P. Tutusaus	Aprilia	1'52.806
30	14	J. Cluzel	Loncin	1'53.345
31	14	A. Pons	Aprilia	1'53.532
32	56	H. Van Den Berg	Aprilia	1'53.560
33	95	R. Muresan	Aprilia	1'53.607
34	75	R. Cardus	Derbi	1'53.698
35	19	R. Lacalendola	Aprilia	1'54.090
36	69	L. Rossi	Honda	1'54.190
37	31	J. Dalmau	Honda	1'54.944
38	78	D. Saez	Aprilia	1'55.022
39	76	I. Maestro	Aprilia	1'55.681

(*): Injured on Friday, E. Rabat (E, KTM), had to withdraw. (cerebral oedema).

RACE: 22 laps = 103.994 km

1	Mike Di Meglio	41'08.708 (151.649 km/h)
2	Pol Espargaro	+ 0.268
3	Gabor Talmacsi	+ 0.338
4	Stefan Bradl	+ 8.765
5	Simone Corsi	+ 10.141
6	Scott Redding	+ 11.178
7	Steve Bonsey	+ 13.671
8	Sandro Cortese	+ 13.755
9	Sergio Gadea	+ 15.541
10	Marc Marquez	+ 18.962
11	Daniel Webb	+ 22.653
12	Dominique Aegerter	+ 24.928
13	Tomoyoshi Koyama	+ 25.013
14	Bradley Smith	+ 25.059
15	Randy Krummenacher	+ 25.188
16	Efren Vazquez	+ 25.352
17	Michael Ranseder	+ 25.541
18	Stefano Bianco	+ 31.365
19	Pere Tutusaus	+ 42.899
20	Jules Cluzel	+ 43.469
21	Hugo Van Den Berg	+ 56.930
22	Takaaki Nakagami	+ 1'01.318
23	Roberto Lacalendola	+ 1'02.867
24	Robert Muresan	+ 1'17.370
25	Louis Rossi	+ 1'18.790
26	Ricard Cardus	+ 1'27.350
27	Daniel Saez	+ 1'28.736

Fastest lap
Olivé, in 1'51.271 (152.934 km/h).
Record: Krummenacher, in 1'50.732 (153.679 km/h/2007).

Outright fastest lap
Talmacsi, in 1'50.012 (154.684 km/h/2007).

CHAMPIONSHIP

1.	M. Di Meglio	112 (2 wins)
2.	S. Corsi	98 (3 wins)
3.	S. Bradl	77
4.	N. Terol	75
5.	P. Espargaró	75
6.	G. Talmacsi	68
7.	J. Olivé	65
8.	S. Gadea	49 (1 win)
9.	B. Smith	49
10.	A. Iannone	47 (1 win)

'At speed with bridge in background' - a work of art signed Lukas Swiderek.

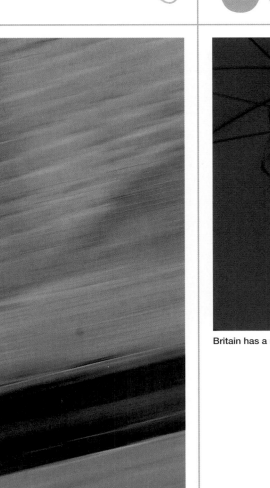

Britain has a new hero! His name is James Toseland and his fans are loud - but cuddly with it.

DONINGTON,
TRADITION

DODGY WEATHER, DEVOTED FANS:
IMPOSSIBLE TO OVERLOOK THE FACT
THAT GREAT BRITAIN IS THE HOME OF
MOTOR SPORT.

THE RACE

THE MID-SEASON TRADITIONS

Nobody would be so foolish as to question the key role played by Great Britain in the history of motorised sports. Once a year, when the Continental Circus returns to its roots, there are thousands of examples there, who come to revive memories of old, which allow the very youngest - and there are more and more of those, with proof this weekend to be found on the 125 cc podium, with two adolescents who had only just turned 15 - to complete their education when it comes to tradition.

Tradition? It starts on the Thursday before practice with "The Day Of Champions," a free event which ends with an auction from which all profits go to the "Riders For Health" charity, which is supported by many, notably Randy Mamola.

Tradition? The fans who, all year long, deprive themselves of holidays and save up for the scary experience of a couple of laps of Donington Park on the pillion of a Desmosedici ridden by the very same Mamola, with profits again going to the same worthy cause.

Tradition? The enthusiasm of the British press who would love to find the answer to the existential question: over 25 years after the last victory for Barry Sheene in the 500 cc class, is there a worthy successor on this Sceptred Isle? The answer came on this penultimate weekend in June, but not in the shape that everyone was dreaming of, namely James Toseland, who was transformed into a comedy of errors all weekend,

but instead it was a little kid by the name of Scott Redding, who was majestic in the 125 cc race. God Save The Queen!

Tradition? Donington is also the GP where one often comes across some new faces. This year one of these belonged to double US Superbike champion, Ben Spies, who was replacing Loris Capirossi, injured in Catalunya.

Tradition? Above all it's the unofficial start of the transfer season. And usually, it gets off to a brisk start. So, let's get it underway with some modest contribution to the gossip that will be confirmed in the coming months and others that will sink without trace. Shall we begin? Gibernau will replace Melandri before the end of the season, but it's Nicky Hayden who will second Stoner next year in the official Ducati team. And on the subject of the Borgo Panigale crew, the second "red" team, run by Luis D'Antin will, in 2009, consist of the returning Gibernau and the young current Ducati tester, Nicola Canepa (a protégé of Carlo Pernat.) More? Dovizioso will pick up the second seat in the works Honda Repsol team and Melandri will be saved yet again, for the last time? by Kawasaki, who have realised that West was worthless. Still more? Vermeulen is in danger at Suzuki, where Spies is favouried and to replace Edwards, who has become too greedy, Herve Poncharal is interested in a rookie, who might be Marco Simoncelli, again from the Pernat squad.

So that's your lot, with the truth…and falsehoods to be revealed in early November.

Very British, don't you think? On home soil, James Toseland (52) laid on quite a show for his followers.

IN JUST ONE WEEKEND STONER WAS RIGHT BACK TO HIS ASSURED SELF OF 2007.

RUNNERS AND RIDERS

Capirossi got up from his fall in the Catalunya GP to find he had broken the fifth metacarpal on his right hand and is replaced by the double US Superbike champion, Ben Spies. Hayden is using the pneumatic valve Honda, Pedrosa's back still hurts from his fall the day after the Catalunya GP, while Lorenzo is back.

QUALIFYING

The track is damp on Saturday afternoon and it's time for the Stoner show, with help from Bridgestone, who take the top three slots with three different makes of bike. The "losers" are Pedrosa (9th) and Toseland (16th) in front of his home crowd, having fallen twice on his last two timed laps!

START

Stoner and the Ducati are perfect. With all eyes on Toseland, he crashes at Redgate Corner. At the end of the opening lap, the reigning champion's lead over Rossi is 549 thousandth. Following on behind are a strong Dovizioso, with Hayden and Pedrosa in attendance.

LAP 4

Pedrosa has passed Hayden to go fourth. At the head of the field, Stoner leads Rossi by 1.063.

LAP 8

Pedrosa has finally found a way past Dovizioso to go third, 8 tenths off Rossi.

LAP 12

Hayden is fourth, after a nice scrap with Dovizioso.

HALF-DISTANCE (15 LAPS)

Things are finally hotting up, because while Stoner still leads comfortably, the duel between Rossi and Pedrosa is superb. Dani passes for the first time at the end of the straight, with Rossi getting back the lead on the downhill section and one lap later, it happens all over again.

LAP 18

In the space of two laps, Edwards has dealt with first Hayden and then Dovizioso, to put the Texan fourth.

LAP 23

Stoner continues on his majestic way, with 5.677 in hand over Rossi, who cannot shake off Pedrosa. In fourth place, Edwards is the quickest man on track.

LAP 24

Lorenzo has come up to the Vermeulen-Hayden duo like a rocket, with sixth place up for grabs.

LAP 26

Lorenzo is sixth, ahead of Hayden who snuck past Vermeulen a few moments earlier.

FINISH (30 LAPS)

No disrespect to Stoner, but one could have believed one was in Magny-Cours for one of those preordained F1 races. Casey led from start to finish, just like the Ferraris could not lose in France. Rossi is the best of the rest, with Pedrosa having dropped back in the final three laps.

CHAMPIONSHIP

As Stoner is not (yet?) the danger, Rossi has done well, as he nibbles 4 points off Pedrosa. Valentino leads by 11.

De Puniet (left) has just got by Melandri; Guintoli will soon do likewise and the two Frenchman will finish in close order. Right: Stoner does a victory wheelie and a new American face, Ben Spies, comes in for Loris Capirossi.

GP GREAT BRITAIN | 22nd June 2008 | Donington | 4.023 m

STARTING GRID

1	1	C. Stoner	Ducati	1'38.232
2	46	V. Rossi	Yamaha	1'38.881
3	7	C. Vermeulen	Suzuki	1'39.018
4	69	N. Hayden	Honda	1'39.270
5	5	C. Edwards	Yamaha	1'39.601
6	4	A. Dovizioso	Honda	1'39.783
7	13	A. West	Kawasaki	1'39.995
8	11	B. Spies	Suzuki	1'40.244
9	2	D. Pedrosa	Honda	1'40.350
10	56	S. Nakano	Honda	1'40.417
11	21	J. Hopkins	Kawasaki	1'40.539
12	50	S. Guintoli	Ducati	1'40.595
13	15	A. De Angelis	Honda	1'40.667
14	14	R. De Puniet	Honda	1'41.110
15	33	M. Melandri	Ducati	1'41.379
16	52	J. Toseland	Yamaha	1'41.751
17	48	J. Lorenzo	Yamaha	1'41.873
18	24	T. Elias	Ducati	1'42.933

RACE: 30 laps = 120.690 km

1	Casey Stoner	44'44.982 (161.820 km/h)
2	Valentino Rossi	+ 5.789
3	Dani Pedrosa	+ 8.347
4	Colin Edwards	+ 12.678
5	Andrea Dovizioso	+ 14.801
6	Jorge Lorenzo	+ 15.690
7	Nicky Hayden	+ 18.196
8	Chris Vermeulen	+ 21.666
9	Shinya Nakano	+ 29.354
10	Anthony West	+ 41.030
11	Toni Elias	+ 44.426
12	Randy De Puniet	+ 46.199
13	Sylvain Guintoli	+ 48.731
14	Ben Spies	+ 49.591
15	Alex De Angelis	+ 1'22.186
16	Marco Melandri	+ 1'30.021
17	James Toseland	+ 1 lap

Fastest lap
Stoner, in 1'28.773 (163.144 km/h).
Record: Pedrosa, in 1'28.714 (163.252 km/h/2006).

Outright fastest lap
Pedrosa, in 1'27.676 (165.185 km/h/2006).

CHAMPIONSHIP

1	V. Rossi	162 (3 wins)
2	D. Pedrosa	151 (2 wins)
3	C. Stoner	117 (2 wins)
4	J. Lorenzo	104 (1 win)
5	C. Edwards	82
6	A. Dovizioso	68
7	N. Hayden	57
8	J. Toseland	53
9	L. Capirossi	51
10	S. Nakano	49

No wonder Kallio and the KTM personnel look happy after Simoncelli and Bautista (opposite) handed them such a gift. Left: best of the rest, Hector Barbera.

MIKA KALLIO CAN'T BELIEVE HIS LUCK AS SIMONCELLI AND BAUTISTA TRIP OVER EACH OTHER ON THE LAST LAP.

RUNNERS AND RIDERS

The paddock was shocked to hear that Dieter Stappert, who this year runs the Yamaha Pertamina Indonesia team, having spent happy days with German teams in the days of Bradl (the father,) Roth and Waldmann, suffered a heart attack at Munich airport and was in a coma from which he had still not awoken on the night of the British GP.

QUALIFYING

Qualifying was played out over a single dry session, on Friday. The highlight was another duel between the two quickest men in the category this season, Bautista and Marco Simoncelli. Barbera and Luthi complete the front row, while Kallio, quickest in the wet on Saturday is "only" fourteenth.

START

A super start from Simoncelli, but not from Luthi, who is tenth at the first split. At the end of the opening lap, Simoncelli leads Takahashi, Bautista, Simon and Barbera.

LAP 3

Bautista is risking everything and gets it wrong at the hairpin, allowing Simoncelli to pull out a lead of 1.021.

LAP 5

This time, Bautista finds a chink in Takahashi's armour and the Spaniard is second, 586 thousandths behind Simoncelli.

LAP 10

Simoncelli still holds off Bautista by 369 thousandths. Kallio who started a long way back in 14th spot, is already up to third.

LAP 12

Pasini falls from tenth place.

HALF-DISTANCE (13 LAPS)

Bautista has just taken the lead, heading Simoncelli by precisely 57 thousandths. Kallio is 2 seconds behind in third, ahead of Barbera and Luthi, the latter being the quickest man on track at this time. He is up to fifth.

LAP 15

Simoncelli has regained the lead, making the most of a slight slip from Bautista.

LAP 20

Bautista again. Kallio has closed to 8 tenths.

LAP 21

They've caught up so that three of them are within 824 thousandths.

LAP 24

328 thousandths separate Bautista, Simoncelli and Kallio, so the last three laps should be hot.

FINISH (27 LAPS)

Simoncelli attempts a suicidal move going into the final lap, forcing Bautista wide to avoid him, allowing Kallio to slip through. The Finn would not make any mistakes and, once again, Bautista has reason to have it in for Simoncelli. Indeed, the two men exchange words at the foot of the podium. Looks like summertime will be showtime!

CHAMPIONSHIP

Kallio has pulled out a further five points on his pursuer and now leads by 8. Debon is third, but 30 points down on the KTM rider.

GP GREAT BRITAIN | 22nd June 2008 | Donington | 4.023 m

STARTING GRID

1	19	A. Bautistá	Aprilia	1'31.834
2	58	M. Simoncelli	Gilera	1'32.004
3	21	H. Barberá	Aprilia	1'32.353
4	12	T. Lüthi	Aprilia	1'32.835
5	72	Y. Takahashi	Honda	1'32.853
6	4	H. Aoyama	KTM	1'32.983
7	60	J. Simón	KTM	1'33.063
8	41	A. Espargaró	Aprilia	1'33.116
9	52	L. Pesek	Aprilia	1'33.276
10	32	F. Lai	Gilera	1'33.281
11	6	A. Debón	Aprilia	1'33.297
12	75	M. Pasini	Aprilia	1'33.302
13	15	R. Locatelli	Gilera	1'33.379
14	36	M. Kallio	KTM	1'33.595
15	54	M. Poggiali	Gilera	1'33.660
16	17	K. Abraham	Aprilia	1'33.859
17	55	H. Faubel	Aprilia	1'33.954
18	14	R. Wilairot	Honda	1'34.039
19	25	A. Baldolini	Aprilia	1'34.074
20	50	E. Laverty	Aprilia	1'34.285
21	10	I. Toth	Aprilia	1'35.571
22	7	R. Gomez	Aprilia	1'37.081
23	63	T. Markham	Yamaha	1'37.675
24	45	D.-T. Pradita	Yamaha	1'38.170

RACE: 27 laps = 108.621 km

1	Mika Kallio	42'14.410 (154.290 km/h)
2	Marco Simoncelli	+ 0.353
3	Alvaro Bautistá	+ 1.237
4	Hector Barberá	+ 8.875
5	Thomas Lüthi	+ 11.359
6	Hiroshi Aoyama	+ 16.124
7	Alex Debón	+ 16.136
8	Julian Simón	+ 18.007
9	Yuki Takahashi	+ 33.271
10	Aleix Espargaró	+ 49.681
11	Roberto Locatelli	+ 52.534
12	Karel Abraham	+ 55.311
13	Lukas Pesek	+ 57.399
14	Manuel Poggiali	+ 57.641
15	Hector Faubel	+ 1'04.329
16	Ratthapark Wilairot	+ 1'06.156
17	Fabrizio Lai	+ 1'15.812
18	Russel Gomez	+ 1 lap
19	Doni Tata Pradita	+ 1 lap

Fastest lap

Simoncelli, in 1'32.474 (156.614 km/h). New record.
Previous: Dovizioso, in 1'33.029 (155.680 km/h/2006).

Outright fastest lap

Lorenzo, in 1'31.659 (158.007 km/h/2006).

CHAMPIONSHIP

1	M. Kallio	131 (3 wins)
2	M. Simoncelli	123 (2 wins)
3	A. Debón	101 (1 win)
4	M. Pasini	98 (1 win)
5	H. Barberá	82
6	H. Aoyama	80
7	A. Bautistá	77 (1 win)
8	Y. Takahashi	70
9	T. Lüthi	57
10	J. Simón	51

Redding only hung onto his magnum of champagne for a few moments: he's too young to drink so he handed it over to Mike di Meglio as a bemused Marc Marquez looked on. Right: the duelling KTM's of Japan's Koyama and Swiss rider Krummenacher.

AT 15 YEARS, 5 MONTHS AND 7 DAYS SCOTT REDDING IS THE YOUNGEST GP WINNER IN HISTORY.

RUNNERS AND RIDERS

Efren Vazquez broke a hand a week earlier, competing in the Spanish championship. He comes to Donington, but the doctors forbid him to race.

QUALIFYING

Significant events in qualifying, as series leader, Mike Di Meglio has a gearbox problem on Friday afternoon and does not get out on track until ten minutes before the end of what will be the only dry session and sets the 21st time. Second blow on Saturday morning in the rain: Pol Espargaro is one of the many riders in this category to hit the deck and he gets up holding his left shoulder and the verdict is a broken clavicle and he heads off the same day to Barcelona to undergo surgery.

START

A good start for Corsi, but Gadea does better to take the lead at Redgate Corner. It comes close to disaster on the descent when Nieto falls, his KTM bouncing back onto the track, but everyone manages to avoid the obstacle. Crossing the line for the first time, Iannone is the leader by 8 tenths from Corsi, Marquez and Gadea.

LAP 2

Talmacsi falls, having been tenth.

LAP 5

Iannone now has 1.874 in hand over Redding, who is a solid second. Behind them, eleven riders are nose to tail, led by little Marquez. In the group, a super showing from Di Meglio, who had started 20th but was already in the top ten.

LAP 9

Redding has closed to under a second of Iannone. Riders are affected by strong cross winds.

LAP 10

Incredible! Di Meglio is now third and with every passing race, the Frenchman looks more and more like the main contender for the title.

HALF-DISTANCE (12 LAPS)

Still Iannone. The Italian leads Redding by 1.064. Di Meglio is third, 6.714 off the leader, with Gadea and Marquez on his tail. The others have lost contact.

LAP 14

Bradl slows on the track.

LAP 16

The crowd goes wild as Redding is right up with the leader at 270 thousandths.

LAP 20

Iannone falls in the downhill section and an Englishman leads his home GP!

FINISH (25 LAPS)

At the age of 15 years, 5 months and 7 days, Scott Redding becomes the youngest winner in the history of GP racing. Naturally, the crowd is going crazy at the idea of a winner from Blighty!

CHAMPIONSHIP

Second, having started twentieth, Di Meglio has a very good day at the office, as his main rivals all suffered, with Corsi fifth and the Frenchman now leads by 23 points.

GP GREAT BRITAIN | 22nd June 2008 | Donington | 4.023 m

STARTING GRID

1	24	S. Corsi	Aprilia	1'37.488
2	1	G. Talmacsi	Aprilia	1'37.520
3	33	S. Gadea	Aprilia	1'37.649
4	45	S. Redding	Aprilia	1'37.766
5	44	P. Espargaro	Derbi	1'37.949 (*)
6	29	A. Iannone	Aprilia	1'37.950
7	18	N. Terol	Aprilia	1'38.034
8	93	M. Marquez	KTM	1'38.044
9	22	P. Nieto	KTM	1'38.104
10	71	T. Koyama	KTM	1'38.153
11	35	R. De Rosa	KTM	1'38.186
12	38	B. Smith	Aprilia	1'38.347
13	12	E. Rabat	KTM	1'38.355
14	99	D. Webb	Aprilia	1'38.473
15	6	J. Olivé	Derbi	1'38.554
16	51	S. Bonsey	Aprilia	1'38.606
17	11	S. Cortese	Aprilia	1'38.724
18	17	S. Bradl	Aprilia	1'38.775
19	34	R. Krummenacher	KTM	1'38.856
20	60	M. Ranseder	Aprilia	1'38.916
21	63	M. Di Meglio	Derbi	1'38.938
22	74	T. Nakagami	Aprilia	1'39.007
23	27	S. Bianco	Aprilia	1'39.037
24	8	L. Zanetti	KTM	1'39.386
25	30	P. Tutusaus	Aprilia	1'39.538
26	16	J. Cluzel	Loncin	1'39.760
27	77	D. Aegerter	Derbi	1'39.806
28	5	A. Masbou	Loncin	1'39.986
29	56	H. Van Den Berg	Aprilia	1'40.357
30	21	R. Lässer	Aprilia	1'40.525
31	95	R. Muresan	Aprilia	1'41.070
32	69	L. Rossi	Honda	1'41.320
33	19	R. Lacalendola	Aprilia	1'42.182
34	64	M. Hoyle	Honda	1'42.316
35	66	C. Behan	Honda	1'42.593
36	65	L. Hinton	Honda	1'42.966
37	67	L. Costello	Honda	1'43.149
38	68	P. Jordan	Honda	1'43.227
	7	E. Vazquez	Aprilia	(**)

(*): Injured on Saturday morning, P. Espargaró (E, Derbi) had to withdraw (fractured left clavicle).
(**): E. Vazquez (E, Aprilia) broke his hand on the Spanish championship (Jerez de la Frontera). He came to Donington, but even Dr Costa refused to allowed him to race.

RACE: 25 laps = 100.575 km

1	Scott Redding	41'39.472 (144.858 km/h)
2	Mike Di Meglio	+ 5.324
3	Marc Marquez	+ 5.806
4	Sergio Gadea	+ 13.990
5	Simone Corsi	+ 16.855
6	Tomoyoshi Koyama	+ 17.181
7	Joan Olivé	+ 18.014
8	Takaaki Nakagami	+ 18.222
9	Sandro Cortese	+ 18.404
10	Bradley Smith	+ 18.891
11	Esteve Rabat	+ 18.976
12	Michael Ranseder	+ 28.269
13	Randy Krummenacher	+ 28.347
14	Raffaele De Rosa	+ 29.403
15	Lorenzo Zanetti	+ 35.763
16	Jules Cluzel	+ 35.868
17	Steve Bonsey	+ 38.158
18	Nicolas Terol	+ 42.766
19	Dominique Aegerter	+ 42.924
20	Stefano Bianco	+ 1'06.296
21	Robin Lässer	+ 1'10.158
22	Pere Tutusaus	+ 1'10.905
23	Louis Rossi	+ 1'29.269
24	Robert Muresan	+ 1 lap
25	Hugo Van Den Berg	+ 1 lap
26	Lee Costello	+ 1 lap
27	Roberto Lacalendola	+ 1 lap

Fastest lap
Redding, in 1'38.704 (146.729 km/h).
Record: Bautistá, in 1'37.312 (148.828 km/h/2006).

Outright fastest lap
Bautista, in 1'36.203 (150.544 km/h/2006).

CHAMPIONSHIP

1	M. Di Meglio	132 (2 wins)
2	S. Corsi	109 (3 wins)
3	S. Bradl	77
4	N. Terol	75
5	P. Espargaró	75
6	J. Olivé	74
7	G. Talmacsi	68
8	S. Gadea	62 (1 win)
9	S. Redding	57 (1 win)
10	B. Smith	55

After another flawless performance Casey Stoner celebrates his third win of the season in his own way.

Assen is also a great big bike park - and the place where Valentino Rossi made his one big mistake.

VALENTINO
GETS IT ALL WRONG

IT DOESN'T HAPPEN OFTEN, BUT IT
DOES HAPPEN: VALENTINO ROSSI WENT
OFF ON THE FIRST LAP AND TOOK
POOR DE PUNIET WITH HIM. STONER
COULDN'T BELIEVE HIS LUCK.

THE RACE

WHEN PROGRESS IS BORING…

Nicky Hayden may be struggling to come to terms with it, but Dani Pedrosa is very happy with the electronic launch control that helps him take the holeshot nearly every time.

Historically, motorised sports were born to meet two key needs: the first is one that dates back to when man first emerged from the primordial swamp, namely the desire for competition. The second, which is just as inbred, is that inventors, or these days, engineers, have always needed a test bed to validate or contradict their work. Without racing in the pioneering days, there would be no band of rubber around the wheels, no effective braking system, no gearbox, no headlights to light up the night and without modern racing, electronic engine management systems would not be as advanced as they are. And of course, all that is a good thing.

However, over the past few weeks, one can seriously ask oneself if constant progress is not in fact making the racing boring. Are you prepared to make a bet? Next time, unless he has a problem in qualifying and is way back on the grid, bet on Pedrosa to lead going into the first corner and you will win! Why? Because Honda's starting system is currently the best and when you add in the fact that Dani is clearly lighter than team-mate Hayden…

It's the same for the exit speed coming out of the turns: in this case you really have to bet on Ducati, which basically means backing Casey Stoner. Ever since the Desmosedici GP8 has run a new electronic set-up, tested on the day after the Catalunya GP, the world champion on his pretty red bike is back to the form he showed last year. "Today, the problem is that if you see in practice that Stoner is taking 2 tenths off you at any specific point, you know you'll have no chance in the race, as it will be a case of 2 tenths times the number of laps to the chequered flag," reckons Valentino Rossi. The Italian is currently focussed on one priority, namely the new Yamaha electronics system, which was due to be tested the

day after the Czech GP, the first race after the summer break. He wants it on the race bike as quickly as possible.

It's a case of the glorious uncertainty of motor sport having to surrender to technical development. You cannot go backwards in the world of technology, but there are worse options.

Worse indeed: because of all these anti aids, anti everything, anti spin, anti locking up, anti slide, the bikes are going quicker and quicker, as they give the impression of being safer. On the downside, when there is an accident, it happens so suddenly that even the best riders in the world can be caught out. At Assen this weekend, two riders - Capirossi and Hayden - were seriously hurt, while in China and Catalunya it was Lorenzo and at the Catalunya tests, Pedrosa had a heavy fall on his back. The result of this carnage is that there were only 16 riders taking the start of a race where it was clear as day that Stoner would win…and that Melandri would be last.

Rossi (left) has just lost it, leaving de Puniet to head back to the pits on foot as former King of Assen Kevin Schwantz looks on.

STONER OUT ON HIS OWN; AFTER HIS FIRST-LAP GAFFE, ROSSI FIGHTS BACK TO 11TH.

RUNNERS AND RIDERS

Capirossi had not been one hundred percent certain of making his comeback at Assen, but he does, here at the Mecca of motorcycle racing. As for the rest, Kawasaki boss Michael Bartholemy assures everyone that West will finish the season with the "greens."

QUALIFYING

Capirossi would have done better to follow the advice of his manager, Carlo Pernat and stay away: he has a terrible fall on Thursday, which leaves the GP veteran with a deep cut to his right arm, where the foot rest had dug in. The wound required twenty stitches. As Spies leaves the paddock that same day, there will only be one Suzuki racing. There will also be just one Kawasaki as, on Friday, Hopkins falls twice, the second time leading to an injured left malleolus.

START

Honda's electronic starting system is as effective as ever, because Dani Pedrosa leads and Hayden immediately swarms over Stoner. De Puniet, running wide with Rossi falls, while "Vale" manages to keep going. Stoner takes the lead before the end of the opening lap, while Rossi is 29.869 behind.

LAP 4

As was to be expected, Stoner is in a world of his own, leading Pedrosa by 2.138.

LAP 12

As he is wont to do, Edwards fights back strongly and is now on Nakano's back wheel and is about to pass him.

HALF-DISTANCE (13 LAPS)

Stoner of course, with a lead of 5.439 over Pedrosa. Hayden is third, 2.142 off his team-mate. Dovizioso is fourth, 7 seconds down, with Vermeulen and Edwards, who will pass the Australian shortly, - right up with him. In last place, Rossi is consistently the second fastest man on track after the leader.

LAP 14

Another victim for Edwards, as he passes Dovizioso to go fourth.

LAP 20

Rossi is no longer last, as he's just passed Melandri. A bit later, Lorenzo helps himself to Vermeulen's spot.

LAP 21

And again for Lorenzo, this time overtaking Nakano.

LAP 23

Rossi is eleventh, as it's Elias' turn to be dealt with.

FINISH (26 LAPS)

If only Rossi hadn't made that mistake on the opening lap, not that Stoner cares, having dominated the GP, head and shoulders above the rest. Pedrosa is second by 11.310. Amazingly in third place it's Edwards, after Hayden runs out of fuel at the final chicane.

CHAMPIONSHIP

The race is wide open again, as Pedrosa moves ahead, by four points, with Stoner closing to 29 points off the leader.

GP NETHERLANDS | 28th June 2008 | Assen | 4.555 m

STARTING GRID

1	1	C. Stoner	Ducati	1'35.520
2	2	D. Pedrosa	Honda	1'35.552
3	46	V. Rossi	Yamaha	1'35.659
4	69	N. Hayden	Honda	1'35.975
5	14	R. De Puniet	Honda	1'35.985
6	5	C. Edwards	Yamaha	1'36.278
7	48	J. Lorenzo	Yamaha	1'36.532
8	7	C. Vermeulen	Suzuki	1'36.768
9	56	S. Nakano	Honda	1'36.804
10	50	S. Guintoli	Ducati	1'36.823
11	4	A. Dovizioso	Honda	1'36.899
12	15	A. De Angelis	Honda	1'36.948
13	52	J. Toseland	Yamaha	1'36.978
14	24	T. Elias	Ducati	1'37.287
15	21	J. Hopkins	Kawasaki	1'37.643 (*)
16	13	A. West	Kawasaki	1'37.793
17	33	M. Melandri	Ducati	1'38.726

(*): Injured on Saturday, J. Hopkins (EU, Kawasaki) had to withdraw (fractured left ankle).

RACE: 26 laps = 118.430 km

1	Casey Stoner	42'12.337 (168.361 km/h)
2	Dani Pedrosa	+ 11.310
3	Colin Edwards	+ 17.125
4	Nicky Hayden	+ 20.477
5	Andrea Dovizioso	+ 27.346
6	Jorge Lorenzo	+ 28.608
7	Chris Vermeulen	+ 32.330
8	Shinya Nakano	+ 34.892
9	James Toseland	+ 38.566
10	Sylvain Guintoli	+ 38.817
11	Valentino Rossi	+ 46.025
12	Toni Elias	+ 48.213
16	Marco Melandri	+ 59.594

Fastest lap

Stoner, in 1'36.738 (169.509 km/h). New record.
Previous: Hayden, in 1'37.106 (168.867 km/h/2006).

Outright fastest lap

Stoner, in 1'35.520 (171.670 km/h/2008).

CHAMPIONSHIP

1	D. Pedrosa	171 (2 wins)
2	V. Rossi	167 (3 wins)
3	C. Stoner	142 (3 wins)
4	J. Lorenzo	114 (1 win)
5	C. Edwards	98
6	A. Dovizioso	79
7	N. Hayden	70
8	J. Toseland	60
9	C. Vermeulen	57
10.	S. Nakano	57

Thomas Luthi shot off the line and led for most of the race but he had no answer to Alvaro Bautista's dazzling form (above).

BAUTISTA WAS BEST, BUT TOM LUTHI WASN'T BAD EITHER.

RUNNERS AND RIDERS

One invited rider, Sweden's Frederik Watz. The day before qualifying, all the riders in the class are called to the Race Director, who reminds them that there are certain rules of behaviour they should adhere to and that yellow cards could be handed out. Simoncelli is the first rider to get one of these, after the accident that knocked out Barbera at Mugello.

QUALIFYING

On Friday, despite the gusting wind, Simoncelli and Debon manage to improve on their previous day's times, but it's Bautista and Barbera who lay claim to the two top slots. That evening, the Grand Prix Commission ratifies what had already been guessed at; namely that as from 1st January 2011, the 250 cc class would be replaced by an open class for 600 cc four stroke prototypes, with a maximum of four cylinders.

START

The start is delayed twice and at 12h30, it's Simoncelli who shows the best reflexes, although he is soon forced to run wide as he is attacked by Luthi. Debon and the Swiss make the most of it and Luthi leads the Spaniard by 164 thousandths at the end of the opening lap.

LAP 3

Luthi now has a lead of 1.497 over Debon, who is pursued by Kallio, Espargaro and Simon.

LAP 6

Luthi's lead is 3.195, but now it's Bautista who is his closest pursuer.

LAP 9

Bautista is the quickest man on track and has closed to 1.420 off Luthi. Further back, the two KTM riders, Aoyama and Kallio are not pulling their punches, which doesn't bother Simoncelli in sixth, wedged between the two orange machines.

LAP 11

Pasini falls.

HALF-DISTANCE (12 LAPS)

Bautista racks up fastest laps and is now 407 thousandths behind Luthi. In third spot, Debon trails by 7.817, followed by Barbera, Simoncelli, Aoyama and Kallio.

LAP 13

Bautista has got past.

LAP 14

Crazy Barbera cuts the chicane while trying to attack Debon. Now, it's Aoyama who is third, 9.891 off Luthi, as Bautista has a one second lead.

LAP 16

It appears to be raining at some points on the track, as Luthi goes by and immediately pulls out a lead of 961 thousandths.

LAP 18

Having grown to over two seconds, Luthi's lead is back to 1.041.

LAP 19

The Spaniard retakes the lead. Simoncelli is now third at 5.931.

FINISH (24 LAPS)

Bautista has 3.876 in hand over Luthi going into the final lap and it's enough to get the job done. Luthi records his best ever 250 finish. Simoncelli is third and for the sixth time, Aoyama has beaten Kallio.

CHAMPIONSHIP

Simoncelli comes out of it very well, as he has closed to within a point of Kallio.

GP NETHERLANDS | 28th June 2008 | Assen | 4.555 m

STARTING GRID

1	19	A. Bautistá	Aprilia	1'39.510
2	21	H. Barberá	Aprilia	1'39.741
3	58	M. Simoncelli	Gilera	1'39.854
4	6	A. Debón	Aprilia	1'40.059
5	41	A. Espargaró	Aprilia	1'40.210
6	12	T. Lüthi	Aprilia	1'40.455
7	60	J. Simón	KTM	1'40.686
8	52	L. Pesek	Aprilia	1'40.742
9	15	R. Locatelli	Gilera	1'40.759
10	72	Y. Takahashi	Honda	1'40.796
11	36	M. Kallio	KTM	1'40.849
12	32	F. Lai	Gilera	1'40.862
13	4	H. Aoyama	KTM	1'40.914
14	75	M. Pasini	Aprilia	1'40.936
15	55	H. Faubel	Aprilia	1'40.972
16	54	M. Poggiali	Gilera	1'41.180
17	14	R. Wilairot	Honda	1'41.543
18	17	K. Abraham	Aprilia	1'41.680
19	25	A. Baldolini	Aprilia	1'42.121
20	50	E. Laverty	Aprilia	1'42.943
21	10	I. Toth	Aprilia	1'43.108
22	64	F. Watz	Aprilia	1'44.481
23	7	R. Gomez	Aprilia	1'44.639
24	45	D.-T. Pradita	Yamaha	1'45.400

RACE: 24 laps = 109.320 km

1	Alvaro Bautistá	40'54.117 (160.363 km/h)
2	Thomas Lüthi	+ 4.597
3	Marco Simoncelli	+ 6.003
4	Alex Debón	+ 9.034
5	Hector Barberá	+ 9.079
6	Hiroshi Aoyama	+ 11.515
7	Mika Kallio	+ 12.874
8	Yuki Takahashi	+ 13.622
9	Roberto Locatelli	+ 21.168
10	Julian Simón	+ 28.789
11	Hector Faubel	+ 37.607
12	Ratthapark Wilairot	+ 37.741
13	Fabrizio Lai	+ 38.729
14	Alex Baldolini	+ 39.165
15	Lukas Pesek	+ 43.037
16	Eugene Laverty	+ 54.171
17	Aleix Espargaró	+ 54.334
18	Frederik Watz	+ 1'24.430
19	Doni Tata Pradita	+ 1 lap
20	Imre Toth	+ 1 lap

Fastest lap

Bautistá, in 1'40.340 (163.424 km/h). New record.
Previous: De Angelis, in 1'40.354 (163.401 km/h/2007).

Outright fastest lap

Bautistá, in 1'39.510 (164.787 km/h/2008).

CHAMPIONSHIP

1	M. Kallio	140 (3 wins)
2	M. Simoncelli	139 (2 wins)
3	A. Debón	114 (1 win)
4	A. Bautistá	102 (2 wins)
5	M. Pasini	98 (1 win)
6	H. Barberá	93
6	H. Aoyama	90
8	Y. Takahashi	78
9	T. Lüthi	77
10	J. Simón	57

ONE RACE, TWO STARTS: TALMACSI'S EXPERIENCE PAID OFF.

RUNNERS AND RIDERS

Pol Espargaro has undergone surgery on his right collar bone and is therefore absent. Another Donington casualty, Danny Webb, is replaced by a 16 year old Dutch rider, Jerry Van De Bunt. Five riders have wild cards, including Sweden's Robert Gull, a protégé of Aki Ajo, and the Dutchmen, Litjens and Iwema, who are riding garagiste-built Seels, running Bridgestone tyres.

QUALIFYING

Everything is decided on Thursday, as Friday's conditions are slower after rain in the morning and only two riders, Bonsey and Marquez, improve their time from the previous day in the top 20. Corsi is quickest and series leader Mike Di Meglio grabs a slot on the front row. Smith is up the sharp end so all is as it should be.

START

A super getaway from Smith, ahead of Corsi and Olive, who goes second immediately. Litjens and Cluzel are fallers on an opening lap that sees Smith come round with a lead of 1.283 over Olive, followed by Cortese, Corsi, Gadea and Terol.

LAP 2

Corsi messes up the chicane and finds himself 19th.

LAP 3

Gadea retires. At the front, Smith now has 1.789 in hand over Olive, who is 3.505 ahead of Terol. Krummenacher falls at the chicane.

LAP 5

Di Meglio and Corsi, the two men dominating the championship, are scrapping....for fifteenth place!

LAP 7

Terol has worked his way up to second place, but he is already trailing Smith by 3.611.

LAP 10

Smith falls, when leading by over 3 seconds. Marquez also hits the deck, it starts to rain and the Race Director hangs out the red flag. The classification is taken from the lap prior to the red flag and they will restart for a five lap sprint race.

SECOND START

Terol gets the best start, while Marquez and Vazquez don't, ahead of Smith, Iannone and Olive, who takes the lead before the end of the lap.

FINISH (5 LAPS)

Olive begins the final lap with a 105 thousandths edge over Corsi. There are six of them covered by less than a second and after a brio show from Rabat, who passes three rivals in one go on the final lap, it's the world champion Talmacsi who has the last word, ahead of Olive and Corsi. Mike di Meglio's surprising record set at the French GP for the shortest race in history does not last long as it now goes to Talmacsi for his 9'04.520 of racing!

CHAMPIONSHIP

With Mike di Meglio only seventh, Corsi, third in this sprint race, closes to within 16 points.

Left: Talmacsi, Olive and Corsi attack the final chicane in what would be the final finishing order. The reigning World Champion (above) celebrates his first win of the campaign as Alexis Masbou reminds us that his sense of balance is built in.

GP NETHERLANDS| 28th June 2008 | Assen | 4.555 m

STARTING GRID

1	24	S. Corsi	Aprilia	1'45.533
2	38	B. Smith	Aprilia	1'45.873
3	6	J. Olivé	Derbi	1'45.896
4	63	M. Di Meglio	Derbi	1'45.897
5	11	S. Cortese	Aprilia	1'45.935
6	45	S. Redding	Aprilia	1'46.028
7	35	R. De Rosa	KTM	1'46.105
8	18	N. Terol	Aprilia	1'46.139
9	33	S. Gadea	Aprilia	1'46.318
10	17	S. Bradl	Aprilia	1'46.329
11	34	R. Krummenacher	KTM	1'46.396
12	77	D. Aegerter	Derbi	1'46.444
13	1	G. Talmacsi	Aprilia	1'46.532
14	27	S. Bianco	Aprilia	1'46.554
15	12	E. Rabat	KTM	1'46.700
16	51	S. Bonsey	Aprilia	1'46.714
17	71	T. Koyama	KTM	1'46.760
18	93	M. Marquez	KTM	1'46.863
19	8	L. Zanetti	KTM	1'46.935
20	22	P. Nieto	KTM	1'46.956
21	60	M. Ranseder	Aprilia	1'47.019
22	7	E. Vazquez	Aprilia	1'47.106
23	29	A. Iannone	Aprilia	1'47.243
24	30	P. Tutusaus	Aprilia	1'47.354
25	56	H. Van Den Berg	Aprilia	1'47.458
26	74	T. Nakagami	Aprilia	1'47.502
27	16	J. Cluzel	Loncin	1'47.617
28	80	J. Litjens	Seel	1'47.670
29	5	A. Masbou	Loncin	1'47.795
30	95	R. Muresan	Aprilia	1'48.027
31	19	R. Lacalendola	Aprilia	1'48.037
32	82	M. Van Der Mark	Honda	1'49.173
33	21	R. Lässer	Aprilia	1'49.207
34	69	L. Rossi	Honda	1'49.995
35	89	E. Dubbink	Honda	1'50.126
36	81	J. Iwema	Seel	1'50.574
37	84	R. Gull	Derbi	1'50.598
38	83	J. Van De Bunt	Aprilia	1'51.569

RACE: 5 laps = 22.775 km (*)

1	Gabor Talmacsi	9'04.520 (150.572 km/h)
2	Joan Olivé	+ 0.128
3	Simone Corsi	+ 0.255
4	Sandro Cortese	+ 0.340
5	Bradley Smith	+ 0.425
6	Esteve Rabat	+ 0.568
7	Mike Di Meglio	+ 0.846
8	Andrea Iannone	+ 0.928
9	Nicolas Terol	+ 1.438
10	Raffaele De Rosa	+ 2.554
11	Stefano Bianco	+ 2.829
12	Stefan Bradl	+ 3.021
13	Tomoyoshi Koyama	+ 3.201
14	Michael Ranseder	+ 3.600
15	Hugo Van Den Berg	+ 4.547
16	Dominique Aegerter	+ 4.592
17	Steve Bonsey	+ 4.819
18	Jules Cluzel	+ 10.548
19	Randy Krummenacher	+ 10.643
20	Pablo Nieto	+ 10.849
21	Pere Tutusaus	+ 11.094
22	Robin Lässer	+ 11.854
23	Alexis Masbou	+ 13.716
24	Louis Rossi	+ 13.828
25	Robert Muresan	+ 16.155
26	Michael Van Der Mark	+ 18.201
27	Robert Gull	+ 25.692
28	Jasper Iwama	+ 29.208
29	Ernst Dubbink	+ 29.949
30	Jerry Van De Bunt	+ 36.419

(*): The race was stopped on the 10th of 22 laps, by the arrival of rain. The championship at this point was used to establish the starting grid of the second race, reduced to 5 laps.

Fastest lap
Di Meglio, in 1'46.661 (153.739 km/h).
Record: Gadea, in 1'45.098 (156.025 km/h/2006).

Outright fastest lap
Kallio, in 1'44.532 (156.870 km/h/2006).

CHAMPIONSHIP

1	M. Di Meglio	141 (2 wins)
2	S. Corsi	125 (3 wins)
3	J. Olivé	94
4	G. Talmacsi	93 (1 win)
5	N. Terol	82
6	S. Bradl	81
7	P. Espargaró	75
8	B. Smith	66
9	S. Gadea	62 (1 win)
10	S. Cortese	58

Like a fly on a window-pane, Pedrosa ends his race among the air barriers - while his Honda takes to the air…

10

Germany, land of contrasts : smiles when there's not much else on, umbrellas in the rain.

KNOCKOUT BLOW
FOR PEDROSA AT THE RING

THE SPANIARD SUFFERED A
DREADFUL FALL ON
GERMANY'S'OTHER' FAMOUS RING,
THE SACHSENRING - ONE THAT LEFT
ITS MARK ON BODY AND SOUL.

THE RACE

FLY-AWAY DANI…

Loris Capirossi was back, still with a hole in his arm after his accident at the Netherlands GP. John Hopkins wasn't, thanks to a broken ankle he was trying to have rebuilt back in the States. And Jorge Lorenzo? The Spaniard caused a stir by doing the unthinkable for a racer: admitting he was afraid. "Yes," he said, "at Le Mans I thought I was going to be killed. And my bed-time reading for these past few weeks has been a book called 'How to conquer fear'."

Because it's a sport practised on two-wheeled machines that can't stay upright on their own, motorcycle racing is dangerous. Danger and risk are important factors in the discipline, they are what makes it so attractive. But as the summer moved uncertainly towards its peak, people in the paddock were asking more and more questions. Had it all got out of hand… again? Those recalcitrant two-stroke 500cc machines were gone, replaced by supposedly more civilized bikes with 'big bang' engines that came

in with less of a rush. And yet nothing had changed. So this was the age of four-stroke technology, was it? Heavier bikes, harder to get the most out of, records would never be broken again… What rubbish! We trimmed down from the 1000cc mark because it was all getting out of hand. What a shame! On every circuit, the best times set by the 1000cc bikes that kick-started the MotoGP class have been wiped out. Not only that, but the preponderance of electronics means performance levels just keep going up and up. And that means the line between staying upright and coming to grief is finer than ever. The proof: the accident that took Pedrosa out. Or, as we put it at the time:

"It was a striking image - the number 2 Honda flying through the air and its rider crumpled against the airfence, wondering helplessly - the scene captured for posterity by the MotoGP Year photographer - if the crazy bike isn't about to bounce right back at him. Just seconds before,

Daniel Pedrosa had been leading the World Championship and leading the wet German GP. Out in front after another perfect start, with seven seconds in hand over Stoner after just six laps. A huge margin… But that yawning gap swallowed up the man himself. Not only did Pedrosa suffer injuries to the ring finger of his left hand, but dislocation and ligament damage to the same finger and his middle finger. The main problem was that Pedrosa couldn't close his left hand, which meant he couldn't get it to work properly. Dani was flown straight home to Barcelona to have it operated on by Professor Xavier Mir, who knows him well, in the course of the following Monday. That being the case, it seems unlikely that Honda's number one rider will be able to make the trip to Laguna Seca." That was Sunday evening, July 13, 2008. On Wednesday 16th, just three days later, Daniel Pedrosa caught his flight to San Francisco…

Too hard on the brakes, and the bike goes down : Daniel Pedrosa ends up in the air barriers as his Honda RC212V heads skyward. The Spaniard was able to get up, but with a badly injured left hand.

STONER LEADS ROSSI AGAIN. PEDROSA'S LAST CHANCES OF THE TITLE HAVE GONE IN THAT HORRIBLE FALL.

RUNNERS AND RIDERS

Loris Capirossi is back, but John Hopkins has flown home to the United States to have another operation on the ankle he broke at Assen and will also miss Laguna Seca. Melandri is still with us; not so Luis D'Antin, embroiled in financial difficulties.

QUALIFYING

The Red Devil is back: Casey Stoner dominates proceedings once more. De Puniet is a fine sixth-fastest and might well have gone quicker had he not been baulked by Nakano on his last qualifying lap. Rossi is seventh - and only third-quickest for Yamaha.

START

It's raining in earnest now and everyone starts on rain tyres, but that doesn't stop Pedrosa getting the best start ahead of Dovizioso, Edwards and Stoner. The Spaniard completes his first lap almost two seconds clear of Dovizioso, who will soon have to give best to Stoner. Rossi is seventh.

LAP 3

Lorenzo goes down soon after being deposed from fifth by Rossi. Up ahead, Pedrosa is now 5.101 seconds in front of Stoner.

LAP 6

High drama as Pedrosa, who was over seven seconds in the lead, comes off under braking at the first corner. Stoner can't believe his luck as he takes the lead, hotly pursued by Dovizioso, Edwards and Rossi.

LAP 8

Rossi passes Edwards; Hayden, back in the pack since the start, pits but comes out again.

LAP 9

Rossi goes second; fastest man on track is Melandri, now in eighth. West has come off but managed to get going again.

LAP 10

Melandri goes down. Up front, Rossi has closed the gap on Stoner to 2.453 seconds. Vermeulen makes up an all-Bridgestone podium at this stage.

HALF-DISTANCE (15 LAPS)

Stoner has things under control, his lead over Rossi now out to 4.410 seconds. Vermeulen is a further 1.4 behind Rossi, with De Angelis right on his wheel, which means we have four Bridgestone riders on four different makes of bike in the first four places in the wet.

LAP 20

Edwards goes down; De Angelis is still right behind Vermeulen.

RACE FINISH (30 LAPS)

Nice snooze? Good. As you may have guessed, nothing much happened in the last third of the race except De Angelis' attack on Vermeulen on the last lap, which Vermeulen was able to fend off.

CHAMPIONSHIP

Rossi is back in the lead, by 16 points from Pedrosa, but with Stoner only 20 points adrift now he knows this is no comfort zone.

Above : Pedrosa has already gone past and there's a bit of argy-bargy behind between Dovizioso (4), Edwards (5), Stoner (1) and Toseland (52). Opposite : Elias caught between the devil and the deep blue sea while Mr and Mrs Stoner (top) can afford to smile.

GP GERMANY | 13th July 2008 | Sachsenring | 3.671 m

STARTING GRID

1	1	C. Stoner	Ducati	1'21.067
2	2	D. Pedrosa	Honda	1'21.420
3	5	C. Edwards	Yamaha	1'21.519
4	4	A. Dovizioso	Honda	1'21.656
5	48	J. Lorenzo	Yamaha	1'21.795
6	14	R. De Puniet	Honda	1'21.821
7	46	V. Rossi	Yamaha	1'21.845
8	69	N. Hayden	Honda	1'21.876
9	56	S. Nakano	Honda	1'21.920
10	15	A. De Angelis	Honda	1'21.977
11	52	J. Toseland	Yamaha	1'22.126
12	24	T. Elias	Ducati	1'22.256
13	65	L. Capirossi	Suzuki	1'22.542
14	7	C. Vermeulen	Suzuki	1'22.601
15	50	S. Guintoli	Ducati	1'22.938
16	33	M. Melandri	Ducati	1'23.131
17	13	A. West	Kawasaki	1'23.158

RACE: 30 laps = 110.130 km

1	Casey Stoner	47'30.057 (139.108 km/h)
2	Valentino Rossi	+ 3.708
3	Chris Vermeulen	+ 14.002
4	Alex De Angelis	+ 14.124
5	Andrea Dovizioso	+ 42.022
6	Sylvain Guintoli	+ 46.648
7	Loris Capirossi	+ 1'04.483
8	Randy De Puniet	+ 1'04.588
9	Shinya Nakano	+ 1'16.773
10	Anthony West	+ 1'29.275
11	James Toseland	+ 1 lap
12	Toni Elias	+ 1 lap
13	Nicky Hayden	+ 2 laps

Fastest lap
Stoner, in 1'32.749 (142.487 km/h).
Record: Pedrosa, in 1'23.082 (159.066 km/h/2007).

Outright fastest lap
Stoner, in 1'21.067 (163.020 km/h/2008).

CHAMPIONSHIP

1	V. Rossi	187 (3 wins)
2	D. Pedrosa	171 (2 wins)
3	C. Stoner	167 (4 wins)
4	J. Lorenzo	114 (1 win)
5	C. Edwards	98
6	A. Dovizioso	90
7	C. Vermeulen	73
8	N. Hayden	73
9	J. Toseland	73
10	S. Nakano	64

A PERFECT RACE FROM SIMONCELLI, AN IMPRESSIVE COMEBACK FOR BAUTISTA. AND KALLIO MISSES OUT AGAIN.

RUNNERS AND RIDERS

Now just a point behind Championship leader Kallio, Simoncelli went to Brno to try out the 2008 factory Gilera-Aprilia, the RSA, and decided to use it for Germany. The Zongshen team were there with two riders, Chow and Sandi, while there were two further wild cards for Hungarian Alen Gyorfi and Germany's Toni Wirsing.

QUALIFYING

Simoncelli is a serious piece of work: left out of pre-season calculations by many, he is boss man of the class even though not yet in the Championship lead. On the RSA he opened a six-tenths gap on the next man up.

START

On a wet track, Simon and Lai catch Simoncelli napping. But the man who lorded it over practice does the business before the end of the opening lap and takes control by two-tenths from Simon. Barbera is third ahead of Kallio, Debon and Lai.

LAP 2

Debon goes down.

LAP 3

Simoncelli now has a 1.746-second lead as Simon and Barbera do battle.

LAP 7

Simoncelli sets a string of fastest laps to take his lead out to more than five seconds. Kallio is right behind Simon

Top : Luthi (12) with Lai and Bautista early in the race. Right : Simoncelli wins for the third time this season after a race that saw Abraham taken out and Bautista come out of it all right.

fighting for third, not far from Barbera, while the two men who donated the Assen round, Bautista and Luthi, are scrapping over seventh.

LAP 10

Kallio is now second, but more than seven seconds adrift of an imperious Simoncelli

LAP 13

The rain suddenly intensifies.

HALF-DISTANCE (15 LAPS)

Simoncelli is controlling the race: his lead is now 7.417 seconds over Kallio, who has a fight on his hands with Barbera and Simon. Seventh-placed Bautista is the fastest man on track and Luthi hasn't been able to hang on.

LAP 17

Aoyama, who was in sixth place, comes off.

LAP 19

As Bautista gets back at Pasini for fifth, Pesek goes down

LAP 21

Nail-biting stuff as Kallio, Barbera and Simon go at it head-to-head, with Pasini and Bautista closing in again.

LAP 26

Barbera, Simon and Bautista head the pursuing group.

LAP 27

Bautista is up to third, right behind Barbera.

RACE FINISH (29 LAPS)

Simoncelli starts the last lap with more than four seconds in hand over Barbera, who is still locked in his duel with Bautista. Contrary to what we might expect from these characters, the last lap goes by without any further mishaps.

CHAMPIONSHIP

Double joy for Simoncelli: his win puts him into the Championship lead and guarantees some summer fun and games on the Adriatic Coast, where he was born and still lives.

GP GERMANY | 13th July 2008 | Sachsenring | 3.671 m

STARTING GRID

1	58	M. Simoncelli	Gilera	1'23.399
2	60	J. Simón	KTM	1'24.057
3	21	H. Barberá	Aprilia	1'24.077
4	36	M. Kallio	KTM	1'24.084
5	19	A. Bautistá	Aprilia	1'24.253
6	6	A. Debón	Aprilia	1'24.398
7	32	F. Lai	Gilera	1'24.460
8	15	R. Locatelli	Gilera	1'24.502
9	4	H. Aoyama	KTM	1'24.544
10	72	Y. Takahashi	Honda	1'24.652
11	55	H. Faubel	Aprilia	1'24.709
12	41	A. Espargaró	Aprilia	1'24.785
13	75	M. Pasini	Aprilia	1'24.797
14	12	T. Lüthi	Aprilia	1'24.811
15	52	L. Pesek	Aprilia	1'24.847
16	17	K. Abraham	Aprilia	1'24.865
17	14	R. Wilairot	Honda	1'25.331
18	90	F. Sandi	Aprilia	1'25.492
19	50	E. Laverty	Aprilia	1'25.840
20	54	M. Poggiali	Gilera	1'25.889
21	25	A. Baldolini	Aprilia	1'26.197
22	10	I. Toth	Aprilia	1'26.862
23	7	R. Gomez	Aprilia	1'27.291
24	45	D.-T. Pradita	Yamaha	1'27.388
25	94	T. Wirsing	Honda	1'27.836
26	93	A. Gyorfi	Honda	1'29.134

RACE: 29 laps = 106.459 km

1	Marco Simoncelli	45'36.703 (140.041 km/h)
2	Hector Barberá	+ 2.257
3	Alvaro Bautistá	+ 2.423
4	Mika Kallio	+ 4.150
5	Julian Simón	+ 4.846
6	Mattia Pasini	+ 8.132
7	Thomas Lüthi	+ 38.302
8	Hiroshi Aoyama	+ 48.926
9	Yuki Takahashi	+ 50.062
10	Roberto Locatelli	+ 51.670
11	Alex Baldolini	+ 1'08.796
12	Fabrizio Lai	+ 1'09.962
13	Aleix Espargaró	+ 1'11.351
14	Hector Faubel	+ 1'11.654
15	Eugene Laverty	+ 1'13.856
16	Ratthapark Wilairot	+ 1'29.976
17	Imre Toth	+ 1 lap
18	Alen Gyorfi	+ 1 lap
19	Doni Tata Pradita	+ 1 lap
20	Toni Wirsing	+ 2 laps

Fastest lap

Barberá, in 1'32.551 (142.792 km/h).
Record: Kallio, in 1'24.762 (155.914 km/h/2007).

Outright fastest lap

Simoncelli, in 1'23.399 (158.462 km/h/2008).

CHAMPIONSHIP

1	M. Simoncelli	164 (3 wins)
2	M. Kallio	153 (3 wins)
3	A. Bautistá	118 (2 wins)
4	A. Debón	114 (1 win)
5	H. Barberá	113
6	M. Pasini	108 (1 win)
7	H. Aoyama	98
8	T. Lüthi	86
9	Y. Takahashi	85
10	J. Simón	68

DI MEGLIO IS THE
CLASS'S MR
PERFECT. WITH
CORSI ONLY FIFTH,
THE FRENCHMAN
OPENED UP A
HANDY LEAD.

RUNNERS AND RIDERS

The start of the second half of the
Championship is traditionally the point at
which the midfield teams drop riders who
have either shown disappointing form or
failed to bring the promised funding with
them. So it was that Stefano Bianco lost
his place in the WTR San Marino line-up
to 16-year-old Swiss Bastien Chesaux,
who had been racing in the German
championship since the previous year. At
Matteoni, out went Italian champion
Roberto Lacalendola, and in for the
Sachsenring came Marco Ravaioli. Pol
Espargaro (injured collarbone, Donington)
and Webb were back in action.

QUALIFYING

Despite yet another spectacular fall,
Bradley Smith qualified second-fastest,
behind reigning World Champion
Talmacsi. Local hero Bradl was third-
quickest and bent on pulling off the
sensation of the year. Corsi completed
the front row.

START

Talmacsi got it wrong, but Bradl didn't,
racing into the lead from Smith and Corsi.
He got a hero's welcome at the end of
the first lap, which he led by 485-
thousandths of a second from Corsi,
followed by Smith, Olive and Terol.

LAP 2

Corsi goes into the lead, while the leading

Sachsenring is all about that
dizzying downhill stretch which the
riders take blind. Di Meglio (63,
above) comes out on top again
while Swiss rider Bastien Chesaux
makes his first GP start. Opposite :
the winning twosome of 2008, Aki
Ajo and Mike Di Meglio.

quartet of Corsi, Olive, Bradl and Smith
carve out a gap of more than a second to
the chasing pack.

LAP 5

With Bradl back in front, less than a
second now covers the top seven as
Talmacsi, Terol and Di Meglio have closed
up.

LAP 7

Terol is dropped.

LAP 9

Olive slows at the side of the track; Smith
is in front from Corsi, Bradl, Talmacsi and
Di Meglio.

HALF-DISTANCE (13 LAPS)

Smith has upped the pace and now has a
0.808 gap on Corsi. World Championship
leader Mike Di Meglio senses the threat
and is now third, 1.445 behind. Bradl and
Talmacsi are not far adrift, while Cortese is
in a lonely sixth place.

LAP 15

Di Meglio has moved up to second, 0.9
behind Smith.

LAP 17

Gadea retires; Di Meglio is right on Smith's
rear wheel and is about to go past him.

LAP 19

Di Meglio has a lead of five-tenths of a
second. Now it's Bradl's turn to lead the
chasing pack, with Smith and Talmacsi
right there.

LAP 23

De Rosa falls; Di Meglio's lead has gone
out to over a second.

RACE FINISH (27 LAPS)

Another mistake-free ride by Di Meglio, the
main man of this 2008 season. Bradl
finishes a superb second ahead of World
Champion Gabor Talmacsi.

CHAMPIONSHIP

With a 30-point lead over Corsi,
Frenchman Di Meglio can go off on holiday
with an easy mind. Outgoing champion
Talmacsi has regained third place overall,
but he is 59 points adrift of the leader.

GP GERMANY | 13th July 2008 | Sachsenring | 3.671 m

STARTING GRID

1	1	G. Talmacsi	Aprilia	1'27.552
2	38	B. Smith	Aprilia	1'27.645
3	17	S. Bradl	Aprilia	1'27.921
4	24	S. Corsi	Aprilia	1'28.038
5	6	J. Olivé	Derbi	1'28.045
6	63	M. Di Meglio	Derbi	1'28.123
7	71	T. Koyama	KTM	1'28.363
8	35	R. De Rosa	KTM	1'28.410
9	11	S. Cortese	Aprilia	1'28.465
10	12	E. Rabat	KTM	1'28.499
11	99	D. Webb	Aprilia	1'28.535
12	33	S. Gadea	Aprilia	1'28.559
13	51	S. Bonsey	Aprilia	1'28.572
14	18	N. Terol	Aprilia	1'28.622
15	44	P. Espargaró	Derbi	1'28.702
16	45	S. Redding	Aprilia	1'28.732
17	34	R. Krummenacher	KTM	1'28.754
18	22	P. Nieto	KTM	1'28.759
19	93	M. Marquez	KTM	1'28.831
20	87	M. Schrötter	Honda	1'28.852
21	77	D. Aegerter	Derbi	1'28.870
22	60	M. Ranseder	Aprilia	1'28.935
23	7	E. Vazquez	Aprilia	1'28.944
24	29	A. Iannone	Aprilia	1'28.964
25	74	T. Nakagami	Aprilia	1'29.007
26	16	J. Cluzel	Loncin	1'29.231
27	8	L. Zanetti	KTM	1'29.232
28	21	R. Lässer	Aprilia	1'29.307
29	56	H. Van Den Berg	Aprilia	1'29.308
30	85	M. Fritz	Seel	1'29.552
31	30	P. Tutusaus	Aprilia	1'29.618
32	95	R. Muresan	Aprilia	1'29.638
33	5	A. Masbou	Loncin	1'29.821
34	88	S. Kreuziger	Honda	1'30.074
35	72	M. Ravaioli	Aprilia	1'30.739
36	86	E. Hübsch	Aprilia	1'30.947
37	41	T. Siegert	Aprilia	1'30.971
38	48	B. Chesaux	Aprilia	1'30.983
39	69	L. Rossi	Honda	1'31.308

RACE: 27 laps = 99.117 km

1	Mike Di Meglio	40'03.710 (148.446 km/h)
2	Stefan Bradl	+ 2.010
3	Gabor Talmacsi	+ 2.733
4	Bradley Smith	+ 2.847
5	Simone Corsi	+ 9.117
6	Sandro Cortese	+ 9.249
7	Nicolas Terol	+ 9.257
8	Scott Redding	+ 30.778
9	Esteve Rabat	+ 32.311
10	Marc Marquez	+ 33.034
11	Dominique Aegerter	+ 33.121
12	Andrea Iannone	+ 33.134
13	Pere Tutusaus	+ 33.171
14	Marcel Schrötter	+ 33.208
15	Pablo Nieto	+ 33.755
16	Efrén Vazquez	+ 34.554
17	Pol Espargaró	+ 37.776
18	Steve Bonsey	+ 37.872
19	Takaaki Nakagami	+ 54.240
20	Marvin Fritz	+ 58.249
21	Alexis Masbou	+ 1'14.202
22	Louis Rossi	+ 1'15.255
23	Robert Muresan	+ 1'16.356
24	Marco Ravaioli	+ 1'16.854
25	Tobias Siegert	+ 1 lap

Fastest lap
Di Meglio, in 1'27.584 (150.890 km/h).
Record: Talmacsi, in 1'26.909 (152.062 km/h/2007).

Outright fastest lap
Talmacsi, in 1'26.839 (152.185 km/h/2007).

CHAMPIONSHIP

1	M. Di Meglio	166 (3 wins)
2	S. Corsi	136 (3 wins)
3	G. Talmacsi	109 (1 win)
4	S. Bradl	101
5	J. Olivé	94
6	N. Terol	91
7	B. Smith	79
8	P. Espargaró	75
9	S. Cortese	68
10	S. Redding	65 (1 win)

Rossi's number 46 Yamaha between barrier and wall : the moment the Championship balance shifted.

Who called it 'the American dream' ?

SHOCK
TREATMENT FOR STONER

'DR' ROSSI WAS RUTHLESS UNDER THE CALIFORNIA SUN ; MEANWHILE HIS PATIENT, THE REIGNING WORLD CHAMPION, HAD A HARD TIME GETTING BACK ON HIS FEET.

THE RACE

SUPERLATIVES ALL ROUND

Three pictures that tell the story of a two-handed fight :
Rossi leads Stoner by a few lengths before the latter comes to grief.
Another triumph beckons for Valentino.

It was all too much, the mid-July race weekend in California. Too big a risk for Daniel Pedrosa, who flew to the New World virtually straight from Barcelona's Dexeus Clinic, where all Dr Mir could do for him was confirm the extent of the damage, in particular the multiple fractures to his left hand.

Too much of a roughing-up for Jorge Lorenzo, too : a week after admitting he had felt fear, he had another heavy crash, this time in the first few metres of the race. Once again he paid the price not just in physical terms - injuring his left ankle - but on the mental side as well.

Last but by no means least, the Rossi-Stoner duel was just too much to take : too wild, too wonderful, too big, too… everything. Too Rossi, in the end, and of course that's the best part of it. It had all been bubbling up inside Valentino for the last few weeks as the reigning World Champion fought back from a tricky start to be the Championship's dominant force once more. At Laguna Seca he really piled it on : four

practice sessions plus warm-up all added up to five fastest times for Stoner. The gap between the heir apparent and the rest was small - just 0.446 seconds after qualifying, and that gap was to Rossi himself. So Rossi went to war, starting on Saturday.

« How do you stop Stoner ? » he was asked. « Easy : just shoot him ! » And as a Spanish colleague reminded him that the officials would never let him go to the front row of the grid with a weapon in his hands, Rossi came back with another quip : « Fine, but I have another way of beating him : I'll take the start 30 seconds earlier ! »

Was this a man who already knew he was beaten? That's what it looked like on Saturday evening, although that really isn't what you expect from Valentino Rossi. But then, we reminded ourselves, no-one can do what's just not possible. And of course we were all wrong…

Valentino Rossi bared his teeth right from the start, the first turn, the first time under brakes, and stayed

that way all race long. He leaned on the rival Ducati whenever he had to, the gap measured in thousandths of a second ; some of the passing manœuvres took your breath away ; there were only the two of them out there, each in charge of his own destiny.

And Rossi came out on top, provoking first a fall from Stoner, and then this reaction : « I've been racing a long time, I've seen a lot of passes that were right on the limit, I've made some myself. But today, at times, some of them went beyond the limit, but of course my mistake is down to me. »

Rossi was having none of it, nor was his crew chief Jeremy Burgess. « If Stoner had been racing in the Eighties and early Nineties, » said Burgess, « against the likes of Schwantz, Rainey and Doohan, he'd have seen passes like that every weekend. » Which, when we translate Burgess-speak, means : « Silly little boy, you're not in the playground now ! » The Doctor had just dished out a lesson of his own.

Happy holidays, everyone…

Rossi and Stoner wheel to wheel once more - but not for long. Colin Edwards (middle) with his family and (right) 37-year-old first-timer Jamie Hacking.

IT'S ALL OR NOTHING FOR ROSSI ; STONER HAS TRIED TO HOLD HIM OFF AND CRASHED OUT IN THE PROCESS.

RUNNERS AND RIDERS

First thunderbolt of the weekend : despite multiple fractures to his left hand and another to his right ankle, on the Wednesday before the GP Pedrosa decided to 'come over and see' if he was able to compete. Jamie Hacking, 37, replaced John Hopkins, still out injured, and with Ben Spies enjoying a wild-card entry this time there were three Suzukis on track.

QUALIFYING

No-one can do what's just not possible : slowest of all on Friday morning,

Pedrosa did manage to go two seconds faster that afternoon but decided come Saturday not to persist, saying that even with a painkilling injection he just couldn't bear it. Unbearable for different reasons was Casey Stoner, who dominated all four practice sessions and then warm-up as well. Among the many fallers was Alex de Angelis, who broke his left thumb.

START

Stoner gets away best from Rossi and Hayden. Immediately there is drama for Lorenzo, who comes off his bike and clutches his left ankle. Another sensation soon after : Rossi catches Stoner out through the Corkscrew !

LAP 4

Stoner goes ahead again on the straight but Rossi is immediately back on the attack. They make contact as Rossi risks all, running off on to the

gravel out of the Corkscrew. There are just thousandths of a second between the two and behind them Hayden, 2.388 seconds adrift, is a mere spectator.

LAP 6

It's still Rossi, now by 0.199 from Stoner.

LAP 11

Melandri has had an off in a gravel trap; Rossi still leads - and third-placed Vermeulen is 10 seonds and more behind.

LAP 14

Stoner gets his braking wrong in the first corner and Rossi grabs six-tenths' breathing space, but within another lap the Ducati is back in touch.

HALF-DISTANCE (16 LAPS)

Rossi is still out in front, with Stoner 0.163 behind. Vermeulen, running in a solid third, is now 15.070 seconds

behind the leader but has three seconds in hand over Hayden and Dovizioso. De Puniet is sixth, another three seconds behind the rookie.

LAP 23

There are precisely six-thousandths of a second between our two front-runners.

LAP 24

Rossi's constant hounding takes its toll as Stoner goes off, drops the bike in the gravel trap and slips back to 13.830 seconds behind !

FINISH (32 LAPS)

It's been one of the wildest races of the last few years but there was always going to be one winner - Valentino Rossi.

CHAMPIONSHIP

25 points is a whole race ; that's the lead Rossi now enjoys over heir apparent Stoner as the break looms. A handy gap to play with...

GP UNITED STATES | 20th July 2008 | Laguna Seca | 3.610 m

STARTING GRID

1	1	C. Stoner	Ducati	1'20.700
2	46	V. Rossi	Yamaha	1'21.147
3	69	N. Hayden	Honda	1'21.430
4	48	J. Lorenzo	Yamaha	1'21.636
5	52	J. Toseland	Yamaha	1'21.848
6	14	R. De Puniet	Honda	1'21.921
7	5	C. Edwards	Yamaha	1'21.947
8	7	C. Vermeulen	Suzuki	1'21.971
9	4	A. Dovizioso	Honda	1'21.974
10	24	T. Elias	Ducati	1'21.999
11	65	L. Capirossi	Suzuki	1'22.039
12	56	S. Nakano	Honda	1'22.092
13	11	B. Spies	Suzuki	1'22.127
14	50	S. Guintoli	Ducati	1'22.719
15	33	M. Melandri	Ducati	1'22.957
16	15	A. De Angelis	Honda	1'23.035
17	12	J. Hacking	Kawasaki	1'23.309
18	13	A. West	Kawasaki	1'24.525

RACE: 32 laps = 115.520 km

1	Valentino Rossi	44'04.311 (157.270 km/h)
2	Casey Stoner	+ 13.001
3	Chris Vermeulen	+ 26.609
4	Andrea Dovizioso	+ 34.901
5	Nicky Hayden	+ 35.663
6	Randy De Puniet	+ 37.668
7	Toni Elias	+ 41.629
8	Ben Spies	+ 41.927
9	James Toseland	+ 43.019
10	Shinya Nakano	+ 44.391
11	Jamie Hacking	+ 46.258
12	Sylvain Guintoli	+ 55.273
13	Alex De Angelis	+ 55.521
14	Colin Edwards	+ 1'02.380
15	Loris Capirossi	+ 1'10.962
16	Anthony West	+ 1 lap

Fastest lap

Stoner, in 1'21.488 (159.483 km/h). New record.
Previous: Stoner, in 1'22.542 (157.447 km/h/2007).

Outright fastest lap

Stoner, in 1'20.700 (161.040 km/h/2008).

CHAMPIONSHIP

1	V. Rossi	212 (4 wins)
2	C. Stoner	187 (4 wins)
3	D. Pedrosa	171 (2 wins)
4	J. Lorenzo	114 (1 win)
5	A. Dovizioso	103
6	C. Edwards	100
7	C. Vermeulen	89
8	N. Hayden	84
9	J. Toseland	72
10	S. Nakano	70

No, it's not Italy, it's the Czech Republic - but Rossimania travels well.

Scenes from everyday life : mounted police and mouth-watering sausages.

ROSSI-STONER :
SAME AGAIN

AT LAGUNA SECA IT WAS THE SAME
OLD STORY : STONER DOMINATED THE
EARLY PROCEEDINGS, ROSSI STAYED
CLOSE AND CASEY CAME OFF.
ANOTHER HAPPY DAY FOR HIS ROYAL
HIGHNESS.

THE RACE

ANYONE FOR POLITICS ?

The short break for 'sea, sex and sun' over, it's back to grim reality, which everyone fights off with a few too many during practice. No more beach, no more babes : welcome back to the real world. And what does it have to say for itself as the summer of 2008 draws to a close ? Well, for all the excitement of that extraordinary Laguna Seca race, the MotoGP class has a bit of a collective hangover. Riders are hurt, or missing, or not what they used to be ; cash-strapped satellite teams are having to be propped up ; the imbalance between tyre suppliers Bridgestone and Michelin, already obvious at Laguna Seca, will be absolutely glaring this weekend in the Czech Republic. And to top it all, there is a growing cloud over the future of the class whose task it is to get riders battle-hardened before they move up to MotoGP. That, of course, is the in-between category, currently a 250cc two-stroke class which, by 2011, plans to switch to 600 four-stroke prototypes.

- MotoGP and its many woes : While John Hopkins and Dani Pedrosa are back (although the Spaniard is still in trouble with that left hand), Hayden is missing, Lorenzo still carries mental scars, as does James Toseland, his confidence dented by his multiple mistakes in his home race at Donington, and Melandri's not much better. MotoGP, it seems, might not be so good for you…

- MotoGP and its money woes : Motor sport is in a period of transition between the good old days when tobacco companies were falling over themselves to be involved and a new era in which promoting new products will gradually become the teams' path to financial stability. Balancing the books is now such a precarious art that with Rossi, Stoner and Pedrosa already fixed up for next year, the other riders and their managers need to revise their expectations downwards.

- MotoGP's other balancing act: Now it's tyre time. They were already at the centre of major discussions 12 months ago, and look what happened then : Rossi (i.e. half of the works Yamaha team !) went from Michelin to Bridgestone. In mid-August this year things are even more black-and-white than they were last year ; Dorna boss Carmelo Ezpeleta is well aware that he can't vouch for the medium-term quality of his product when there is such imbalance between the various competitors. No decision at Brno - but the chance (should that be risk ?) of moving to a one-make series as early as 2009 is growing ever greater.

- MotoGP and the class below : 2009 is the penultimate year for the two-stroke 250cc class which so many talents have emerged from. As of 2011, in a decision taken this Spring, we go to four-stroke technology and 600cc engines. Or at least we should - by the cut-off date of July 31, when constructors were supposed to have put forward their proposals, no-one had.

Worrying times ? You can say that again…

Good odds for anyone having a flutter : not on the winner, as he celebrates his fifth victory of the season, but certainly if you were on the other podium finishers, Toni Elias (left) and Loris Capirossi

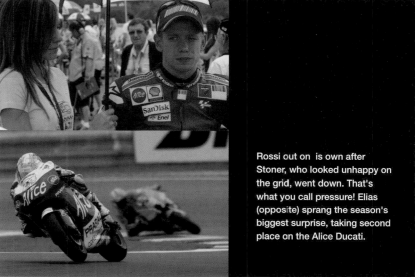

Rossi out on is own after Stoner, who looked unhappy on the grid, went down. That's what you call pressure! Elias (opposite) sprang the season's biggest surprise, taking second place on the Alice Ducati.

ANOTHER EPISODE IN THE TYRE WARS SAGA, ANOTHER WIN FOR BRIDGESTONE - EVEN WITHOUT STONER...

RUNNERS AND RIDERS

There's one big name missing, and that's Hayden, who has damaged an ankle in a training run during the X-Games. Meanwhile Hopkins is back. On the eve of practice Stoner and Rossi exchange a handshake to show that peace has broken out following the war of words sparked by that fantastic race at Laguna Seca. For the first time this season Nakano is on the same Honda machinery as Pedrosa.

QUALIFYING

The resurfaced Czech track will play its part all weekend : right from opening practice the Michelin riders claim their hardest front tyres won't last more than a few laps. In rainy qualifying Bridgestone have it all their own way - there is just one man from the Bibendum camp (De Puniet in seventh) among the top 11 riders.

START

A perfect one from Stoner as Rossi struggles to shake off Hopkins, so the World Champion enjoys a 1.142 -second lead over the Italian at the end of the opening lap. Hopkins is third, 2.459 seconds away - and West fourth !

LAP 3

The Michelin mauling begins : Pedrosa is now ninth, De Puniet down in 11th.

LAP 6

No miracles for De Puniet as his front tyre gets away from him.

LAP 7

Drama as Stoner goes down - Rossi had come back to within 1.057. The World Champion gets going but stops again soon after.

LAP 8

Capirossi has just got past Hopkins and Vermeulen and is briefly up to second until his teammate slips through a tiny gap and takes it back.

LAP 9

The old fox won't let go : Capirossi goes second again.

LAP 10

There are rich pickings on offer for a betting man : not because Rossi's in the lead, of course, but because Elias is now second from Capirossi.

HALF-DISTANCE (11 LAPS)

Rossi has a 16.770-second lead over Elias, who is looking to drop Capirossi. Now West is fourth ahead of Hopkins and Vermeulen. The last Michelin rider in the running, Dovizioso, has just lost seventh to Nakano.

FINISH (22 LAPS)

His Royal Highness starts the last lap of another convincing demonstration with 17.164 seconds in hand over Elias, now no longer threatened by Capirossi. There are five different marques in the top five places while Dovizioso in ninth is the first Michelin runner home.

CHAMPIONSHIP

With a 50-point gap, 'Vale' now has two races in hand over Stoner.

GP CZECH REPUBLIC | 17th August 2008 | Brno | 5.403 m

STARTING GRID

1	1	C. Stoner	Ducati	2'11.657
2	46	V. Rossi	Yamaha	2'12.846
3	21	J. Hopkins	Suzuki	2'12.959
4	7	C. Vermeulen	Suzuki	2'13.002
5	15	A. De Angelis	Honda	2'13.352
6	13	A. West	Kawasaki	2'14.064
7	14	R. De Puniet	Honda	2'14.535
8	56	S. Nakano	Honda	2'14.718
9	65	L. Capirossi	Suzuki	2'14.805
10	50	S. Guintoli	Ducati	2'14.861
11	33	M. Melandri	Ducati	2'15.880
12	2	D. Pedrosa	Honda	2'16.032
13	24	T. Elias	Ducati	2'16.510
14	4	A. Dovizioso	Honda	2'17.632
15	5	C. Edwards	Yamaha	2'20.074

Not qualified but allowed to race:

	52	J. Toseland	Yamaha	2'23.303
	48	J. Lorenzo	Yamaha	2'23.701

RACE: 22 laps = 118.866 km

1	Valentino Rossi	43'28.841 (164.025 km/h)
2	Toni Elias	+ 15.004
3	Loris Capirossi	+ 21.689
4	Shinya Nakano	+ 25.859
5	Anthony West	+ 29.465
6	Chris Vermeulen	+ 30.608
7	Marco Melandri	+ 36.453
8	Alex De Angelis	+ 36.750
9	Andrea Dovizioso	+ 38.822
10	Jorge Lorenzo	+ 39.573
11	John Hopkins	+ 39.610
12	Sylvain Guintcli	+ 40.892
13	James Toseland	+ 1'11.490
14	Colin Edwards	+ 1'21.133
15	Daniel Pedrosa	+ 1'37.038
16	Randy De Puniet	+ 1'38.407

Fastest lap
Stoner, in 1'57.199 (165.963 km/h). New record.
Previous: Capirossi, in 1'58.157 (164.618 km/h/2006).

Outright fastest lap
Rossi, ein 1'56.191 (167.403 km/h/2006).

CHAMPIONSHIP

1	V. Rossi	237 (5 wins)
2	C. Stoner	187 (4 wins)
3	D. Pedrosa	172 (2 wins)
4	J. Lorenzo	120 (1 win)
5	A. Dovizioso	110
6	C. Edwards	102
7	C. Vermeulen	99
8	N. Hayden	84
9	S. Nakano	83
10	L. Capirossi	77

DEBON, BAUTISTA, SIMONCELLI AND BARBERA: GREAT SCRAP, GUYS !

RUNNERS AND RIDERS

Championship leader Marco Simoncelli didn't spend the whole break on the Adriatic beach : he also got his driving licence, which he promptly lost just 24 hours later for an illegal overtaking move ! One man missing was Hungarian Imre Toth after fracturing the ring finger on his right hand in a motocross accident a week earlier.

QUALIFYING

Once again Simoncelli sorted things out to suit himself, this despite a spectacular off in the driest session of the whole weekend. In the end the Gilera man was ahead of Alex Debon and Hector Barbera, with Mattia Pasini fourth from Tom Luthi and Bautista 'only' 10th. Poggiali didn't go out in the first day's rain and did only three laps on Saturday, meaning he missed the qualifying cut. Though he earned a reprieve he didn't take the race start.

START

Simoncelli's reactions are best, followed by Luthi who takes the lead soon after but hands it back to the title leader. First time across the line there is just 0.265 between the two men who are seven-tenths clear of their first pursuer, Debon.

LAP 4

After a touch with Debon Luthi makes a mistake and goes down in a gravel trap - it's all over for the Swiss rider. Up front, Simoncelli, Debon and Kallio have opened up a gap of nearly two seconds on fourth-placed man Bautista.

LAP 7

Debon has been hounding Simoncelli and now finds a chink in the Italian's armour.

LAP 8

Bautista is fastest man on track and just half a second behind Kallio.

HALF-DISTANCE (10 LAPS)

Simoncelli has just retaken the lead and is 0.165 ahead of Debon, on whom Bautista has quickly closed the gap ; Kallio is now back in fourth with Barbera eight-tenths away in fifth.

LAP 15

Top three Debon, Bautista and Simoncelli are covered by less than four-tenths of a second as Barbera closes in on Kallio.

LAP 17

Debon still has it in his grasp but things are really hotting up between Simoncelli and Bautista.

LAP 19

Simoncelli makes a do-or-die move and retakes the lead ; Barbera has just set fastest race lap so it's a three-way Spanish fight behind the Italian.

FINISH (20 LAPS)

In a crazy final lap both Debon (round the outside) and Bautista (up the inside) catch Simoncelli napping.

CHAMPIONSHIP

Despite being beaten Simoncelli extends his lead as Kallio is now 16 points adrift.

Well may Debon give Bautista a spray (left) : he's just taken his second win at this level. Below : Pasini, Takahashi and Faubel fight for sixth while it all ends in tears for Luthi (opposite) when it all seemed to be going so well.

GP CZECH REPUBLIC | 17th August 2008 | Brno | 5.403 m

STARTING GRID

1	58	M. Simoncelli	Gilera	2'10.723
2	6	A. Debón	Aprilia	2'11.489
3	21	H. Barberá	Aprilia	2'11.578
4	75	M. Pasini	Aprilia	2'12.168
5	12	T. Lüthi	Aprilia	2'12.762
6	60	J. Simón	KTM	2'13.074
7	36	M. Kallio	KTM	2'13.698
8	72	Y. Takahashi	Honda	2'13.944
9	52	L. Pesek	Aprilia	2'13.970
10	19	A. Bautistá	Aprilia	2'14.577
11	25	A. Baldolini	Aprilia	2'14.664
12	50	E. Laverty	Aprilia	2'14.918
13	32	F. Lai	Gilera	2'15.103
14	55	H. Faubel	Aprilia	2'15.416
15	17	K. Abraham	Aprilia	2'15.659
16	4	H. Aoyama	KTM	2'15.785
17	15	R. Locatelli	Gilera	2'15.836
18	41	A. Espargaró	Aprilia	2'16.552
19	90	F. Sandi	Aprilia	2'17.550
20	14	R. Wilairot	Honda	2'18.009
21	94	T. Wirsing	Honda	2'18.764
22	45	D.-T. Pradita	Yamaha	2'19.018

Not qualified but allowed to race:

	7	R. Gomez	Aprilia	2'21.402
	54	M. Poggiali	Gilera	2'34.770

RACE: 20 laps = 108.060 km

1	Alex Debón	41'08.168 (157.613 km/h)
2	Alvaro Bautistá	+ 0.280
3	Marco Simoncelli	+ 0.325
4	Hector Barberá	+ 0.827
5	Mika Kallio	+ 1.249
6	Yuki Takahashi	+ 13.713
7	Mattia Pasini	+ 13.826
8	Hector Faubel	+ 16.026
9	Roberto Locatelli	+ 19.084
10	Aleix Espargaró	+ 20.692
11	Ratthapark Wilairot	+ 29.495
12	Julian Simón	+ 29.772
13	Hiroshi Aoyama	+ 31.944
14	Lukas Pesek	+ 36.314
15	Alex Baldolini	+ 43.751
16	Eugene Laverty	+ 46.564
17	Fabrizio Lai	+ 55.591
18	Federico Sandi	+ 55.704
19	Doni Tata Pradita	+ 1'24.324
20	Toni Wirsing	+ 1'39.423
21	Russel Gomez	+ 1'59.990

Fastest lap

Debón, in 2'02.354 (158.971 km/h).
Record: Lorenzo, in 2'02.299 (159.043 km/h/2007).

Outright fastest lap

Lorenzo, in 2'01.368 (160.263 km/h/2007).

CHAMPIONSHIP

1	M. Simoncelli	180 (3 wins)
2	M. Kallio	164 (3 wins)
3	A. Debón	139 (2 wins)
4	A. Bautistá	138 (2 wins)
5	H. Barberá	126
6	M. Pasini	117 (1 win)
7	H. Aoyama	101
8	Y. Takahashi	95
9	T. Lüthi	86
10	J. Simón	72

LIKE FATHER, LIKE SON : YOUNG GERMAN STEFAN BRADL CLAIMS HIS FIRST WIN AS DI MEGLIO GETS HIS SUMS RIGHT.

RUNNERS AND RIDERS

We were thunderstruck to learn, on the eve of practice, that Spanish rider Esteve Rabat, ninth in the German GP, had been disqualified for a fuel discrepancy. Otherwise it was business as usual, apart from the five wild cards, including German Red Bull MotoGP Academy rider Jonas Folger, who turned 15 the Wednesday before the GP, and Czech female Andrea Touskova.

QUALIFYING

Thanks to the quirky weather the grid was set in one session, on Friday, on a slippery track. When it's like that there's no substitute for experience and reigning World Champion Talmacsi left them all for dead. Terol, Iannone and Smith made up the front row with Championship leader Mike Di Meglio ideally placed to keep a watching brief from fifth on the grid.

START

Smith makes the best one from Terol, Talmacsi and Espargaro. Koyama won't make it to the end of the first lap, nor will Nakagami, De Rosa or Webb. Smith finishes it 0.237 ahead of Terol.

LAP 2

Bradl, only 13th in qualifying, is already up into fourth, in fact there is a breakaway quartet at the front made up of Smith, Talmacsi, Terol and the young German. Di Meglio is fifth, eight-tenths behind.

LAP 3

Bradl has gone to the front.

LAP 5

No change after the break : Mike is still the leader of the pack - the Frenchman is back in front from Talmacsi and Bradl.

LAP 7

Marquez goes down ; Bradl leads from Talmacsi, Terol and Di Meglio.

HALF-DISTANCE (10 LAPS)

Bradl is still out there ; the German is 0.746 clear of Terol with Talmacsi, Olive, a hard-charging Cortese and Di Meglio in pursuit.

LAP 13

A perfect lap from Bradl means the race leader, for the first time, is over a second clear (1.438 ahead of Derbi duo Olive and Di Meglio).

LAP 15

No change up front and there are only four men - Di Meglio, Terol, Talmacsi and Olive -- still in contention for the other two podium places as Cortese and Smith have been dropped.

LAP 16

Di Meglio has broken away from the group and is now just 1.179 behind Bradl.

FINISH (19 LAPS)

A first win for Bradl, and the first by a German since Steve Jenkner in the wet in the Netherlands in 2003. It's another great day's work for Di Meglio as Corsi can only come home 10th.

CHAMPIONSHIP

Things are looking good at Ajo as Di Meglio moves to a 44-point lead, while Bradl is up to third.

Bradl leads the pack, the young German on his ultra-quick Aprilia heading for a first victory. Gabor Talmacsi (below) meanwhile boasts a special helmet in honour of Hungary.

GP CZECH REPUBLIC | 17th August 2008 | Brno | 5.403 m

STARTING GRID

1	1	G. Talmacsi	Aprilia	2'09.870
2	18	N. Terol	Aprilia	2'10.588
3	29	A. Iannone	Aprilia	2'10.589
4	38	B. Smith	Aprilia	2'10.652
5	63	M. Di Meglio	Derbi	2'10.791
6	11	S. Cortese	Aprilia	2'11.024
7	44	P. Espargaró	Derbi	2'11.030
8	24	S. Corsi	Aprilia	2'11.227
9	33	S. Gadea	Aprilia	2'11.276
10	6	J. Olivé	Derbi	2'11.341
11	35	R. De Rosa	KTM	2'11.353
12	93	M. Marquez	KTM	2'11.353
13	17	S. Bradl	Aprilia	2'11.515
14	71	T. Koyama	KTM	2'11.518
15	12	E. Rabat	KTM	2'11.676
16	99	D. Webb	Aprilia	2'11.688
17	45	S. Redding	Aprilia	2'11.719
18	51	S. Bonsey	Aprilia	2'11.776
19	7	E. Vazquez	Aprilia	2'12.256
20	8	L. Zanetti	KTM	2'12.277
21	74	T. Nakagami	Aprilia	2'12.286
22	21	R. Lässer	Aprilia	2'12.675
23	94	J. Folger	KTM	2'12.921
24	77	D. Aegerter	Derbi	2'13.033
25	60	M. Ranseder	Aprilia	2'13.099
26	34	R. Krummenacher	KTM	2'13.119
27	16	J. Cluzel	Loncin	2'13.755
28	22	P. Nieto	KTM	2'13.782
29	37	K. Pesek	Aprilia	2'14.033
30	30	J. Tutusaus	Aprilia	2'14.192
31	95	R. Muresan	Aprilia	2'14.590
32	5	A. Masbou	Loncin	2'14.631
33	72	M. Ravaioli	Aprilia	2'14.769
34	48	B. Chesaux	Aprilia	2'15.131
35	56	H. Van Den Berg	Aprilia	2'15.285
36	96	L. Sembera	Aprilia	2'15.909
37	69	L. Rossi	Honda	2'16.321
38	97	M. Prazek	Aprilia	2'16.744
39	98	A. Touskova	Honda	2'18.214

RACE: 19 laps = 102.657 km

1	Stefan Bradl	41'05.176 (149.914 km/h)
2	Mike Di Meglio	+ 0.881
3	Joan Olivé	+ 4.070
4	Gabor Talmacsi	+ 4.118
5	Nicolas Terol	+ 7.048
6	Bradley Smith	+ 9.334
7	Sandro Cortese	+ 12.813
8	Pol Espargaró	+ 16.491
9	Andrea Iannone	+ 17.637
10	Simone Corsi	+ 17.855
11	Scott Redding	+ 18.964
12	Sergio Gadea	+ 29.920
13	Esteve Rabat	+ 38.445
14	Dominique Aegerter	+ 54.637
15	Robin Lässer	+ 54.797
16	Pablo Nieto	+ 55.723
17	Lukas Sembera	+ 56.786
18	Efrén Vazquez	+ 59.166
19	Lorenzo Zanetti	+ 59.330
20	Pere Tutusaus	+ 59.340
21	Michael Ranseder	+ 1'00.307
22	Marco Ravaioli	+ 1'07.401
23	Randy Krummenacher	+ 1'11.701
24	Jules Cluzel	+ 1'19.343
25	Hugo Van Den Berg	+ 1'30.988
26	Alexis Masbou	+ 1'31.018
27	Robert Muresan	+ 1'31.149
28	Bastien Chesaux	+ 1'33.222
29	Louis Rossi	+ 1'33.600
30	Michal Prazek	+ 1 lap
31	Andrea Touslova	+ 1 lap

Fastest lap
Di Meglio, in 2'08.391 (151.496 km/h).
Record: Cecchinello, in 2'07.836 (152.154 km/h/2003).

Outright fastest lap
Talmacsi, in 2'06.8619 (153.323 km/h/2007).

CHAMPIONSHIP

1	M. Di Meglio	186 (3 wins)
2	S. Corsi	142 (3 wins)
3	S. Bradl	126 (1 win)
4	G. Talmacsi	122 (1 win)
5	J. Olivé	110
6	N. Terol	102
7	B. Smith	89
8	P. Espargaró	83
9	S. Cortese	77
10	S. Redding	70 (1 win)

Rossi, De Puniet (14), Elias and Lorenzo (partly hidden) set out after Stoner. Some of them wouldn't get very far.

13

Alice has a serious look. Did she forget to come by way of Tavullia, where the Rossi fan club is in full swing ?

VALENTINO
A HOME WINNER AT LAST

JUST A FEW KILOMETRES FROM THE LION'S DEN, TAVULLIA, MISANO HAD NEVER BEEN KIND TO ROSSI - UNTIL NOW.

THE RACE

THERE ARE KINGDOMS - AND THEN THERE ARE KINGDOMS...

So which is Valentino Rossi's kingdom ? Tavullia, of course! Tavullia, a town of 7300 souls, whose best-known citizen was made mayor for a day. But Rossi lords it over another kingdom - and that's the track. Or tracks, to put it better, the ones that stage World Championship events. He is monarch of all he surveys with the public too, media included : they only have eyes for him. But Rossi's kingdom spreads wider still. It embraces a substantial legacy (one that underwent much-publicised major fiscal surgery a year ago), and a doctorate in communication studies bestowed on him a few years ago by the University of Urbino. Rossi the great communicator? As evidence, there was his encounter with another king, Diego Armando Maradona, with Pele the best-known footballer in the world. And words were at the centre of their meeting. « You are History itself, » the Argentine told him on the grid, only for the rider to reply, « No, no, it's you who have made History ! » And with those words went an image, a kiss on the hand from the man who always thought he was God. It meant a lot to Rossi, who said later : « Why did he kiss my right hand ? Because it's the one that turns the throttle. What could I do in response ? Maybe I should have kissed that magical left foot of his… » Two kings, all right, together in the court of Rossi.

But there was still room for more mundane things, and there was no shortage of those on that

Two kings together : Diego Armando Maradona and Valentino Rossi. Below : the king of motorcycling in his pomp.

roasting hot weekend on the Adriatic coast. Another mistake from Casey Stoner among them: like many a man before him (Biaggi and Gibernau among them), the outgoing champion had succumbed to the shock treatment meted out by the Doctor at Laguna Seca. And then there was the Hopkins business : a rider on a fat salary unable to turn up for the first day's practice because a night's drinking had left him in no fit state to do so. The upshot ? Vague threats, an official press release harking back to some old injury, and last place. Any self-respecting business would have sacked him on the spot !

But there was worse to come : the announcement from the works Honda team, no more than an hour after the race, telling us that Dani Pedrosa would no longer be racing on Michelins. That really did it: we know Kawasaki's Japanese staff will put up with anything from the people who control their budgets, and Honda's didn't dare stand up to the outfit run by Pedrosa's mentor Alberto Puig, with Dorna boss Carmelo Ezpeleta's blessing - a boss who seemed somehow to have forgotten that mixing private and personal interests isn't part of his brief. It's a small world, a petty world, and it's a world that's an insult to its real king. After all he has done Valentino Rossi deserves better than being tainted by such spineless goings-on.

ROSSI 3, STONER 0, MEANING A 75-POINT LEAD FOR THE ITALIAN ON A HOT WEEKEND FOR JOHN HOPKINS…

RUNNERS AND RIDERS

Nicky Hayden was back. After the Czech Republic we had learned that Melandri had done a deal with Kawasaki for next year ; meanwhile Loris Capirossi was setting a new record with his 277th Grand Prix start.

QUALIFYING

While Stoner was taking his seventh straight pole by half a second from Valentino Rossi (Tavullia's mayor for a day !), no-one took much notice - they were all too busy with the marital and alcoholic antics of John Hopkins.

START

Drama straight away as Hayden pulls out for fear of aggravating the injury to his right ankle. The star name among the weekend guests is footballer Diego Armando Maradona. Stoner, Pedrosa, Rossi and De Puniet get away best, but Valentino is already on guard, so first time over the line it's Stoner by 1.701 from Pedrosa with Rossi third, four-tenths behind the Honda rider. De Puniet has a heavy fall in the first corner.

LAP 2

Rossi takes Pedrosa but the gap to Stoner is already 3.077. Down goes Alex de Angelis.

LAP 5

Lorenzo has caught Pedrosa out ; Elias, coming right back to form, is in touch.

LAP 6

Elias has got past while, up ahead, the gap from Stoner to Rossi has stayed the same.

LAP 8

As in Brno, Stoner - who had three seconds in hand over Rossi - goes to ground. That leaves Rossi in the lead, 2.9 ahead of Lorenzo and just over four seconds clear of Elias.

HALF-DISTANCE (14 LAPS)

Now the two Yamahas are in control, Rossi leading Lorenzo by 3.155. Elias is third, with Pedrosa seven-tenths behind him. Dovizioso is fighting Toseland and a hard-charging Vermeulen for fifth, but they are nine seconds adrift.

LAP 19

Toseland is up to fifth.

LAP 22

Now Vermeulen has taken over fifth, while Capirossi is closing in on Dovizioso.

LAP 27

Óld boy' Capirossi, in his record 277th GP, has got past 'new boy' Dovizioso.

FINISH (28 LAPS)

Maradona celebrates as Rossi - with his 94th win, his 55th in MotoGP (added to 13 in 500cc) - beats Agostini's record to prove that he's not just top man in Tavullia, but king of the MotoGP world. Lorenzo is second (good effort, Michelin!) and Elias is again on the podium as he was in Brno.

CHAMPIONSHIP

A 75-point gap means Rossi now has three races in hand over Stoner. The outgoing champion is obviously still coming to terms with the treatment he got from the Doctor at Laguna Seca.

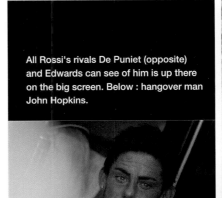

All Rossi's rivals De Puniet (opposite) and Edwards can see of him is up there on the big screen. Below : hangover man John Hopkins.

GP SAN MARINO | **31st August 2008** | **Misano** | **4.226 m**

STARTING GRID

1	1	C. Stoner	Ducati	1'33.378
2	46	V. Rossi	Yamaha	1'33.888
3	48	J. Lorenzo	Yamaha	1'33.964
4	14	R. De Puniet	Honda	1'34.236
5	24	T. Elias	Ducati	1'34.322
6	2	D. Pedrosa	Honda	1'34.398
7	7	C. Vermeulen	Suzuki	1'34.461
8	56	S. Nakano	Honda	1'34.494
9	52	J. Toseland	Yamaha	1'34.652
10	5	C. Edwards	Yamaha	1'34.795
11	65	L. Capirossi	Suzuki	1'34.926
12	50	S. Guintoli	Ducati	1'34.961
13	15	A. De Angelis	Honda	1'35.153
14	4	A. Dovizioso	Honda	1'35.381
15	33	M. Melandri	Ducati	1'35.418
16	69	N. Hayden	Honda	1'35.584
17	21	J. Hopkins	Kawasaki	1'35.980
18	13	A. West	Kawasaki	1'37.047

RACE: 28 laps = 118.328 km

1	Valentino Rossi	44'41.884 (158.836 km/h)
2	Jorge Lorenzo	+ 3.163
3	Toni Elias	+ 11.705
4	Daniel Pedrosa	+ 17.470
5	Chris Vermeulen	+ 23.409
6	James Toseland	+ 26.208
7	Loris Capirossi	+ 26.824
8	Andrea Dovizioso	+ 27.591
9	Marco Melandri	+ 33.169
10	Colin Edwards	+ 36.529
11	Sylvain Guintoli	+ 42.081
12	Shinya Nakano	+ 43.808
13	Anthony West	+ 54.874
14	John Hopkins	+ 55.154

Fastest lap

Rossi, in 1'34.904 (160.305 km/h).
New record (new circuit layout).

Outright fastest lap

Stoner, in 1'33.378 (162.924 km/h/2008).

CHAMPIONSHIP

1	V. Rossi	262 (6 wins)
2	C. Stoner	187 (4 wins)
3	D. Pedrosa	185 (2 wins)
4	J. Lorenzo	140 (1 win)
5	A. Dovizioso	118
6	C. Vermeulen	110
7	C. Edwards	108
8	S. Nakano	87
9	L. Capirossi	86
10	J. Toseland	85

THAT HOT LATIN TEMPERAMENT ! BARBERA AND SIMONCELLI ARE ABOUT TO COME TO GRIEF.

RUNNERS AND RIDERS

It had been on the cards since Brno: now Manuel Poggiali had retired for the second time, to be replaced by recent 125 runner Grotzky. For Blusens, the young Manuel Hernandez replaced Paul Gomez.

QUALIFYING

There were Barbera and Simoncelli, and then there were the rest. The two men dominated qualifying, the Spaniard coming out on top. In 10th, 11th and 12th Kallio, Bautista and Debon were over a second off the pole-winning time.

START

Takahashi gets away best from Barbera and Simoncelli. The two big names of the weekend both get past on the first lap and open a five-second gap to third place.

LAP 3

Debon goes down, Faubel can't miss him. but Luthi miraculously gets through.

LAP 4

Two birds with one stone : KTM loses both riders as Kallio comes into contact with Aoyama. Meanwhile Simoncelli has taken the lead.

LAP 6

Simoncelli leads by 0.328.

LAP 7

Simoncelli, Barbera and Takahashi are fightint it out wheel to wheel as Pasini brings the pursuing pack closer.

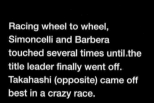

Racing wheel to wheel, Simoncelli and Barbera touched several times until.the title leader finally went off. Takahashi (opposite) came off best in a crazy race.

LAP 9

Simoncelli and Barbera run off-track, so Takahashi leads ; Pasini and Bautista are right there.

LAP 10

It's all happening as Pasini now finds himself in front and just 2.240 seconds cover the first seven. Two seconds further back Locatelli and Luthi are the fastest men on track.

LAP 12

Pasini clips Barbera and goes down, leaving the Spaniard in another wheel-to-wheel fight with Simoncelli.

HALF-DISTANCE (13 LAPS)

Simoncelli has got back in front, just 0.182 ahead of Barbera, with Takahashi third a further 0.374 away. Fourth is Bautista, half-a-second behind the Japanese rider, but he will soon be right back in touch.

LAP 18

Battling with Simon for seventh, Luthi misses his braking ; Bautista is now in second place.

LAP 19

Bautista is in the lead, but you could throw a blanket over the front four. Espargaro retires.

LAP 22

Luthi slows down, while Barbera and Simoncelli are still at it hammer and tongs up front.

LAP 23

Simoncelli goes down.

FINISH (26 LAPS)

What a crazy afternoon ! Bautista goes into the final lap leading by two seconds from Takahashi, the main beneficiary of all the carnage.

CHAMPIONSHIP

Simoncelli is still comfortably in front, since Kallio had a no-score. But Bautista came out of it best, moving to within a point of the Finnish KTM rider and just 27 adrift of the leader.

GP SAN MARINO | 31st August 2008 | Misano | 4.226 m

STARTING GRID

1	21	H. Barberá	Aprilia	1'38.047
2	58	M. Simoncelli	Gilera	1'38.124
3	41	A. Espargaró	Aprilia	1'38.813
4	72	Y. Takahashi	Honda	1'38.822
5	4	H. Aoyama	KTM	1'38.869
6	12	T. Lüthi	Aprilia	1'38.961
7	60	J. Simón	KTM	1'39.009
8	55	H. Faubel	Aprilia	1'39.058
9	75	M. Pasini	Aprilia	1'39.130
10	36	M. Kallio	KTM	1'39.165
11	19	A. Bautistá	Aprilia	1'39.217
12	6	A. Debón	Aprilia	1'39.402
13	52	L. Pesek	Aprilia	1'39.749
14	15	R. Locatelli	Gilera	1'39.828
15	14	R. Wilairot	Honda	1'39.875
16	32	F. Lai	Gilera	1'39.963
17	50	E. Laverty	Aprilia	1'40.317
18	17	K. Abraham	Aprilia	1'40.360
19	25	A. Baldolini	Aprilia	1'40.732
20	90	F. Sandi	Aprilia	1'41.205
21	43	M. Hernandez	Aprilia	1'41.513
22	94	T. Wirsing	Honda	1'42.620
23	35	S. Grotzkyj	Gilera	1'42.756
24	45	D.-T. Pradita	Yamaha	1'42.992
25	10	I. Toth	Aprilia	1'43.841

Not qualified:

93	R. Gyorfi	Honda	1'46.446

RACE: 26 laps = 109.876 km

1	Alvaro Bautistá	43'15.831 (152.380 km/h)
2	Yuki Takahashi	+ 2.088
3	Hector Barberá	+ 3.752
4	Roberto Locatelli	+ 7.472
5	Julian Simón	+ 10.862
6	Marco Simoncelli	+ 21.180
7	Thomas Lüthi	+ 29.440
8	Ratthapark Wilairot	+ 33.882
9	Lukas Pesek	+ 35.051
10	Karel Abraham	+ 45.405
11	Fabrizio Lai	+ 47.260
12	Federico Sandi	+ 1'10.664
13	Manuel Hernandez Jnr	+ 1'10.882
14	Toni Wirsing	+ 1'33.332
15	Simone Grotzkyj	+ 1 lap
19	Doni Tata Pradita	+ 1 lap

Fastest lap

Simoncelli, in 1'38.993 (153.993 km/h). New record (new circuit layout).

Outright fastest lap

Barberá, in 1'38.047 (155.166 km/h/2008).

CHAMPIONSHIP

1	M. Simoncelli	190 (3 wins)
2	M. Kallio	164 (3 wins)
3	A. Bautistá	163 (3 wins)
4	H. Barberá	142
5	A. Debón	139 (2 wins)
6	M. Pasini	117 (1 win)
7	Y. Takahashi	115
8	H. Aoyama	101
9	T. Lüthi	95
10	J. Simón	83

SLY OLD FOX TALMACSI IS NEVER BEATEN ; MEANWHILE DI MEGLIO HAS USED UP ONE OF IS WILD CARDS.

RUNNERS AND RIDERS

There were changes in the reigning World Champion team with Pere Tutusaus being replaced by 16-year-old Adrián Martin. Luca Vitali, son of Garelli veteran Maurizio, now working for AGC with Valentino Rossi, replaced Robert Muresan.

QUALIFYING

Talmacsi claimed his third straight pole ahead of Smith, Espargaro and Redding ; the top nine were covered by less than a second. For the first time in a long while there was a Honda on the fourth row, put there by guest rider Riccardo Moretti.

START

Smith reacted quickest, but Talmacsi elbowed his way through the first chicane. First time across the line the World Champion had a 0.604 second lead over the British rider.

LAP 2

Redding falls.

LAP 4

As he did in the Czech Republic two weeks earlier, Bradl is picking his way nicely through the field, now up to fourth after starting from 11th spot. Title leader Di Meglio, meanwhile, is sixth. Up front, Talmacsi has almost eight seconds

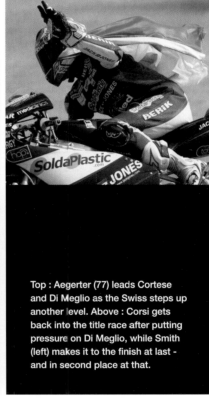

Top : Aegerter (77) leads Cortese and Di Meglio as the Swiss steps up another level. Above : Corsi gets back into the title race after putting pressure on Di Meglio, while Smith (left) makes it to the finish at last - and in second place at that.

in hand over Smith.

LAP 6

Talmacsi has just set fastest lap ; he and Smith are well in front of the rest. Five seconds behind them Bradl, Terol, Corsi, Di Meglio and Iannone are fighting it out for third place.

HALF-DISTANCE (12 LAPS)

As Talmacsi misses his braking Smith takes full advantage by grabbing the lead by just 0.443 seconds. The third-place group, where Di Meglio is being shown no quarter (right, Mr Corsi ?), is 8.714 adrift ; Corsi himself is on the podium at this stage from Di Meglio and Bradl.

LAP 15

Drama : Mike Di Meglio is hounded into a mistake by Corsi just as Talmacsi regains the lead.

LAP 16

More drama : this time Bradl retires, which leaves just Corsi and Olive squabbling over third place. But the fight for fifth is hotting up between Terol, Marquez, Rabat, Iannone, Cortese and Aegerter.

LAP 18

Talmacsi has got away again, now 1.166 ahead of Smith, while Olive and Corsi are going at it wheel-to-wheel.

FINISH (23 LAPS)

Smith has got the message : Talmacsi starts his final lap with 3.739 seconds in hand as attention switches to goings-on behind them. And it's a thrilling sight as Corso dives past Olive at an impossible angle before the Spaniard loses it.

CHAMPIONSHIP

Of course Di Meglio is still out in front, but Corsi has cut his lead to 28 points. The Frenchman has used up one of his jokers …

GP SAN MARINO | 31st August 2008 | Misano | 4.226 m

STARTING GRID

1	1	G. Talmacsi	Aprilia	1'43.729
2	38	B. Smith	Aprilia	1'43.920
3	44	P. Espargaró	Derbi	1'44.334
4	45	S. Redding	Aprilia	1'44.339
5	24	S. Corsi	Aprilia	1'44.450
6	63	M. Di Meglio	Derbi	1'44.543
7	11	S. Cortese	Aprilia	1'44.555
8	93	M. Marquez	KTM	1'44.668
9	18	N. Terol	Aprilia	1'44.706
10	6	J. Olivé	Derbi	1'44.821
11	17	S. Bradl	Aprilia	1'44.840
12	33	S. Gadea	Aprilia	1'45.033
13	29	A. Iannone	Aprilia	1'45.082
14	77	D. Aegerter	Derbi	1'45.119
15	35	R. De Rosa	KTM	1'45.324
16	47	R. Moretti	Honda	1'45.370
17	51	S. Bonsey	Aprilia	1'45.394
18	7	E. Vazquez	Aprilia	1'45.418
19	12	E. Rabat	KTM	1'45.539
20	99	D. Webb	Aprilia	1'45.566
21	60	M. Ranseder	Aprilia	1'45.607
22	71	T. Koyama	KTM	1'45.641
23	40	L. Savadori	Aprilia	1'46.017
24	16	J. Cluzel	Loncin	1'46.099
25	74	T. Nakagami	Aprilia	1'46.136
26	8	L. Zanetti	KTM	1'46.278
27	21	R. Lässer	Aprilia	1'46.310
28	94	J. Folger	KTM	1'46.341
29	5	A. Masbou	Loncin	1'46.410
30	49	G. Sabatino	Aprilia	1'46.500
31	43	G. Ferro	Honda	1'46.559
32	72	M. Ravaioli	Aprilia	1'46.670
33	69	L. Rossi	Honda	1'46.781
34	22	P. Nieto	KTM	1'46.801
35	26	A. Martin	Aprilia	1'47.023
36	42	L. Vitali	Aprilia	1'47.078
37	34	R. Krummenacher	KTM	1'47.100
38	48	B. Chesaux	Aprilia	1'47.863
39	56	H. Van Den Berg	Aprilia	1'47.863

RACE: 23 laps = 97.198 km

1	Gabor Talmacsi	40'03.679 (145.573 km/h)	
2	Bradley Smith	+ 5.402	
3	Simone Corsi	+ 14.388	
4	Marc Marquez	+ 17.058	
5	Nicolas Terol	+ 17.321	
6	Andrea Iannone	+ 17.482	
7	Sandro Cortese	+ 17.485	
8	Dominique Aegerter	+ 18.657	
9	Esteve Rabat	+ 19.148	
10	Sergio Gadea	+ 34.650	
11	Efrén Vazquez	+ 34.855	
12	Joan Olivé	+ 39.394	
13	Michael Ranseder	+ 47.304	
14	Daniel Webb	+ 53.241	
15	Jonas Folger	+ 43.349	
16	Jules Cluzel	+ 1'01.903	
17	Marco Ravaioli	+ 1'04.165	
18	Tomoyoshi Koyama	+ 1'06.235	
19	Takaaki Nakagami	+ 1'06.260	
20	Robin Lässer	+ 1'07.200	
21	Gabriele Ferro	+ 1'21.814	
22	Bastien Chesaux	+ 1'22.521	
23	Louis Rossi	+ 1'35.247	
24	Hugo Van Den Berg	+ 1'39.723	
25	Luca Vitali	+ 1 lap	
26	Randy Krummenacher	+ 2 laps	

Fastest lap

Talmacsi, in 1'43.839 (146.511 km/h).
New record (new circuit layout).

Outright fastest lap

Talmacsi, in 1'43.729 (146.666 km/h/2008).

CHAMPIONSHIP

1	M. Di Meglio	186 (3 wins)
2	S. Corsi	158 (3 wins)
3	G. Talmacsi	147 (2 wins)
4	S. Bradl	126 (1 win)
5	J. Olivé	114
6	N. Terol	113
7	B. Smith	109
8	S. Cortese	86
9	P. Espargaró	83
10.	A. Iannone	77 (1 win)

A legendary setting made of red bricks : this is Indianapolis, shrine of North-American motor racing, opening its doors to MotoGP for the first time.

The Yankees go for the rookies. Us ? We prefer the hostesses…

ROSSI,
COME HAIL OR COME SHINE

NOT EVEN HURRICANE IKE COULD UNSETTLE VALENTINO ROSSI, WHO WAS IN THE RIGHT PLACE - THE LEAD - AT THE RIGHT TIME, WHEN THE RACE WAS STOPPED.

THE RACE

ROSSI FIGHTS OFF IKE

History with a capital H was made at Indianapolis. Just think about it : motorbikes in the temple of US motor sport, the imposing Brickyard, home of all that's great and good in four-wheel racing in the land of Uncle Sam. The races that built the Indianapolis legend may have little in common with what we see on the Old Continent but nevertheless, Indy is Indy, a mythic place you can't go to without the emotions being stirred.

This, then, was the hallowed ground where the stars of the motorcycling world fetched up in mid-September. All sorts of questions were in the air : questions about safety, of course, others about the state of the track surface - make that surfaces, since the lay-out on which our two-wheeled acrobats were being asked to perform was a mixture of the speedway and the F1 circuit.

Questions, questions : this was, after all, the time of the year when other considerations come into play. While the talk was largely of the here and now - Sunday's race - there were those who used the long trip out there to sort out their own futures. Marco Melandri off to Kawasaki… Alex de Angelis staying put at Gresini… Hayden on his way to Ducati… De Puniet confirmed as a Cecchinello rider… Canepa scheduled to make his debut in the second-string Ducati team… plans for Gibernau to get a fifth Desmosedici in a team put together by

the Nieto family : and so it went on. People talked, signed promissory notes and put their names to contracts.

And then there was a surprise visitor to see us all, one by the funny name of Ike - not much of a name for someone who had created havoc in the Caribbean, then headed for Florida and New Orleans before pushing further inland. He brought huge volumes of water with him, this Ike, with rain lashing down on Friday, easing a little on Saturday for qualifying, then turning the Sunday schedule on its head. Race day, that is : the day when a man well used to crushing the opposition laid on another show of strength, answering the call again as he took on the supernatural challenge of a hurricane.

We could all see how the story would go : Valentino Rossi took it easy for three laps before eventually taking control. His lone challenger this season, Casey Stoner, had already realised he was powerless, especially after another heavy Friday fall. Dani Pedrosa, the spoilt brat who had demanded Bridgestone tyres a fortnight earlier at Misano, was a pale imitation of his usual self. Yes, we did catch a glimpse of Nicky Hayden, a proud American kid ; but once again, it was really all about Rossi. And when it came to Rossi, there really was nothing anyone could do. Just ask Hurricane Ike…

Another track ticked off for Valentino Rossi, at the height of his powers.

AN EARLY END TO THE RACE CAN'T STOP ROSSI HAMMERING ANOTHER NAIL HOME.

RUNNERS AND RIDERS

As expected, Ben Spies was on the third Suzuki ; there was a debut, too - on Bridgestones - for Dani Pedrosa, the Spaniard having tested the Japanese rubber after the San Marino GP.

QUALIFYING

As the latest episode of the Rossi-Stoner saga unfolded, for once it wasn't the outgoing champion who came out on top but Rossi, taking his first pole for some time - by just 48-1000ths. Behind them, albeit four-tenths away, Lorenzo showed he had got over his mid-season crisis of confidence.

START

Though the rain has stopped the track is still very wet. Through the first corner Rossi takes things more cautiously than some of the big names, like Stoner, Hayden and Dovizioso, the latter taking the lead on a tip-toe first lap, leading Hayden over the line first time round.

LAP 3

Hayden goes past and immediately opens up a gap of 0.402. Lorenzo's third place brings a smile to Bibendum's face.

LAP 6

The Doctor had just been taking a temperature - not a patient's, the track's - and now he ups the pace ; after passing Lorenzo on lap 4, Rossi has just sneaked past Dovizioso and is only 0.990 behind Hayden.

LAP 9

Hayden still leads, but Rossi is now within 0.440. Behind those two there is a big gap back to Lorenzo at 4.206, Dovizioso at 5.177 and Stoner at 5.570.

HALF-DISTANCE (14 LAPS)

Valentino Rossi marks the halfway point by taking the lead, with Hayden six-tenths behind, and Lorenzo almost seven seconds in arrears, the Spaniard in front of Stoner, Dovizioso and the excellent Ben Spies.

LAP 17

Rossi has things under control, now leading Hayden by 1.109. Further back, Guintoli and Vermeulen have found a way past Bridgestone... oops, sorry, Pedrosa.

LAP 19

It's raining harder again. Rossi has almost tripled the gap to Hayden, and now it's Lorenzo's turn to close in on the man about to be a former Honda rider.

LAP 21

Riding a race bike has become impossible : Race Control brings out the red flag. After some discussion among those most concerned, notably Rossi and Stoner, they all decide to head back inside to get warm. The result will be taken from the order on the previous lap.

FINISH (20 LAPS)

Rossi's seventh win of the season and his fourth in a row : need we say more ?

CHAMPIONSHIP

Rossi has an 87-point lead on Stoner with 100 to play for. Unless an earthquake intervenes, the man who fought off Hurricane Ike will soon be crowned World Champion for the eighth time.

Left : Mr Colin Edwards, US-style. Above : Hayden, Rossi and Lorenzo make up the first Indianapolis MotoGP podium. Right : Pedrosa gets to grips with Bridgestone tyres.

GP INDIANAPOLIS | 14th September 2008 | Indianapolis | 4.216 m

STARTING GRID

1	46	V. Rossi	Yamaha	1'40.776
2	1	C. Stoner	Ducati	1'40.860
3	48	J. Lorenzo	Yamaha	1'41.177
4	69	N. Hayden	Honda	1'41.271
5	11	B. Spies	Suzuki	1'41.464
6	14	R. De Puniet	Honda	1'41.492
7	4	A. Dovizioso	Honda	1'41.744
8	2	D. Pedrosa	Honda	1'41.754
9	24	T. Elias	Ducati	1'41.886
10	52	J. Toseland	Yamaha	1'41.897
11	5	C. Edwards	Yamaha	1'41.934
12	15	A. De Angelis	Honda	1'41.969
13	65	L. Capirossi	Suzuki	1'42.305
14	50	S. Guintoli	Ducati	1'42.405
15	7	C. Vermeulen	Suzuki	1'42.551
16	21	J. Hopkins	Kawasaki	1'42.673
17	56	S. Nakano	Honda	1'42.732
18	33	M. Melandri	Ducati	1'43.807
19	13	A. West	Kawasaki	1'43.931

RACE: 20 laps (*) = 84.320 km

1	Valentino Rossi	37'20.095 (135.508 km/h)
2	Nicky Hayden	+ 5.972
3	Jorge Lorenzo	+ 7.858
4	Casey Stoner	+ 28.162
5	Andrea Dovizioso	+ 28.824
6	Ben Spies	+ 29.645
7	Sylvain Guintoli	+ 36.223
8	Daniel Pedrosa	+ 37.258
9	Chris Vermeulen	+ 38.442
10	Alex De Angelis	+ 42.437
11	Anthony West	+ 47.179
12	Toni Elias	+ 55.962
13	Randy De Puniet	+ 57.366
14	John Hopkins	+ 58.353
15	Colin Edwards	+ 1'00.613
16	Loris Capirossi	+ 1'05.620
17	Shinya Nakano	+ 1'05.854
18	James Toseland	+ 1'07.968
19	Marco Melandri	+ 1'21.023

(*): The race was red flagged on lap 21 of 28 (rain.) By common consent, the riders and organizers decided to consider the race over and valid for points.

Fastest lap

Rossi, in 1'49.668 (138.395 km/h).
New record (new circuit layout).

Outright fastest lap

Rossi, in 1'40.776 (150.607 km/h/2008).

CHAMPIONSHIP

1	V. Rossi	287 (7 wins)
2	C. Stoner	200 (4 wins)
3	D. Pedrosa	193 (2 wins)
4	J. Lorenzo	156 (1 win)
5	A. Dovizioso	129
6	C. Vermeulen	117
7	C. Edwards	109
8	N. Hayden	104
9	S. Nakano	87
10	T. Elias	86

It was raining cats and dogs at the start and Hiroshi Aoyama didn't like it one little bit. Top : the big loser in this pointless Grand Prix was Thomas Luthi, who had a horrible Saturday morning fall.

A TRANSATLANTIC CROSSING, ALL IN VAIN OR, LIKE LUTHI, JUST TO PICK UP AN INJURY.

RUNNERS AND RIDERS

It was a surprise to find Stefano Bianco in the second-string Gilera team, Campetella, in place of Fabrizio Lai, who had to have an operation after the San Marino GP. Bianco had started the season in the 125s but the Italian lost his place to Swiss rider Bastien Chesaux from the German GP because his sponsors didn't honour their commitment. Immediately after the San Marino race Bautista extended his Aspar Martinez contract to stay on for another year in the class. Two wild cards went to Americans Barrett Long and Kyle Ferris.

QUALIFYING

As Hurricane Ike took its effect on Friday it poured with rain and it was Czech rider Karel Abraham who caused a stir by setting quickest time - though we should point out that most of the big names didn't venture out, given that the water was several centimetres deep in places. Pasini, for one, hadn't beaten the cut-off point by the end of the first day's practice. Saturday brought some improvement on the meteorological front, but not for Swiss rider Thomas Luthi : the former 125cc World Champion high-sided on his second free practice lap, fell heavily and was knocked out. He was back at the track next day complaining of severe headaches and with an open wound on his left thumb ; it meant a four-hour operation the following Tuesday during which he needed skin grafts. Fearing infection, he decided to give the next two races in Japan and Australia a miss.

START

Just after one p.m. on Sunday September 14 the rain that had brought the 125cc race to a premature halt turned into a full-scale storm. The 250 race start was immediately delayed and as the minutes ticked by the organisers realised there was nothing they could do. Everyone went back inside and the 250 race was initially rescheduled for the end of the day, after the MotoGP itself. But with conditions worse than ever it was eventually cancelled after due consultation with the teams. They'd come all the way to North America for nothing.

CHAMPIONSHIP

Obviously things stayed as they were, with people commenting that Mika Kallio - often quite at home in tricky going - had been hard done by, whereas Marco Simoncelli hadn't. After all, it meant one race fewer to face the howling pack…

GP INDIANAPOLIS | 14th September 2008 | Indianapolis | 4.216 m

STARTING GRID

1	58	M. Simoncelli	Gilera	1'45.168
2	21	H. Barberá	Aprilia	1'45.537
3	36	M. Kallio	KTM	1'45.563
4	6	A. Debón	Aprilia	1'45.601
5	4	H. Aoyama	KTM	1'45.850
6	19	A. Bautistá	Aprilia	1'46.174
7	75	M. Pasini	Aprilia	1'46.322
8	55	H. Faubel	Aprilia	1'46.360
9	52	L. Pesek	Aprilia	1'46.370
10	60	J. Simón	KTM	1'46.687
11	72	Y. Takahashi	Honda	1'46.739
12	41	A. Espargaró	Aprilia	1'46.835
13	14	R. Wilairot	Honda	1'46.847
14	15	R. Locatelli	Gilera	1'47.049
15	17	K. Abraham	Aprilia	1'47.974
16	27	S. Bianco	Gilera	1'48.620
17	43	M. Hernandez	Aprilia	1'49.024
18	45	D.-T. Pradita	Yamaha	1'49.089
19	35	S. Grotzkyj	Gilera	1'49.666
20	10	I. Toth	Aprilia	1'49.758
21	25	A. Baldolini	Aprilia	1'50.694
22	50	E. Laverty	Aprilia	1'51.097
23	29	B. Long	Yamaha	1'52.384

Not qualified (107%):

38	K. Ferris	Yamaha	1'53.899
12	T. Lüthi	Aprilia	2'06.570 (*)

(*): T. Luthi (CH, Aprilia) was a faller (serious concussion) during Saturday morning's free practice. He did not take part in the afternoon qualifying, on a dry track.

RACE: 26 laps = 109.616 km

Initially put back to the end of the programme, after the MotoGP, the 250 cc race was then cancelled because of the weather.

Fastest lap
Simoncelli, in 1'32.474 (156.614 km/h). New record.
Previous: Dovizioso, in 1'33.029 (155.680 km/h/2006).

Outright fastest lap
Lorenzo, in 1'31.659 (158.007 km/h/2006).

CHAMPIONSHIP

1	M. Simoncelli	190 (3 wins)
2	M. Kallio	164 (3 wins)
3	A. Bautistá	163 (3 wins)
4	H. Barberá	142
5	A. Debón	139 (2 wins)
6	M. Pasini	117 (1 win)
7	Y. Takahashi	115
8	H. Aoyama	101
9	T. Lüthi	95
10	J. Simón	83

Bradl and Cortese fight out a German duel, but two Iberians, Terol (above) and Pol Espargaro are on the top two steps of this historic first podium at the famous Indianapolis Speedway.

IT'S A YOUNG MAN'S WORLD, AS WITNESS TEROL, ESPARGARO, BRADL AND REDDING.

RUNNERS AND RIDERS

KTM having suggested that Randy Krummenacher take some rest - physical and mental - his place went to German Jonas Folger. There was a change in the French Federation team too as Louis Rossi heard the day before he was due to leave that his post had gone to Cyril Carillo. American PJ Jacobsen took over the third Aspar Martinez Aprilia, while two wild cards went to another American, Kristian Lee Turner, and Italian Davide Stirpe.

QUALIFYING

Pol Espargaro and Mike Di Meglio made it a Derbi 1-2, while reigning champion Gabor Talmacsi fell, fractured his left scaphoid and finished up 16th.

START

After qualifying eighth-fastest, Swiss rider Dominique Aegerter waved a 'Get well soon' board to compatriot Thomas Luthi, injured the previous day in the 250 class. Andrea Iannone came through from the second row but Espargaro it was who took the lead, finishing the first lap with a 0.911-second advantage over Redding.

LAP 2

Nicolas Terol takes advantage of a slip-up by Redding to grab second spot, 1.859 behind Espargaro.

LAP 4

Iannone pulls out ; Espargaro's lead is out to 2.249.

LAP 6

There's a big scrap going on for fourth between Corsi, Di Meglio, Marquez and Cortese.

LAP 7

Corsi comes into contact with Di Meglio at the end of the main straight, but the main men in the title race stay upright.

LAP 9

As Pol Espargaro makes his first false move Terol seizes his chance to take the lead. Behind them, Stefan Bradl has caught up with the group fighting for fourth.

HALF-DISTANCE (12 LAPS)

Terol is now 1.455 seconds ahead of Espargaro with Redding third, 5.087 back. Just over a second further away is a group led by Bradl and including Cortese, Di Meglio, Marquez and Corsi.

LAP 15

Just as the rain comes, Di Meglio has trouble with his throttle and slips to ninth.

LAP 16

As the conditions grow steadily worse Espargaro fights back past Terol, who counter-attacks at once. The Bradl group is now in touch.

LAP 17

Now it's raining heavily and Race Control shows the red flag. The result goes by the order on the previous lap, i.e. 16 laps or two-thirds distance. The race is run and Terol has his first win.

CHAMPIONSHIP

Di Meglio finished 10th but lost just three points to Corsi, leaving the Frenchman still 25 points in the lead.

GP INDIANAPOLIS | 14th September 2008 | Indianapolis | 4.216 m

STARTING GRID

1	44	P. Espargaró	Derbi	1'50.475
2	63	M. Di Meglio	Derbi	1'50.844
3	17	S. Bradl	Aprilia	1'50.878
4	99	D. Webb	Aprilia	1'51.000
5	29	A. Iannone	Aprilia	1'51.031
6	18	N. Terol	Aprilia	1'51.179
7	24	S. Corsi	Aprilia	1'51.211
8	77	D. Aegerter	Derbi	1'51.260
9	45	S. Redding	Aprilia	1'51.274
10	11	S. Cortese	Aprilia	1'51.551
11	38	B. Smith	Aprilia	1'51.572
12	6	J. Olivé	Derbi	1'51.985
13	93	M. Marquez	KTM	1'52.069
14	74	T. Nakagami	Aprilia	1'52.076
15	51	S. Bonsey	Aprilia	1'52.086
16	1	G. Talmacsi	Aprilia	1'52.170
17	35	R. De Rosa	KTM	1'52.358
18	71	T. Koyama	KTM	1'52.635
19	60	M. Ranseder	Aprilia	1'52.759
20	22	P. Nieto	KTM	1'53.053
21	12	E. Rabat	KTM	1'53.115
22	21	R. Lässer	Aprilia	1'53.137
23	33	S. Gadea	Aprilia	1'53.140
24	7	E. Vazquez	Aprilia	1'53.155
25	54	P. Jacobsen	Aprilia	1'53.209
26	72	M. Ravaioli	Aprilia	1'53.239
27	5	A. Masbou	Loncin	1'53.478
28	8	L. Zanetti	KTM	1'53.683
29	94	J. Folger	KTM	1'53.774
30	56	H. Van Den Berg	Aprilia	1'53.931
31	16	J. Cluzel	Loncin	1'54.414
32	95	R. Muresan	Aprilia	1'54.732
33	74	D. Stirpe	KTM	1'55.279
34	48	B. Chesaux	Aprilia	1'55.440
35	36	C. Carillo	Honda	1'55.697
36	90	K.-L. Turner	Aprilia	1'56.703

RACE: 16 laps (*) = 67.456 km

1	Nicolas Terol	29'51.350 (135.563 km/h)
2	Pol Espargaró	+ 1.708
3	Stefan Bradl	+ 3.984
4	Scott Redding	+ 4.277
5	Sandro Cortese	+ 4.413
6	Marc Marquez	+ 4.454
7	Simone Corsi	+ 6.261
8	Bradley Smith	+ 7.782
9	Steve Bonsey	+ 12.035
10	Mike Di Meglio	+ 12.251
11	Dominique Aegerter	+ 15.465
12	Joan Olivé	+ 18.312
13	Raffaele De Rosa	+ 20.137
14	Gabor Talmacsi	+ 24.651
15	Daniel Webb	+ 27.592
16	Jules Cluzel	+ 35.432
17	Robin Lässer	+ 37.082
18	Sergio Gadea	+ 38.549
19	Tomoyoshi Koyama	+ 38.571
20	Efrén Vazquez	+ 40.991
21	Hugo Van Den Berg	+ 1'06.197
22	PJ Jacobsen	+ 1'06.327
23	Bastien Chesaux	+ 1'07.067
24	Jonas Folger	+ 1'14.709
25	Robert Muresan	+ 1'20.413
26	Alexis Masbou	+ 1'21.880
27	Davide Stirpe	+ 1'22.026
28	Cyril Carrillo	+ 1'22.159
29	Kristian Lee Turner	+ 2'11.524

(*): The race was red flagged on the 17th lap of 23 because of rain. The order was taken from the previous lap; with two-thirds of race distance covered, the result was declared official.

Fastest lap
Bradl, in 1'50.460 (137.403 km/h).
Record (new circuit layout)

Outright fastest lap
Bradl, in 1'50.460 (137.403 km/h/2008).

CHAMPIONSHIP

1	M. Di Meglio	192 (3 wins)
2	S. Corsi	167 (3 wins)
3	G. Talmacsi	149 (2 wins)
4	S. Bradl	142 (1 win)
5	N. Terol	138 (1 win)
6	J. Olivé	118
7	B. Smith	117
8	P. Espargaró	103
9	S. Cortese	97
10	S. Redding	83 (1 win)

Rossi all on his own : Motegi saw Valentino clinch his eighth world title in style.

Naughty little things - they just love all the riders.

ROSSI PUTS TWO
TOUGH YEARS BEHIND HIM

HE'S A ONE-OFF : VALENTINO ROSSI
SAYS SORRY FOR THE DELAY AFTER
TWO TITLELESS YEARS. THE KING IS
BACK, LONG LIVE THE KING !

THE RACE

PURE ROSSI

One team, three crowns : Rossi is riders' champion, Yamaha takes the constructors' title and Fiat-Yamaha is top team. No wonder it all had to be authenticated by the law before the celebrations could start.

Rossi was just perfect. More than perfect, in fact : in a race he really wanted to get right, a race where he left his closest rivals behind in majestic style, the message rang out loud and clear : 'I'm the King, boys, and I'm back: the Doctor is still the man !'

On Sunday Spetember 28 2008 the bells of Tavullia rang out at 7 :44, gladdening the heart of parish priest Don Cesare. The most famous member of his flock had just won again in the land of the rising sun.

Valentino Rossi had taken back what was rightfully his : the world title in the premier class of motorcycle racing. He had missed out the last two times around, once with more than his fair share of bad luck against Nicky Hayden two years before, again when the dominance of the Stoner-Ducati-Bridgestone package combined with serious personal problems to bring him down. But Rossi apologised by putting on a T-shirt made for the

occasion that said 'Sorry for the delay' on the front and sported a recipe for 'World-class soup' on the back.

In 2008, Rossi was once again the Vale we all know and love, rather than the money-making machine (for himself and others) his entourage had turned him into. Out went the Rossi 'brand', with its ring of watchdogs saying no to anything that didn't rake in a few more millions. Gone, too, was the spectre of tax evasion that had everyone in Italy believing he lived in a tiny apartment in London. As if perfidious Albion and her morning mists could accommodate a young man brought up in the sun and the sunny Southern temperament…

Reducing his riches by a few million - the ones he had to give back to the Italian authorities - Valentino Rossi went back to being himself. That's something he knows you can't put a price on. Just as he knows that nothing can take the place of family and real friends, the tribe, as he calls them,

the ones who were with him before his prodigious talent had brought him his first GP win - and his first millions.

2008 had also seen him pull off a huge technical gamble. He it was who insisted, the previous autumn, that his employer Yamaha allow him to switch tyre suppliers from Michelin to Bridgestone. And Motegi, a track which had never been kind to him (one solitary victory, and that's nothing when your name is Valentino Rossi), was further proof that he was right. It wasn't a matter of asking for star treatment, not at all. Unsure what to make of Stoner's dominance, he just wanted to be judged on equal terms. But then, Valentino Rossi has no equal, has he ? That's why he was head and shoulders above the rest throughout the 2008 campaign.

And now Rossi is homing in on a century of victories. Look out, Mr Agostini with those 122 wins of yours : Vale isn't finished yet !

WIN NUMBER EIGHT FOR THE SEASON GIVES VALENTINO ROSSI THE TITLE AS STONER HAS TO SETTLE FOR SECOND-BEST.

RUNNERS AND RIDERS

Jorge Lorenzo is a happy man, taking advantage of the Japanese trip to visit the Yamaha factory. Rossi, for his part, is in confident mood : his favourite mascots, his Mum Stefania and his half-brother Luca, are in Motegi. The relationship between Luca

Montiron's JiR team and Team Scot breaks down : Scot will stay on in MotoGP with current 250cc rider Yuki Takahashi which means, effectively, that Dovizioso's switch to the works Repsol Honda team is confirmed. Suzuki have a third rider in Kousuke Akiyoshi.

QUALIFYING

Michelin's qualifying rubber works admirably and Lorenzo takes another pole, with Nicky Hayden third-quickest. Big development on Sunday morning : the official decision to go to a one-tyre series from next year, with a tender to go out at the beginning of October.

START

Akiyoshi doesn't get far as Stoner takes charge and finishes the first lap with a 0.214-second lead over Pedrosa, 0.844 to Hayden, 1.212 to Lorenzo and 1.277 to Rossi.

LAP 2

Things happen thick and fast : Rossi passes Lorenzo just as Pedrosa catches Stoner out, then Rossi picks off Hayden as well, so the Doctor is third and already virtually certain to be World Champion for the eighth time.

LAP 6

Poor little Dani's head must be spinning - Stoner and Rossi have swept past him in the space of two corners. The two big names are now just 0.171 apart. Pedrosa, reeling, drops to seven-tenths behind while further back Hayden is already nearly two seconds adrift.

LAP 8

Lorenzo takes Hayden.

HALF-DISTANCE (12 LAPS)

Stoner's still out there, with Rossi four-tenths behind ; Pedrosa is now

3.619 down, but Lorenzo has closed the gap on his compatriot to 1.2.

LAP 14

'I fancy win number 96,' says Valentino Rossi to himself as he sweeps past Stoner.

FINISH (24 LAPS)

There's no catching the Maestro : he starts the final lap of yet another history-making race 1.966 seconds clear of the man who will have to hand back his crown. At precisely 14 :44 on this Sunday September 28 2008 Valentino Rossi is crowned champion for the eighth time.

CHAMPIONSHIP

So it's all done and dusted mathematically. Rossi can't be caught, nor can Yamaha in the constructors' standings, or Fiat-Yamaha in the teams'. That's what you call total dominance.

Stoner can see light at the end of the tunnel - but Rossi is right there. Above : champagne for the King as Hayden (opposite) bids farewell to Honda.

GP JAPAN | 28th September 2008 | Motegi | 4.801 m

STARTING GRID

1	48	J. Lorenzo	Yamaha	1'45.543
2	1	C. Stoner	Ducati	1'45.831
3	69	N. Hayden	Honda	1'45.971
4	46	V. Rossi	Yamaha	1'46.060
5	2	D. Pedrosa	Honda	1'46.303
6	65	L. Capirossi	Suzuki	1'46.450
7	5	C. Edwards	Yamaha	1'46.496
8	14	R. De Puniet	Honda	1'46.554
9	56	S. Nakano	Honda	1'46.616
10	52	J. Toseland	Yamaha	1'46.863
11	21	J. Hopkins	Kawasaki	1'46.888
12	7	C. Vermeulen	Suzuki	1'46.904
13	4	A. Dovizioso	Honda	1'46.907
14	24	T. Elias	Ducati	1'46.958
15	50	S. Guintoli	Ducati	1'47.400
16	33	M. Melandri	Ducati	1'47.475
17	13	A. West	Kawasaki	1'47.669
18	15	A. De Angelis	Honda	1'47.680
19	64	K. Akiyoshi	Suzuki	1'48.671

RACE: 24 laps = 115.224 km

1	Valentino Rossi	43'09.599 (160.181 km/h)
2	Casey Stoner	+ 1.943
3	Daniel Pedrosa	+ 4.866
4	Jorge Lorenzo	+ 6.165
5	Nicky Hayden	+ 24.593
6	Loris Capirossi	+ 25.685
7	Colin Edwards	+ 25.918
8	Shinya Nakano	+ 26.003
9	Andrea Dovizioso	+ 26.219
10	John Hopkins	+ 37.131
11	James Toseland	+ 37.574
12	Randy De Puniet	+ 38.020
13	Marco Melandri	+ 39.768
14	Sylvain Guintoli	+ 45.846
15	Anthony West	+ 55.748
16	Toni Elias	+ 59.320
17	Alex De Angelis	+ 1'12.398

Fastest lap

Stoner, in 1'47.091 (161.391 km/h). New record.
Previous: Rossi, in 1'47.288 (161.095 km/h/2006).

Outright fastest lap

Lorenzo, in 1'45.543 (163.758 km/h/2008).

CHAMPIONSHIP

1	V. Rossi	312 (8 wins)
2	C. Stoner	220 (4 wins)
3	D. Pedrosa	209 (2 wins)
4	J. Lorenzo	169 (1 win)
5	A. Dovizioso	136
6	C. Edwards	118
7	C. Vermeulen	117
8	N. Hayden	115
9	L. Capirossi	96
10	S. Nakano	95

The two main men of the season, Simoncelli and Bautista, hard at it - although the Spaniard wasn't always at his best at the start. Chalk another one up (opposite) to Marco-the-Haircut.

PUTTING HIS MISANO MISTAKE IN THE PAST, MARCO SIMONCELLI IS BACK ON TOP.

RUNNERS AND RIDERS
Following an operation on his left thumb the day after he got back to Switzerland, Thomas Luthi's doctors are worried about possible infection so he decides to miss this Grand Prix and Australia. Lai is back on the Gilera, while Ireland's Laverty is off having some fun in Supersport : he finished third in the World Championship round at Vallelunga the previous weekend and his Aprilia has been taken over by

Spain's Daniel Arcas, already seen in Catalunya. The five wild cards include two Hondas and three Yamahas.

QUALIFYING
Debon is quickest on the opening day from Simoncelli and Barbera ; the latter has a heavy Saturday morning fall and fractures three vertebrae. Simoncelli takes pole from Aoyama, Debon and Kallio. Meanwhile the news comes that Pasini's Polaris World team (like Smith's in 125) will not continue next year. The other big news is that the Grand Prix Commission has ratified the decision taken several weeks earlier and the 250cc two-stroke class will be replaced from 2011 by a four-stroke, 600cc category.

START
Simoncelli and Debon are first away ; the title leader is quickly into the

lead. Grotzkyj hasn't made it through the first corner, Kallio is down in sixth first time over the line, unable to repeat his dominant form here in recent years.

LAP 2
There's Simoncelli… and the rest : the Gilera rider is 0.893 ahead of Debon, who has an aggressive Simon coming after him.

LAP 3
Simon is through, and there's a fine scrap between Kallio and Bautista for sixth.

LAP 7
It's still Simoncelli ; Simon is three-tenths behind, Debon more than two seconds away and Bautista is up to fourth.

HALF-DISTANCE (12 LAPS)
Setting fastest lap after fastest lap, Bautista has now overtaken Debon for third, behind Simoncelli and

Simon, who is 0.306 behind the leader.

LAP 14
Wow ! Bautista is second, less than a second down on Simoncelli.

LAP 16
It's wheel to wheel stuff between Simoncelli and Bautista, and Debon is about to take Simon.

LAP 21
This is the turning-point, and it ruins the show as the two front-runners catch two back-markers : Simoncelli gets past first time, Bautista can't.

FINISH (23 LAPS)
With 0.668 in hand at the start of the last lap, Simoncelli takes his fourth win of the season.

CHAMPIONSHIP
Simoncelli has a 32-point lead, with Bautista now second : the title looks Riviera-bound.

GP JAPAN | 28th September 2008 | Motegi | 4.801 m

		STARTING GRID		
1	58	M. Simoncelli	Gilera	1'51.473
2	4	H. Aoyama	KTM	1'51.719
3	6	A. Debón	Aprilia	1'51.758
4	36	M. Kallio	KTM	1'51.765
5	19	A. Bautistá	Aprilia	1'51.821
6	55	H. Faubel	Aprilia	1'51.973
7	60	J. Simón	KTM	1'52.033
8	72	Y. Takahashi	Honda	1'52.197
9	41	A. Espargaró	Aprilia	1'52.228
10	15	R. Locatelli	Gilera	1'52.259
11	75	M. Pasini	Aprilia	1'52.464
12	21	H. Barberá	Aprilia	1'52.861 (*)
13	52	L. Pesek	Aprilia	1'53.130
14	66	S. Tomizawa	Honda	1'53.289
15	14	R. Wilairot	Honda	1'53.356
16	32	F. Lai	Gilera	1'53.496
17	65	T. Takahashi	Honda	1'53.660
18	25	A. Baldolini	Aprilia	1'54.276
19	35	S. Grotzkyj	Gilera	1'54.688
20	45	D.-T. Pradita	Yamaha	1'55.015
21	43	M. Hernandez	Aprilia	1'55.675
22	92	D. Arcas	Aprilia	1'56.283
23	67	K. Watanabe	Yamaha	1'56.587
24	68	Y. Ito	Yamaha	1'57.053
25	10	I. Toth	Aprilia	1'57.115
26	69	T. Endoh	Yamaha	1'57.451

	RACE: 23 laps = 110.423 km	
1	Marco Simoncelli	43'09.385 (153.520 km/h)
2	Alvaro Bautistá	+ 0.348
3	Alex Debón	+ 8.414
4	Julian Simón	+ 9.151
5	Mika Kallio	+ 17.041
6	Yuki Takahashi	+ 19.632
7	Aleix Espargaró	+ 19.892
8	Mattia Pasini	+ 20.442
9	Hiroshi Aoyama	+ 22.303
10	Roberto Locatelli	+ 22.387
11	Hector Faubel	+ 32.851
12	Lukas Pesek	+ 48.621
13	Ratthapark Wilairot	+ 48.803
14	Shoya Tomizawa	+ 49.572
15	Fabrizio Lai	+ 58.045
16	Alex Baldolini	+ 58.362
17	Takumi Takahashi	+ 1'15.062
18	Doni Tata Pradita	+ 1'49.930
19	Manuel Hernandez	+ 1'58.603
20	Daniel Arcas	+ 1 lap
21	Takumi Endoh	+ 1 lap
22	Imre Toth	+ 1 lap
23	Yuuki Ito	+ 3 laps

Fastest lap
Bautistá, in 1'51.412 (155.132 km/h). New record.
Previous: Nakano, in 1'52.253 (153.970 km/h/2000).

Outright fastest lap
S. Aoyama, in 1'51.327 (155.250 km/h/2007).

	CHAMPIONSHIP	
1	M. Simoncelli	215 (4 wins)
2	A. Bautistá	183 (3 wins)
3.	M. Kallio	175 (3 wins)
4	A. Debón	155 (2 wins)
5	H. Barberá	142
6	M. Pasini	125 (1 win)
7	Y. Takahashi	125
8	H. Aoyama	108
9	J. Simón	96
10	T. Lüthi	95

DI MEGLIO LOSES - AND WINS AT THE SAME TIME AS CORSI, ONLY SEVENTH, IS FINALLY BROKEN.

RUNNERS AND RIDERS
Reigning champion Gabor Talacsi was on hand after an operation on the scaphoid he fractured at Indianapolis ; back in the Aspar Team was Adrian Martin, whom we had already seen at Misano ; and the French Federation announced that it was shutting down its team, for whom L. Rossi and Camillo had ridden this season.

QUALIFYING
Three Derbis filled the top three spots on the provisional grid on a drying track on the opening day, those of Olive, ahead of Smith's Aprilia, then Olive's two partners Di Meglio and Aegerter. In normal conditions on Saturday the title leader claimed his first career pole ahead of Bradl, Terol and Cortese.

START
Di Meglio and Terol are quickest off the mark, taking the lead and avoiding an accident that sees riders go down like ninepins as Pol Espargaro hits Marquez. The little Spaniard's KTM collects virtually everyone else, including Aegerter, who was fifth, on the outside as he goes down. Iannone, Cluzel and Rabat all fail to make it to the end of the opening lap, led by Terol from Talmacsi, Bradl and Di Meglio.

LAP 3
The first gap opens up behind a group of five (Bradl, Terol, Talmacsi, Di Meglio and Cortese), blanketed by just 0.758 of a second.

LAP 4
Joan Olive, fastest man on track, has joined the group and got past Cortese. Behind them, but already three seconds down, Cortese is also trying to bridge the gap.

LAP 7
Bradl and Di Meglio still lead ; there's a six-man fight going on, while further back it's Smith who heads the chasing group.

HALF-DISTANCE (10 LAPS)
Bradl is 0.062 ahead of Di Meglio and 0.246 in front of Talmacsi. Olive is 1.054 seconds away, with Terol eight-tenths behind him and going wheel to wheel with Cortese. Smith and Corsi haven't closed that gap.

LAP 11
A mistake from Bradl lets Di Meglio and Tamacsi through.

LAP 14
Another decisive one, as the three front men, Di Meglio, Talmacsi and Bradl, covered by just 0.207, break away from Olive, Cortese and Terol.

LAP 17
Smith falls while lying 17th.

LAP 18
Bradl goes back in front.

FINISH (20 LAPS)
The German starts the last lap with a 0.413-second advantage over Di Meglio, and it's enough, although the Frechman does claw back to within two-tenths. A heroic third place goes to Talmacsi.

CHAMPIONSHIP
With Corsi back in seventh it's been a good day's work for Di Meglio, whose lead is out to 36 points with just 75 left to play for.

Di Meglio fights with Talmacsi and Olive (left). Above : French is the order of the day at Motegi, not only for Mike Di Meglio as he edges closer to the crown but also for Cyril Carillo, replacing Louis Rossi in the FFM line-up.

GP JAPAN | 28th September 2008 | Motegi | 4.801 m

STARTING GRID

1	63	M. Di Meglio	Derbi	1'58.678
2	17	S. Bradl	Aprilia	1'59.059
3	18	N. Terol	Aprilia	1'59.104
4	11	S. Cortese	Aprilia	1'59.132
5	1	G. Talmacsi	Aprilia	1'59.179
6	45	S. Redding	Aprilia	1'59.351
7	77	D. Aegerter	Derbi	1'59.463
8	44	P. Espargaró	Derbi	1'59.562
9	29	A. Iannone	Aprilia	1'59.565
10	33	S. Gadea	Aprilia	1'59.695
11	71	T. Koyama	KTM	1'59.739
12	6	J. Olivé	Derbi	1'59.756
13	93	M. Marquez	KTM	1'59.783
14	38	B. Smith	Aprilia	1'59.784
15	24	S. Corsi	Aprilia	1'59.919
16	7	E. Vazquez	Aprilia	1'59.956
17	51	S. Bonsey	Aprilia	2'00.112
18	99	D. Webb	Aprilia	2'00.125
19	35	R. De Rosa	KTM	2'00.404
20	74	T. Nakagami	Aprilia	2'00.434
21	12	E. Rabat	KTM	2'01.121
22	5	A. Masbou	Loncin	2'01.247
23	8	L. Zanetti	KTM	2'01.279
24	60	M. Ranseder	Aprilia	2'01.395
25	21	R. Lässer	Aprilia	2'01.458
26	57	I. Namihira	Honda	2'01.944
27	50	I. Iwata	Honda	2'01.946
28	22	P. Nieto	KTM	2'02.000
29	26	A. Martin	Aprilia	2'02.069
30	72	M. Ravaioli	Aprilia	2'02.148
31	94	J. Folger	KTM	2'02.270
32	58	Y. Yanagisawa	Honda	2'02.488
33	95	R. Muresan	Aprilia	2'02.656
34	62	K. Watanabe	Honda	2'02.708
35	59	H. Ono	Honda	2'02.833
36	16	J. Cluzel	Loncin	2'03.058
37	36	C. Carillo	Honda	2'03.426
38	56	H. Van Den Berg	Aprilia	2'03.494
39	48	B. Chesaux	Aprilia	2'04.091

RACE: 20 laps = 96.020 km

1	Stefan Bradl	39'57.228 (144.196 km/h)
2	Mike Di Meglio	+ 0.151
3	Gabor Talmacsi	+ 0.281
4	Joan Olivé	+ 5.945
5	Nicolas Terol	+ 6.072
6	Sandro Cortese	+ 6.135
7	Simone Corsi	+ 6.455
8	Scott Redding	+ 25.393
9	Sergio Gadea	+ 25.537
10	Daniel Webb	+ 26.192
11	Tomoyoshi Koyama	+ 27.307
12	Raffaele De Rosa	+ 39.536
13	Takaaki Nakagami	+ 43.745
14	Efrén Vazquez	+ 51.629
15	Alexis Masbou	+ 51.899
16	Jonas Folger	+ 51.931
17	Lorenzo Zanetti	+ 51.962
18	Pablo Nieto	+ 52.589
19	Dominique Aegerter	+ 56.837
20	Steve Bonsey	+ 56.977
21	Marco Ravaioli	+ 58.626
22	Yuuichi Yanagisawa	+ 59.926
23	Robin Lässer	+ 1'09.782
24	Hiroki Ono	+ 1'14.883
25	Adrián Martin	+ 1'26.120
26	Cyril Carrillo	+ 1'29.130

Fastest lap
Talmacsi, in 1'58.815 (145.466 km/h).
Record: Kallio, in 1'57.666 (146.886 km/h/2006).

Outright fastest lap
Pasini, in 1'56.954 (147.781 km/h/2007).

CHAMPIONSHIP

1	M. Di Meglio	212 (3 wins)
2	S. Corsi	176 (3 wins)
3	S. Bradl	167 (2 wins)
4	G. Talmacsi	165 (2 wins)
5	N. Terol	149 (1 win)
6	J. Olivé	131
7	B. Smith	117
8	S. Cortese	107
9	P. Espargaró	103
10	S. Redding	91 (1 win)

Randy De Puniet chases 2008 World Champion Valentino Rossi.

G'day from Down Under.

IT'S STONER ISLAND

THINGS MIGHT HAVE BEEN
DIFFERENT IF VALENTINO ROSSI
HADN'T STARTED FROM SO FAR
BACK, BUT ONCE AGAIN CASEY WAS
KING ON HIS HOME TRACK.

THE RACE

ONE UP FOR THE MICHELIN MAN !

Which of the two Yamaha M1's do you prefer : the Bridgestone-shod one or the one that still has faith in the Michelin man ? The question won't arise in 23009...

A week earleier it was, of course, Bridgestone rider Mr Valentino Rossi who was crowned World Champion. And a year earlier it was another Bridgestone rider, Casey Stoner, who was his predecessor, and who then headed him home by six seconds in this third-last Grand Prix of the season at Phillip Island. That's all a matter of fact and it all reflects well on the Japanese manufacturer who came, and learned, and progressed, and eventually got right on top of things.

Nevertheless, on this first weekend of 2008, the honours went to the Michelin man, and deservedly so. It was the Clermont-Ferrand company that had the guts not to respond to the tender issued 10 days earlier to decide the sole supplier of tyres to the premier class starting next year.

It was Michelin, pioneers of product development through sport, who reminded everyone - as they had done two years earlier in the same situation in Formula 1, where Bridgestone was also named sole supplier - that without competition, there is no sport. And that sport is the ideal proving-ground, and the lessons learned there are passed on to the customer. And when you stifle competition, sport loses much of its savour.

And the press release duly came out : « The Prix Commission, composed of Messrs. Carmelo Ezpeleta (Dorna, Chairman), Claude Danis (FIM), Hervé Poncharal (IRTA) and Takanao Tsubouchi (MSMA, in the presence of M. Paul Butler (Secretary of the meeting), in a meeting held today at the circuit of Phillip Island, have been informed that Bridgestone has sent a proposal to FIM and Dorna to be the single tyre supplier in MotoGP for 2009. This proposal will be studied and an announcement will be made on 16th of October 2008 in Sepang, Malaysia. »

And yes, we realised then that the bell had tolled. Racing had just lost one of its key players, and one of its most loyal. The one with the keenest sense of tradition. All credit to the Michelin man, and very little to the rest : Carmelo Ezpeleta, who was forgetting that the rights he holds in the World Championship are commercial ones ; the FIM, reluctant to ruffle their main partner's feathers by reminding them that those rights do not cover technical decisions ; the teams, now just money-making machines who lay on the on-track show but off it are just there to bow and scrape ; and then Bridgestone, who should have had the good taste not to respond to the tender - in the name of sport.

For what we now have to look forward to is special helmets saying « Bridgestone's 10th straight win in MotoGP », or « Bridgestone has won the last 20 races in motorcycle racing's premier class ! », or « Put your faith in Bridgestone, unbeaten in 50 Grands Prix », or words to that effect - or worse...

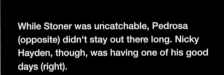
While Stoner was uncatchable, Pedrosa (opposite) didn't stay out there long. Nicky Hayden, though, was having one of his good days (right).

A PRACTICE SCARE FOR ROSSI, A PERFECT RACE FOR STONER

RUNNERS AND RIDERS

Not much going on, except that there is no confirmation yet of who will be on the third Kawasaki on the grid in 2009, the one prepared by Jorge Aspar Martinez's team. Kawasaki chiefs would like it to be Shinya Nakano ; the Spanish team manager, who is naturally bringing in Spanish sponsors, would prefer a fellow-countryman.

QUALIFYING

An on-song Casey Stoner dominates free practice, the second session in the rain, and then takes pole. Mind you, it wasn't easy for him in the hour of qualifying, nor for the Bridgestone riders generally : Lorenzo, Hayden, De Puniet and Toseland all elbowed their way in between last year's winner and Dani Pedrosa. And Rossi ? A heavy fall left him severely bruised and down in 12th.

START

First away are Stoner, Pedrosa and Hayden, but as early as Turn 2 the Spaniard is down ; Vermeulen visits a gravel trap a little further on, as does Guintoli. A chaotic first lap, which faller De Angelis doesn't finish, sees Stoner and Hayden already opening up a gap to the chasing pack led by Toseland, Lorenzo and Edwards. Rossi meanwhile is eighth.

LAP 3

There are two-tenths between Stoner and Hayden, with Lorenzo now third, 2.903 seconds behind.

LAP 4

Rossi is still on it - now he's fifth.

LAP 6

Moments ago Toseland got past Lorenzo ; now it's the World Champion's turn to catch him out.

LAP 8

Why stop when things are going so well ? Rossi passes Toseland and is in a podium spot - but the Englishman briefly fights back.

HALF-DISTANCE (13 LAPS)

Hayden hasn't been able to match Stoner's pace and the American is now 2.329 seconds down on the Australian. Rossi in third is 8.330 seconds behind, with Toseland and Dovizioso hanging on to his coat-tails.

LAP 22

Rossi is now within 2.9 seconds of Hayden and there is a wonderful scrap going on among a group of four riders for fourth place.

LAP 24

Now just 1.630 between Hayden and Rossi. Dovizioso has passed Lorenzo, who in turn has caught Toseland napping.

FINISH (27 LAPS)

Rossi is right with his nearest rival Hayden as they start the final lap and will pass him for second place as Lorenzo has the last word in the battle for fourth.

CHAMPIONSHIP

With the title and runner-up spot decided, the interest in the last two races switches to Pedrosa and Lorenzo as they fight it out for third ; the rookie is now within 27 points.

GP AUSTRALIA | 5th October 2008 | Phillip Island | 4.448 m

STARTING GRID

1	1	C. Stoner	Ducati	1'28.665
2	48	J. Lorenzo	Yamaha	1'28.734
3	69	N. Hayden	Honda	1'28.756
4	14	R. De Puniet	Honda	1'28.808
5	52	J. Toseland	Yamaha	1'29.031
6	2	D. Pedrosa	Honda	1'29.277
7	5	C. Edwards	Yamaha	1'29.513
8	4	A. Dovizioso	Honda	1'29.558
9	56	S. Nakano	Honda	1'29.710
10	15	A. De Angelis	Honda	1'29.925
11	65	L. Capirossi	Suzuki	1'29.942
12	46	V. Rossi	Yamaha	1'30.014
13	24	T. Elias	Ducati	1'30.202
14	50	S. Guintoli	Ducati	1'30.297
15	7	C. Vermeulen	Suzuki	1'30.545
16	21	J. Hopkins	Kawasaki	1'31.157
17	33	M. Melandri	Ducati	1'31.939
18	13	A. West	Kawasaki	1'31.995

RACE: 27 laps = 120.096 km

1	Casey Stoner	40'56.643 (175.990)	
2	Valentino Rossi	+ 6.504	
3	Nicky Hayden	+ 7.205	
4	Jorge Lorenzo	+ 11.500	
5	Shinya Nakano	+ 11.914	
6	James Toseland	+ 12.243	
7	Andrea Dovizioso	+ 12.780	
8	Colin Edwards	+ 25.920	
9	Randy De Puniet	+ 26.037	
10	Loris Capirossi	+ 26.799	
11	Toni Elias	+ 27.027	
12	Anthony West	+ 47.808	
13	John Hopkins	+ 48.333	
14	Sylvain Guintoli	+ 48.899	
15	Chris Vermeulen	+ 48.935	
16	Marco Melandri	+ 1'11.767	

Fastest lap
Hayden, in 1'30.059 (177.803 km/h). New record.
Previous: Melandri, in 1'30.332 (177.266 km/h/2005).

Outright fastest lap
Stoner, in 1'28.665 (180.598 km/h/2008).

CHAMPIONSHIP

1	V. Rossi	332 (8 wins)
2	C. Stoner	245 (5 wins)
3	D. Pedrosa	209 (2 wins)
4	J. Lorenzo	182 (1 win)
5	A. Dovizioso	145
6	N. Hayden	131
7	C. Edwards	126
8.	C. Vermeulen	118
9	S. Nakano	106
10	L. Capirossi	102

SIMONCELLI A STEP CLOSER TO THE CROWN.

RUNNERS AND RIDERS
Still no Thomas Luthi ; Barbera is still confined to his hospital bed in Japan after the latest checks reveal signs of fractures to three vertebrae. Bianco comes in to replace him - but only for the first day. Karel Abraham is back after flying home to the Czech Republic after Japan for a scaphoid operation.

QUALIFYING
The first day's rain brings a flurry of fallers, Debon, Aoyama and Lai among them. In Saturday's sunshine Simoncelli becomes the fastest man in 250cc history, putting nearly eight-tenths between him and Kallio. Bautista and Aoyama have the Finn in their sights.

START
Aoyama goes down the hill in the lead from Bautista, Simoncelli and Kallio. First time across the line it's Bautista in front.

LAP 2
Taking no chances with his main rival, Simoncelli is back within 0.076 of Bautista ; Kallio and the others have been dropped.

LAP 4
The first little brush between the two leaders while behind them, Simon leads the charge.

LAP 5
Faubel goes down.

LAP 6
Bautista is back in front and third-placed Simon is back in striking distance.

Top : typical Phillip Island as a gull keeps a close watch on Bautista, Simoncelli, Kallio and Aoyama. Faubel (above) was out by lap 5 while Simoncelli (right) claimed another win.

LAP 7
Simoncelli again, but the group has reformed with nothing between the front five.

LAP 8
Aoyama has been dropped.

LAP 12
In the same spot where they touched eight laps earlier, Simoncelli and Bautista do it again, much to the delight of KTM as Simon goes to the front from Kallio - and much to the chagrin of Piaggio group sporting director Giampiero Sacchi, looking on from the sidelines.

HALF-DISTANCE (13 LAPS)
The Championship front-runners have seen sense and got a grip on things again, Simoncelli showing the way as he now has a 0.402-second lead over Bautista. Simon is now over a second adrift.

LAP 15
Pasini falls off while running in seventh.

LAP 16
A technical problem sees Aoyama retire ; returning to the pits, he aims a right hook at one of the panels in the garage.

LAP 21
Setting new lap records one after the other, Bautista has got back to within 0.140 of Simoncelli, but the Italian shrugs it off.

FINISH (23 LAPS)
The Gilera rider is three-tenths clear as the last lap starts, and that's enough for the man who has managed to eliminate errors from his game.

CHAMPIONSHIP
He's nearly there : 37 points clear of Bautista and 49 ahead of Kallio with only 50 left to play for.

GP AUSTRALIA | 5th October 2008 | Phillip Island | 4.448 m

STARTING GRID

1	58	M. Simoncelli	Gilera	1'32.075
2	36	M. Kallio	KTM	1'32.862
3	19	A. Bautistá	Aprilia	1'32.917
4	4	H. Aoyama	KTM	1'33.048
5	55	H. Faubel	Aprilia	1'33.167
6	60	J. Simón	KTM	1'33.250
7	72	Y. Takahashi	Honda	1'33.294
8	6	A. Debón	Aprilia	1'33.349
9	41	A. Espargaró	Aprilia	1'33.368
10	75	M. Pasini	Aprilia	1'33.376
11	15	R. Locatelli	Gilera	1'33.508
12	14	R. Wilairot	Honda	1'33.538
13	32	F. Lai	Gilera	1'33.696
14	52	L. Pesek	Aprilia	1'33.871
15	90	F. Sandi	Aprilia	1'34.544
16	10	I. Toth	Aprilia	1'34.997
17	17	K. Abraham	Aprilia	1'35.464
18	25	A. Baldolini	Aprilia	1'36.036
19	43	M. Hernandez	Aprilia	1'36.116
20	92	D. Arcas	Aprilia	1'36.921
21	35	S. Grotzkyj	Gilera	1'37.006
22	45	D.-T. Pradita	Yamaha	1'37.050

Not qualified:

	89	H. Chow	Aprilia	1'41.115
	27	S. Bianco	Aprilia	1'47.654

RACE: 25 laps = 111.200 km

1	Marco Simoncelli	39'02.553 (170.890 km/h)
2	Alvaro Bautistá	+ 0.223
3	Mika Kallio	+ 14.450
4	Julian Simón	+ 14.478
5	Alex Debón	+ 26.226
6	Roberto Locatelli	+ 26.392
7	Yuki Takahashi	+ 26.434
8	Aleix Espargaró	+ 40.546
9	Ratthapark Wilairot	+ 1'00.219
10	Fabrizio Lai	+ 1'20.825
11	Karel Abraham	+ 1'22.802
12	Alex Baldolini	+ 1'22.864
13	Imre Toth	+ 1'23.995
14	Lukas Pesek	+ 1'39.740
15	Simone Grozkyj	+ 1 lap
16	Daniel Arcas	+ 1 lap
17	Doni Tata Pradita	+ 1 lap

Fastest lap
Bautistá, in 1'32.710 (172.729 km/h). New record.
Previous: Porto, in 1'33.381 (171.478 km/h/2004).

Outright fastest lap
S. Simoncelli, in 1'32.075 (173.910 km/h/2008).

CHAMPIONSHIP

1	M. Simoncelli	240 (5 wins)
2	A. Bautistá	203 (3 wins)
3	M. Kallio	191 (3 wins)
4	A. Debón	166 (2 wins)
5	H. Barberá	142
6	Y. Takahashi	134
7	M. Pasini	125 (1 win)
8	J. Simón	109
9	H. Aoyama	108
10	T. Lüthi	95

MIKE DI MEGLIO'S DATE WITH DESTINY

RUNNERS AND RIDERS

Krummenacher was back with Red Bull KTM while over at ISPA Spain's Enrique Jerez came in for Koyama, injured at Motegi. Five Australians, including one of the Leigh-Smith twins, Blake, had wild card entries.

QUALIFYING

The best way of dealing with adversity is to dominate your adversaries. From day one, in the rain and cold, Mike Di Meglio showed his impending date with destiny didn't mean he was going to do this by the numbers. Third on the opening day, Australian rider Ranseder had to pull out after a heavy Saturday morning fall.

START

Smith is first to move when the red lights go out - but he is also first to fall off just a few hundred metres later. Swiss rider Aegerter also has an impressive off. First time over the line it's Cortese from Iannone, Di Meglio and Marquez.

LAP 2

Falls for Cortese and Raffaele De Rosa ; Di Meglio has taken charge and Talmacsi, in whose shoes he is about to follow, is hanging on to second.

LAP 4

Di Meglio makes his first break, now 0.603 clear of Talmacsi.

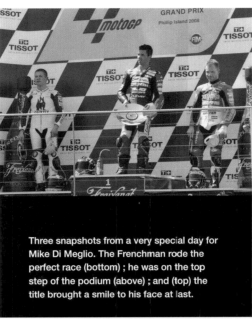

Three snapshots from a very special day for Mike Di Meglio. The Frenchman rode the perfect race (bottom) ; he was on the top step of the podium (above) ; and (top) the title brought a smile to his face at last.

LAP 9

Total domination by the man who has only 20 minutes more to wait till he's home free : Di Meglio is now 2.898 in front of a quartet made up of Talmacsi, Olive, Bradl and Iannone.

HALF-DISTANCE (12 LAPS)

The Frenchman is riding a flawless race, now enjoying a 4.111-second advantage over his closest pursuer, Stefan Bradl. Olive is third, just ahead of Iannone and Talmacsi. Then there is a big gap to seventh-placed Gadea, 9.763 seconds adrift.

LAP 13

Olive goes down, picks the bike up but slips to 12th.

LAP 16

Time to start doing the sums : Bradl in second place has dropped Talmacsi, and if the race finished now Di Meglio would have a 50-point lead. With just two races remaining the German could still draw level on points and race wins, but not on countback to the number of second places.

FINISH (23 LAPS)

Now it's time to break into the Marseillaise as France's new World Champion starts the last lap more than 11 seconds to the good.

CHAMPIONSHIP

Aki Ajo was the man who discovered Mika Kallio back home in Finland, but now, with a French rider of Sicilian background, he has achieved something he never could with his fellow-countryman.

GP AUSTRALIA | 5th October 2008 | Phillip Island | 4.448 m

STARTING GRID

1	63	M. Di Meglio	Derbi	1'37.553
2	38	B. Smith	Aprilia	1'37.791
3	17	S. Bradl	Aprilia	1'38.034
4	18	N. Terol	Aprilia	1'38.110
5	29	A. Iannone	Aprilia	1'38.242
6	11	S. Cortese	Aprilia	1'38.361
7	35	R. De Rosa	KTM	1'38.473
8	24	S. Corsi	Aprilia	1'38.476
9	1	G. Talmacsi	Aprilia	1'38.501
10	77	D. Aegerter	Derbi	1'38.600
11	45	S. Redding	Aprilia	1'38.767
12	93	M. Marquez	KTM	1'38.822
13	51	S. Bonsey	Aprilia	1'38.848
14	33	S. Gadea	Aprilia	1'38.864
15	99	D. Webb	Aprilia	1'38.912
16	44	P. Espargaró	Derbi	1'38.928
17	22	P. Nieto	KTM	1'38.935
18	12	E. Rabat	KTM	1'38.986
19	6	J. Olivé	Derbi	1'39.109
20	8	L. Zanetti	KTM	1'39.688
21	34	R. Krummenacher	KTM	1'39.860
22	56	H. Van Den Berg	Aprilia	1'39.960
23	5	A. Masbou	Loncin	1'39.969
24	21	R. Lässer	Aprilia	1'40.163
25	95	R. Muresan	Aprilia	1'40.352
26	7	E. Vazquez	Aprilia	1'40.441
27	74	T. Nakagami	Aprilia	1'40.480
28	16	J. Cluzel	Loncin	1'41.365
29	48	B. Chesaux	Aprilia	1'41.473
30	72	M. Ravaioli	Aprilia	1'41.477
31	26	A. Martin	Aprilia	1'41.694
32	36	C. Carillo	Honda	1'41.821
33	28	E. Jerez	KTM	1'41.856
34	91	J. Metcher	Honda	1'42.805
35	70	R. Moller	Honda	1'43.802
36	46	B. Gross	Yamaha	1'43.946

Not qualified:

32	B. Leigh-Smith	Honda	1'44.478
92	J. Horne	Honda	1'46.597
60	M. Ranseder	Aprilia	1'49.537

RACE: 23 laps = 102.304 km

1	Mike Di Meglio	37'55.589 (161.845 km/h)
2	Stefan Bradl	+ 10.255
3	Gabor Talmacsi	+ 13.106
4	Andrea Iannone	+ 13.149
5	Pol Espargaró	+ 26.796
6	Sandro Cortese	+ 27.123
7	Esteve Rabat	+ 27.181
8	Simone Corsi	+ 27.871
9	Marc Marquez	+ 28.287 (*)
10	Scott Redding	+ 35.087
11	Efrén Vazquez	+ 57.392
12	Lorenzo Zanetti	+ 57.413
13	Pablo Nieto	+ 57.451
14	Joan Olivé	+ 57.539
15	Robin Lässer	+ 1'42.441
16	Marco Ravaioli	+ 1'06.320
17	Adrián Martin	+ 1'26.120
18	Cyril Carrillo	+ 1'42.455
19	Enrique Jerez	+ 1'43.792
20	Jed Metcher	+ 1 lap
21	Randy Krummenacher	+ 2 laps

(*): Spain's Marc Marquez (KTM) was given a one-second penalty by race officials for 'an action prejudicial to the interests of the sport' under article 3.3.1.2.

Fastest lap
Bradl, in 1'37.908 (163.549 km/h).
Record: Bautistá, in 1'36.927 (165.204 km/h/2006).

Outright fastest lap
Kallio, in 1'36.625 (165.721 km/h/2006).

CHAMPIONSHIP

1	M. Di Meglio	237 (4 wins)
2	S. Bradl	187 (2 wins)
3	S. Corsi	184 (3 wins)
4	G. Talmacsi	181 (2 wins)
5	N. Terol	149 (1 win)
6	J. Olivé	133
7	B. Smith	117
8	S. Cortese	117
9	P. Espargaró	114
10	S. Redding	97 (1 win)

Once again Daniel Pedrosa got the best start. Once again, someone else would win...

Still life… and there's still life.

ROSSI,
GOES AFTER AGO !

ANOTHER WIN FOR THE WORLD
CHAMPION, WHO NOW HAS THE
LEGENDARY '122' IN HIS SIGHTS - THE
NUMBER OF GP WINS BY THE GREAT
GIACOMO AGOSTINI

THE RACE

SHUTTING DOWN THE PIPELINE

Spotlight on a major problem : where is the World Championship going ? There's no shortage of talent coming through, such as Andrea Dovizioso (top), but what's going to happen to the rest of them now that KTM have pulled out of the 250cc class ?

Imagine what would happen if petrol producers took it into their heads to shut off the taps. There would be panic all around. What if the were to say, « That's it, we're not doing it any more. Sort it out among yourselves ! » And at a time when the global economy is taking a hammering, what if the people who rule the planet all got together and decided to stop all production of raw materials. « That's it, make what you can of what you've got. All getting a bit long in the tooth ? Too bad… »

All right, we may be exaggerating a bit, and the world's not about to come to an end just because motorcycle racing's premier class is facing a number of major challenges. But the atmosphere in Sepang spoke volumes for the paddock and the general air of depression around the place.

Why was that ? Well, things really aren't all that bright on the economic front. You can't keep spending more and more money in a milieu that's generating less and less of it, with Suzuki sponsor Rizla the latest to pull the plug. And yet the so-called financial crisis - and it is financial rather than economic - and the roller-coaster markets of the last few weeks don't go all the way to explaining the current state of affairs.

For example, they can't tell us why, when promoters can't lay on a full MotoGP grid, they've done their best to turn away the very people putting most into the lower classes. Everyone realises that the kinds of budgets put together by 'Aspar' Martinez in Spain or Daniel-M. Epp with Thomas Luthi in Switzerland would be a shot in the arm for the premier class. But did they have to let things get to where they are now - a Piaggio group monopoly in 250cc ? Couldn't they have found a way to help KTM keep their project going? Couldn't they see that giving up on the class meant shutting off the pipeline that would bring new players into the MotoGP class ? After all, being able to see what's coming is what governing's all about.

But no. Instead, they just pat themselves on the back and tell us there will be a fifth Ducati Desmosedici out there next year. Unfortunately, it will be for a rider who actually retired 12 months ago. As long-term solutions go, they could have come up with something better than that…

Sadly, too, they keep throwing millions at guys who don't want to know any more (not to name names, but Melandri's comes to mind), forgetting a basic rule of architecture handed down to us by the Egyptians : if you want to build a pyramid that lasts, make sure it has as broad a base as it can.

In the medium term, that base has gone. The two main men in the 250cc Championship, World Champion Marco Simoncelli and runner-up Alvaro Bautista, plan to spend another year in the in-between category. In a year's time, maybe with the addition of Thomas Luthi if he can start winning consistently in his third season in 250, they will be the last products of a nursery system that led all the way from the 125cc class up to MotoGP itself.

ROSSI : THE MASTER OUT ON HIS OWN...

RUNNERS AND RIDERS

There is a third Suzuki for test rider Nobuatsu Aoki, and there is plenty of movement behind the scenes : at the same time as a fifth Ducati Desmosedici for Gibernau with Onde 2000, the Nietos' new team, is confirmed, we also learn that there will not be a third Kawasaki. They wanted Shinya Nakano, but Jorge 'Aspar' Martinez, whose team it was to be, wanted a Spanish rider.

QUALIFYING

The forecast is for heavy rain on Saturday, so free practice is a tactical affair and it's Anthony West who sets fastest time through the three sessions with the help of a set of qualifying tyres. Why was that ? That's an easy one : the Kawasaki people remembered what happened two years before, when the rain was so bad on Saturday afternoon that qualifying was cancelled and the grid went according to free practice times. Sadly for team green, the track dried and it all came down to the last few minutes, and Pedrosa was the master of that little game, claiming his first Bridgestone pole. Rossi and Lorenzo made up the front row, with Stoner back in a lowly seventh.

START

Lorenzo fluffs it, Pedrosa doesn't and takes the lead ahead of Dovizioso, already a stand-out. Nakano, 15th in qualifying, is already up there in sixth by the end of the opening lap.

LAP 2

Rossi has got past Dovizioso and is just 0.414 behind Pedrosa. Toseland has just gone down, while Elias has to serve a drive-through for jumping the start.

HALF-DISTANCE (10 LAPS)

After keeping a close eye on Pedrosa and never letting the gap to drift out past half a second, Rossi now takes charge, leading Pedrosa by 0.286. Dovizioso, 5.368 seconds down, is third and locked in combat with Hayden, Stoner, Lorenzo and Nakano.

LAP 11

Lorenzo comes off, picks the bike up but pulls out a few metres further on.

LAP 15

White flags indicate rain somewhere on the circuit, meaning the riders can change bikes if they want to. Up front, Rossi now has a 3.046 gap on Pedrosa.

FINISH (21 LAPS)

Another master-class from Rossi, but hats off, too, to Andrea Dovizioso for holding off Hayden to the end to claim his first MotoGP podium.

CHAMPIONSHIP

Although only sixth, Stoner secures runner-up position behind Rossi, with Pedrosa now 27 points adrift of the 2007 champion.

Is that West (13) out in front ? This battle is a long way behind the leader of the pack, Valentino Rossi. And as the maestro would have noticed that over the years, MotoGP Yearbook photographer Lukas Swiderel has grown a bit more than he has...

GP MALAYSIA | 19th October 2008 | Sepang | 5.548 m

STARTING GRID

1	2	D. Pedrosa	Honda	2'01.548
2	46	V. Rossi	Yamaha	2'01.957
3	48	J. Lorenzo	Yamaha	2'02.171
4	69	N. Hayden	Honda	2'02.192
5	5	C. Edwards	Yamaha	2'02.245
6	4	A. Dovizioso	Honda	2'02.836
7	1	C. Stoner	Ducati	2'02.953
8	65	L. Capirossi	Suzuki	2'03.078
9	14	R. De Puniet	Honda	2'03.110
10	21	J. Hopkins	Kawasaki	2'03.184
11	7	C. Vermeulen	Suzuki	2'03.271
12	52	J. Toseland	Yamaha	2'03.282
13	13	A. West	Kawasaki	2'03.392
14	33	M. Melandri	Ducati	2'03.835
15	56	S. Nakano	Honda	2'04.001
16	50	S. Guintoli	Ducati	2'04.378
17	15	A. De Angelis	Honda	2'04.679
18	9	N. Aoki	Suzuki	2'04.835
19	24	T. Elias	Ducati	2'05.120

RACE: 21 laps = 116.508 km

1	Valentino Rossi	43'06.007 (162.191 km/h)
2	Daniel Pedrosa	+ 4.008
3	Andrea Dovizioso	+ 8.536
4	Nicky Hayden	+ 8.858
5	Shinya Nakano	+ 10.583
6	Casey Stoner	+ 13.640
7	Loris Capirossi	+ 15.936
8	Colin Edwards	+ 18.802
9	Chris Vermeulen	+ 23.174
10	Randy De Puniet	+ 25.516
11	John Hopkins	+ 27.609
12	Anthony West	+ 41.399
13	Sylvain Guintoli	+ 45.617
14	Alex De Angelis	+ 49.003
15	Toni Elias	+ 59.139
16	Marco Melandri	+ 1'03.328

Fastest lap

Rossi, in 2'02.249 (163.378 km/h).
Record: Stoner, in 2'02.108 (163.566 km/h/2007).

Outright fastest lap

Rossi, in 2'00.605 (165.605 km/h/2006).

CHAMPIONSHIP

1	V. Rossi	357 (9 wins)
2	C. Stoner	255 (5 wins)
3	D. Pedrosa	229 (2 wins)
4	J. Lorenzo	182 (1 win)
5	A. Dovizioso	161
6	N. Hayden	144
7	C. Edwards	134
8	C. Vermeulen	125
9	S. Nakano	117
10	L. Capirossi	111

SIMONCELLI DOES IT TOUGH ON WAY TO TITLE

RUNNERS AND RIDERS

Luthi was back, even though still in some pain from the left hand that was injured in Indianapolis and needed a four-hour reconstruction. Injured at Motegi, Barbera had at last been able to travel home to Spain. The headlines were political: on Thursday KTM announced they were withdrawing from the class for 2009. « I am heart-broken, » said engineer Harald Bartol, though he knew full well the the 250 class, which will disappear in two years, had no real future.

QUALIFYING

As if in response to that sad news, the KTM riders had a fine time of it, especially Hiroshi Aoyama, quickest on Friday afternoon. Saturday morning's rain meant the track was slower than the previous day, though it had dried by the time qualifying began that afternoon. In those condtions, not many were able to improve, although Simolncelli, no great fan of the Sepang circuit, did enough to get himself on to the front row.

START

A few hours before race start news came that Dieter Stappert, the Yamaha-Pertamina manager whose team enjoyed great success with Reinhold Roth, Helmut Bradl and Ralf Waldmann, had died. Kallio is away fastest, but Espargaro slips by in the first corner and leads them over the line first time with Simoncelli second and Bautista 'only' seventh.

LAP 3

Simon, on song as the season draws to a close, is in front from Simoncelli, with Espargaro, Aoyama and Bautista next up.

LAP 4

Faubel goes down, Simoncelli leads.

LAP 5

Kallio is out with mechanical problems.

HALF-DISTANCE (10 LAPS)

Bautista, needing to start putting pressure on Simoncelli, leads from Aoyama, Simoncelli and Simon.

LAP 11

Simon slows down - another KTM retirement. With just three riders in the leading group, Simoncelli is to all intents and purposes World Champion.

LAP 14

Aprilias can be fragile too : now Pasini pulls out.

FINISH (20 LAPS)

Bautista has done his fair share, and so has Simoncelli after making sure of third place. He's near collapse and dehydrated, but the Italian with the crazy hair can now happily pull on the World Champion's top. The Gilera man started the season on an LE, then adapted beautifully to the works RSA.

CHAMPIONSHIP

A 28-point lead with one race to go : Simoncelli's name follows Lorenzo's on the honour roll of a class which, sadly, will soon be no more.

A dehydrated Marco Simoncelli enjoys a well-earned champagne spray. In the race, Bautista (seen here in the lead) gave it everything he had but it wasn't enough to spoil the Simoncelli party.

GP MALAISIA | 19th October 2008 | Sepang | 5.548 m

STARTING GRID

1	4	H. Aoyama	KTM	2'06.893
2	19	A. Bautistá	Aprilia	2'07.073
3	58	M. Simoncelli	Gilera	2'07.109
4	36	M. Kallio	KTM	2'07.118
5	14	R. Wilairot	Honda	2'07.410
6	41	A. Espargaró	Aprilia	2'07.455
7	60	J. Simón	KTM	2'07.668
8	72	Y. Takahashi	Honda	2'07.766
9	6	A. Debón	Aprilia	2'07.920
10	55	H. Faubel	Aprilia	2'08.009
11	75	M. Pasini	Aprilia	2'08.386
12	32	F. Lai	Gilera	2'08.483
13	52	L. Pesek	Aprilia	2'08.649
14	12	T. Lüthi	Aprilia	2'08.653
15	15	R. Locatelli	Gilera	2'09.150
16	10	I. Toth	Aprilia	2'09.301
17	25	A. Baldolini	Aprilia	2'09.759
18	17	K. Abraham	Aprilia	2'10.060
19	35	S. Grotzkyj	Gilera	2'10.490
20	45	D.-T. Pradita	Yamaha	2'11.437
21	43	M. Hernandez	Aprilia	2'11.665
22	92	D. Arcas	Aprilia	2'13.770

RACE: 20 laps = 110.960 km

1	Alvaro Bautistá	42'56.428 (155.042 km/h)
2	Hiroshi Aoyama	+ 2.586
3	Marco Simoncelli	+ 8.343
4	Yuki Takahashi	+ 11.032
5.	Aleix Espargaró	+ 13.846
6	Alex Debón	+ 14.274
7	Roberto Locatelli	+ 15.101
8	Ratthapark Wilairot	+ 16.987
9	Thomas Lüthi	+ 25.356
10	Lukas Pesek	+ 26.846
11	Fabrizio Lai	+ 49.907
12	Karel Abraham	+ 50.088
13	Alex Baldolini	+ 1'05.816
14	Simone Grozkyj	+ 1'15.544
15	Imre Toth	+ 1'19.905
16	Manuel Hernandez	+ 1'35.890
17	Daniel Arcas	+ 2'00.717
18	Doni Tata Pradita	+ 2'28.842

Fastest lap
Bautistá, in 2'08.012 (156.022 km/h). New record.
Previous: Pedrosa, in 2'08.015 (156.019 km/h/2004).

Outright fastest lap
H. Aoyama, in 2'06.893 (157.398 km/h/2008).

CHAMPIONSHIP

1	M. Simoncelli	256 (5 wins)
2	A. Bautistá	228 (4 wins)
3	M. Kallio	191 (3 wins)
4	A. Debón	176 (2 wins)
5	Y. Takahashi	147
6	H. Barberá	142
7	H. Aoyama	128
8	M. Pasini	125 (1 win)
9	J. Simón	109
10	T. Lüthi	102

Talmacsi leads through the first corner. Rabat (above) genuflects on track as a relaxed Mike Di Meglio arrives at the circuit.

TALMACSI TITLE GONE, HEAD HIGH

RUNNERS AND RIDERS
Michael Ranseder, injured in Australia, went home to Austria, at the same time signing a contract with Jan Witteveen and Gary Taylor's new Chinese project, the Maxtra team. Koyama, who missed Phillip Island and was not too happy with his employers ISPA, was back thanks to a wild card, as was Jonas Folger. Despite needing an operation on one of the fingers on his left hand after his first-lap fall in Australia, Dominique Aegerter was able to race.

QUALIFYING
Typically Malaysian weather greeted the riders, with the only dry session taking place on Friday afternoon, when Andrea Iannone was quickest ahead of Talmacsi, Webb and Pol Espargaro. Struggling with grip, World Champion Mike Di Melgio was down in ninth. Marc Marquez had a big off on Friday morning, the young Spaniard getting his legs caught between swing arm and wheel and breaking his tibia.

START
Unable to fire up the bike and take his front-row spot, Webb starts the warm-up lap from pit lane, then - contrary to the regulations - takes up his grid spot. Talmacsi is quickest away, followed by Iannone, the two men immediately opening up a slight gap on their pursuers.

LAP 5
The two leaders are still rubbing wheels ; Smith is now up to third while Webb gets a drive-through penalty for his start-line gaffe.

LAP 6
Talmacsi ups the pace and drops Iannone as Smith, now 4.614 seconds back in third, grapples with Bradl, Cortese, Pol Espargaro and World Champion Mike Di Meglio.

HALF-DISTANCE (9 LAPS)
Talmacsi's lead has now gone out to nine seconds ; his closest pursuer is now Smith, Iannone having fallen back into the chasing group.

LAP 10
Bradl retires ; Smith has broken away from the riders around him, and now Cortese and Di Meglio are squabbling over third.

LAP 12
It's all happening as Corsi gets back in touch with the chasing group.

LAP 15
Talmacsi is simply managing the gap to Smith, and now Corsi has taken over third place.

LAP 17
Rabat goes down.

FINISH (19 LAPS)
A faultless race from Talmacsi, but further back there is a red-hot battle between Corsi, Cortese and Di Meglio, the three finishing respectively third, fourth and fifth.

CHAMPIONSHIP
The day's big loser is Bradl, tumbling to fourth, but Valencia should be lively as Talmacsi and Corsi fight over second place behind newly-crowned Mike Di Meglio.

GP MALAISIA | 19th October 2008 | Sepang | 5.548 m

STARTING GRID

1	29	A. Iannone	Aprilia	2'14.676
2	1	G. Talmacsi	Aprilia	2'15.206
3	99	D. Webb	Aprilia	2'15.365
4	44	P. Espargaró	Derbi	2'15.676
5	33	S. Gadea	Aprilia	2'15.684
6	6	J. Olivé	Derbi	2'15.860
7	71	T. Koyama	KTM	2'15.922
8	24	S. Corsi	Aprilia	2'16.001
9	63	M. Di Meglio	Derbi	2'16.030
10	17	S. Bradl	Aprilia	2'16.263
11	45	S. Redding	Aprilia	2'16.272
12	18	N. Terol	Aprilia	2'16.314
13	38	B. Smith	Aprilia	2'16.397
14	5	A. Masbou	Loncin	2'16.517
15	51	S. Bonsey	Aprilia	2'16.557
16	7	E. Vazquez	Aprilia	2'16.586
17	22	P. Nieto	KTM	2'16.678
18	11	S. Cortese	Aprilia	2'16.731
19	35	R. De Rosa	KTM	2'16.849
20	8	L. Zanetti	KTM	2'17.272
21	74	T. Nakagami	Aprilia	2'17.418
22	77	D. Aegerter	Derbi	2'17.622
23	16	J. Cluzel	Loncin	2'18.296
24	72	M. Ravaioli	Aprilia	2'18.303
25	12	E. Rabat	KTM	2'18.334
26	36	C. Carillo	Honda	2'18.413 (*)
27	26	A. Martin	Aprilia	2'18.655
28	21	R. Lässer	Aprilia	2'19.002
29	94	J. Folger	KTM	2'19.576
30	56	H. Van Den Berg	Aprilia	2'19.612
31	95	R. Muresan	Aprilia	2'19.688
32	34	R. Krummenacher	KTM	2'19.735
33	28	E. Jerez	KTM	2'19.963
34	48	B. Chesaux	Aprilia	2'20.115

(*): French rider C. Carillo (Honda) suffered a fractured left radius in a heavy fall on Saturday morning.

M. Marquez (E, KTM) suffered a fractured left shin in a fall on Friday morning.

RACE: 19 laps = 105.412 km

1	Gabor Talmacsi	43'00.716 (147.045 km/h)
2	Bradley Smith	+ 3.416
3	Simone Corsi	+ 6.896
4	Sandro Cortese	+ 6.925
5	Mike Di Meglio	+ 7.115
6	Pol Espargaró	+ 15.122
7	Joan Olivé	+ 21.805
8	Dominique Aegerter	+ 21.869
9	Nicolas Terol	+ 21.958
10	Andrea Iannone	+ 23.615
11	Tomoyoshi Koyama	+ 23.651
12	Sergio Gadea	+ 35.224
13	Lorenzo Zanetti	+ 40.502
14	Pablo Nieto	+ 51.404
15	Adrián Martin	+ 55.726
16	Jules Cluzel	+ 56.537
17	Jonas Folger	+ 1'07.140
18	Marco Ravaioli	+ 1'07.573
19	Randy Krummenacher	+ 1'07.741
20	Robin Lässer	+ 1'08.849
21	Bastien Chesaux	+ 1'46.609
22	Robert Muresan	+ 1 lap

Fastest lap
Cortese, in 2'14.589 (148.398 km/h).
Record: Bautistá, in 2'13.118 (150.038 km/h/2006).

Outright fastest lap
Dovizioso, in 2'12.684 (150.529 km/h/2004).

CHAMPIONSHIP

1	M. Di Meglio	248 (4 wins)
2	G. Talmacsi	206 (3 wins)
3	S. Corsi	200 (3 wins)
4	S. Bradl	187 (2 wins)
5	N. Terol	156 (1 win)
6	J. Olivé	142
7	B. Smith	137
8	S. Cortese	130
9	P. Espargaró	124
10	S. Redding	97 (1 win)

The season's final race-winner Casey Stoner makes smoke to celebrate.

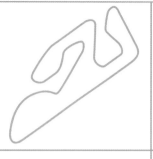

Maybe it would be a good idea if the riders were made of rubber themselves - it might be easier to resist temptation.

STONER:
TOPPED AND TAILED

THE 2007 WORLD CHAMPION WON THE
SEASON-OPENER UNDER LIGHTS IN QATAR
AND DID THE SAME TO BRING THE CURTAIN
DOWN IN VALENCIA.

THE RACE

TURNING A PAGE OF HISTORY

With Stoner and Pedrosa leading from the word go, it was not to be a happy last event for the Michelin man. Farewll, too - for the time being, we hope - to Sylvain Guintoli. Maybe he's just too nice a guy to get on well in this class ?

So there was to be no dramatic last-minute turn of events, the kind the soap opera script-writers like. The heroine didn't change her mind at the eleventh hour, she stuck to her guns, she didn't confound her rivals' schemes, or hit back at the people who were after her hide and couldn't be bothered to hide the fact.

No, the heroine didn't change her mind ; the final curtain fell. That's all, folks. The Michelin man had shut up the Grand Prix shop, beaten one last time, by three riders on three different makes of bike. The results don't lie. So a page of History had been turned. Only time will tell if they were right to drive our heroine away.

Since Monday October 27, 2008, on Valencia's Cheste circuit, all MotoGP participants are on the same rubber. The economic crisis has forced the class to cut back its winter testing too. It's a class that's lost its leading lady, but not its king (Valentino Rossi), nor some of its princes (Casey Stoner, Dani Pedrosa, the promising Andrea Dovizioso and Jorge Lorenzo).

But when the leading lights go out, it's up to the lesser mortals to step forward. We may have faith in the five men mentioned already - but what about the other players ?

Nicky Hayden, for one : it will be interesting to see how he handles the switch from Honda to a Ducati some say is so hard to ride.

Colin Edwards? Nice guy - but his future is behind him.

Chris Vermeulen? So much promise - but will it ever be fulfilled ?

Loris Capirossi? One man who will never sell you short.

James Toseland? A bit of a question-mark : after a flying start he struggled to get his second wind, though everyone is taken with his style - it's a one-off.

Toni Elias? The guy only stirs his stumps two or three times a year - at contract time.

Alex De Angelis? The biggest also-ran of recent years.

Randy De Puniet? Oh dear, more questions than answers, as ever : he's super-quick, but he just can't get his head together.

John Hopkins? Well, we all thought he was a star in the making at Suzuki, but he decided to take the Kawasaki money - and put the brakes on his progress.

Marco Melandri? No point kicking a man when he's down. Suffice it to say that he's found another backer willing to put up a million-dollar contract…

And the rest ? Some old names, like Gibernau, some new, like Kallio, whom we know well from the 125and 250 classes, and Canepa, who's a good lad.

And some have come and gone - Nakano, for instance, or West, and especially Guintoli, and it's a pity about him because he's a nice bloke. Maybe too nice to feel at home amongst this lot.

Happy holidays…

STONER LEADS FROM SIRT LAP TO LAST. SO MUCH FOR EXCITEMENT...

RUNNERS AND RIDERS

Nothing new to note, with all 18 of the year's contracted riders taking the start. The Fiat-Yamahas came to the line with a special livery in Lorenzo's honour, including the colours of the countries where the Spaniard had been a race-winner. And on race day the Repsol Hondas were all-white to mark the oil company's 40 years in racing. A new team was confirmed for 2009 the day before practice got under way, with Gibernau lining up for Onde 2000.

QUALIFYING

Stoner finally saw off Pedrosa to claim his ninth pole position of the season, but a troubled Rossi was only 10th - and Melandri marked his last race start for Ducati with the slowest time of all, meaning the two Desmosedicis were at opposite ends of the grid. This was also Nicky Hayden's swan-song for Honda, as the American reminded us with a few parting shots for 'certain people' (read Alberto Puig).

START

Pedrosa makes his usual good get-away, but Stoner immediately goes to the front. Edwards crosses the line first time in third place from Hayden and Dovizioso. After an off-track excursion De Puniet is last and over 11 seconds adrift.

LAP 2

Hayden has got past Edwards, Rossi is seventh but will soon overtake his old pal Capirossi.

LAP 4

Rossi pulls a classic pass on Dovizioso under braking for fifth as Stoner now leads Pedrosa by 0.569.

LAP 6

Rossi passes Edwards, Dovizioso follows suit ; soon after, the World Champion gobbles up Hayden to go third, 3.394 seconds behind Pedrosa.

HALF-DISTANCE (15 LAPS)

There's not much to get excited about for those trackside or watching on the couch at home. Stoner now has a 2.603-second lead over Pedrosa, who in turn has 4.076 on Rossi. There's some fun going on further back as Lorenzo, De Angelis, Toseland, Melandri and Hopkins fight it out for ninth.

LAP 24

No, we haven't forgotten you - it's just that there's not a lot to report other than Melandri taking 10th spot from De Angelis.

LAP 29

Melandri has just slipped up ; Lorenzo takes eighth from Capirossi.

FINISH (30 LAPS)

Stoner is a handy 5.141 seconds clear of Pedrosa as they start the last lap and the 2007 World Champion ends the season as he began it - with another win. Otherwise it was a pretty dull affair.

CHAMPIONSHIP

Rossi, Stoner, Pedrosa, Lorenzo and Dovizioso: the top five in the 2008 Championship reflect the state of affairs with three big names and two outstanding rookies up there. And behind them…
Well, have a good winter break, everyone !

Pedrosa, his Honda liveried in honour of Repsol's 40 years in racing, fought off Valentino Rossi ; Sylvain Guintoli (below) passes the World Champion's pit.

GP VALENCIA | 26th October 2008 | Cheste | 4.005 m

STARTING GRID				
1	1	C. Stoner	Ducati	1'31.502
2	2	D. Pedrosa	Honda	1'31.555
3	69	N. Hayden	Honda	1'31.703
4	5	C. Edwards	Yamaha	1'32.212
5	52	J. Toseland	Yamaha	1'32.518
6	14	R. De Puniet	Honda	1'32.572
7	48	J. Lorenzo	Yamaha	1'32.594
8	65	L. Capirossi	Suzuki	1'32.614
9	4	A. Dovizioso	Honda	1'32.734
10	46	V. Rossi	Yamaha	1'32.962
11	24	T. Elias	Ducati	1'32.983
12	7	C. Vermeulen	Suzuki	1'33.017
13	50	S. Guintoli	Ducati	1'33.352
14	21	J. Hopkins	Kawasaki	1'33.681
15	56	S. Nakano	Honda	1'33.767
16	15	A. De Angelis	Honda	1'33.848
17	13	A. West	Kawasaki	1'33.879
18	33	M. Melandri	Ducati	1'34.174

RACE: 30 laps = 120.150 km		
1	Casey Stoner	46'46.114 (154.141 km/h)
2	Daniel Pedrosa	+ 3.390
3	Valentino Rossi	+ 12.194
4	Andrea Dovizioso	+ 24.159
5	Nicky Hayden	+ 26.232
6	Colin Edwards	+ 32.209
7	Shinya Nakano	+ 34.571
8	Jorge Lorenzo	+ 35.661
9	Loris Capirossi	+ 38.228
10	Alex De Angelis	+ 47.583
11	James Toseland	+ 52.107
12	Sylvain Guintoli	+ 52.350
13	Chris Vermeulen	+ 52.833
14	John Hopkins	+ 53.227
15	Randy De Puniet	+ 53.411
16	Marco Melandri	+ 1'08.387
17	Anthony West	+ 1'11.181
18	Toni Elias	+ 1'37.055

Fastest lap
Stoner, in 1'32.582 (155.732 km/h). New record.
Previous: Pedrosa, in 1'32.748 (155.453 km/h/2007).

Outright fastest lap
Rossi, in 1'31.002 (158.436 km/h/2006).

CHAMPIONSHIP		
1	V. Rossi	373 (9 wins)
2	C. Stoner	280 (6 wins)
3	D. Pedrosa	249 (2 wins)
4	J. Lorenzo	190 (1 win)
5	A. Dovizioso	174
6	N. Hayden	155
7	C. Edwards	144
8	C. Vermeulen	128
9	S. Nakano	126
10	L. Capirossi	118

WORLD CHAMPION MARCO SIMONCELLI CELEBRATES HIS TITLE IN FINE STYLE

RUNNERS AND RIDERS

As we all wondered how many riders would be competing in this class in 2009, in came Hungarian Alen Gyorfi as substitute for Barbera. There were wild cards for Italy's Sandi and German rider Wirsing.

QUALIFYING

We got just one dry day, Saturday, and it gave us a superb duel between Alex Debon and Marco Simoncelli. The World Champion came out on top by just 10-thousandths of a second.

Simon and Kallio, the latter having destroyed a KTM the day before, made up the front row. On Saturday afternoon Luthi's number 12 Aprilia sported the livery of his sponsor the Emmi group's new energy drink.

START

Kallio and Simon are quickest away from Debon and a red-hot Locatelli, from eighth on the grid. Sandi doesn't finish the opening lap, Abraham gets there in the end after losing a lot of time.

LAP 2

Kallio has 0.104 on Simon, 0.344 on Locatelli, but Luthi, whose bike just stopped, has slipped back five spots.

LAP 4

The season's two main men Bautista and Simoncelli have caught the leading trio, meaning there are now five riders blanketed by just one second.

LAP 7

Simon leads as Simoncelli and Bautista battle for third place.

LAP 9

Simocelli has taken charge and now has 0.334 in hand over Kallio, followed by Simon and Takahashi as Bautista drops back.

HALF-DISTANCE (13 LAPS)

Pesek has just gone down ; up front, World Champion Simoncelli has a 0.397-second edge over Kallio, who has Takahashi right with him. Simon is fourth as Bautista and Locatelli squabble over fifth.

LAP 18

Just 0.305 covers Simoncelli, Kallio and Takahashi but behind them there is a big gap to Simon, now nearly three seconds down, as Bautista is unable to shake off Locatelli.

LAP 20

Simon breaks down ; up front,

Kallio has just set fastest race lap and is 0.154 adrift of Simoncelli.

LAP 22

Debon goes down, and Simoncelli is now a comfortable seven-tenths in front.

LAP 25

Takahashi has let them go - but not Kallio, now less than two-tenths behind Simoncelli.

FINISH (27 LAPS)

They go into the last lap with just 0.230 between them until the Finn gets it all wrong, recovering to 11th place. It's the icing on the cake for World Champion Simoncelli.

CHAMPIONSHIP

Ride of the day comes from Locatelli, an excellent fourth, good enough to pip both Simon and Luthi as the Swiss rider drops out of the top 10.

This was the big battle of the day between Simoncelli (58) and Kallio, but the Finn got it all wrong on the last lap. Thomas Luthi's Aprilia (opposite) as you will never see it again : in the colours of the Swiss rider's sponsor's energy drink. Above : the last podium of the year.

GP VALENCIA | 26th October | Cheste | 4.005 m

STARTING GRID

1	58	M. Simoncelli	Gilera	1'35.408
2	6	A. Debón	Aprilia	1'35.418
3	60	J. Simón	KTM	1'35.964
4	36	M. Kallio	KTM	1'36.194
5	4	H. Aoyama	KTM	1'36.267
6	19	A. Bautistá	Aprilia	1'36.419
7	14	R. Wilairot	Honda	1'36.568
8	15	R. Locatelli	Gilera	1'36.573
9	55	H. Faubel	Aprilia	1'36.635
10	72	Y. Takahashi	Honda	1'36.654
11	12	T. Lüthi	Aprilia	1'36.832
12	41	A. Espargaró	Aprilia	1'36.841
13	52	L. Pesek	Aprilia	1'36.892
14	75	M. Pasini	Aprilia	1'37.047
15	32	F. Lai	Gilera	1'37.400
16	25	A. Baldolini	Aprilia	1'37.455
17	35	S. Grotzkyj	Gilera	1'37.803
18	10	I. Toth	Aprilia	1'38.245
19	90	F. Sandi	Aprilia	1'38.592
20	17	K. Abraham	Aprilia	1'38.641
21	43	M. Hernandez	Aprilia	1'38.874
22	92	D. Arcas	Aprilia	1'40.593
23	45	D.-T. Pradita	Yamaha	1'40.593
24	93	A. Gyorfi	Aprilia	1'41.075
25	94	T. Wirsing	Honda	1'41.974

RACE: 27 laps = 108.135 km

1	Marco Simoncelli	43'29.003 (149.208 km/h)
2	Yuki Takahashi	+ 5.164
3	Alvaro Bautistá	+ 8.648
4	Roberto Locatelli	+ 15.605
5	Hiroshi Aoyama	+ 20.991
6	Hector Faubel	+ 22.212
7	Aleix Espargaró	+ 23.199
8	Ratthapark Wilairot	+ 23.321
9	Mattia Pasini	+ 37.424
10	Thomas Lüthi	+ 38.887
11	Mika Kallio	+ 44.065
12	Alex Baldolini	+ 1'10.999
13	Imre Toth	+ 1'31.950
14	Daniel Arcas	+ 1'39.110
15	Simone Grozkyj	+ 1'41.209
16	Manuel Hernandez	+ 1 lap
17	Karel Abraham	+ 1 lap
18	Federico Sandi	+ 1 lap
19	Doni Tata Pradita	+ 1 lap

Fastest lap

Kallio, in 1'35.890 (150.359 km/h).
Record: Kallio, in 1'35.659 (150.722 km/h/2007).

Outright fastest lap

H. Aoyama, in 1'35.109 (151.594 km/h/2006).

CHAMPIONSHIP

1	M. Simoncelli	281 (6 wins)
2	A. Bautistá	244 (4 wins)
3	M. Kallio	196 (3 wins)
4	A. Debón	176 (2 wins)
5	Y. Takahashi	167
6	H. Barberá	142
7	H. Aoyama	139
8	M. Pasini	132 (1 win)
9	R. Locatelli	110
10	J. Simón	109

AS CORSI MAKES SURE OF THE RUNNER-UP SPOT, PABLO NIETO CALLS IT A DAY

RUNNERS AND RIDERS

There was no replacement for Marc Marquez following his injury in Malaysia, while Michael Ranseder's Aprilia went to Italian and European champion Lorenzo Savadori. It was new for old, sort of, in the French Federation team, where Louis Rossi, shown the door after Indianapolis, was back on the Honda with Carrillo being injured at Sepang.

QUALIFYING

« Pole or bust », joked former World Champion Gabor Talmacsi's crew as they approached his final 125cc race in good spirits. The Hungarian duly obliged. Pol Espargaro gave us a major scare when he went down after contact with Rabat, but the young Spaniard emerged relatively unscathed, though unable to take the race start.

START

Talmacsi and Nicolas Terol are in front by the first corner, Terol leading at the end of the opening lap from Talmacsi, Sergio Gadea, Simone Corsi and Mike Di Meglio.

LAP 3

Stefan Bradl goes down and takes Gadea with him, leaving Corsi and Terol out front on their own. Sandro Cortese has taken over in third. Aegerter, confirmed as a works Derbi rider for next year the previous day, retires after a fall of his own.

LAP 5

There are just 220-thousandths between Corsi and Terol, with World Champion Di Meglio in third and fastest man among the leading group.

LAP 7

Di Meglio is right behind Terol and bringing Cortese with him, while Talmacsi has just come off.

LAP 9

Di Meglio is now second in a five-man leading bunch made up of Corsi, Di Meglio, Terol, Cortese and Smith. Raffaele De Rosa goes down.

HALF-DISTANCE (12 LAPS)

That's what you call a World Champion ! Di Meglio has gone to the front, with Corsi right behind him. Cortese is third, 0.778 away, with Terol virtually riding pillion in fourth. Fifth man Smith has been dropped but has four seconds in hand over Bonsey, his nearest pursuer.

LAP 15

We have a leading group again as only 0.530 covers Di Meglio, Corsi, Cortese and Terol. Meanwhile Olive is out.

LAP 18

As Corsi and Di Meglio go at it hammer and tongs, Smith has got back in touch.

FINISH (24 LAPS)

A mistake by Di Meglio, losing the front on the second-last lap, has let Simone Corsi into the lead for the final lap, 0.214 ahead of team-mate Terol and 0.540 clear of the World Champion. That's the finishing order.

CHAMPIONSHIP

Corsi finishes as runner-up as the other contenders, Talmacsi and Bradl, end their seasons with a no-score.

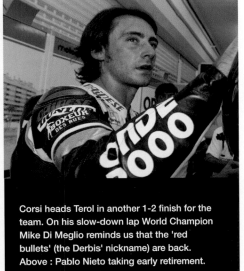

Corsi heads Terol in another 1-2 finish for the team. On his slow-down lap World Champion Mike Di Meglio reminds us that the 'red bullets' (the Derbis' nickname) are back. Above : Pablo Nieto taking early retirement.

GP VALENCIA | 26th October | Cheste | 4.005 m

STARTING GRID

1	1	G. Talmacsi	Aprilia	1'41.451
2	33	S. Gadea	Aprilia	1'41.641
3	24	S. Corsi	Aprilia	1'41.951
4	18	N. Terol	Aprilia	1'42.049
5	38	B. Smith	Aprilia	1'42.095
6	51	S. Bonsey	Aprilia	1'42.099
7	63	M. Di Meglio	Derbi	1'42.163
8	29	A. Iannone	Aprilia	1'42.237
9	77	D. Aegerter	Derbi	1'42.503
10	17	S. Bradl	Aprilia	1'42.589
11	11	S. Cortese	Aprilia	1'42.636
12	12	E. Rabat	KTM	1'42.654
13	99	D. Webb	Aprilia	1'42.908
14	6	J. Olivé	Derbi	1'42.969
15	71	T. Koyama	KTM	1'43.017
16	8	L. Zanetti	KTM	1'43.037
17	45	S. Redding	Aprilia	1'43.133
18	22	P. Nieto	KTM	1'43.358
19	35	R. De Rosa	KTM	1'43.499
20	74	T. Nakagami	Aprilia	1'43.706
21	34	R. Krummenacher	KTM	1'43.843
22	7	E. Vazquez	Aprilia	1'44.018
23	5	A. Masbou	Loncin	1'44.061
24	26	A. Martin	Aprilia	1'44.193
25	16	J. Cluzel	Loncin	1'44.232
26	40	L. Savadori	Aprilia	1'44.333
27	28	E. Jerez	KTM	1'44.405
28	75	R. Cardus	Deri	1'44.530
29	23	J. Miralles	Aprilia	1'44.785
30	44	P. Espargaró	Derbi	1'44.954
31	72	M. Ravaioli	Aprilia	1'45.132
32	21	R. Lässer	Aprilia	1'45.231

33	78	D. Saez	Aprilia	1'45.290
34	95	R. Muresan	Aprilia	1'45.380
35	69	L. Rossi	Honda	1'45.495
36	30	P. Tutusaus	Aprilia	1'45.774
37	94	J. Folger	KTM	1'45.976
38	56	H. Van Den Berg	Aprilia	1'46.098
39	48	B. Chesaux	Aprilia	1'46.749
40	25	C. Trabalon	Aprilia	1'48.306

RACE: 24 laps = 96.120 km

1	Simone Corsi	40'45.715 (141.485 km/h)
2	Nicolas Terol	+ 0.106
3	Mike Di Meglio	+ 0.223
4	Bradley Smith	+ 0.776
5	Sandro Cortese	+ 1.333
6	Andrea Iannone	+ 21.578
7	Tomoyoshi Koyama	+ 29.387
8	Scott Redding	+ 29.419
9	Pablo Nieto	+ 38.059
10	Esteve Rabat	+ 38.481
11	Lorenzo Zanetti	+ 38.941
12	Efren Vazquez	+ 48.466
13	Lorenzo Savadori	+ 48.802
14	Alexis Mabou	+ 50.340
15	Enrique Jerez	+ 50.575
16	Takaaki Nakagami	+ 52.220
17	Randy Krummenacher	+ 55.047
18	Jonas Folger	+ 55.139
19	Jules Cluzel	+ 55.546
20	Marco Ravaioli	+ 1'00.289
21	Robert Muresan	+ 1'10.142
22	Bastien Chesaux	+ 1'26.165

23	Louis Rossi	+ 1'26.407
24	Daniel Saez	+ 1'41.720
25	Cristian Trabalon	+ 1 lap

Fastest lap
Di Meglio, in 1'40.901 (142.892 km/h).
Record: Faubel, in 1'39.380 (145.079 km/h/2007).

Outright fastest lap
Talmacsi, in 1'39.029 (145.029 km/h/2007).

CHAMPIONSHIP

1	M. Di Meglio	263 (4 wins)
2	S. Corsi	225 (4 wins)
3	G. Talmacsi	206 (3 wins)
4	S. Bradl	187 (2 wins)
5	N. Terol	176 (1 win)
6	B. Smith	150
7	J. Olivé	142
8	S. Cortese	141
9	P. Espargaró	124
10	A. Iannone	106

1			2	3	4	5	6	7	8	9	10
1	ROSSI VALENTINO	ITA	373	18	2	10	9	16	18	1	-
2	STONER CASEY	AUS	280	18	9	13	6	11	15	1	2
3	PEDROSA DANIEL	SPA	249	17	2	9	2	11	15	1	2
4	LORENZO JORGE	SPA	190	17	4	8	1	6	13	1	4
5	DOVIZIOSO ANDREA	ITA	174	18	-	-	-	1	17	3	1
6	HAYDEN NICKY	USA	155	16	-	5	-	2	15	2	1
7	EDWARDS COLIN	USA	144	18	1	5	-	2	16	3	2
8	VERMEULEN CHRIS	AUS	128	18	-	1	-	2	15	3	2
9	NAKANO SHINYA	JPN	126	18	-	-	-	-	17	4	-
10	CAPIROSSI LORIS	ITA	118	16	-	1	-	1	14	3	1
11	TOSELAND JAMES	GBR	105	18	-	1	-	-	14	6	2
12	ELIAS TONI	SPA	92	18	-	-	-	2	15	2	1
13	GUINTOLI SYLVAIN	FRA	67	18	-	-	-	-	17	6	-
14	DE ANGELIS ALEX	RSM	63	18	-	-	-	-	11	4	5
15	DE PUNIET RANDY	FRA	61	18	-	-	-	-	12	6	5
16	HOPKINS JOHN	USA	57	15	-	1	-	-	12	5	3
17	MELANDRI MARCO	ITA	51	18	-	-	-	-	10	5	2
18	WEST ANTHONY	AUS	50	18	-	-	-	-	12	5	1
19	SPIES BEN	USA	20	3	-	-	-	-	3	6	-
20	HACKING JAMIE	USA	5	1	-	-	-	-	1	11	-
21	OKADA TADAYUKI	JPN	2	1	-	-	-	-	1	14	-

1 Final Championship Classification **2** Number of points **3** Number of qualifications (out of 18 GP) **4** Number of pole positions **5** Number of front row starts
6 Number of victories **7** Number of podiums **8** Score points (top 15) **9** Best race finish **10** Number of retirements

FINAL CONSTRUCTOR'S WORLDS CHAMPIONSHIP CLASSIFICATION

1	YAMAHA	402
2	DUCATI	321
3	HONDA	315
4	SUZUKI	161
5	KAWASAKI	88

ROOKIE OF THE YEAR

1	LORENZO JORGE	190
2	DOVIZIOSO ANDREA	174
3	TOSELAND JAMES	105
4	DE ANGELIS ALEX	63

FINAL TEAMS WORLDS CHAMPIONSHIP CLASSIFICATION

1	FIAT YAMAHA TEAM	563
2	REPSOL HONDA TEAM	404
3	DUCATI MARLBORO TEAM	331
4	TECH 3 YAMAHA	249
5	RIZLA SUZUKI MOTOGP	248
6	S.CARLO HONDA GRESINI	189
7	JIR TEAM SCOT MOTOGP	174
8	ALICE TEAM	159
9	KAWASAKI RACING TEAM	112
10	LCR HONDA MOTOGP	61

1			2	3	4	5	6	7	8	9	10
1 SIMONCELLI MARCO	ITA		281	16	7	14	6	12	14	1	2
2 BAUTISTÁ ALVARO	SPA		244	16	5	11	4	11	14	1	2
3 KALLIO MIKA	FIN		196	16	-	11	3	6	13	1	3
4 DEBÓN ALEX	ESP		176	16	2	9	2	4	12	1	4
5 TAKAHASHI YUKI	JPN		167	16	-	1	-	3	15	2	1
6 BARBERÁ HECTOR	SPA		142	12	2	10	-	4	11	2	1
7 AOYAMA HIROSHI	JPN		139	16	1	3	-	2	13	2	2
8 PASINI MATTIA	ITA		132	16	-	2	1	4	10	1	6
9 LOCATELLI ROBERTO	ITA		110	16	-	-	-	-	14	4	2
10 SIMÓN JULIAN	SPA		109	16	-	3	-	-	13	4	3
11 LÜTHI THOMAS	SWI		108	14	-	3	-	2	11	2	3
12 ESPARGARÓ ALEIX	SPA		92	16	-	1	-	-	13	5	2
13 WILAIROT RATTHAPARK	THA		73	16	-	-	-	-	14	8	-
14 FAUBEL HECTÓR	SPA		64	16	-	-	-	-	11	6	5
15 PESEK LUKAS	CZE		43	16	-	-	-	-	10	9	6
16 ABRAHAM KAREL	CZE		40	14	-	-	-	-	7	7	5
17 BALDOLINI ALEX	ITA		35	16	-	-	-	-	10	11	4
18 LAI FABRIZIO	ITA		33	16	-	-	-	-	10	10	4
19 POGGIALI MANUEL	RSM		16	9	-	-	-	-	4	6	4
20 TOTH IMRE	HUN		9	15	-	-	-	-	5	13	4
21 LAVERTY EUGENE	IRL		6	12	-	-	-	-	4	13	5
22 SANDI FEDERICO	ITA		6	7	-	-	-	-	2	12	2
23 HERNANDEZ MANUEL	SPA		5	7	-	-	-	-	2	13	2
24 GROTZKYJ SIMONE	ITA		5	5	-	-	-	-	4	14	1
25 ARCAS DANIEL	SPA		2	5	-	-	-	-	1	14	1
26 TOMIZAWA SHOYA	JPN		2	1	-	-	-	-	1	14	-
27 WIRSING TONI	GER		2	4	-	-	-	-	1	14	1
28 PRADITA DONI TATA	INA		1	16	-	-	-	-	1	15	-

1 Final Championship Classification   2 Number of points   3 Number of qualifications (out of 16 GP)   4 Number of pole positions   5 Number of front row starts
6 Number of victories   7 Number of podiums   8 Score points (top 15)   9 Best race finish   10 Number of retirements

FINAL CONSTRUCTOR'S WORLDS CHAMPIONSHIP CLASSIFICATION

1 APRILIA	343
2 GILERA	300
3 KTM	245
4 HONDA	174
5 YAMAHA	1

ROOKIE OF THE YEAR

1 PASINI MATTIA	132
2 FAUBEL HECTOR	64
3 PESEK LUKAS	43
4 PRADITA DONI TATA	1

MICHEL MÉTRAUX TROPHY (BEST PRIVATE RIDER)

1 TAKAHASHI YUKI	JPN	167
2 SIMÓN JULIAN	SPA	109
3 ESPARGARÓ ALEIX	SPA	92
4 WILAIROT RATTHAPARK	THA	73
5 FAUBEL HECTÓR	SPA	64
6 PESEK LUKAS	CZE	43
7 ABRAHAM KAREL	CZE	40
8 BALDOLINI ALEX	ITA	35
9 LAI FABRIZIO	ITA	33
10 POGGIALI MANUEL	RSM	16
11 TOTH IMRE	HUN	9
12 LAVERTY EUGENE	IRL	6
13 GROTZKYJ SIMONE	ITA	5
14 HERNANDEZ MANUEL	SPA	3
15 ARCAS DANIEL	SPA	2
16 PRADITA DONI TATA	INA	1

1		2	3	4	5	6	7	8	9	10
1 DI MEGLIO MIKE	FRA	264	17	2	8	4	9	16	1	1
2 CORSI SIMONE	ITA	225	17	3	6	4	7	16	1	1
3 TALMACSI GABOR	HUN	206	17	4	10	3	9	14	1	3
4 BRADL STEFAN	GER	187	17	-	6	2	6	13	1	4
5 TERÓL NICOLAS	SPA	176	17	-	8	1	5	14	1	2
6 SMITH BRADLEY	GBR	150	17	3	9	-	4	12	2	4
7 OLIVÉ JOAN	SPA	142	16	-	1	-	4	13	2	4
8 CORTESE SANDRO	GER	141	17	-	1	-	-	16	4	-
9 ESPARGARÓ POL	SPA	124	14	2	5	-	3	11	2	2
10 IANNONE ANDREA	ITA	106	17	1	2	1	1	12	1	4
11 REDDING SCOTT	GBR	105	17	-	4	1	1	11	1	5
12 GADEA SERGIO	SPA	83	17	1	3	1	1	9	1	6
13 MARQUEZ MARC	SPA	63	13	-	-	-	1	7	3	4
14 RABAT ESTEVE	SPA	49	16	-	-	-	-	8	6	4
15 BONSEY STEVE	USA	46	17	-	1	-	-	6	4	7
16 AEGERTER DOMINIQUE	SWI	45	17	-	-	-	-	8	8	2
17 KOYAMA TOMOYOSHI	JPN	41	16	-	-	-	-	8	6	5
18 DE ROSA RAFFAELE	ITA	37	17	1	1	-	-	8	9	9
19 WEBB DANIEL	GBR	35	15	-	3	-	-	6	5	8
20 VAZQUEZ EFRÉN	SPA	31	15	-	-	-	-	8	10	3
21 NIETO PABLO	SPA	25	16	-	-	-	-	5	5	7
22 ZANETTI LORENZO	ITA	22	17	-	-	-	-	5	7	8
23 RANSEDER MICHAEL	AUT	22	14	-	-	-	-	7	7	4
24 NAKAGAMI TAKAAKI	JPN	12	17	-	-	-	-	3	8	6
25 KRUMMENACHER R.	SWI	10	13	-	-	-	-	3	10	2
26 TUTUSAUS PERE	SPA	9	12	-	-	-	-	3	12	1
27 BIANCO STEFANO	ITA	8	8	-	-	-	-	2	11	3
28 MASBOU ALEXIS	FRA	4	17	-	-	-	-	3	14	7
29 SAVADORI LORENZO	ITA	3	2	-	-	-	-	1	13	-
30 SCHRÖTTER MARCEL	GER	3	1	-	-	-	-	1	13	-
31 LÄSSER ROBIN	GER	2	15	-	-	-	-	2	15	5
32 JEREZ ENRIQUE	SPA	1	3	-	-	-	-	1	15	1
33 MARTIN ADRIÁN	SPA	1	5	-	-	-	-	1	15	2
34 FOLGER JONAS	GER	1	6	-	-	-	-	1	15	1
35 VAN DEN BERG HUGO	NED	1	17	-	-	-	-	1	15	9

1 Final Championship Classification **2** Number of points **3** Number of qualifications (out of 17 GP) **4** Number of pole positions **5** Number of front row starts **6** Number of victories **7** Number of podiums **8** Score points (top 15) **9** Best race finish **10** Number of retirements

FINAL CONSTRUCTOR'S WORLDS CHAMPIONSHIP CLASSIFICATION

1	APRILIA	401
2	DERBI	319
3	KTM	123
4	LONCIN	4
5	HONDA	3

ROOKIE OF THE YEAR

1	REDDING SCOTT	GBR	105
2	MARQUEZ MARC	SPA	63
3	VAZQUEZ EFREN	SPA	31
4	NAKAGAMI TAKAAKI	JPN	9
5	LÄSSER ROBIN	GER	2

MICHEL MÉTRAUX TROPHY (BEST PRIVATE RIDER)

1	TERÓL NICOLAS	SPA	176
2	IANNONE ANDREA	ITA	106
3	REDDING SCOTT	GBR	105
4	MARQUEZ MARC	SPA	63
5	RABAT ESTEVE	SPA	49
6	BONSEY STEVE	USA	46
7	AEGERTER DOMINIQUE	SWI	45
8	DE ROSA RAFFAELE	ITA	37
9	WEBB DANIEL	GBR	35
10	VAZQUEZ EFRÉN	SPA	31
11	ZANETTI LORENZO	ITA	22
12	RANSEDER MICHAEL	AUT	22
13	NAKAGAMI TAKAAKI	JPN	12
14	TUTUSAUS PERE	SPA	9
15	BIANCO STEFANO	ITA	8
16	SAVADORI LORENZO	ITA	3
17	LÄSSER ROBIN	GER	2
18	MARTIN ADRIÁN	SPA	1
19	VAN DEN BERG HUGO	NED	1

THE RESULTS OF
THE OTHER CHAMPIONSHIPS

THE MOST COMPREHENSIVE STATISTICS
SECTION GOING, FROM THE SUPERBIKE
WORLD CHAMPIONSHIP TO THE SWISS
NATIONAL SERIES, TAKING IN GERMANY,
FRANCE, ITALY, THE UNITED STATES, GREAT
BRITAIN AND SPAIN.

SUPERBIKE WORLD CHAMPIONSHIP

February 23 - Doha - Qatar

Race I: 1. T. Bayliss (AUS, Ducati), 18 laps, 36'11.468 (160.548 km/h); 2. M. Biaggi (I, Ducati), 0.396; 3. T. Corser (AUS, Yamaha), 1.878; 4. R. Xaus (E, Ducati), 4.487; 5. M. Neukirchner (D, Suzuki), 7.505; 6. C. Checa (E, Honda), 9.639; 7. A. Gonzales-Nieto (E, Suzuki), 9.725; 8. Y. Kagayama (J, Suzuki), 19.537; 9. M. Fabrizio (I, Ducati), 23.156; 10.J. Smrz (CZ, Ducati), 24.429; 11. R. Rolfo (I, Honda), 27.595; 12. K. Sofuoglu (TUR, Honda), 27.979; 13. G. Lavilla (E, Honda), 28.237; 14. N. Haga (J, Yamaha), 30.205; 15. R. Laconi (F, Kawasaki), 31.882. 25 finishers. Fastest lap: N. Haga (J, Yamaha), 1'59.217 (162.460 km/h).

Race II: 1. A. Gonzales-Nieto (E, Suzuki), 18 laps, 36'12.963 (160.437 km/h); 2. R. Xaus (E, Ducati), 0.301; 3. M. Biaggi (I, Ducati), 1.321; 4. T. Bayliss (AUS, Ducati), 6.452; 5. M. Fabrizio (I, Ducati), 7.627; 6. L. Lanzi (I, Ducati), 9.117; 7. T. Corser (AUS, Yamaha), 10.806; 8. M. Neukirchner (D, Suzuki), 11.661; 9. J. Smrz (CZ, Ducati), 13.269; 10. K. Sofuoglu (TUR, Honda), 14.563; 11. C. Checa (E, Honda), 15.953; 12. M. Tamada (J, Kawasaki), 16.748; 13. N. Haga (J, Yamaha), 18.356; 14. G. Lavilla (E, Honda), 26.311; 15. R. Rolfo (I, Honda), 26.560. 22 finishers. Fastest lap: A. Gonzales-Nieto (E, Suzuki), 1'59.156 (162.543 km/h).

March 2 - Phillip Island - Australia

Race I: 1. T. Bayliss (AUS, Ducati), 22 laps, 34'22.933 (170.652 km/h); 2. T. Corser (AUS, Yamaha), 4.221; 3. M. Fabrizio (I, Ducati), 4.738; 4. R. Xaus (E, Ducati), 5.171; 5. A. Gonzales-Nieto (E, Suzuki), 5.543; 6. C. Checa (E, Honda), 5.895; 7. M. Neukirchner (D, Suzuki), 5.964; 8. N. Haga (J, Yamaha), 14.826; 9. R. Kiyonari (J, Honda), 18.899; 10. R. Rolfo (I, Honda), 20.633; 11. G. Lavilla (E, Honda), 21.601; 12. K. Muggeridge (AUS, Honda), 29.281; 13. L. Lanzi (I, Ducati), 29.500; 14. K. Sofuoglu (TUR, Honda), 30.030; 15. S. Nakatomi (J, Yamaha), 30.223. 18 finishers. Fastest lap: T. Bayliss (AUS, Ducati), 1'32.516 (172.965 km/h).

Race II: 1. T. Bayliss (AUS, Ducati), 22 laps, 34'35.284 (169.637 km/h); 2. C. Checa (E, Honda), 1.127; 3. A. Gonzales-Nieto (E, Suzuki), 4.395; 4. R. Xaus (E, Ducati), 6.621; 5. M. Neukirchner (D, Suzuki), 11.550; 6. R. Kiyonari (J, Honda), 11.620; 7. N. Haga (J, Yamaha), 12.049; 8. G. Lavilla (E, Honda), 12.134; 9. R. Holland (AUS, Honda), 13.462; 10. K. Muggeridge (AUS, Honda), 15.519; 11. K. Sofuoglu (TUR, Honda), 16.225; 12. D. Checa (E, Yamaha), 21.959; 13. S. Gimbert (F, Yamaha), 21.989; 14. M. Tamada (J, Kawasaki), 29.106; 15. S. Nakatomi (J, Yamaha), 29.219. 21 finishers. Fastest lap: M. Biaggi (I, Ducati), 1'33.477 (171.186 km/h).

April 6 - Spain - Valencia

Race I: 1. L. Lanzi (I, Ducati), 23 laps, 37'01.894 (149.248 km/h); 2. T. Bayliss (AUS, Ducati), 2.987; 3. T. Corser (AUS, Yamaha), 7.287; 4. A. Gonzales-Nieto (E, Suzuki), 11.992; 5. C. Checa (E, Honda), 12.824; 6. K. Muggeridge (AUS, Honda), 13.125; 7. G. Lavilla (E, Honda), 13.191; 8. R. Laconi (F, Kawasaki), 13.906; 9. M. Tamada (J, Kawasaki), 17.254; 10. R. Rolfo (I, Honda), 18.606; 11. S. Nakatomi (J, Yamaha), 19.858; 12. K. Sofuoglu (TUR, Honda), 23.350; 13. R. Holland (AUS, Honda), 23.577; 14. J. Smrz (CZ, Ducati), 24.082; 15. D. Checa (E, Yamaha), 26.611. 20 finishers. Fastest lap: N. Haga (J, Yamaha), 1'35.131 (151.559 km/h).

Race II: 1. N. Haga (J, Yamaha), 23 laps, 37'03.759 (149.123 km/h); 2. T. Bayliss (AUS, Ducati), 1.551; 3. C. Checa (E, Honda), 2.903; 4. R. Kiyonari (J, Honda), 7.277; 5. T. Corser (AUS, Yamaha), 8.051; 6. Y. Kagayama (J, Suzuki), 9.223; 7. R. Xaus (E, Ducati), 10.164; 8. M. Biaggi (I, Ducati), 10.614; 9. R. Laconi (F, Kawasaki), 17.234; 10. A. Gonzales-Nieto (E, Suzuki), 18.100; 11. G. Lavilla (E, Honda), 18.288; 12. L. Lanzi (I, Ducati), 18.826; 13. M. Fabrizio (I, Ducati), 21.770; 14. J. Smrz (CZ, Ducati), 22.872; 15. K. Sofuoglu (TUR, Honda), 25.224. 25 finishers. Fastest lap: C. Checa (E, Honda), 1'35.322 (151.256 km/h).

April 27 - Netherlands - Assen

Race I: 1. T. Bayliss (AUS, Ducati), 22 laps, 36'50.907 (163.171 km/h); 2. C. Checa (E, Honda), 2.132; 3. M. Neukirchner (D, Suzuki), 2.179; 4. Y. Kagayama (J, Suzuki), 10.919; 5. T. Corser (AUS, Yamaha), 11.051; 6. J. Smrz (CZ, Ducati), 11.979; 7. R. Kiyonari (J, Honda), 15.184; 8. M. Tamada (J, Kawasaki), 18.395; 9. G. Lavilla (E, Honda), 18.634; 10. M. Biaggi (I, Ducati), 20.699; 11. R. Laconi (F, Kawasaki), 25.759; 12. K. Sofuoglu (TUR, Honda), 26.064; 13. A. Badovini (I, Kawasaki), 35.582; 14. K. Muggeridge (AUS, Honda), 36.266; 15. S. Nakatomi (J, Yamaha), 37.215. 22 finishers. Fastest lap: M. Neukirchner (D, Suzuki), 1'39.395 (164.978 km/h).

Race II: 1. T. Bayliss (AUS, Ducati), 22 laps, 36'46.238 (163.516 km/h); 2. N. Haga (J, Yamaha), 0.082; 3. C. Checa (E, Honda), 6.336; 4. R. Xaus (E, Ducati), 7.575; 5. M. Neukirchner (D, Suzuki), 8.011; 6. Y. Kagayama (J, Suzuki), 13.999; 7. G. Lavilla (E, Honda), 15.215; 8. J. Smrz (CZ, Ducati), 16.376; 9. M. Tamada (J, Kawasaki), 17.269; 10. T. Corser (AUS, Yamaha), 18.380; 11. A. Gonzales-Nieto (E, Suzuki), 18.926; 12. M. Biaggi (I, Ducati), 21.452; 13. K. Muggeridge (AUS, Honda), 23.794; 14. R. Rolfo (I, Honda), 29.847; 15. S. Nakatomi (J, Yamaha), 30.252. 23 finishers. Fastest lap: T. Bayliss (AUS, Ducati), 1'39.562 (164.701 km/h).

May 11 - Italy - Monza

Race I: 1. M. Neukirchner (D, Suzuki), 18 laps, 32'02.851 (195.224 km/h); 2. N. Haga (J, Yamaha), 0.058; 3. T. Bayliss (AUS, Ducati), 0.672; 4. Y. Kagayama (J, Suzuki), 0.771; 5. M. Biaggi (I, Ducati), 3.869; 6. R. Kiyonari (J, Honda), 5.995; 7. A. Gonzales-Nieto (E, Suzuki), 8.788; 8. C. Checa (E, Honda), 9.374; 9. M. Fabrizio (I, Ducati), 10.667; 10. J. Smrz (CZ, Ducati), 10.771; 11. G. Lavilla (E, Honda), 12.180; 12. T. Corser (AUS, Yamaha), 14.719; 13. S. Nakatomi (J, Yamaha), 32.734; 14. L. Lanzi (I, Ducati), 36.550; 15. S. Gimbert (F, Yamaha), 36.607. 19 finishers. Fastest lap: N. Haga (J, Yamaha), 1'45.882 (196.963 km/h).

Race II: 1. N. Haga (J, Yamaha), 18 laps, 32'07.576 (194.745 km/h); 2. M. Neukirchner (D, Suzuki), 0.009; 3. R. Kiyonari (J, Honda), 0.051; 4. A. Gonzales-Nieto (E, Suzuki), 4.489; 5. M. Fabrizio (I, Ducati), 10.272; 6. K. Muggeridge (AUS, Honda), 10.376; 7. R. Xaus (E, Ducati), 10.496; 8. T. Corser (AUS, Yamaha), 12.498; 9. A. Badovini (I, Kawasaki), 19.429; 10. G. Lavilla (E, Honda), 26.373; 11. L. Lanzi (I, Ducati), 26.544; 12. S. Nakatomi (J, Yamaha), 26.895; 13. R. Holland (AUS, Honda), 27.761; 14. S. Gimbert (F, Yamaha), 29.661; 15. M. Beck (USA, Yamaha), 1'29.001. 16 finishers. Fastest lap: N. Haga (J, Yamaha), 1'46.363 (196.072 km/h).

June 1st - United States - Miller Park

Race I: 1. C. Checa (E, Honda), 20 laps, 37'04.991 (158.789 km/h); 2. T. Corser (AUS, Yamaha), 2.809; 3. M. Fabrizio (I, Ducati), 6.546; 4. M. Neukirchner (D, Suzuki), 7.764; 5. A. Gonzales-Nieto (E, Suzuki), 16.475; 6. J. Smrz (CZ, Ducati), 17.126; 7. K. Muggeridge (AUS, Honda), 17.284; 8. Y. Kagayama (J, Suzuki), 17.416; 9. M. Biaggi (I, Ducati), 18.117; 10. R. Kiyonari (J, Honda), 20.467; 11. L. Lanzi (I, Ducati), 21.742; 12. K. Sofuoglu (TUR, Honda), 27.533; 13. G. Lavilla (E, Honda), 32.609; 14. R. Xaus (E, Ducati), 33.165; 15. R. Holland (AUS, Honda), 34.182. 24 finishers. Fastest lap: C. Checa (E, Honda), 1'50.091 (160.460 km/h).

Race II: 1. C. Checa (E, Honda), 21 laps, 38'44.105 (159.618 km/h); 2. M. Neukirchner (D, Suzuki), 3.547; 3. M. Fabrizio (I, Ducati), 6.613; 4. M. Biaggi (I, Ducati), 7.878; 5. Y. Kagayama (J, Suzuki), 10.568; 6. N. Haga (J, Yamaha), 11.539; 7. R. Kiyonari (J, Honda), 18.381; 8. A. Gonzales-Nieto (E, Suzuki), 20.646; 9. R. Laconi (F, Kawasaki), 21.264; 10. L. Lanzi (I, Ducati), 24.863; 11. K. Muggeridge (AUS, Honda), 25.672; 12. A. Badovini (I, Kawasaki), 31.711; 13. M. Tamada (J, Kawasaki), 35.628; 14. K. Sofuoglu (TUR, Honda), 42.816; 15. G. Lavilla (E, Honda), 45.034. 22 finishers. Fastest lap: C. Checa (E, Honda), 1'49.703 (161.028 km/h).

June 15 - Germany - Nürburgring

Race I: 1. N. Haga (J, Yamaha), 20 laps, 39'19.427 (156.760 km/h); 2. T. Bayliss (AUS, Ducati), 2.025; 3. M. Neukirchner (D, Suzuki), 2.792; 4. T. Corser (AUS, Yamaha), 5.458; 5. C. Checa (E, Honda), 10.225; 6. R. Xaus (E, Ducati), 10.462; 7. M. Fabrizio (I, Ducati), 17.018; 8. A. Gonzales-Nieto (E, Suzuki), 20.520; 9. M. Tamada (J, Kawasaki), 21.162; 10. K. Muggeridge (AUS, Honda), 22.650; 11. J. Smrz (CZ, Ducati), 22.845; 12. R. Kiyonari (J, Honda), 25.555; 13. M. Biaggi (I, Ducati), 25.879; 14. R. Laconi (F, Kawasaki), 26.288; 15. S. Gimbert (F, Yamaha), 32.824. 20 finishers. Fastest lap: T. Bayliss (AUS, Ducati), 1'57.276 (157.690 km/h).

Race II: 1. N. Haga (J, Yamaha), 14 laps, 27'26.594 (157.237 km/h); 2. T. Corser (AUS, Yamaha), 0.150; 3. M. Neukirchner (D, Suzuki), 5.316; 4. T. Bayliss (AUS, Ducati), 7.651; 5. C. Checa (E, Honda), 7.951; 6. M. Fabrizio (I, Ducati), 9.027; 7. M. Biaggi (I, Ducati), 9.420; 8. R. Xaus (E, Ducati), 9.916; 9. A. Gonzales-Nieto (E, Suzuki), 12.862; 10. R. Laconi (F, Kawasaki), 13.559; 11. R. Kiyonari (J, Honda), 13.960; 12. K. Muggeridge (AUS, Honda), 16.172; 13. M. Tamada (J, Kawasaki), 17.946; 14. G. Lavilla (E, Honda), 22.815; 15. D. Checa (E, Yamaha), 23.758. 24 finishers. Fastest lap: N. Haga (J, Yamaha), 1'56.892 (158.208 km/h).

June 29 - San Marino - Misano

Race I: 1. M. Neukirchner (D, Suzuki), 24 laps, 39'27.918 (154.197 km/h); 2. T. Corser (AUS, Yamaha), 0.542; 3. T. Bayliss (AUS, Ducati), 2.249; 4. R. Xaus (E, Ducati), 3.028; 5. C. Checa (E, Honda), 5.408; 6. L. Lanzi (I, Ducati), 5.518; 7. J. Smrz (CZ, Ducati), 6.202; 8. G. Lavilla (E, Honda), 18.279; 9. S. Nakatomi (J, Yamaha), 19.072; 10. N. Haga (J, Yamaha), 19.132; 11. Y. Kagayama (J, Suzuki), 28.098; 12. A. Gonzales-Nieto (E, Suzuki), 34.385; 13. S. Aoyama (J, Honda), 34.572; 14. R. Kiyonari (J, Honda), 34.902M; 15. D. Checa (E, Yamaha), 39.979. 18 finishers. Fastest lap: J. Smrz (CZ, Ducati), 1'37.694 (155.727 km/h).

Race II: 1. R. Xaus (E, Ducati), 24 laps, 39'19.710 (154.734 km/h); 2. M. Biaggi (I, Ducati), 1.035; 3. T. Bayliss (AUS, Ducati), 4.158; 4. N. Haga (J, Yamaha), 5.466; 5. T. Corser (AUS, Yamaha), 6.759; 6. L. Lanzi (I, Ducati), 13.468; 7. M. Neukirchner (D, Suzuki), 15.221; 8. C. Checa (E, Honda), 16.687; 9. J. Smrz (CZ, Ducati), 17.030; 10. A. Gonzales-Nieto (E, Suzuki), 17.681; 11. M. Fabrizio (I, Ducati), 21.356; 12. Y. Kagayama (J, Suzuki), 28.676; 13. R. Kiyonari (J, Honda), 31.304; 14. G. Lavilla (E, Honda), 32.339; 15. S. Nakatomi (J, Yamaha), 33.716. 19 finishers. Fastest lap: T. Corser (AUS, Yamaha), 1'37.580 (155.909 km/h).

July 20 - Czech Republic - Brno

Race I: 1. T. Bayliss (AUS, Ducati), 20 laps, 40'22.724 (160.570 km/h); 2. T. Corser (AUS, Yamaha), 1.468; 3. M. Fabrizio (I, Ducati), 3.272; 4. M. Biaggi (I, Ducati), 3.475; 5. R. Kiyonari (J, Honda), 3.791; 6. N. Haga (J, Yamaha), 9.120; 7. M. Neukirchner (D, Suzuki), 9.358; 8. C. Checa (E, Honda), 11.787; 9. Y. Kagayama (J, Suzuki), 17.228; 10. K. Sofuoglu (TUR, Honda), 17.705; 11. K. Muggeridge (AUS, Honda), 22.347; 12. S. Nakatomi (J, Yamaha), 25.563; 13. N. Canepa (I, Ducati), 25.699; 14. A. Gonzales-Nieto (E, Suzuki), 34.064; 15. G. Lavilla (E, Honda), 36.545. 21 finishers. Fastest lap: T. Bayliss (AUS, Ducati), 2'00.298 (161.688 km/h).

Race II: 1. T. Bayliss (AUS, Ducati), 20 laps, 40'16.436 (160.988 km/h); 2. M. Fabrizio (I, Ducati), 0.928; 3. M. Biaggi (I, Ducati), 1.259; 4. T. Corser (AUS, Yamaha), 1.785; 5. M. Neukirchner (D, Suzuki), 3.942; 6. R. Kiyonari (J, Honda), 7.910; 7. N. Haga (J, Yamaha), 11.297; 8. A. Gonzales-Nieto (E, Suzuki), 11.375; 9. Y. Kagayama (J, Suzuki), 13.103; 10. K. Sofuoglu (TUR, Honda), 18.978; 11. J. Smrz (CZ, Ducati), 19.106; 12. R. Rolfo (I, Honda), 20.556; 13. L. Lanzi (I, Ducati), 21.775; 14. G. Lavilla (E, Honda), 26.372; 15. S. Nakatomi (J, Yamaha), 26.922. 21 finishers. Fastest lap: M. Fabrizio (I, Ducati), 1'59.979 (162,118 km/h).

August 3 - Great Britain - Brands Hatch

Race I: 1. R. Kiyonari (J, Honda), 25 laps, 36'18.607 (152.933 km/h); 2. T. Bayliss (AUS, Ducati), 0.137; 3. M. Biaggi (I, Ducati), 0.180; 4. Y. Kagayama (J, Suzuki), 5.733; 5. A. Gonzales-Nieto (E, Suzuki), 6.499; 6. C. Checa (E, Honda), 6.984; 7. M. Neukirchner (D, Suzuki), 8.300; 8. T. Corser (AUS, Yamaha), 10.732; 9. J. Smrz (CZ, Ducati), 16.547; 10. R. Rolfo (I, Honda), 16.569; 11. L. Lanzi (I, Ducati), 18.366; 12. M. Fabrizio (I, Ducati), 22.308; 13. K. Sofuoglu (TUR, Honda), 26.788; 14. G. Lavilla (E, Honda), 26.856; 15. C. Walker (GB, Honda), 32.877. 23 finishers. Fastest lap: R. Kiyonari (J, Honda), 1'26.560 (153.965 km/h).

Race II: 1. R. Kiyonari (J, Honda), 25 laps, 36'14.904 (153.193 km/h); 2. N. Haga (J, Yamaha), 1.848; 3. T. Corser (AUS, Yamaha), 8.883; 4. M. Neukirchner (D, Suzuki), 11.180; 5. A. Gonzales-Nieto (E, Suzuki), 12.928; 6. M. Fabrizio (I, Ducati), 13.696; 7. T. Sykes (GB, Suzuki), 13.872; 8. C. Checa (E, Honda), 14.009; 9. J. Smrz (CZ, Ducati), 19.065; 10. L. Lanzi (I, Ducati), 19.864; 11. T. Bayliss (AUS, Ducati), 20.479; 12. M. Biaggi ((I, Ducati), 20.621; 13. G. Lavilla (E, Honda), 20.722; 14. R. Rolfo (I, Honda), 24.512; 15. C. Walker (GB, Honda), 32.090. 25 finishers. Fastest lap: M. Fabrizio (I, Ducati), 1'26.362 (154.318 km/h).

September 7 - Europa - Donington

Race I: 1. T. Bayliss (AUS, Ducati), 19 laps, 29'55.384 (153.267 km/h); 2. T. Sykes (GB, Suzuki), 1.266; 3. M. Biaggi (I, Ducati), 28.636; 4. G. Lavilla (E, Honda), 33.566; 5. Y. Kagayama (J, Suzuki), 35.966; 6. J. Smrz (CZ, Ducati), 36.034; 7. A. Gonzales-Nieto (E, Suzuki), 36.442; 8. L. Haslam (GB, Honda), 41.633; 9. K. Muggeridge (AUS, Honda), 42.075; 10. J. Ellison (GB, Honda), 43.476; 11. D. Checa (E, Yamaha), 1'12.578; 12. A. Badovini (I, Kawasaki), 1'13.147; 13. S. Nakatomi (J, Yamaha), 1'34.664; 14. S. Aoyama (J, Honda), 1'56.726. 14 finishers. Fastest lap: T. Bayliss (AUS, Ducati), 1'31.814 (157.741 km/h).

Race II: 1. R. Kiyonari (J, Honda), 23 laps, 40'26.508 (137.277 km/h); 2. C. Crutchlow (GB, Honda), 2.261; 3. T. Corser (AUS, Yamaha), 9.727; 4. J. Ellison (GB, Honda), 20.227; 5. M. Fabrizio (I, Ducati), 27.475; 6. M. Biaggi (I, Ducati), 28.051; 7. G. Lavilla (E, Honda), 30.922; 8. R. Xaus (E, Ducati), 38.353; 9. C. Checa (E, Honda), 50'196; 10. T. Sykes (GB, Suzuki), 57.346; 11. L. Lanzi (I, Ducati), 1'03.093; 12. J. Smrz (CZ, Ducati), 1'06.697; 13. R. Rolfo (I, Honda), 1'08.057; 14. M. Neukirchner (D, Suzuki), 1'15.276; 15. R. Laconi (F, Kawasaki), 1'38.848. 19 finishers. Fastest lap: J. Ellison (GB, Honda), 1'43.405 (140.059 km/h).

September 21 - Italy - Vallelunga

Race I: 1. N. Haga (J, Yamaha), 24 laps, 39'25.030 (150.148 km/h); 2. M. Biaggi (I, Ducati), 0.129; 3. T. Corser (AUS, Yamaha), 0.535; 4. M. Neukirchner (D, Suzuki), 5.188; 5. C. Checa (E, Honda), 6.693; 6. T. Bayliss (AUS, Ducati), 7.993; 7. M. Fabrizio (I, Ducati), 16.976; 8. R. Rolfo (I, Honda), 18.359; 9. Y. Kagayama (J, Suzuki), 19.214; 10. S. Nakatomi (J, Yamaha), 19.386; 11. L. Lanzi (I, Ducati), 21.230; 12. A. Gonzales-Nieto (E, Suzuki), 24.956; 13. J. Smrz (CZ, Ducati), 25.186; 14. G. Lavilla (E, Honda), 31.799; 15. A. Badovini (I, Kawasaki), 33.949. 22 finishers. Fastest lap: C. Checa (E, Honda), 1'37.537 (151.696 km/h).

Race II: 1. N. Haga (J, Yamaha), 24 laps, 39'10.265 (151.091 km/h); 2. M. Fabrizio (I, Ducati), 1.507; 3. T. Corser (AUS, Yamaha), 2.268; 4. M. Neukirchner (D, Suzuki), 11.813; 5. C. Checa (E, Honda), 17.922; 6. A. Gonzales-Nieto (E, Suzuki), 18.281; 7. Y. Kagayama (J, Suzuki), 19.368; 8. S. Nakatomi (J, Yamaha), 19.717; 9. R. Laconi (F, Kawasaki), 23.868; 10. R. Rolfo (I, Honda), 24.198; 11. J. Smrz (CZ, Ducati), 25.426; 12. R. Xaus (E, Ducati), 28.384; 13. R. Kiyonari (J, Honda), 30.436; 14. S. Gimbert (F, Yamaha), 36.490; 15. C. Walker (GB, Honda), 42.903. 22 finishers. Fastest lap: T. Corser (AUS, Yamaha), 1'37.072 (152.423 km/h).

October 5 - France - Magny-Cours

Race I: 1. N. Haga (J, Yamaha), 23 laps, 38'33.367 (157.878 km/h); 2. A. Gonzales-Nieto (E, Suzuki), 6.223; 3. T. Bayliss (AUS, Ducati), 6.875; 4. M. Biaggi (I, Ducati), 7.237; 5. M. Neukirchner (D, Suzuki), 8.925; 6. T. Corser (AUS, Yamaha), 10.714; 7. C. Checa (E, Honda), 16.176; 8. Y. Kagayama (J, Suzuki), 22.661; 9. K. Sofuoglu (TUR, Suzuki), 27.224; 10. G. Lavilla (E, Honda), 31.300; 11. R. Laconi (F, Kawasaki), 35.558; 12. K. Muggeridge (AUS, Honda), 35.774; 13. S. Gimbert (F, Yamaha), 36.078; 14. S. Nakatomi (J, Yamaha), 36.289; 15. C. Walker (GB, Honda), 40.472. 20 finishers. Fastest lap: C. Checa (E, Honda), 1'39.834 (159.060 km/h).

Race II: 1. T. Bayliss (AUS, Ducati), 23 laps, 38'33.579 (157.864 km/h); 2. N. Haga (J, Yamaha), 0.909; 3. T. Corser (AUS, Yamaha), 2.966; 4. C. Checa (E, Honda), 7.175; 5. R. Xaus (E, Ducati), 12.822; 6. M. Biaggi (I, Ducati), 13.004; 7. Y. Kagayama (J, Suzuki), 18.876; 8. A. Gonzales-Nieto (E, Suzuki), 19.512; 9. M. Neukirchner (D, Suzuki), 19.627; 10. R. Rolfo (I, Honda), 21.425; 11. L. Lanzi (I, Ducati), 25.133; 12. G. Lavilla (E, Honda), 30.538; 13. J. Smrz (CZ, Ducati), 35.334; 14. M. Fabrizio (I, Ducati), 38.453; 15. C. Walker (GB, Honda), 40.008. 23 finishers. Fastest lap: T. Bayliss (AUS, Ducati), 1'39.818 (159.086 km/h).

November 2 - Portugal - Portimaõ

Race I: 1. T. Bayliss (AUS, Ducati), 22 laps, 38'48.373 (156.198 km/h); 2. C. Checa (E, Honda), 2.207; 3. T. Corser (AUS, Yamaha), 6.972; 4. J. Rea (GB, Honda), 15.228; 5. A. Gonzales-Nieto (E, Suzuki), 16.126; 6. G. Lavilla (E, Honda), 18.152; 7. L. Haslam (GB, Honda), 18.939; 8. R. Kiyonari (J, Honda), 20.942; 9. R. Xaus (E, Ducati), 32.018; 10. R. Laconi (F, Kawasaki), 32.871; 11. A. Badovini (I, Kawasaki), 36.778; 12. R. Rolfo (I, Honda), 36.848; 13. S. Nakatomi (J, Yamaha), 41.667; 14. K. Muggeridge (AUS, Honda), 41.806. 21 finishers. Fastest lap: T. Bayliss (AUS, Ducati), 1'44.776 (157.777 km/h).

Race II: 1. T. Bayliss (AUS, Ducati), 22 laps, 38'26.125 (157.705 km/h); 2. M. Fabrizio (I, Ducati),

3.638; 3. L. Haslam (GB, Honda), 4.356; 4. M. Neukirchner (D, Suzuki), 4.983; 5. A. Gonzales-Nieto (E, Suzuki), 6.775; 6. T. Corser (AUS, Yamaha), 7.403; 7. C. Checa (E, Honda), 7.578; 8. G. Lavilla (E, Honda), 16.113; 9. C. Crutchlow (GB, Honda), 16.284; 10. R. Laconi (F, Kawasaki), 16.446; 11. R. Kiyonari (J, Honda), 21.633; 12. J. Smrz (CZ, Ducati), 22.098; 13. M. Biaggi (I, Ducati), 24.089; 14. N. Haga (J, Yamaha), 24.117; 15. J. Rea (GB, Honda), 31.003. 29 finishers. Fastest lap: T. Bayliss (AUS, Ducati), 1'43.787 (158.280 km/h).

FINAL CLASSIFICATION

1. Troy Bayliss (AUS)	Ducati	460 points
2. Troy Corser (AUS)	Yamaha	342
3. Noriyuki Haga (J)	Yamaha	327

4. C. Checa (E, Honda), 313; 5. M. Neukirchner (D, Suzuki), 311; 6. A. Gonzales-Nieto (E, Suzuki), 256; 7. M. Biaggi (I, Ducati), 238; 8. M. Fabrizio (I, Ducati), 223; 9. R. Kiyonari (J, Honda), 206; 10. R. Xaus (E, Ducati), 178. 33 finishers.

CONSTRUCTORS

1. Ducati	570 points
2. Yamaha	487
3. Honda	415

4. Suzuki, 408; 5. Kawasaki, 94. 5 finishers.

SUPERSPORT WORLD CHAMPIONSHIP

February 23 - Doha - Qatar

1. B. Parkes (AUS, Yamaha), 18 laps, 37'05.271 (156.666 km/h); 2. J. Lascorz (E, Honda), 0.048; 3. C. Jones (GB, Honda), 0.755; 4. J. Brookes (AUS, Honda), 9.502; 5. M. Lagrive (F, Honda), 11.962; 6. B. Veneman (NL, Suzuki), 17.428; 7. R. Harms (DK, Honda), 17.660; 8. D. Salom (E, Yamaha), 17.888; 9. C. Walker (GB, Kawasaki), 25.883; 10. G. Vizziello (I, Honda), 32.236; 11. G. Leblanc (F, Honda), 32.573; 12. I. Clementi (I, Triumph), 35.117; 13. M. Praia (POR, Honda), 36.390; 14. V. Kallio (SF, Honda), 36.608; 15. K. Fujiwara (J, Kawasaki), 37.096. 24 finishers. Fastest lap: F. Foret (F, Yamaha), 2'02.626 (157.944 km7h).

March 2 - Phillip Island - Australia

1. A. Pitt (AUS, Honda), 21 laps, 33'51.257 (165.435 km/h); 2. J. Brookes (AUS, Honda), 0.062; 3. R. Harms (DK, Honda), 0.597; 4. F. Foret (F, Yamaha), 0.780; 5. J. Rea (GB, Honda), 0.976; 6. G. McCoy (AUS, Triumph), 1.228; 7. J. Lascorz (E, Honda), 6.590; 8. G. Vizziello (I, Honda), 10.266; 9. M. Roccoli (I, Yamaha), 10.594; 10. G. Nannelli (I, Honda), 10.991; 11. I. Clementi (I, Triumph), 16.068; 12. M. Aitchison (AUS, Triumph), 16.245; 13. G. Gowland (GB, Honda), 16.355; 14. C. Walker (GB, Kawasaki), 16.526; 15. V. Kallio (SF, Honda), 17.270. 30 finishers. Fastest lap: R. Harms (DK, Honda), 1'35.429 (167.685 km/h).

April 6 - Spain - Valencia

1. J. Lascorz (E, Honda), 23 laps, 37'58.607 (145.534 km/h); 2. F. Foret (F, Yamaha), 1.125; 3. C. Jones (GB, Honda), 1.530; 4. B. Parkes (AUS, Yamaha), 10.514; 5. G. Nannelli (I, Honda), 17.492; 6. J. Rea (GB, Honda), 17.602; 7. M. Roccoli (I, Yamaha), 19.636; 8. A. Rodriguez (E, Yamaha), 19.694; 9. C. Walker (GB, Kawasaki), 25.230; 10. M. Aitchison (AUS, Triumph), 25.702; 11. K. Fujiwara (J, Kawasaki), 32.370; 12. G. Vizziello (I, Honda), 33.591; 13. M. Lagrive (F, Honda), 34.706; 14. V. Kallio (SF, Honda), 39.956; 15. M. Praia (POR, Honda), 40.227. 23 finishers. Fastest lap: B. Parkes (AUS, Yamaha), 1'37.590 (147.741 km/h).

April 27 - Netherlands - Assen

1. A. Pitt (AUS, Honda), 21 laps, 36'10.751 (158.635 km/h); 2. J. Rea (GB, Honda), 0.014; 3. J. Lascorz (E, Honda), 0.150; 4. F. Foret (F, Yamaha), 0.201; 5. B. Parkes (AUS, Yamaha), 0.283; 6. J. Brookes (AUS, Honda), 0.447; 7. B. Veneman (NL, Suzuki), 2.060; 8. G. Vizziello (I, Honda), 2.346; 9. C. Jones (GB, Honda), 2.714; 10. M. Lagrive (F, Honda), 3.073; 11. M. Aitchison (GB, Triumph), 4.070; 12. C. Walker (GB, Kawasaki), 4.863; 13. R. Harms (DK, Honda), 5.088; 14. I. Clementi (I, Triumph), 16.644; 15. I. Dionisi (I, Triumph), 21.630. 27 finishers. Fastest lap: G. Vizziello (I, Honda), 1'42.130 (160.560 km/h).

May 11 - Italy - Monza

1. F. Foret (F, Yamaha), 16 laps, 29'38.261 (187.642 km/h); 2. J. Brookes (AUS, Honda), 1.199; 3. B. Parkes (AUS, Yamaha), 6.736; 4. A. Pitt (AUS, Honda), 11.398; 5. R. Harms (DK, Honda), 11.477; 6. C. Jones (GB, Honda), 11.716; 7. M. Roccoli (I, Yamaha), 11.757; 8. M. Lagrive (F, Honda), 12.186; 9. J. Lascorz (E, Honda), 14.847; 10. A. Rodriguez (E, Yamaha), 15.175; 11. M. Aitchison (AUS, Triumph), 21.256; 12. C. Migliorati (I, Kawasaki), 24.899; 13. G. Nannelli (I, Honda), 25.077; 14. V. Kallio (SF, Honda), 25.160; 15. K. Fujiwara (J, Kawasaki), 26.429. 27 finishers. Fastest lap: F. Foret (F, Yamaha), 1'50.430 (188.851 km/h).

June 15 - Germany - Nürburgring

1. A. Pitt (AUS, Honda), 19 laps, 38'26.584 (152.334 km/h); 2. J. Brookes (AUS, Honda), 0.387; 3. B. Parkes (AUS, Yamaha), 1.379; 4. F. Foret (F, Yamaha), 10.279; 5. C. Jones (GB, Honda), 11.624; 6. J. Rea (GB, Honda), 19.211; 7. D. Van Keymeulen (B, Suzuki), 28.775; 8. A. Tode (D, Triumph), 28.890; 9. C. Walker (GB, Kawasaki), 28.990; 10. V. Kallio (SF, Honda), 37.853; 11. K. Fujiwara (J, Kawasaki), 43.101; 12. J. Lascorz (E, Honda), 51.843; 13. M. Praia (POR, Honda), 54.459; 14. G. Vizziello (I, Honda), 54.653; 15. J. Crowe (AUS, Yamaha), 54.705. 21 finishers. Fastest lap: B. Parkes (AUS, Yamaha), 2'00.452 (153.532 km/h).

June 29 - San Marino - Misano

1. A. Pitt (AUS, Honda), 22 laps, 37'08.387 (150.198 km/h); 2. C. Jones (GB, Honda), 5.347; 3. J. Rea (GB, Honda), 9.183; 4. F. Foret (F, Yamaha), 13.784; 5. R. Harms (DK, Honda), 15.863; 6. M. Aitchison (AUS, Triumph), 15.967; 7. M. Roccoli (I, Yamaha), 21.689; 8. B. Veneman (NL, Suzuki), 24.070; 9. I. Clementi (I, Triumph), 26.075; 10. B. Parkes (AUS, Yamaha), 30.387; 11. G. Vizziello (I, Honda), 32.578; 12. C. Walker (GB, Kawasaki), 34.648; 13. G. Nannelli (I, Honda), 36.040; 14. J. Brookes (AUS, Honda), 37.896; 15. D. Marrancone (I, Yamaha), 40.167. 28 finishers. Fastest lap: B. Parkes (AUS, Yamaha), 1'40.187 (151.852 km/h).

July 20 - Czech Republic - Brno

1. J. Rea (GB, Honda), 18 laps, 37'35.093 (155.255 km/h); 2. A. Pitt (AUS, Honda), 0.020; 3. J. Brookes (AUS, Honda), 1.433; 4. B. Parkes (AUS, Yamaha), 1.853; 5. B. Veneman (NL, Suzuki), 2.237; 6. G. Nannelli (I, Honda), 12.032; 7. R. Holland (AUS, Honda), 12.221; 8. M. Lagrive (F, Honda), 12.787; 9. V. Kallio (SF, Honda), 15.334; 10. M. Roccoli (I, Yamaha), 15.780; 11. C. Walker (GB, Kawasaki), 23.645; 12. G. Vizziello (I, Honda), 23.758; 13. I. Clementi (I, Triumph), 24.074; 14. D. Van Keymeulen (B, Suzuki), 24.621; 15. D. Salom (E, Yamaha), 26.866. 24 finishers. Fastest lap: A. Pitt (AUS, Honda), 2'04.062 (156.783 km/h).

August 3 - Great Britain - Brands Hatch (*)

1. J. Rea (GB, Honda), 15 laps, 22'29.935 (148.087 km/h); 2. C. Jones (*) (GB, Honda), 0.209; 3. A. Pitt (AUS, Honda), 0.664; 4. B. Parkes (AUS, Yamaha), 2.816; 5. J. Brookes (AUS, Honda), 6.789; 6. B. Veneman (NL, Suzuki), 9.094; 7. G. Nannelli (I, Honda), 15.048; 8. M. Roccoli (I, Yamaha), 15.623; 9. R. Frost (GB, Triumph), 18.393; 10. H. Kennaugh (RSA, Yamaha), 19.528; 11. S. Plater (GB, Triumph), 20.034; 12. G. Vizziello (I, Honda), 22.696; 13. V. Kallio (SF, Honda), 25.049; 14. J. Lascorz (E, Honda), 27.102; 15. G. Gowland (GB, Honda), 35.504. 28 finishers. Fastest lap: A. Pitt (AUS, Honda), 1'28.399 (150.762 km/h).

(*): The race was stopped under red flag twice, the second one because the accident which caused death of C. Jones (GB, Honda).

September 7 - Europe - Donington

1. J. Brookes (AUS, Honda), 22 laps, 34'53.607 (152.188 km/h); 2. A. Pitt (AUS, Honda), 0.872; 3. J. Rea (GB, Honda), 4.846; 4. B. Veneman (NL, Suzuki), 5.066; 5. H. Kennaugh (RSA, Yamaha), 8.604; 6. R. Harms (DK, Honda), 8.990; 7. J. Lascorz (E, Honda), 15.660; 8. D. Van Keymeulen (B, Suzuki), 16.674; 9. M. Lagrive (F, Honda), 17.081; 10. B. Parkes (AUS, Yamaha), 20.474; 11. G. Vizziello (I, Honda), 21.110; 12. E. Laverty (IRL, Yamaha), 26.338; 13. M. Aitchison (AUS, Triumph), 26.597; 14. K. Fujiwara (J, Kawasaki), 29.104; 15. C. Martin (GB, Kawasaki), 30.603. 24 finishers. Fastest lap: J. Brookes (AUS, Honda), 1'34.079 (153.943 km/h).

September 21 - Italy - Vallelunga

1. J. Rea (GB, Honda), 22 laps, 36'48.656 (147.380 km/h); 2. B. Parkes (AUS, Yamaha), 2.971; 3. E. Laverty (IRL, Yamaha), 6.461; 4. J. Lascorz (E, Honda), 7.135; 5. B. Veneman (NL, Suzuki), 10.945; 6. R. Harms (DK, Honda), 14.412; 7. G. Nannelli (I, Honda), 14.557; 8. D. Van Keymeulen (B, Suzuki), 19.286; 9. M. Aitchison (AUS, Triumph), 23.854; 10. J. Hayes (USA, Honda), 31.193; 11. I. Clementi (I, Triumph), 31.327; 12. J. Brookes (AUS, Honda), 39.771; 13. M. Praia (POR, Honda), 40.957; 14. T. Toti (I, Suzuki), 41.196; 15. G. Vizziello (I, Honda), 41.337. 27 finishers. Fastest lap: B. Parkes (AUS, Yamaha), 1'39.417 (148.828 km/h).

October 5 - France

1. A. Pitt (AUS, Honda), 22 laps, 37'57.929 (153.364 km/h); 2. B. Veneman (NL, Suzuki), 1.250; 3. J. Brookes (AUS, Honda), 1.514; 4. M. Lagrive (F, Honda), 1.685; 5. D. Van Keymeulen (B, Suzuki), 5.075; 6. M. Roccoli (I, Yamaha), 13.171; 7. G. Nannelli (I, Honda), 13.386; 8. F. Foret (F, Yamaha), 19.563; 9. J. Hayes (USA, Honda), 19.677; 10. J. Rea (GB, Honda), 21.686; 11. G. Vizziello (I, Honda), 22.599; 12. K. Fujiwara (J, Kawasaki), 24.967; 13. P. Vostarek (CZ, Honda), 28.888; 14. I. Clementi (I, Triumph), 29.351; 15. R. Harms (DK, Honda), 38.000. 22 finishers. Fastest lap: B. Parkes (AUS, Yamaha), 1'42.593 (154.782 km/h).

November 2 - Portugal - Portimaõ

1. K. Sofuoglu (TUR, Honda), 20 laps, 35'39.851 (154.508 km/h); 2. A. Pitt (AUS, Honda), 3.844; 3. J. Lascorz (E, Honda), 7.403; 4. J. Hayes (USA, Honda), 7.445; 5. B. Parkes (AUS, Yamaha), 17.271; 6. G. Nannelli (I, Honda), 17.297; 7. S. Sanna (I, Honda), 25.803; 8. G. Vizziello (I, Honda), 29.749; 9. M. Aitchison (AUS, Triumph), 29.960; 10. F. Foret (F, Yamaha), 30.155; 11. J. Brookes (AUS, Honda), 30.697; 12. M. Praia (POR, Honda), 30.719; 13. G. McCoy (AUS, Triumph), 40.033; 14. R. Holland (AUS, Honda), 40.839; 15. D. Van Keymeulen (B, Suzuki), 44.266. 26 finishers. Fastest lap: K. Sofuoglu (TUR, Honda), 1'46.082 (166.834 km/h).

FINAL CLASSIFICATION

1. Andrew Pitt (AUS)	Honda	214 points
2. Jonathan Rea (GB)	Honda	164
3. Joshua Brookes (AUS)	Honda	150

4. B. Parkes (AUS, Yamaha), 150; 5. J. Lascorz (E, Honda), 121; 6. F. Foret (F, Yamaha), 111; 7. C. Jones (GB, Honda), 100; 8. B. Veneman (NL, Suzuki), 92; 9. R. Harms (DK, Honda), 71; 10. G. Nannelli (I, Honda), 70. 41 finishers.

CONSTRUCTORS

1. Honda	315 points
2. Yamaha	203
3. Suzuki	102

4. Triumph, 77; 5. Kawasaki, 46. 5 finishers.

ENDURANCE WORLD CHAMPIONSHIP

April 19-20 - Le Mans 24 Hours - France

1. Costes/Dietrich/Veneman (F/F/NL, Suzuki), 770 laps, 24 h 01'26.500 (150.425 km/h); 2. Philippe/Lagrive/Da Costa (F, Suzuki)), 11 laps; 3. Fastre/Leblanc/Dos Santos (F, Yamaha), 14 laps; 4. J. Tangre/C. Michel/C. Tangre (F, Suzuki), 15 laps; 5. Jonchière/K. Foray/De Carolis (F, Suzuki), 17 laps; 6. Seidel/D. Sutter/Miksovsky (D/CH/POL, Honda), 19 laps; 7. Morillon/Mizera/Saiger (F/F/D, Kawasaki), 21 laps; 8. Aj Al Haimi/Al Mannai/Delhalle (QAT/QAT/F, Suzuki), 22 laps; 9. Devoyon/F. Jond/Chèvre (F/F/CH, Suzuki); 10. S. Hernandez/Guersillon/Auger (F, Suzuki), 23 laps; 11. D. Ribalta/Vallcañeras/Lopez (E, Yamaha), 25 laps; 12. Haydon/Mc Bride/D. Cudlin (GB, Yamaha); 13. J. Millet/Brivet/Gantner (F/F/CH, Yamaha), 26 laps; 14. Hutchins/A. Cudlin/Weynand (GB, Kawasaki), 30 laps; 15. Baratin/Lalevée/Gnemmi (F, Yamaha), 33 laps. 34 finishers.

May 10 - 6 Hours of Albacete - Spain

1. Philippe/Dietrich/Da Costa (F, Suzuki), 177 laps, 6 h 01'09.291 (104.060 km/h); 2. Sarda/K. Noyes/B. Martinez (E, Suzuki), 2 laps; 3. Morillon/Muff/Saiger (F/CH/D, Kawasaki); 4. Jerman/Martin/Plater (SLO/GB/GB, Yamaha), 4 laps; 5. J. Millet/Brivet/Gantner (F/F/CH, Yamaha), 5 laps; 6. Aj Al Haimi/Al Mannai/Delhalle (QAT/QAT/F, Suzuki), 6 laps (1ers SST); 7. Nowland/Pridmore (AUS/USA, Yamaha); 8. Mazuecos/Nigon/Carrasco (E/F/E, Kawasaki), 7 laps; 9. Devoyon/Chèvre (F/CH, Suzuki); 10. Dos Santosd/Huvier/Lalevée (F, Yamaha); 11. Ribalta/Vallcañeras/Romás (E, Yamaha); 12. Grelaud/Pierre/Hedelin (F, Suzuki), 8 laps; 13. Jaulneau/Lagrive/Parisse (F, Suzuki), 12 laps; 14. Seidel/Lozano/Miksobsky (D/E/POL, Honda); 15. Vossel/Hooegenraad/Velthuijzen (NL, Yamaha), 13 laps. 21 finishers.

July 27- 8 Hours of Suzuka - Japan

1. Kiyonari/C. Checa (J/E, Honda), 214 laps, 8 h 00'20.726 (155.600 km/h); 2. Sakai/Watanabe (J, Suzuki), 1'18.900; 3. Konishi/Takahashi (J, Honda), 4 laps; 4. Akiyoshi/Kagayama (J, Suzuki), 5 laps; 5. Sato/Nakasuga/Takeda (J, Yamaha); 6. Yamaguchi/Crutchlow/Challoran (J/GB/GB, Honda), 6 laps; 7. Konno/Teramoto (J, Suzuki), 7 laps; 8. Hatano/Ogata/Namekata (J, Suzuki), 9 laps; 9. Kameya/L. Haslam (J/GB, Honda); 10. Tsuda/Brookes (J/AUS, Honda), 10 laps; 11. Jerman/Martin/Plater (SLO/AUS/GB, Yamaha); 12. Ribaltá/Vallcañeras (E, Yamaha); 13. Penzkofer/S. Smart/D. Cudlin (D/GB/AUS, Yamaha); 14. Da Costa/Lagrive (F, Suzuki), 12 laps; 15. Takeishi/Tsuruta/Eguchi (J, Kawasaki). 54 finishers.

August 9 - 8 Hours of Oschersleben - Germany

1. Silvá/Mazuecos(Nigon (E/E/F, Kawasaki), 305 laps, 8 h 00'04.577 (139.783 km/h); 2. Jerman/Martin/Plater (SLO/AUS/GB, Yamaha), 1 lap; 3. Philippe/M. Lagrive/Da Costa (F, Suzuki), 2 laps; 4. Gowland/D. Cudlin/Scarnato (GB/AUS/F, Yamaha); 5. Ribaltá/Valcañeras (E, Yamaha), 3 laps; 6. Nowland/Pridmore (AUS/USA, Yamaha); 7. S. Hernandez/Guersillon/Auger (F, Suzuki), 5 laps; 8. Seidel/Mikskovsky (D/CZ, Honda), 7 laps; 9. Hutchins/A. Cudlin/Weynand (GB/AUS/B, Kawasaki), 9 laps; 10. Tessari/Holmes/A. Aldrovandi (I/USA/I, Yamaha), 10 laps; 11. Al Naimi/Al Mannai/Delhalle (QAT/QAT/F, Suzuki), 11 laps; 12. Hinterreiter/R. Cooper (A/GB, BMW); 13. Penzkofer/Mertens/Fastre (D/B/B, BMW); 14. Huvier/Lalevée/Dos Santos (F, Yamaha), 12 laps; 15. Röthig/Mizera/Eckhardt (D/F/D, Suzuki), 15 laps. 38 finishers.

September 13-14 - Bol d'Or - France

1. Philippe/Lagrive/Da Costa (F, Suzuki), 747 laps, 14 h 01'30.409; 2. Costes/Dietrich/Four (F, Suzuki), 6 laps; 3. Jerman/Martin/Giabbani (SLO/AUS/F, Yamaha), 9 laps; 4. Silvá/Mazuecos/Nigon (E/E/F, Kawasaki), 14 laps; 5. Gowland/Teuchert/Cudlin (GB/D/AUS, Yamaha), 15 laps; 6. Gimbert/D. Checa/Plater (F/E/GB, Yamaha), 16 laps; 7. Ribalta/Vallcañeras/Luis (E, Yamaha), 22 laps; 8. F. Foray/Jonchière/K. Foray (F, Suzuki), 25 laps; 9. Morillon/Muff/Saiger (F/CH/A, Kawasaki), 26 laps; 10. Seidel/Vehniäinen/Resch (D/SF/A, Honda), 27 laps; 11. Devoyon/Chèvre/Jond (F, Suzuki); 12. Al Naimi/De Carolis/Delhalle (QAT/F/F, Suzuki), 28 laps; 13. Molinier/Brière/Savary (F/F/CH, Suzuki), 29 laps; 14. Huvier/Sainz Zozaya/Lerat-Vanstaen (F/E/F, Yamaha), 34 laps; 15. Brivet/Piot/Dos Santos (F, Yamaha). 36 finishers.

November 8 - 8 Hours of Losail - Qatar

This race took place after printing of "The Motorcycle Yearbook" had been completed.

FIM SUPERSTOCK CUP 1000

April 6 - Spain - Valencia

1. B. Roberts (AUS, Ducati), 13 laps, 21'17.585 (146.710 km/h); 2. D. Giugliano (I, Suzuki), 3.795; 3. X. Siméon (B, Suzuki), 6.865; 4. A. Polita (I, Ducati), 7.272; 5. C. Corti (I, Yamaha), 7.680; 6. M. Pirro (I, Yamaha), 11.646; 7. M. Berger (F, Honda), 13.281; 8. C. Seaton (AUS, Suzuki), 17.294; 9. B. Burrell (GB, Honda), 17.487; 10. M. Magnoni (I, Yamaha), 18.254; 11. F. Perotti (I, Suzuki), 19.910; 12. F. Foray (F, Suzuki), 24.142; 13. K. Foray (F, Yamaha), 24.451; 14. S. Barrier (F, Yamaha), 24.896; 15. Y. Tiberio (F, Kawasaki), 24.934. 33 finishers. Fastest lap: B. Roberts (AUS, Ducati), 1'36.681 (149.130 km/h).

April 27 - Netherlands - Assen

1. M. Berger (F, Honda), 13 laps, 22'24.450 (158.559 km/h); 2. M. Pirro (I, Yamaha), 0.904; 3. X. Siméon (B, Suzuki), 2.848; 4. A. Polita (I, Ducati), 4.811; 5. A. Antonelli (I, Honda), 5.481; 6. R. Schouten (NL, Yamaha), 9.544; 7. M. Smrz (CZ, Honda), 16.932; 8. D. Giugliano (I, Suzuki), 17.289; 9. K. Foray (F, Yamaha), 16.672; 10. M. Rothlaan (EST, Honda), 19.588; 11. D. Colucci (I, Ducati), 19.898; 12. M. Baiocco (I, Kawasaki), 23.074; 13. D. De Boer (NL, Suzuki), 25.288; 14. G. Jones (GB, Suzuki), 25.595; 15. Y. Tiberio (F, Kawasaki), 29.279. 29 finishers. Fastest lap: M. Pirro (I, Yamaha), 1'42.076 (160.645 km/h).

May 11 - Italy - Monza

1. X. Siméon (B, Suzuki), 11 laps, 20'14.707 (188.854 km/h); 2. M. Smrz (CZ, Honda), 2.109; 3. A. Polita (I, Ducati), 2.147; 4. B. Roberts (AUS, Ducati), 6.656; 5. M. Magnoni (I, Yamaha), 10.849; 6. F. Perotti (I, Suzuki), 11.070; 7. F. Foray (F, Suzuki), 11.143; 8. K. Foray (F, Yamaha), 14.501; 9. G. Jones (AUS, Suzuki), 15.802; 10. M. Savary (CH, Suzuki), 16.593; 11. A. Aldrovandi (I, Kawasaki), 19.172; 12. A. Antonelli (I, Honda), 19.315; 13. F. Backlund (S, Suzuki), 28.267; 14. G. Junod (CH, Yamaha), 28.874; 15. J. Gallina (I, Kawasaki), 29.029. 22 finishers. Fastest lap: M. Smrz (CZ, Honda), 1'49.418 (190.598 km/h).

June 15 - Germany - Nürburgring

1. B. Roberts (AUS, Ducati), 11 laps, 22'17.805 (152.059 km/h); 2. D. Giugliano (I, Suzuki), 0.307; 3. X. Siméon (B, Suzuki), 0.444; 4. M. Pirro (I, Yamaha), 8.763; 5. M. Smrz (CZ, Honda), 9.786; 6. C. Corti (I, Yamaha), 10.713; 7. M. Berger (F, Honda), 13.766; 8. F. Foray (F, Suzuki), 18.348; 9. M. Magnoni (I, Yamaha), 19.419; 10. Y. Tiberio (F, Kawasaki), 22.772; 11. C. Seaton (AUS, Suzuki), 23.827; 12. B. Burrell (GB, Honda), 23.962; 13. A. Antonelli (I, Honda), 25.179; 14. G. Jones (AUS, Suzuki), 25.778; 15. M. Savary (CH, Suzuki), 25.924. 34 finishers. Fastest lap: B. Roberts (AUS, Ducati), 1'59.970 (154.149 km/h).

June 29 - San Marino - Misano

1. A. Polita (I, Ducati), 14 laps, 23'37.092 (150.301 km/h); 2. M. Pirro (I, Yamaha), 1.471; 3. M. Berger (F, Honda), 2.382; 4. B. Roberts (AUS, Ducati), 5.234; 5. X. Siméon (B, Suzuki), 6.999; 6. A. Antonelli (I, Honda), 7.826; 7. D. Colucci (I, Ducati), 11.349; 8. F. Foray (F, Suzuki), 13.493; 9. C. Seaton (AUS, Suzuki), 14.110; 10. K. Foray (F, Yamaha), 15.238; 11. L. Verdini (I, Yamaha), 17.081; 12. C. Corti (I, Yamaha), 17.546; 13. B. Burrell (GB, Honda), 18.799; 14. S. Barrier (F, Yamaha), 23.705; 15. M. Baiocco (I, Kawasaki), 23.818. 31 finishers. Fastest lap: A. Polita (I, Ducati), 1'39.806 (152.432 km/h).

July 20 - Czech Republic - Brno

1. M. Berger (F, Honda), 12 laps, 24'58.402 (155.772 km/h); 2. B. Roberts (AUS, Ducati), 3.043; 3. A. Polita (I, Ducati), 3.100; 4. A. Antonelli (I, Honda), 3.367; 5. X. Siméon (B, Suzuki), 5.709; 6. M. Pirro (I, Yamaha), 10.032; 7. C. Seaton (AUS, Suzuki), 13.380; 8. M. Smrz (CZ, Honda), 19.510; 9. D. Giugliano (I, Suzuki), 19.724; 10. M. Magnoni (I, Yamaha), 20.249; 11. G. Jones (AUS, Suzuki), 20.796; 12. D. Colucci (I, Ducati), 20.959; 13. M. Baiocco (I, Kawasaki), 21.042; 14. R. Schouten (NL, Yamaha), 21.432; 15. B. Burrell (GB, Honda), 21.609. 30 finishers. Fastest lap: M. Berger (F, Honda), 2'03.676 (157.272 km/h).

August 3 - Great Britain - Brands Hatch

1. M. Berger (F, Honda), 14 laps, 21'56.050 (141.773 km/h); 2. S. Morais (RSA, Kawasaki), 4.172; 3. A. Antonelli (I, Honda), 5.808; 4. B. Roberts (AUS, Ducati), 18.391; 5. A. Polita (I, Ducati), 18.629; 6. M. Pirro (I, Yamaha), 19.049; 7. B. Burrell (GB, Honda), 19.468; 8. C. Corti (I, Yamaha), 24.682; 9. C. Seaton (AUS, Suzuki), 26.331; 10. F. Foray (F, Suzuki), 38.554; 11. G. Jones (AUS, Suzuki), 43.675; 12. M. Savary (CH, Suzuki), 43.891; 13. R. Mähr (A, KTM), 44.375; 14. P. Pekkanen (SF, KTM), 46.011; 15. Y. Tiberio (F, Kawasaki), 48.886. 29 finishers. Fastest lap: S. Morais (RSA, Kawasaki), 1'31.448 (145.735 km/h).

September 7 - Europa - Donington

1. X. Siméon (B, Suzuki), 12 laps, 21'30.092 (134.714 km/h); 2. A. Polita (I, Ducati), 16.109; 3. D. Giugliano (I, Suzuki), 34.318; 4. B. Roberts (AUS, Ducati), 37.319; 5. J. Kirkham (GB, Yamaha), 44.199; 6. M. Berger (F, Honda), 45.533; 7. M. Baiocco (I, Kawasaki), 47.888; 8. F. Backlund (S, Suzuki), 49.623; 9. B. Burrell (GB, Honda), 50.461; 10. S. Stibilj (SLO, Honda), 51.416; 11. D. Colucci (I, Ducati), 52.516; 12. R. Schouten (NL, Yamaha), 1'01.720; 13. D. De Boer (NL, Suzuki), 1'02.726; 14. N. Rosso (I, Honda), 1'02.946; 15. G. Junod (CH, Yamaha), 1'05.181. 26 finishers. Fastest lap: X. Siméon (B, Suzuki), 1'46.033 (136.588 km/h).

October 5 - France - Magny-Cours

1. M. Smrz (CZ, Honda), 14 laps, 24'07.794 (153.554 km/h); 2. F. Foray (F, Suzuki), 0.463; 3. C. Corti (I, Yamaha), 0.543; 4. A. Polita (I, Ducati), 1.001; 5. X. Siméon (B, Suzuki), 1.792; 6. J. Millet (F, Yamaha), 2.556; 7. S. Barrier (F, Yamaha), 8.425; 8. K. Foray (F, Yamaha), 8.701; 9. M. Savary (CH, Suzuki), 12.636; 10. M. Pirro (I, Yamaha), 12.776; 11. M. Berger (F, Honda), 14.352; 12. C. Seaton (AUS, Suzuki), 22.002; 13. D. Colucci (I, Ducati), 23.114; 14. B. Burrell (GB, Honda), 23.739; 15. D. Giugliano (I, Suzuki), 27.654. 35 finishers. Fastest lap: M. Smrz (CZ, Honda), 1'42.725 (154.584 km/h).

November 2 - Portugal - Portimaõ

1. B. Roberts (AUS, Ducati), 12 laps, 22'23.040 (147.706 km/h); 2. C. Seaton (AUS, Suzuki), 2.995; 3. M. Berger (F, Honda), 3.938; 4. M. Pirro (I, Yamaha), 4.773; 5. M. Smrz (CZ, Honda), 17.166; 6. A. Polita (I, Ducati), 17.482; 7. S. Barrier (F, Yamaha), 10.452; 8. C. Corti (I, Yamaha), 19.878; 9. F. Foray (F, Suzuki), 22.892; 10. B. Burrell (GB, Honda), 23.050; 11. X. Siméon (B, Suzuki), 31.698; 12. S. Saltarelli (I, Suzuki), 32.952; 13. J. Millet (F, Yamaha), 35.502; 14. F. Backlund (S, Suzuki), 37.798; 15. S. Morais (RSA, Kawasaki), 42.098. 33 finishers. Fastest lap: B. Roberts (AUS, Ducati), 1'49.482 (150.995 km/h).

FINAL CLASSIFICATION

1. Brendan Robeerts (AUS)	Ducati	147 points
2. Maxime Berger (F)	Honda	140
3. Alessandro Polita (I)	Ducati	137

4. X. Siméon (B, Suzuki), 136; 5. M. Pirro (I, Yamaha), 102; 6. M. Smrz (CZ, Honda), 84; 7. D. Giugliano (I, Suzuki), 72; 8. F. Foray (F, Suzuki), 62; 9. C. Seaton (AUS, Suzuki), 60; 10. A. Antonelli (I, Yamaha), 57. 37 finishers.

CONSTRUCTORS

1. Ducati	195 points
2. Honda	182
3. Suzuki	175

4. Yamaha, 135; 5. Kawasaki, 50; 6. KTM, 3. 6 finishers.

SIDE-CARS WORLD CHAMPIONSHIP

May 25 - Donington - Great Britain

1. Päivärinta/Karttiala (SF, LCR-Suzuki), 20 laps, 41'17.463; 2. Reeves/Farrance (GB, LCR-Suzuki), 6.224; 3. S. Hegarty/M. Hegarty (GB, LCR-Suzuki), 1'25.344; 4. B. Birchall/T. Birchall (GB, LCR-Suzuki), 1'32.267; 5. Gatt/Randall (GB, LCR-Suzuki), 1'34.110; 6. Schofield/Aalto (GB/SF, LCR-Suzuki), 1 lap; 7. Delannoy/Cluze (F, LCR-Suzuki); 8. Moser/Wäfler (A/CH, LCR-Suzuki); 9. Shand/Belsey (GB, LCR-Suzuki); 10. G. Knight/D. Knight (GB, LCR-Suzuki); 11. Spendal/Hill (SLO/GB, LCR-Suzuki); 12. Remse/D. Biggs (SLO/GB, LCR-Yamaha); 13. Norbury/Knapton (GB, LCR-Suzuki), 2 laps; 14. Percy/Swift (GB, LCR-Suzuki); 15. Rutz/Aeberli (CH, LCR-Yamaha). 15 finishers. Fastest lap: Päivärinta/Karttiala (SF, LCR-Suzuki), 1'59.835.

June 22 - Sachsenring - Germany

Race I: 1. Päivärinta/Karttiala (SF, LCR-Suzuki), 11 laps, 17'54.016 (135.316 km/h); 2. Delannoy/Cluze (F, LCR-Suzuki), 24.508; 3. B. Birchall/T. Birchall (GB, LCR-Suzuki), 26.983; 4. Reeves/Farrance (GB, LCR-Suzuki), 27.807; 5. Moser/Wäfler (A/CH, LCR-Suzuki), 40.044; 6. S. Hegarty/M. Hegarty (GB, LCR-Suzuki), 41.174; 7. Schofield/Aalto (GB/SF, LCR-Suzuki), 48.401; 8. Schlosser/Hänni (CH, LCR-Suzuki), 49.893; 9. Centner/Wolfram (D, LCR-Suzuki), 1'19.166; 10. Reuterholt/Ikonen (S, ART-Suzuki), 1'21.880; 11. G. Knight/D. Knight (GB, LCR-Suzuki), 1'31.723; 12. Remse/D. Biggs (SLO/GB, LCR-Yamaha), 1'44.189; 13. Norbury/Knapton (GB, LCR-Suzuki), 1'48.530; 14. Percy/Swift (GB, LCR-Suzuki), 1'54.657; 15. Rutz/Aeberli (CH, LCR-Yamaha), 2'32.799. 15 finishers. Fastest lap: Päivärinta/Karttiala (SF, LCR-Suzuki), 1'31.894.

Race II: 1. Reeves/Farrance (GB, LCR-Suzuki), 22 laps, 33'06.743 (146.302 km/h); 2. Delannoy/Cluze (F, LCR-Suzuki), 1.263; 3. Päivärinta/Karttiala (SF, LCR-Suzuki), 4.852; 4. B. Birchall/T. Birchall (GB, LCR-Suzuki), 12.374; 5. Schlosser/Hänni (CH, LCR-Suzuki), 17.891; 6. Moser/Wäfler (A/CH, LCR-Suzuki), 20.949; 7. Norbury/Knapton (GB, LCR-Suzuki), 22.016; 8. Schofield/Aalto (GB/SF, LCR-Suzuki), 49.704; 9. Spendal/Hill (SLO/GB, LCR-Suzuki), 1'17.754; 10. Centner/Wolfram (D, LCR-Suzuki), 1'25.857; 11. G. Knight/D. Knight (GB, LCR-Suzuki), 1 lap; 12. Percy/Swift (GB, LCR-Suzuki); 13. Remse/D. Biggs (SLO/GB, LCR-Yamaha). 13 finishers. Fastest lap: Delannoy/Cluze (F, LCR-Suzuki), 1'28.437.

June 28 - Assen - Netherlands

1. Reeves/Farrance (GB, LCR-Suzuki), 18 laps, (156.297 km/h); 2. Päivärinta/Karttiala (SF, LCR-Suzuki), 2,298; 3. Delannoy/Cluze (F, LCR-Suzuki), 17.223; 4. B. Birchall/T. Birchall (GB, LCR-Suzuki), 24.077; 5. Schlosser/Hänni (CH, LCR-Suzuki), 24.446; 6. S. Hegarty/M. Hegarty (GB, LCR-Suzuki), 35.504; 7. Moser/Wäfler (A/CH, LCR-Suzuki), 45.956; 8. Norbury/Knapton (GB, LCR-Suzuki), 1'03.306; 9. G. Knight/D. Knight (GB, LCR-Suzuki), 1'33.547; 10. Reuterholt/Ikonen (S, ART-Suzuki), 1'43.451; 11. Schofield/Aalto (GB/SF, LCR-Suzuki), 1'45.953; 12. Ducouret/Herman (F, LCR-Suzuki), 1 lap; 13. Spendal/Hill (SLO/GB, LCR-Suzuki); 14. Rutz/Aeberli (CH, LCR-Yamaha); 15. Bevers/Vermeer (NL, LCR-Suzuki), 2 laps. 15 finishers. Fastest lap: Reeves/Farrance (GB, LCR-Suzuki), 1'43.347 (158.669 km/h).

13 July - Sachsenring - Germany

1. Päivärinta/Karttiala (SF, LCR-Suzuki), 20 laps, 33'42.401 (130.692 km/h); 2. Reeves/Farrance (GB, LCR-Suzuki), 13.098; 3. B. Birchall/T. Birchall (GB, LCR-Suzuki), 31.299; 4. Delannoy/Cluze (F, LCR-Suzuki), 31.573; 5. Schlosser/Hänni (CH, LCR-Suzuki), 47.403; 6. S. Hegarty/M. Hegarty (GB, LCR-Suzuki), 1'04.365; 7. Norbury/Knapton (GB, LCR-Suzuki), 1'21.886; 8. Moser/Wäfler (A/CH, LCR-Suzuki), 1'32.008; 9. Roscher/Krieg (D, LCR-Suzuki), 1 lap; 10. Schofield/Aalto (GB/SF, LCR-Suzuki); 11. Centner/Wolfram (D, LCR-Suzuki); 12. Reuterholt/Ikonen (S, ART-Suzuki); 13. Spendal/Hill (SLO/GB, LCR-Suzuki); 14. G. Knight/D. Knight (GB, LCR-Suzuki); 15. Percy/Swift (GB, LCR-Suzuki), 2 laps. 16 finishers. Fastest lap : Päivärinta/Karttiala (SF, LCR-Suzuki), 1'39.586 (132.705 km/h).

August 17 - Grobnik - Croatia

Race I: 1. Reeves/Farrance (GB, LCR-Suzuki), 5 laps, 7'44.043; 2. Päivärinta/Karttiala (SF, LCR-Suzuki), 0.473; 3. B. Birchall/T. Birchall (GB, LCR-Suzuki), 4.557; 4. Delannoy/Cluze (F, LCR-Suzuki), 4.763; 5. Schlosser/Hänni (CH, LCR-Suzuki), 6.565; 6. Moser/Wäfler (A/CH, LCR-Suzuki), 13.213. 6 finishers.

Race II: 1. B. Birchall/T. Birchall (GB, LCR-Suzuki), 20 laps, 31'19.725; 2. Päivärinta/Karttiala (SF, LCR-Suzuki), 0.828; 3. Reeves/Farrance (GB, LCR-Suzuki), 6.301; 4. Schlosser/Hänni (CH, LCR-Suzuki), 12.043; 5. Moser/Wäfler (A/CH, LCR-Suzuki), 44.394; 6. Norbury/Knapton (GB, LCR-Suzuki), 51.471; 7. Spendal/Hill (SLO/GB, LCR-Suzuki), 1'08.861; 8. Schofield/Aalto (GB/SF, LCR-Suzuki), 1'10.049; 9. G. Knight/D. Knight (GB, LCR-Suzuki), 1'32.583; 10. Reuterholt/Ikonen (S, ART-Suzuki), 1'39.262; 11. Ozimo/Zanini (I, LCR-Suzuki), 1 lap; 12. Percy/Swift (GB, LCR-Suzuki); 13. Remse/D. Biggs (SLO/GB, LCR-Yamaha). 13 finishers.

September 21 - Le Mans - France

1. Reeves/Farrance (GB, LCR-Suzuki), 18 laps, 30'57.962 (145.785 km/h); 2. Päivärinta/Karttiala (SF, LCR-Suzuki), 2.881; 3. Delannoy/Cluze (F, LCR-Suzuki), 13.209; 4. B. Birchall/T. Birchall (GB, LCR-Suzuki), 15.239; 5. Schlosser/Hänni (CH, LCR-Suzuki), 27.451; 6. S. Hegarty/M. Hegarty (GB, LCR-Suzuki), 39.874; 7. Moser/Wäfler (A/CH, LCR-Suzuki), 53.597; 8. Schofield/Aalto (GB/SF, LCR-Suzuki), 55.603; 9. Ducouret/Herman (F, LCR-Suzuki), 1'12.673; 10. Spendal/Hill (SLO/GB, LCR-Suzuki), 1 lap; 11. Reuterholt/Ikonen (S, ART-Suzuki); 12. Barbier/Debroise (F, LCR-Suzuki); 13. Percy/Swift (GB, LCR-Suzuki); 14. Rutz/Aeberli (CH, LCR-Yamaha); 15. Makkula/Nikkanen (SF, LCR-Suzuki). Fastest lap: Päivärinta/Karttiala (SF, LCR-Suzuki), 1'41.791 (147,832 km/h). 19 finishers.

FINAL CLASSIFICATION

1. Päivärinta/Karttiala (SF)	LCR-Suzuki 171 points
2. Reeves/Farrance (GB)	LCR-Suzuki 169
3. B. Birchall/T. Birchall (GB)	LCR-Suzuki 125

4. Delannoy/Cluze (F, LCR-Suzuki), 107 ; 5. Schlosser/Hänni (CH, LCR-Suzuki), 76; 6. Moser/Wäfler (A/CH, LCR-Suzuki), 76; 7. S. Hegarty/M. Hegarty (GB, LCR-Suzuki), 65; 8. Schofield/Aalto (GB/SF, LCR-Suzuki), 58; 9. Norbury/Knapton (GB, LCR-Suzuki), 50; 10. Spendal/Hill (SLO/GB, LCR-Suzuki), 36; 11. G. Knight/D. Knight (GB, LCR-Suzuki), 34; 12. Reuterholt/Ikonen (S, ART-Suzuki), 28; 13. Centner/Wolfram (D, LCR-Suzuki), 24; 14. Percy/Swift (GB, LCR-Suzuki), 21; 15. Remse/D. Biggs (SLO/GB, LCR-Yamaha), 14. 24 finishers.

EUROPEAN CUP AND CHAMPIONSHIP

The EMU (European Motorcycle Union) was working to a new formula, with the European title going to the winner of a single event on October 12 at Albacete in Spain. The five first place-getters in a number of championships - France, Italy, the Netherlands, Spain, Alpe Adria, Scandinavia, Eastern Europe - and the winners of a series of races under the 'European Cup' banner qualified for the final.

125CC

October 12 - Albacete - Spain

1. L. Savadori (I, Aprilia), 18 laps, 29'03.477 (131.53 km/h); 2. J. Litjens (NL, Seel), 4.422; 3. R. Cardus (E, Derbi), 4.671; 4. R. Moretti (I, Honda), 4.732; 5. P. Tutusaus (E, Aprilia), 15.823; 6. J. Iwema (NL, Seel), 19.166; 7. M. Schrötter (D, Honda), 20.739; 8. E. Lopez (E, Aprilia), 20.829; 9. J. Miralles Jnr (E, Aprilia), 21.123; 10. L. Sembera (CZ, Aprilia), 26.109; 11. C. Carillo (F, Honda), 26.183; 12. F. Lamborghini (I, Aprilia), 27.202; 13. C. Dunikowski (F, Aprilia), 30.704; 14. M. Van Der Mark (NL, Honda), 38.145; 15. L. Vitali (I, Aprilia), 45.098. 32 finishers.

SUPERSPORT

October 12 - Albacete - Spain

1. A. Rodriguez (E, Yamaha), 20 laps, 31'04.762 (136.64 km/h); 2. K. Coghlan (GB, Honda), 3.766; 3. D.

Rivas (E, Suzuki), 4.496; 4. D. Salom (E, Yamaha), 6.219; 5. J.-L. Carrion (E, Honda), 12.388; 6. M.-A. Cortes (E, Yamaha), 12.494; 7. R. Schouten (NL, Yamaha), 20.525; 8. J. Alabarce (E, Kawasaki), 20.777; 9. I. Moreno (E, Yamaha), 32.520; 10. M. Filla (CZ, Yamaha), 39.183; 11. M. Gines (F, Yamaha), 39.371; 12. F. Gamell (E, Kawasaki), 39.747; 13. A. Brannetti (I, Yamaha), 43.592; 14. D. Marrancone (I, Yamaha), 44.129; 15. R. Gomez (E, Yamaha), 50.229. 30 finishers.

SUPERSTOCK 1000

October 12 - Albacete - Spain

1. C. Morales (E, Yamaha), 20 laps, 30'45.886 (138.04 km/h); 2. B. Martinez (E, Yamaha), 2.287; 3. J. Del Amor (E, Yamaha), 2.374; 4. J. Teuchert (D, Yamaha), 13.601; 5. X. Siméon (B, Suzuki), 18.406; 6. D. Lozano (E, Honda), 18.425; 7. I. Silvá (E, Yamaha), 23.339; 8. S. Cruciani (I, Ducati), 23.469; 9. A. Meklau (A, Suzuki), 26.780; 10. J. Torres (E, Yamaha), 32.194; 11. F. Pellizzon (I, Kawasaki), 36.875; 12. A. Lopez (E, Yamaha), 38.663; 13. C. Tangre (F, Suzuki), 48.811; 14. N. Prinz (D, Yamaha), 50.215; 15. L. Verdini (I, Yamaha), 59.215. 30 finishers.

SUPERSTOCK 600

April 6 - Spain - Valencia

1. L. Baz (F, Yamaha), 9 laps, 15'22.756 (140.624 km/h); 2. D. Petrucci (I , Yamaha), 1.166; 3. D. Linfoot (GB, Yamaha), 1.435; 4. D. Beretta (I, Suzuki), 2.310; 5. G. Gregorini (I, Honda), 3.631; 6. L. Biliotti (I, Honda), 4.277; 7. H. Johansson (S, Yamaha), 5.246; 8. E. La Marra (I, Suzuki), 6.343; 9. G. Rea (GB, Yamaha), 7.669; 10. R. Costantini (I, Yamaha), 10.697; 11. P. Vostárek (CZ, Honda), 11.873; 12. V. Lonbois (B, Suzuki), 12.874; 13. N. Calero (E, Yamaha), 13.563; 14. M. Sembera (CZ, Honda), 13.684; 15. T. Grant (GB, Triumph), 13.841. 30 finishers.

April 27 - Netherlands - Assen

1. D. Linfoot (GB, Yamaha), 10 laps, 17'40.133 (154.679 km/h); 2. P. Vostarek (CZ, Honda), 3.188; 3. V. Lonbois (B, Suzuki), 5.707; 4. D. Beretta (I, Suzuki), 6.454; 5. L. Baz (F, Yamaha), 7.023; 6. G. Black (GB, Yamaha), 10.874; 7. M. Bussolotti (I, Yamaha), 15.993; 8. E. La Marra (I, Suzuki), 16.151; 9. G. Rea (GB, Yamaha), 16.252; 10. F. Karlsen (N, Yamaha), 17.718: 11. H. Johansson (S, Yamaha), 18.070; 12. D. Paton (GB, Honda), 18.708; 13. A. Boscoscuro (I, Kawasaki), 21.267; 14. K. Tirsgaard (DK, Suzuki), 21.336; 15. M. Lussiana (F, Yamaha), 29.133. 24 finishers.

May 11 - Italy - Monza

1. L. Baz (F, Yamaha), 8 laps, 15'28.647 (179.658 km/h); 2. M. Bussolotti (I, Yamaha), 1.159; 3. D. Beretta (I, Suzuki), 1.364; 4. D. Petrucci (I, Yamaha), 1.435; 5. L. Biliotti (I, Honda), 2.008; 6. P. Vostarek (CZ, Honda), 3.140; 7. E. La Marra (I, Suzuki), 4.697; 8. G. Rea (GB, Yamaha), 6.512; 9. G. Capitini (I, Yamaha), 8.173; 10. G. Gregorini (I, Honda), 8.301; 11. Y. Guerra (E, Yamaha), 8.599; 12. K. Tirsgaard (DK, Suzuki), 29.739; 13. S. Lowes (GB, Honda), 32.763; 14. C. Von Gunten (CH, Suzuki), 33.141; 15. S. Grotzkyj (I, Honda), 35.342. 16 finishers.

June 15 - Germany - Nürburgring

1. P. Vostarek (CZ, Honda), 9 laps, 18'54.960 (146.647 km/h); 2. L. Baz (F, Yamaha), 0.083; 3. G. Rea (GB, Yamaha), 1.445; 4. G. Gregorini (I, Honda), 1.766; 5. M. Bussolotti (I, Yamaha), 2.038; 6. D. Linfoot (GB, Yamaha), 2.067; 7. G. Black (GB, Yamaha), 10.034; 8. D. Petrucci (I, Yamaha), 10.740; 9. M. Lussiana (F, Yamaha), 11.068; 10. R. Costantini (I, Yamaha), 13.100; 11. K. Tirsgaard (DK, Suzuki), 13.778; 12. O. Jezek (CZ, Kawasaki), 15.431; 13. V. Lonbois (B, Suzuki), 15.644; 14. M. Sembera (CZ, Honda), 16.855; 15. J. Guarnoni (F, Yamaha), 17.421. 28 finishers.

June 29 - San Marino - Misano

1. P. Vostarek (CZ, Honda), 10 laps, 17'12.285 (147.378 km/h); 2. M. Bussolotti (I, Yamaha), 1.959; 3. L. Baz (F, Yamaha), 2.733; 4. V. Lonbois (B, Suzuki), 7.175; 5. D. Beretta (I, Suzuki), 10.101; 6. D. Linfoot (GB, Yamaha), 13.302; 7. D. Petrucci (I, Yamaha), 13.380; 8. G. Black (GB, Yamaha), 15.749; 9. G. Rea (GB, Yamaha), 17.750; 10. H. Johansson (S, Yamaha), 18.121; 11. E. La Marra (I, Suzuki), 18.429; 12. G. Gregorini (I, Honda), 19.764; 13. S. Grotzkyj (I, Honda), 22.318; 14. R. Costantini (I, Yamaha), 23.783; 15. D. Fanelli (I, Triumph), 23.883. 26 finishers.

July 20 - Czech Republic - Brno

1. P. Vostarek (CZ, Honda), 9 laps, 19'12.257 (151.925 km/h); 2. L. Baz (F, Yamaha), 0.349; 3. G. Rea (GB, Yamaha), 16.862; 4. D. Linfoot (GB, Yamaha), 17.037; 5. M. Bussolotti (I, Yamaha), 17.072; 6. G. Black (GB, Yamaha), 17.226; 7. O. Jezek (CZ, Kawasaki), 17,454; 8. L. Biliotti (I, Honda), 22.382; 9. N. Pouhair (F, Yamaha), 24.735; 10. D. Petrucci (I, Yamaha), 26.447; 11. M. Lussiana (F, Yamaha), 26.856; 12. S. Lowes (GB, Honda), 27.034; 13. E. La Marra (I, Suzuki), 29.155; 14. J. Guarnoni (F, Yamaha), 29.539; 15. F. Karlsen (N, Yamaha), 29.940. 26 finishers.

August 3 - Great Britain - Brands Hatch

1. L. Baz (F, Yamaha), 11 laps, 16'56.504 (144.219 km/h); 2. G. Rea (GB, Yamaha), 1.586; 3. D. Beretta (I, Suzuki), 1.744; 4. D. Petrucci (I, Yamaha), 9.700; 5. M. Bussolotti (I, Yamaha), 9.730; 6. E. La Marra (I, Suzuki), 10.062; 7. M. Gines (F, Yamaha), 10.125; 8. G. Black (GB, Yamaha), 15.357; 9. R. Costantini (I, Yamaha), 16.067; 10. L. Hunt (GB, Yamaha), 18.840; 11. J. Guarnoni (I, Yamaha), 19.549; 12. M. Sembera (CZ, Honda), 19.696; 13. D. Paton (GB, Honda), 20.106; 14. D. Fanelli (I, Triumph), 20.381; 15. J. Hamilton (IRL, Kawasaki), 23.851. 30 finishers.

September 7 - Europa - Donington

1. M. Bussolotti (I, Yamaha), 10 laps, 18'11.205 (132.723 km/h); 2. A. Lowes (GB, Kawasaki), 5.559; 3. G. Rea (GB, Yamaha), 11.227; 4. D. Linfoot (GB, Yamaha), 11.298; 5. P. Vostarek (CZ, Honda), 29.434; 6. S. Lowes (GB, Honda), 30.765; 7. V. Lonbois (B, Suzuki), 32.599; 8. L. Johnston (GB, Honda), 37.778; 9. L. Biliotti (I, Honda), 38.491; 10. E. La Marra (I, Suzuki), 43.184; 11. J. Burns (GB, Yamaha), 48.676; 12. L. Baz (F, Yamaha), 49.669; 13. C. Von Gunten (CH, Suzuki), 51.636; 14. J. Day (USA, Honda), 52.503; 15. G. Gregorini (I, Honda), 53.156. 22 finishers.

October 5 - France - Magny-Cours

1. D. Linfoot (GB, Yamaha), 10 laps, 17'44.716 (149.144 km/h); 2. L. Baz (F, Yamaha), 0.232; 3. M. Gines (F, Yamaha), 0.392; 4. V. Lonbois (B, Suzuki), 0.616; 5. M. Bussolotti (I, Yamaha), 1.091; 6. G. Rea (GB, Yamaha), 1.734; 7. D. Beretta (I, Suzuki), 3.377; 8. G. Black (GB, Yamaha), 14.671; 9. K. Tirsgaard (DK, Suzuki), 14.747; 10. E. Masson (F, Yamaha), 14.927; 11. D. Petrucci (I, Yamaha), 15.117; 12. J. Guarnoni (F, Yamaha), 21.192; 13. Y. Guerra (E, Yamaha), 24.562; 14. R. Costantini (I, Yamaha), 25.432; 15. M. Sembera (CZ, Honda), 25.909. 24 finishers.

November 2 - Portugal - Portimaõ

1. G. Rea (GB, Yamaha), 10 laps, 18'18.478 (150.492 km/h); 2. L. Baz (F, Yamaha), 0.060; 3. M. Bussolotti (I, Yamaha), 3.161; 4. V. Lonbois (B, Suzuki), 3.819; 5. J. Day (USA, Honda), 10.038; 6. D. Beretta (I, Suzuki), 12.283; 7. D. Petrucci (I, Yamaha), 14.822; 8. F. Massei (I, Honda), 15.215; 9. M. Lussiana (F, Yamaha), 16.046; 10. J. Guarnoni (F, Yamaha), 16.416; 11. D. Linfoot (GB, Yamaha), 24.940; 12. J. Litjens (NL, Yamaha), 25.267; 13. K. Tirsgaard (DK, Suzuki), 26.040; 14. M. Gines (F, Yamaha), 27.131; 15. F. Karlsen (N, Yamaha), 30.629. 29 finishers

FINAL CLASSIFICATION

1. Loris Baz (F)	Yamaha	186 points
2. Marco Bussolotti (I)	Yamaha	134
3. Gino Rea (GB)	Yamaha	132

4. P. Vostarek (CZ, Honda), 121; 5. D. Linfoot (GB, Yamaha), 117; 6. D. Beretta (I, Suzuuki), 88; 7. D. Petrucci (I, Yamaha), 83; 8. V. Lonbois (B, Suzuki), 71; 9. G. Black (GB, Yamaha), 53; 10. E. La Marra (I, Suzuki), 49. 41 finishers.

USA CHAMPIONSHIP

SUPERSPORT

March 8 - Daytona

1. B. Bostrom (Yamaha); 2. Herrin (Yamaha); 3. R.-L. Hayden (Kawasaki); 4. Davies (GB, Kawasaki); 5. Young (Suzuki); 6. Cardeñas (COL, Suzuki); 7. Rapp (Kawasaki); 8. Zemke (Honda); 9. T. Hayden (Suzuki); 10. Eslick (Suzuki).

April 20 - Birmingham

1. Herrin (Yamaha); 2. B. Bostrom (Yamaha); 3. Zemke (Honda); 4. Young (Suzuki); 5. Rapp (Kawasaki); 6. Cardeñas (COL, Suzuki); 7. Hayes (Honda); 8. Eslick (Suzuki); 9. C. West (Suzuki); 10. C. Davies (GB, Kawasaki).

April 27 - Fontana

1. B. Bostrom (Yamaha); 2. Zemke (Honda); 3. Herrin (Yamaha); 4. Hayes (Honda); 5. C. West (Suzuki); 6. Eslick (Suzuki); 7. Young (Suzuki); 8. C. Davies (GB, Kawasaki); 9. Rapp (Kawasaki); 10. Fouchek (Honda).

May 18 - Sonoma

1. B. Bostrom (Yamaha); 2. Zemke (Honda); 3. Eslick (Suzuki); 4. Young (Suzuki); 5. Hayes (Honda); 6. Herrin (Yamaha); 7. C. West (Suzuki); 8. Beck (Yamaha); 9. Aa. Gobert (AUS, Honda); 10. C. Davies (GB, Kawasaki).

June 1st - Tooele

1. Zemke (Honda); 2. Hayes (Honda); 3. C. West (Suzuki); 4. Aa. Gobert (AUS, Honda); 5. Beck (Yamaha); 6. Young (Suzuki); 7. Aquino (Yamaha); 8. G.-D. Carter (Suzuki); 9. C. Davies (GB, Kawasaki); 10. Fouchek (Honda).

June 8 - Elkhart Lake

1. B. Bostrom (Yamaha); 2. Zemke (Honda); 3. Hayes (Honda); 4. Young (Suzuki); 5. C. West (Suzuki); 6. G.-D. Carter (Suzuki); 7. C. Davies (GB, Kawasaki); 8. Aa. Gobert (AUS, Honda); 9. Rizmayer (H, Suzuki); 10. Eslick (Suzuki).

July 20 - Laguna Seca

1. B. Bostrom (Yamaha); 2. Zemke (Honda); 3. Rapp (Kawasaki); 4. Eslick (Suzuki); 5. Fong (Suzuki); 6. Hayes (Honda); 7. Cardeñas (Suzuki); 8. Aquino (Yamaha); 9. Beck (Yamaha); 10. Herrin (Yamaha).

August 3 - Lexington

1. B. Bostrom (Yamaha); 2. Cardeñas (COL, Suzuki); 3. Hayes (Honda); 4. Young (Suzuki); 5. Zemke (Honda); 6. Rapp (Kawasaki); 7. C. West (Suzuki); 8. Fong (Suzuki); 9. C. Davies (GB, Kawasaki); 10. Aquino (Yamaha).

August 17 - Alton

1. Hayes (Honda); 2. B. Bostrom (Yamaha); 3. Herrin (Yamaha); 4. Young (Suzuki); 5. Zemke (Honda); 6. Fouchek (Honda); 7. Aquino (Yamaha); 8. Eslick (Suzuki); 9. C. West (Suzuki); 10. Wood (Yamaha).

August 31 - Road Atlanta

1. Hayes (Honda); 2. Zemke (Honda); 3. B. Bostrom (Yamaha); 4. Cardeñas (COL, Suzuki); 5. C. West (Suzuki); 6. Herrin (Yamaha); 7. Beck (Yamaha); 8. Day (Yamaha); 9. Aa. Gobert (AUS, Honda); 10. Westby (Yamaha).

September 28 - Laguna Seca

1. Young (Suzuki); 2. B. Bostrom (Yamaha); 3. Herrin (Yamaha); 4. Davies (GB, Kawasaki); 5. Zemke (Honda); 6. C. West (Suzuki); 7. Aquino (Yamaha); 8. Fong (Suzuki); 9. Cardeñas (COL, Suzuki); 10. Beck (Yamaha).

FINAL CLASSIFICATION

1. Ben Bostrom	Yamaha	361 points
2. Jake Zemke	Honda	330
3. Joshua Hayes	Honda	286

4. B. Young (Suzuki), 267; 5. J. Herrin (Yamaha), 263; 6. C. Davies (GB, Kawasaki), 239; 7. C. West (Suzuki), 236; 8. Aa. Gobert (AUS, Honda), 220; 9. M. Beck (Yamaha), 190; 10. D. Eslick (Suzuki), 180. 86 finishers.

SUPERSTOCK

March 8 - Daytona

1. Yates (Suzuki); 2. Young (Suzuki); 3. May (Suzuki); 4. Ulrich (Suzuki); 5. Peris (Suzuki); 6. Barnes (Suzuki); 7. Mazzotta (Suzuki); 8. Pietri (VEN, Suzuki); 9. Wood (Suzuki); 10. Jensen (Suzuki).

April 20 - Birmingham

1. Yates (Suzuki); 2. Holden (Honda); 3. Ulrich (Suzuki); 4. Szoke (Kawasaki); 5. Thompson (Suzuki); 6. McCormick (Kawasaki); 7. May (Suzuki); 8. F. Martin (Suzuki); 9. Jensen (Suzuki); 10. Kienast (Suzuki).

April 27 - Fontana

1. Holden (Honda); 2. Yates (Suzuki); 3. Young (Suzuki); 4. Pietri (VEN, Suzuki); 5. Pridmore (Suzuki); 6. Peris (Suzuki); 7. Ulrich (Suzuki); 8. Jensen (Suzuki); 9. May (Suzuki); 10. Anthony (Suzuki).

May 18 - Sonoma

1. Holden (Honda); 2. Yates (Suzuki); 3. Peris (Suzuki); 4. Peris (Suzuki); 5. Young (Suzuki); 6. Pietri (VEN, Suzuki); 7. Ulrich (Suzuki); 8. Elleby (Suzuki); 9. Jensen (Suzuki); 10. Anthony (Suzuki).

June 1st - Tooele

1. May (Suzuki); 2. Yates (Suzuki); 3. Holden (Honda); 4. Peris (Suzuki); 5. Anthony (Suzuki); 6. Pietri (VEN, Suzuki); 7. Ulrich (Suzuki); 8. Elleby (Suzuki); 9. Thompson (Suzuki); 10. Mazzotta (Suzuki).

June 8 - Elkhart Lake

1. Young (Suzuki); 2. Yates (Suzuki); 3. Pietri (VEN, Suzuki); 4. Seeley (IRL, Suzuki); 5. Barnes (Suzuki); 6. Holden (Honda); 7. Peris (Suzuki); 8. Jensen (Suzuki); 9. May (Suzuki); 10. Anthony (Suzuki).

August 3 - Lexington

1. Yates (Suzuki); 2. Young (Suzuki); 3. Holden (Honda); 4. May (Suzuki); 5. Peris (Suzuki); 6. Jensen (Suzuki); 7. Thompson (Suzuki); 8. K. Noyes (E, Suzuki); 9. Pietri (VEN, Suzuki); 10. Anthony (Suzuki).

August 17 - Alton

1. Yates (Suzuki); 2. Holden (Honda); 3. Peris (Suzuki); 4. Young (Suzuki); 5. May (Suzuki); 6. Toye (Kawasaki); 7. Starnes (Suzuki); 8. Jensen (Suzuki); 9. Ulrich (Suzuki); 10. Anthony (Suzuki).

August 31 - Road Atlanta

1. May (Suzuki); 2. Yates (Suzuki); 3. Young (Suzuki); 4. Holden (Honda); 5. Elleby (Suzuki); 6. Thompson (Suzuki); 7. Ulrich (Suzuki); 8. Caylor (Suzuki); 9. Mazzotta (Suzuki); 10. Starnes (Suzuki).

September 28 - Laguna Seca

1. Yates (Suzuki); 2. Young (Suzuki); 3. May (Suzuki); 4. Peris (Suzuki); 5. Thompson (Suzuki); 6. Elleby (Suzuki); 7. Anthony (Suzuki); 8. Pietri (VEN, Suzuki); 9. Toye (Honda); 10. Mazzotta (Suzuki).

FINAL CLASSIFICATION

1. Aaron Yates	Suzuki	348 points
2. Geoff May	Suzuki	284
3. Jake Holden	Honda	269

4. B. Young (Suzuki), 265; 5. C. Peris (Suzuki), 211; 6. C. Ulrich (Suzuki), 202; 7. R. Elleby (Suzuki), 196; 8. D. Anthony (Suzuki), 193; 9. R. Pietri (VEN, Suzuki), 187; 10. B. Thompson (Suzuki), 173. 75 finishers.

SUPERBIKE

March 18 - Daytona
1. Mladin (AUS, Suzuki); 2. Spies (Suzuki); 3. Di Salvo (Yamaha); 4. T. Hayden (Suzuki); 5. Hacking (Kawasaki); 6. Yates (Suzuki); 7. Hodgson (GB, Honda); 8. R.-L. Hayden (Kawasaki); 9. Young (Suzuki); 10. May (Suzuki).

April 20 - Birmingham
Race I: 1. Mladin (AUS, Suzuki); 2. Di Salvo (Yamaha); 3. T. Hayden (Suzuki); 4. Hacking (Denver); 5. Hodgson (GB, Honda); 6. M. Duhamel (CAN, Honda); 7. E. Bostrom (Yamaha); 8. May (Suzuki); 9. Peris (Suzuki); 10. Szoke (Kawasaki).
Race II: 1. Mladin (AUS, Suzuki); 2. Spies (Suzuki); 3. T. Hayden (Suzuki); 4. Di Salvo (Yamaha); 5. Hodgson (GB, Honda); 6. E. Bostrom (Yamaha); 7. Yates (Suzuki); 8. M. Duhamel (CAN, Honda); 9. Lynn (Honda); 10. May (Suzuki).

April 27 - Fontana
Race I: 1. Spies (Suzuki); 2. Mladin (AUS, Suzuki); 3. T. Hayden (Suzuki); 4. Hodgson (GB, Honda); 5. E. Bostrom (Yamaha); 6. Hacking (Kawasaki); 7. M. Duhamel (CAN, Honda); 8. Di Salvo (Yamaha); 9. Lynn (Honda); 10. Holden (Honda).
Race II: 1. Spies (Suzuki); 2. Mladin (AUS, Suzuki); 3. T. Hayden (Suzuki); 4. Hodgson (GB, Honda); 5. Di Salvo (Yamaha); 6. E. Bostrom (Yamaha); 7. Hacking (Kawasaki); 8. Jensen (Suzuki); 9. Lynn (Honda); 10. Mizdal (Suzuki).

May 18 - Sonoma
Race I: 1. Spies (Suzuki); 2. Mladin (AUS, Suzuki); 3. Hacking (Kawasaki); 4. E. Bostrom (Yamaha); 5. Yates (Suzuki); 6. Hodgson (GB, Honda); 7. Di Salvo (Yamaha); 8. Lynn (Honda); 9. May (Suzuki); 10. M. Duhamel (CAN, Honda).
Race II: 1. Spies (Suzuki); 2. Mladin (AUS, Suzuki); 3. Hacking (Kawasaki); 4. Yates (Suzuki); 5. Hodgson (Honda); 6. E. Bostrom (Yamaha); 7. M. Duhamel (CAN, Honda); 8. May (Suzuki); 9. Peris (Suzuki); 10. Elleby (Suzuki).

June 1st - Tooele
Race I: 1. Spies (Suzuki); 2. Hacking (Kawasaki); 3. Hodgson (GB, Honda); 4. Yates (Suzuki); 5. M. Duhamel (CAN, Honda); 6. E. Bostrom (Yamaha); 7. Di Salvo (Yamaha); 8. Peris (Suzuki); 9. Anthony (Suzuki); 10. Jensen (Suzuki).
Race II: 1. Spies (Suzuki); 2. Hacking (Kawasaki); 3. Hodgson (GB, Honda); 4. Mladin (AUS, Suzuki); 5. Yates (Suzuki); 6. M. Duhamel (CAN, Honda); 7. May (Suzuki); 8. Di Salvo (Yamaha); 9. E. Bostrom (Yamaha); 10. Peris (Suzuki).

June 8 - Elkhart Lake
Race I: 1. Spies (Suzuki); 2. Mladin (AUS, Suzuki); 3. Hacking (Kawasaki); 4. Hodgson (GB, Honda); 5. M. Duhamel (CAN, Honda); 6. Yates (Suzuki); 7. Di Salvo (Yamaha); 8. E. Bostrom (Yamaha); 9. May (Suzuki); 10. Seeley (IRL, Suzuki).
Race II: 1. Mladin (AUS, Suzuki); 2. Spies (Suzuki); 3. Hacking (Kawasaki); 4. Hodgson (GB, Honda); 5. E. Bostrom (Yamaha); 6. M. Duhamel (CAN, Honda); 7. May (Suzuki); 8. Yates (Suzuki); 9. Seeley (IRL, Suzuki); 10. Peris (Suzuki).

July 20 - Laguna Seca
1. Mladin (AUS, Suzuki); 2. Spies (Suzuki); 3. Yates (Suzuki); 4. Hacking (Kawasaki); 5. T. Hayden (Suzuki); 6. R.-L. Hayden (Kawasaki); 7. Hodgson (GB, Honda); 8. Di Salvo (Yamaha); 9. E. Bostrom (Yamaha); 10. Mi. Duhamel (CAN, Honda).

August 3 - Lexington
Race I: 1. Mladin (AUS, Suzuki); 2. Spies (Suzuki); 3. Hacking (Kawasaki); 4. Di Salvo (Yamaha); 5. T. Hayden (Suzuki); 6. R.-L. Hayden (Kawasaki); 7. E. Bostrom (Yamaha); 8. May (Suzuki); 9. Peris (Suzuki); 10. Jensen (Suzuki).
Race II: 1. Mladin (AUS, Suzuki); 2. Spies (Suzuki); 3. Hacking (Kawasaki); 4. Hodgson (GB, Honda); 5. T. Hayden (Suzuki); 6. Mi. Duhamel (CAN, Honda); 7. Di Salvo (Yamaha); 8. May (Suzuki); 9. Peris (Suzuki); 10. K. Noyes (E, Suzuki).

August 17 - Alton
Race I: 1. Mladin (AUS, Suzuki); 2. Spies (Suzuki); 3. T. Hayden (Suzuki); 4. E. Bostrom (Yamaha); 5. Di Salvo (Yamaha); 6. Mi. Duhamel (CAN, Honda); 7. May (Suzuki); 8. R.-L. Hayden (Kawasaki); 9. Peris (Suzuki); 10. K. Noyes (E, Suzuki).
Race II: 1. Mladin (AUS, Suzuki); 2. Spies (Suzuki); 3. T. Hayden (Suzuki); 4. E. Bostrom (Yamaha); 5. Mi. Duhamel (CAN, Honda); 6. Hacking (Kawasaki); 7. Hodgson (GB, Honda); 8. May (Suzuki); 9. Di Salvo (Yamaha); 10. Lynn (Honda).

August 31- Road Atlanta
Race I: 1. Mladin (AUS, Suzuki); 2. Spies (Suzuki); 3. T. Hayden (Suzuki); 4. Yates (Suzuki); 5. E. Bostrom (Yamaha); 6. Di Salvo (Yamaha); 7. Mi. Duhamel (CAN, Honda); 8. May (Suzuki); 9. Thompson (Suzuki); 10. Lynn (Honda).
Race II: 1. Spies (Suzuki); 2. Mladin (AUS, Suzuki); 3. T. Hayden (Suzuki); 4. Mi. Duhamel (CAN, Honda); 5. Di Salvo (Yamaha); 6. E. Bostrom (Yamaha); 7. Hodgson (GB, Honda); 8. Yates (Suzuki); 9. Lynn (Honda); 10. May (Suzuki).

September 28- Laguna Seca
1. Mladin (AUS, Suzuki); 2. Spies (Suzuki); 3. T. Hayden (Suzuki); 4. Yates (Suzuki); 5. Hodgson (GB, Honda); 6. E. Bostrom (Yamaha); 7. Mi. Duhamel (CAN, Honda); 8. Di Salvo (Yamaha); 9. Szoke (Kawasaki); 10. Peris (Suzuki).

FINAL CLASSIFICATION
1. Ben Spies — Suzuki — 652 points
2. Matthew Mladin — Suzuki — 557
3. Jason Di Salvo — Yamaha — 463
4. E. Bostrom (Yamaha), 445; 5. J. Hacking (Kawasaki), 421; 6. N. Hodgson (GB, Honda), 419 ; 7. Mi. Duhamel (CAN, Honda), 412 ; 8. T. Hayden (Suzuki), 372 ; 9. A. Yates (Suzuki), 365 ; 10. G. May (Suzuki), 357. 50 finishers.

FORMULA XTREME

March 8 - Daytona
1. Davies (GB, Honda); 2. Rapp (Kawasaki); 3. Pegram (Ducati); 4. Cardeñas (COL, Suzuki); 5. Cooper (BMW); 6. Parriott (BMW); 7. Fong (Suzuki); 8. Skubic (Yamaha); 9. Atlas (Honda); 10. Amantini (VEN, Kawasaki).

April 20 - Birmingham
1. Zemke (Honda); 2. Cardeñas (COL, Suzuki); 3. C. Davies (GB, Honda); 4. Pegram (Ducati); 5. Rapp (Kawasaki); 6. Aa. Gobert (AUS, Honda); 7. Hayes (Honda); 8. Eslick (Suzuki); 9, G.-D. Carter (Suzuki); 10. Sassaman (Yamaha).

April 27 - Fontana
1. Zemke (Honda); 2. Hayes (Honda); 3. Pegram (Ducati); 4. Rapp (Kawasaki); 5. C. Davies (GB, Kawasaki); 6. Cardeñas (COL, Suzuki); 7. Aa. Gobert (AUS, Honda); 8. Eslick (Suzuki); 9. Moore (Kawasaki); 10. Amantini (VEN, Kawasaki).

May 18 - Sonoma
1. Zemke (Honda); 2. Hayes (Honda); 3. Rapp (Kawasaki); 4. C. West (Suzuki); 5. Pegram (Ducati); 6. Eslick (Suzuki); 7. Moore (Kawasaki); 8. Carter (Suzuki); 9. Amantini (VEN, Kawasaki); 10. Parriott (BMW).

June 1st - Tooele
1. Zemke (Honda); 2. Hayes (Honda); 3. Rapp (Kawasaki); 4. Pegram (Ducati); 5. Aa. Gobert (AUS, Honda); 6. C. West (Suzuki); 7. Beck (Yamaha); 8. G.-D. Carter (Suzuki); 9. Moore (Kawasaki); 10. Herrmann (Yamaha).

June 8 - Elkhart Lake
1. Aa. Gobert (AUS, Honda); 2. Zemke (Honda); 3. Pegram (Ducati); 4. Rapp (Kawasaki); 5. Eslick (Suzuki); 6. C. Davies (GB, Kawasaki); 7. Farrell (Kawasaki); 8. Sassaman (Yamaha); 9. Clay (Yamaha); 10. Barnes (Suzuki).

August 3 - Lexington
1. Hayes (Honda); 2. Zemke (Honda); 3. Cardeñas (COL, Suzuki); 4. C. Davies (GB, Kawasaki); 5. Rapp (Kawasaki); 6. Pegram (Ducati); 7. Eslick (Suzuki); 8. Aa. Gobert (AUS, Honda); 9. Beck (Yamaha); 10. Moore (Kawasaki).

August 17 - Alton
1. Hayes (Honda); 2. Zemke (Honda); 3. Cardeñas (COL, Suzuki); 4. Aa. Gobert (AUS, Honda); 5. Rapp (Kawasaki); 6. C. Davies (GB, Kawasaki); 7. Wood (Yamaha); 8. Pegram (Ducati); 9. Knapp (Yamaha); 10. Moore (Kawasaki).

August 31- Road Atlanta
1. Hayes (Honda); 2. Zemke (Honda); 3. Cardeñas (COL, Suzuki); 4. Rapp (Kawasaki); 5. Davies (GB, Kawasaki); 6. Pegram (Ducati); 7. Aa. Gobert (AUS, Honda); 8. Beck (Yamaha); 9. Knapp (Yamaha); 10. Westby (Triumph).

September 28 - Laguna Seca
1. Zemke (Honda); 2. Hayes (Honda); 3. Rapp (Kawasaki); 4. Cardeñas (COL, Suzuki); 5. Davies (GB, Kawasaki); 6. Pegram (Ducati); 7. Beck (Yamaha); 8. C. West (Suzuki); 9. Aa. Gobert (AUS, Honda); 10. Meiring (Yamaha).

FINAL CLASSIFICATION
1. Jake-P. Zemke — Honda — 336 points
2. Joshua Hayes — Honda — 287
3. Steve Rapp — Kawasaki — 278
4. L. Pegram (Ducati), 265; 5. Aa. Gobert (AUS, Honda), 224; 6. C. Davies (GB, Kawasaki), 224; 7. M. Cardeñas (COL, Suzuki), 213; 8. F. Amantini (VEN, Kawasaki), 177; 9. C. Siebenhaar (Suzuki), 159; 10. N. Moore (Kawasaki), 140. 95 finishers.

GERMAN CHAMPIONSHIP

125CC

April 27 - Lausitz
1. Schrötter (Honda); 2. B. Chesaux (CH, Aprilia); 3. Litjens (NL, Seel); 4. Hübsch (Aprilia); 5. Unger (Aprilia); 6. Fritz (Seel); 7. Kartheininger (Honda); 8. K. Pesek (CZ, Aprilia); 9. Kreuziger (Aprilia); 10. Leigh-Smith (AUS, Honda).

May 18 - Oschersleben
1. Litjens (NL, Seel); 2. Fritz (Seel); 3. Van Der Mark (NL, Honda); 4. Sembera (CZ, Aprilia); 5. Kreuziger (Aprilia); 6. Dubbink (NL, Honda); 7. Bühn (Seel); 8. Vinales (E, Aprilia); 9. B. Chesaux (CH, Aprilia); 10. Gull (S, Derbi).

June 1st - Nürburgring
1. Schrötter (Honda); 2. Litjens (NL, Seel); 3. Fritz (Seel); 4. Hübsch (Aprilia); 5. Siegert (Aprilia); 6. B. Chesaux (CH, Aprilia); 7. Eckner (Seel); 8. K. Meyer (Honda); 9. Dubbink (NL, Honda); 10. Iwema (NL, Seel).
22 June - Sachsenring
1. Schrötter (Honda); 2. Folger (KTM); 3. Litjens (NL, Seel); 4. Gull (S, Derbi); 5. Hübsch (Aprilia); 6. Van Der Mark (NL, Honda); 7. Kreuziger (Aprilia); 8. Finsterbusch (Aprilia); 9. Dubbink (NL, Honda); 10. Viñales (E, Aprilia).

July 6 - Salzburgring - Autriche
1. Fritz (Seel); 2. Iwema (NL, Seel); 3. Kartheininger (Honda); 4. Litjens (NL, Seel); 5. Schrötter (Honda); 6. Van Der Mark (NL, Honda); 7. Grünwaki (Honda); 8. Viñales (E, Aprila); 9. Siegert (Aprilia); 10. Bühn (Seel).

August 3 - Schleiz
1. Schrötter (Honda); 2. Litjens (NL, Seel); 3. Van Der Mark (NL, Honda); 4. Iwema (NL, Seel); 5. Oliveira Falcão (POR, Aprilia); 6. Unger (Aprilia); 7. Grünwald (Honda); 8. Kreuziger (Aprilia); 9. Hübsch (Aprilia); 10. Raemy (CH, Honda).

August 10 - Oschersleben
1. Schrötter (Honda); 2. Litjens (NL, Seel); 3. Van Der Mark (NL, Honda); 4. Siegert (Aprilia); 5. Van Der Aa (NL, Seel); 6. Bühn (Sdeel); 7. Puffe (Seel); 8. Dubbink (NL, Honda); 9. Van Houwelingen (NL, Honda); 10. Raemy (CH, Honda).

September 7 - Hockenheim
1. Van Der Mark (NL, Honda); 2. Schrötter (Honda); 3. Iwema (NL, Seel); 4. Siegert (Aprilia); 5. Litjens (NL, Seel); 6. Grünwald (Honda); 7. Raemy (CH, Honda); 8. Finsterbusch (Aprilia); 9. Dubbink (NL, Honda); 10. K. Meyer (Honda).

FINAL CLASSIFICATION
1. Marcel Schrötter — Honda — 156 points
2. Joey Litjens (NL) — Seek — 145
3. Michael Van Der Mark (NL) — Honda — 99
4. M. Fritz (Seel), 71; 5. J. Iwema (NL, Seel), 61; 6. E. Hübsch (Aprilia), 53; 7. S. Kreuziger (Aprilia), 48; 8. T. Siegert (Aprilia), 44; 9. E. Dubbink (NL, Honda), 44; 10. B. Chesaux (CH, Aprilia), 38. 32 finishers.

SUPERSPORT

April 27 - Lausitz
Race I: 1. Tode (Triumph); 2. Ivanov (RUS, Yamaha); 3. Cudlin (AUS, Yamaha); 4. Diss (F, Kawasaki); 5. Penzkofer (Yamaha); 6. Leonov (RUS, Yamaha); 7. Eckhardt (Yamaha); 8. Kaufmann (Suzuki); 9. Hafenegger (Triumph); 10. Minnerop (Yamaha).
Race II: 1. Tode (Triumph); 2. Cudlin (AUS, Yamaha); 3. Penzkofer (Yamaha); 4. Hafenegger (Triumph); 5. Ivanov (RUS, Yamaha); 6. Diss (F, Kawasaki); 7. Jezek (CZ, Yamaha); 8. Eckhardt (Yamaha); 9. Leonov (RUS, Yamaha); 10. Kaufmann (Suzuki).

May 18 - Oschersleben
Race I: 1. Günther (Triumph); 2. Tode (Triumph); 3. Kaufmann (Suzuki); 4. Cudlin (AUS, Yamaha); 5. Penzkofer (Yamaha); 6. Leonov (RUS, Yamaha); 7. Ivanov (RUS, Yamaha); 8. Diss (F, Kawasaki); 9. Hafenegger (Triumph); 10. Filla (CZ, Kawasaki).
Race II: 1. Tode (Triumph); 2. Kaufmann (Suzuki); 3. Cudlin (AUS, Yamaha); 4. Diss (F, Kawasaki); 5. Ivanov (RUS, Yamaha); 6. Penzkofer (Yamaha); 7. Günther (Triumph); 8. Eckhardt (Yamaha); 9. Filla (CZ, Yamaha); 10. Hommel (Honda).

June 1st - Nürburgring
Race I: 1. Tode (Triumph); 2. Van Keymeulen (B, Suzuki); 3. Diss (F, Kawasaki); 4. Kaufmann (Suzuki); 5. Cudlin (AUS, Yamaha); 6. Jezek (CZ, Yamaha); 7. Wahr (Suzuki); 8. Vostarek (CZ, Honda); 9. Hafenegger (Triumph); 10. Minnerop (Yamaha).

Race II: 1. Ivanov (RUS, Yamaha); 2. Hafenegger (Triumph); 3. Diss (F, Kawasaki); 4. Van Keymeulen (B, Suzuki); 5. Kaufmann (Suzuki); 6. Eckhardt (Yamaha); 7. Raschle (CH, Kawasaki); 8. Wahr (Suzuki); 9. Jezek (CZ, Kawasaki); 10. Cudlin (AUS, Yamaha).

June 22 - Sachsenring

1. Ivanov (RUS, Yamaha); 2. Tode (Triumph); 3. Penzkofer (Yamaha); 4. Diss (F, Kawasaki); 5. Cudlin (AUS, Yamaha); 6. Vostarek (CZ, Honda); 7. Wahr (Suzuki); 8. Richter (Honda); 9. Kaufmann (Suzuki); 10. Raschle (CH, Kawasaki).

July 6 - Salzburgring - Autriche

Race I: 1. Cudlin (AUS, Yamaha); 2. Penzkofer (Yamaha); 3. Leonov (RUS, Yamaha); 4. Diss (F, Kawasaki); 5. Eckhardt (Yamaha); 6. Tode (Triumph); 7. Kaufmann (Suzuki); 8. Sommer (Triumph); 9. Wahr (Suzuki); 10. Jezek (CZ, Kawasaki).

August 3 - Schleiz

Race I: 1. Ivanov (RUS, Yamaha); 2. Tode (Triumph); 3. Cudlin (AUS, Yamaha); 4. Wahr (Suzuki); 5. Diss (F, Kawasaki); 6. Kaufmann (Suzuki); 7. Raschle (CH, Kawasaki); 8. Reichelt (Suzuki); 9. Leonov (RUS, Yamaha); 10. Richter (Honda).

Race II: 1. Ivanov (RUS, Yamaha); 2. Tode (Triumph); 3. Penzkofer (Yamaha); 4. Diss (F, Kawasaki); 5. Wahr (Suzuki); 6. Kaufmann (Suzuki); 7. Cudlin (AUS, Yamaha); 8. Eckhardt (Yamaha); 9. Richter (Honda); 10. Michels (Suzuki).

August 10 - Oschersleben

Race I: 1. Tode (Triumph); 2. Cudlin (AUS, Yamaha); 3. Penzkofer (Yamaha); 4. Diss (F, Kawasaki); 5. Eckhardt (Yamaha); 6. Leonov (RUS, Yamaha); 7. Hommel (Honda); 8. Kaufmann (Suzuki); 9. Ivanov (RUS, Yamaha); 10. Wahr (Suzuki).

Race II: 1. Kaufmann (Suzuki); 2. Penzkofer (Yamaha); 3. Tode (Triumph); 4. Leonov (RUS, Yamaha); 5. Ivanov (RUS, Yamaha); 6. Hommel (Honda); 7. Eckhardt (Yamaha); 8. Ackermann (F, Kawasaki); 9. Michels (Suzuki); 10. Raschle (CH, Kawasaki).

September 7 - Hockenheim

Race I: 1. Penzkofer (Yamaha); 2. Hommel (Honda); 3. Cudlin (AUS, Yamaha); 4. Eckhardt (Yamaha); 5. Tode (Triumph); 6. Richter (Honda); 7. Diss (F, Kawasaki); 8. Kaufmann (Suzuki); 9. Ivanov (RUS, Yamaha); 10. Vincon (Suzuki).

Race II: 1. Diss (F, Kawasaki); 2. Wahr (Suzuki); 3. Ivanov (RUS, Yamaha); 4. Leonov (RUS, Yamaha); 5. Tode (Triumph); 6. Cudlin (AUS, Yamaha); 7. Kaufmann (Suzuki); 8. Hommel (Honda); 9. Richter (Honda); 10. Eckhardt (Yamaha).

FINAL CLASSIFICATION

1. Arne Tode	Triumph	247,5 points
2. Vladimir Ivanov (RUS)	Yamaha	188,5
3. Damian Cudlin (AUS)	Yamaha	184

4. S. Diss (F, Kawasaki), 177,5; 5. H. Kaufmann (Suzuki), 161; 6. R. Penzkofer (Yamaha), 154,5; 7. V. Leonov (RUS, Yamaha), 95; 8. K. Wahr (Suzuki), 89; 9. P. Eckhardt (Yamaha), 88,5; 10. P. Hafenegger (Triumph), 68,5. 30 finishers.

SUPERBIKE

April 27 - Lausitz

Race I: 1. Bauer (A, Honda); 2. Teuchert (Yamaha); 3. Meklau (A, Suzuki); 4. Giuseppetti (Ducati); 5. Daemen (B, Suzuki); 6. Rizmayer (H, Suzuki); 7. Szkopek (POL, Yamaha); 8. Andersen (N, MV-Agusta); 9. Stamm (CH, Suzuki); 10. Vehniäinen (SF, Yamaha).

Race II: 1. Bauer (A, Honda); 2. Teuchert (Yamaha); 3. Meklau (A, Suzuki); 4. Daemen (B, Suzuki); 5. Kellner (Ducati); 6. Szkopek (POL, Yamaha); 7. Stamm (CH, Suzuki); 8. Zaiser (A, Ducati); 9. Giuseppetti (Ducati); 10. Vehniäinen (SF, Yamaha).

May 18 - Oschersleben

Race I: 1. Bauer (A, Honda); 2. Teuchert (Yamaha); 3. Daemen (B, Suzuki); 4. Meklau (A, Suzuki); 5. Andersen (N, MV-Agusta); 6. Stamm (CH, Suzuki); 7. Lammert (Suzuki); 8. Zaiser (A, Ducati); 9. Kellner (Ducati); 10. Knobloch (A, Ducati).

Race II: 1. Bauer (A, Honda); 2. Teuchert (Yamaha); 3. Damen (B, Suzuki); 4. Meklau (A, Suzuki); 5. Stamm (CH, Suzuki); 6. Lammert (Suzuki); 7. Depoorter (B, Suzuki); 8. Knobloch (A, Ducati); 9. Vehniäinen (SF, Yamaha); 10. Von Hammerstein (Honda).

June 1st - Nürburgring

Race I: 1. Bauer (A, Honda); 2. Meklau (A, Suzuki); 3. Daemen (B, Suzuki); 4. Lammert (Suzuki); 5. Zaiser (A, Ducati); 6. Vehniänen (SF, Yamaha); 7. X. Siméon (B, Suzuki); 8. Prinz (Yamaha); 9. Depoorter (B, Suzuki); 10. Muff (CH, Suzuki).

Race II: 1. Bauer (A, Honda); 2. Daemen (B, Suzuki); 3. Meklau (A, Suzuki); 4. Lammert (Suzuki); 5. Stamm (CH, Suzuki); 6. X. Siméon (B, Suzuki); 7. Muff (CH, Suzuki); 8. Knobloch (A, Ducati); 9. Kellner (Ducati); 10. Depoorter (B, Suzuki).

June 22 - Sachsenring

Race I: 1. Teuchert (Yamaha); 2. Bauer (A, Honda); 3. Meklau (A, Suzuki); 4. Daemen (B, Suzuki); 5. K.-B. Andersen (N, MV-Agusta); 6. Stamm (CH, Suzuki); 7. Lammert (Suzuki); 8. Giuseppetti (Ducati); 9. Zaiser (A, Ducati); 10. Rizmayer (H, Suzuki).

Race II: 1. Teuchert (Yamaha); 2. Meklau (A, Suzuki); 3. Stamm (CH, Suzuki); 4. Daemen (B, Suzuki); 5. Zaiser (A, Ducati); 6. K.-B. Andersen (N, MV-Agusta); 7. Depoorter (B, Suzuki); 8. Rizmayer (H, Suzuki); 9. Kellner (Ducati); 10. Knobloch (A, Ducati).

July 6 - Salzburgring - Austria

Race I: 1. Teuchert (Yamaha); 2. Bauer (A, Honda); 3. Daemen (B, Suzuki); 4. Meklau (A, Suzuki); 5. K.-B. Andersen (N, MV-Agusta); 6. Rizmayer (H, Suzuki); 7. Depoorter (B, Suzuki); 8. Giabbani (F, Kawasak); 9. Prinz (Yamaha); 10. Stamm (CH, Suzuki).

Race II: 1. Daemen (B, Suzuki); 2. Teuchert (Yamaha); 3. Bauer (A, Honda); 4. K.-B. Andersen (N, MV-Agusta); 5. Knobloch (A, Ducati); 6. Meklau (A, Suzuki); 7. Prinz (Yamaha); 8. Zaiser (A, Ducati); 9. Giabbani (F, Kawasaki); 10. Stamm (CH, Suzuki).

August 3 - Schleiz

Race I: 1. Bauer (A, Honda); 2. Teuchert (Yamaha); 3. Daemen (B, Suzuki); 4. Meklau (A, Suzuki); 5. Giabbani (F, Kawasaki); 6. Giuseppetti (Ducati); 7. Stamm (CH, Suzuki); 8. Rizmayer (H, Suzuki); 9. Pawelec (POL, Yamaha); 10. Knobloch (A, Ducati).

Race II: 1. Bauer (A, Honda); 2. Teuchert (Yamaha); 3. Meklau (A, Suzuki); 4. Daemen (B, Suzuki); 5. Giabbani (F, Kawasaki); 6. Knobloch (A, Ducati); 7. Andersen (N, MV-Agusta); 8. Lammert (Suzuki); 9. Depoorter (B, Suzuki); 10. Stamm (CH, Suzuki).

August 10 - Oschersleben

Race I: 1. Teuchert (Yamaha); 2. Giabbani (F, Kawasaki); 3. Bauer (A, Honda); 4. Meklau (A, Suzuki); 5. Pawelec (POL, Yamaha); 6. Lammert (Suzuki); 7. Stamm (CH, Suzuki); 8. Knobloch (A, Ducati); 9. Lozano (E, Honda); 10. Prinz (Yamaha).

Race II: 1. Teuchert (Yamaha); 2. Stamm (CH, Suzuki); 3. Rizmayer (H, Suzuki); 4. Giabbani (F, Kawasaki); 5. Daemen (B, Suzuki); 6. Bauer (A, Honda); 7. Meklau (A, Suzuki); 8. Vehniäinen (SF, Yamaha); 9. Kellner (Ducati); 10. Pawelec (POL, Yamaha).

September 7 - Hockenheim

Race I: 1. Bauer (A, Honda); 2. Teuchert (Yamaha); 3. Giabbani (F, Kawasaki); 4. Lammert (Suzuki); 5. Rizmayer (H, Suzuki); 6. Muff (CH, Suzuki); 7. Prinz (Yamaha); 8. Meklau (A, Suzuki); 9. Knobloch (A, Ducati); 10. Andersen (N, MV-Agusta).

Race II: 1. Giabbani (F, Kawasaki); 2. Teuchert (Yamaha); 3. Bauer (A, Honda); 4. Meklau (A, Suzuki); 5. Prinz (Yamaha); 6. Muff (CH, Suzuki); 7. Lammert (Suzuki); 8. Giuseppetti (Ducati); 9. Stamm (CH, Suzuki); 10. Knobloch (A, Ducati).

FINAL CLASSIFICATION

1. Martin Bauer (A)	Honda	323 points
2. Jörg Teuchert	Yamaha	305
3. Andy Meklau (A)	Suzuki	226

4. W. Daemen (B, Suzuki), 199; 5. R. Stamm (CH, Suzuki), 152; 6. D. Lammert (Suzuki), 98; 7. G. Giabbani (F, Kawasaki), 96; 8. Rizmayer (H, Suzuki), 93; 9. Knobloch (A, Ducati), 89; 10. K.-B. Andersen (N, MV-Agusta), 85. 35 finishers.

SIDE-CARS

April 27 - Lausitz

1. Schlosser/Hänni (CH, LCR-Suzuki); 2. Moser/Wäfler (A, LCR-Suzuki); 3. Roscher/Hildebrand (LCR); 4. Hock/Becker (Hock-Suzuki); 5. Schröder/Burkard (CH, LCR-Suzuki); 6. M. Grabmüller/B. Grabmüller (A, LCR-Suzuki); 7. Kornas/Kölsch (RSR); 8. Centner/Höss (LCR-Suzuki); 9. Zimmermann/Ziegler (LCR); 10. Brändle/Helbig (CH, LCR-Suzuki).

May 18 - Oschersleben

1. Kornas/Kölsch (RSR); 2. M. Grabmüller/B. Grabmüller (A, LCR-Suzuki); 3. Hock/Becker (Hock-Suzuki); 4. Hainbucher/Adelsberger (A, RSR-Suzuki); 5. Göttlich/Koloska (LCR-Suzuki); 6. Schröder/Burkard (CH, LCR-Suzuki); 7. Brändle/Helbig (CH, LCR-Suzuki); 8. Eilers/Freund (RSR-Honda); 9. Brüner/Van de Ketterij (Suzuki); 10. S. Dodd/D. Dodd (LCR-Yamaha).

June 1st - Nürburgring

1. Hock/Becker (Hock-Suzuki); 2. Hainbucher/Adelsberger (A, RSR-Suzuki); 3. Schröder/Burkard (CH, LCR-Suzuki); 4. Göttlich/Koloska (LCR-Suzuki); 5. Brändle/Helbig (LCR-Suzuki); 6. S. Dodd/D. Dodd (LCR-Yamaha); 7. Brüner/Van de Ketterij (Suzuki); 8. Kiser/Engelmann (CH, LCR-Kawasaki); 9. Green/Kclloch (GB, LCR-Honda); 10. Rutz/Aeberli (CH, LCR-Yamaha).

June 22 - Sachsenring

1. Kornas/Kölsch (RSR); 2. Hainbucher/Adelsberger (A, RSR-Suzuki); 3. M. Grabmüller/B. Grabmüller (A, LCR-Suzuki); 4. Schröder/Burkard (CH, LCR-Suzuki); 5. Brändle/Helbig (LCR-Suzuki); 6. Göttlich/Koloska (LCR-Suzuki); 7. Zimmermann/Ziegler (LCR); 8. Rutz/Aeberli (CH, LCR-Yamaha); 9. S. Dodd/D. Dodd (LCR-Yamaha); 10. Nagel/Knoof (LCR-Suzuki).

6 July - Salzburgring - Autriche

1. Moser/Wäfler (A, LCR-Suzuki); 2. M. Grabmüller/B. Grabmüller (A, LCR-Suzuki); 3. Hainbucher/Adelsberger (A, RSR-Suzuki); 4. Schröder/Burkard (CH, LCR-Suzuki); 5. Hock/Becker (Hock-Suzuki); 6. Göttlich/Koloska (LCR-Suzuki); 7. Ozimo/Zanarini (I, LCR-Suzuki); 8. S. Dodd/D. Dodd (LCR-Yamaha); 9. Rutz/Aeberli (CH, LCR-Yamaha); 10. Bereuter/Hofer (CH, LCR-Swissauto).

August 3 - Schleiz

1. Schlosser/Hänni (CH, LCR-Suzuki); 2. Hock/Becker (Hock-Suzuki); 3. Kornas/Kölsch (RSR); 4. Hainbucher/Adelsberger (A, RSR-Suzuki); 5. Schröder/Burkard (CH, LCR-Suzuki); 6. Brändle/Helbig (CH, LCR-Suzuki); 7. Göttlich/Koloska (LCR-Suzuki); 8. Zimmermann/Ziegler (LCR); 9. Rutz/Aeberli (CH, LCR-Yamaha); 10. Eilers/De Backer (RSR-Honda).

August 10 - Oschersleben

1. Roscher/Hänni (D/CH, LCR); 2. M. Grabmüller/A. Grabmüller (A, LCR-Suzuki); 3. Schröder/Burkard (CH, LCR-Suzuki); 4. Reuterholt/Ikonen (S, ART-Suzuki); 5. Göttlich/Koloska (LCR-Suzuki); 6. Hainbucher/Adelsberger (A, RSR-Suzuki); 7. Kiser/Engelmann (CH, LCR-Kawasaki); 8. Kornas/Kölsch (RSR); 9. Brändle/Helbig (CH, LCR-Suzuki); 10. Hock/Becker (Hock-Suzuki).

September 7 - Hockenheim

1. Moser/Wäfler (A, LCR-Suzuki); 2. M. Grabmüller/A. Grabmüller (A, LCR-Suzuki); 3. Kornas/Kölsch (RSR); 4. Schröder/Burkard (CH, LCR-Suzuki); 5. Hainbucher/Adelsberger (A, RSR-Suzuki); 6. Hock/Becker (Hock-Suzuki); 7. Ozimo/Zanarini (I, LCR-Suzuki); 8. Göttlich/Koloska (LCR-Suzuki); 9. Zimmermann/Ziegler (LCR); 10. Brändle/Helbig (CH, LCR-Suzuki).

FINAL CLASSIFICATION

1. Hainbucher/Adelsberger (A)	RSR-Suzuki1	20 points
2. M. Grabmüller/A. Grabmüller (A)	LCR-Suzuki	119
3. Hock/Becker	Hock-Suzuki	117

4. Schröder/Burkard (CH, LCR-Suzuki), 116; 5. Kornas/Kölsch (RSR), 113; 6. Göttlich/Koloska (LCR-Suzuki), 86; 7. Brändle/Helbig (CH, LCR-Suzuki), 67; 8. S. Dodd/D. Dodd (LCR-Yamaha), 56; 9. Roscher/Hildebrand (LCR), 50; 10. Rutz/Aeberli (CH, LCR-Yamaha), 47. 21 finishers.

SPANISH CHAMPIONSHIP

125

2007

November 18 - Valencia

1. Redding (GB, Aprilia); 2. Masbou (F, Honda); 3. E. Vazquez (Aprilia); 4. S. Bradl (D, Aprilia); 5. Nakagami (J, Honda); 6. Tutusaus (Aprilia); 7. D. Saez (Aprilia); 8. Maestro (Aprilia); 9. Schrötter (D, Honda); 10. A. Martin (Aprilia).

November 25 - Jerez de la Frontera

1. Redding (GB, Aprilia); 2. S. Bradl (D, Aprilia); 3. Masbou (F, Honda); 4. E. Vazquez (Aprilia); 5. Nakagami (J, Honda); 6. Maestro (Aprilia); 7. Salvadori (I, Aprilia); 8. Marquez (KTM); 9. Salom (Aprilia); 10. Jerez (Honda).

FINAL CLASSIFICATION

1. Stefan Bradl (D)	Aprilia	123 points
2. Scott Redding (GB)	Aprilia	115
3. Efrén Vázquez	Aprilia	92

4. P. Tutusaus (Aprilia), 88; 5. I. Maestro (Aprilia), 66; 6. T. Nakagami (J, Honda), 65; 7. J.-L. Salom (Aprilia), 49; 8. D. Saez (Aprilia), 46; 9. M. Marquez (KTM), 39; 10. A. Masbou (F, Honda), 36. 36 finishers.

2008

April 20 - Valencia

1. Schrötter (D, Honda); 2. A. Martin (Aprilia); 3. L.-J. Salom (Aprilia); 4. R. Cardus (Derbi); 5. J. Miralles Jnr (Aprilia); 6. Trabalon (Aprilia); 7. Beaubier (USA, KTM); 8. Kent (GB, KTM); 9. Llados (Aprilia); 10. Litjens (NL, Aprilia).

May 25 - Catalunya

1. Litjens (NL, Seel); 2. Saez (Aprilia); 3. A. Pons (Aprilia); 4. Redding (GB, Aprilia); 5. E. Vazquez (Aprilia); 6. Maestro (Aprilia); 7. Dalmau (Honda); 8. Casuso (Aprilia); 9. R. Cardus (Derbi); 10. Iwema (NL, Seel).

June 15 - Jerez de la Frontera

1. L.-J. Salom (Aprilia); 2. Tutusaus (Aprilia); 3. E. Vazquez (Aprilia); 4. Savadori (I, Aprilia); 5. A. Martin (Aprilia); 6. Moncayo (Derbi); 7. Trabalón (Aprilia); 8. Climent (Aprilia); 9. J. Miralles Jnr (Aprilia); 10. Otani (J, Honda).

July 27 - Albacete
1. E. Vazquez (Aprilia); 2. Moncayo (Derbi); 3. Tutusaus (Aprilia); 4. R. Cardus (Derbi); 5. Otani (J, Honda); 6. Sambera (CZ, Aprilia); 7. J. Fernandez (Aprilia); 8. Lopez (Aprilia); 9. K. Smith (GB, Aprilia); 10. Borch (N, Aprilia).

September 21 - Albacete
1. Moncayo (Derbi); 2. E. Vazquez (Aprilia); 3. L-J. Salom (Aprilia); 4. R. Cardus (Derbi); 5. Savadori (I, Aprilia); 6. Tutusaus (Aprilia); 7. Otani (J, Honda); 8. Litjens (NL, Seel); 9. A. Martin (Aprilia); 10. Fagerhaug (N, Aprilia).

The two last races (Valencia on November 9 and Jerez de la Frontera on the 16) took place after printing of "The Motorcycle Yearbook" had been completed. Result and final classification of the 2008 Spanish championship in the next issue.

SUPERSPORT
2007

November 18 - Valencia
1. Lascorz (Honda); 2. Gowland (GB, Honda); 3. Brookes (AUS, Honda); 4. Leblanc (F, Honda); 5. Salom (Yamaha); 6. R. Gomez (Suzuki); 7. V. Kallio (Honda); 8. Bonache (Suzuki); 9. A. Rodriguez (Yamaha); 10. Bonastre (Yamaha).

November 25- Jerez de la Frontera
1. R. Gómez (Suzuki); 2. Gowland (GB, Honda); 3. Lascorz (Honda); 4. A. Rodriguez (Yamaha); 5. Bonastre (Yamaha); 6. Carrion (Honda); 7. Bonache (Suzuki); 8. Ortega (Suzuki); 9. Alabarce (Kawasaki); 10. Rivas (Suzuki).

FINAL CLASSIFICATION
1. Graeme Gowland (GB)   Honda   112 points
2. Russel Gómez   Suzuki   109
3. Ángel Rodríguez   Yamaha   99
4. A. Bonastre (Yamaha); 5. J. Lascorz (Honda); 6. J. Alabarce (Kawasaki); 7. D. Arcas (Honda); 8. D. Bonache (Suzuki); 9. J.-L. Carrión (Honda); 10. F.-J. Hidalgo (Honda). 38 finishers.

2008

20 April - Valencia
1. A. Rodriguez (Yamaha); 2. D. Salom (Yamaha); 3. Coghlan (GB, Honda); 4. Rivas (Suzuki); 5. Arcas (Honda); 6. Barragan (Honda); 7. Bonastre (Honda); 8. Carrion (Honda); 9. Tizón (Suzuki); 10. Ortega (Suzuki).

May 25 - Catalunya
1. A. Rodriguez (Yamaha); 2. Tizón (Suzuki); 3. Cortes (Yamaha); 4. Bonastre (Honda); 5. Rivas (Suzuki); 6. Moreno (Yamaha); 7. Monto (Yamaha); 8. Aguilar (Suzuki); 9. Lascorz (Honda); 10. Carrion (Honda).

June 15 - Jerez de la Frontera
1. A. Rodriguez (Yamaha); 2. Coghlan (GB, Honda); 3. Rivas (Suzuki); 4. Albarce (Kawasaki); 5. Cortés (Yamaha); .6 Tizón (Suzuki); 7. Carrión (Honda); 8. Arcas (Honda); 9. Saseta (Honda); 10. Ramos (Kawasaki).

July 27 - Albacete
1. A. Rodriguez (Yamaha); 2. Coghlan (GB, Honda); 3. Tizón (Suzuki); 4. Alabarce (Kawasaki); 5. Moreno (Yamaha); 6. Hidalgo (Honda); 7. Carrion (Honda); 8. Cortes (Yamaha); 9. Pedro (Yamaha); 10. Ramos (Kawasaki).

September 21- Albacete
1. A. Rodriguez (Yamaha); 2. Tizón (Suzuki); 3. Carrion (Honda); 4. Coghlan (GB, Honda); 5. Ortega (Suzuki); 6. Alabarce (Kawasaki); 7. Bonastre (Honda); 8. Ramos (Honda); 9. Cortes (Yamaha); 10. Gamell (Kawasaki).

The two last races (Valencia on November 9 and Jerez de la Frontera on the 16) took place after printing of "The Motorcycle Yearbook" had been completed. Result and final classification of the 2008 Spanish championship in the next issue.

FORMULA EXTREME
2007

November 18 - Valencia
1. De Gea (Suzuki); 2. Sarda (Suzuki); 3. Fuertes (Suzuki); 4. Mazuecos (Kawasaki); 5. Lozano (Honda); 6. B. Martinez (Yamaha); 7. Morales (Yamaha); 8. K. Noyes (Suzuki); 9. Del Amor (Yamaha); 10. Rocamora (Suzuki).

November 25 - Jerez de la Frontera
1. Morales (Yamaha); 2. Del Amor (Yamaha); 3. De Gea (Suzuki); 4. K. Noyes (Suzuki); 5. Mazuecos (Kawasaki); 6. X. Siméon (B, Suzuki); 7. Lozano (Honda); 8. Torres (Yamaha); 9. Cardoso (Yamaha); 10. B. Martinez (Yamaha).

FINAL CLASSIFICATION
1. José David De Gea   Suzuki   151 points
2. Carmelo Morales   Yamaha   129
3. Javier Del Amor   Yamaha   108
4. J. Sardá (Suzuki), 63; 5. S. Fuertes (Suzuki), 63; 6. D. Lozano (Honda), 58; 7. J. Mazuecos (Kawasaki), 55; 8. J. Torres (Yamaha), 54; 9. K. Noyes (Suzuki), 52; 10. J.-L. Cardoso (Yamaha), 38. 27 finishers.

2008

April 20 - Valencia
1. B. Martinez (Yamaha); 2. Cardoso (Suzuki); 3. K. Noyes (Suzuki); 4. Rocamora (Suzuki); 5. Silvá (Kawasaki); 6. Morales (Yamaha); 7. Lozano (Honda); 8. Torres (Honda); 9. Del Amor (Yamaha); 10. Bonache (Suzuki).

May 25 - Catalunya
1. Rocamora (Suzuki); 2. Luis (Yamaha); 3. Cardoso (Suzuki); 4. Del Amor (Yamaha); 5. Carrasco (Kawasaki); 6. Lozano (Honda); 7. Torres (Honda); 8. Tirado (Yamaha); 9. M. Hernandez Jnr (Suzuki); 10.Fuertes (Suzuki).

June 15 - Jerez de la Frontera
1. Morales (Yamaha); 2. Del Amor (Yamaha); 3. Cardoso (Suzuki); 4. Silvá (Kawasaki); 5. K. Noyes (Suzuki); 6. B. Martinez (Yamaha); 7. Fuertes (Suzuki); 8. Monge (Kawasaki); 9. Lozano (Honda); 10. Fores (Kawasaki).

July 27 - Albacete
1. Morales (Yamaha); 2. Del Amor (Yamaha); 3. Cardoso (Suzuki); 4. K. Noyes (Suzuki); 5. Carrasco (Kawasaki); 6. B. Martinez (Yamaha); 7. Lozano (Honda); 8. Torres (Honda); 9. Silvá (Yamaha); 10. Bonache (Suzuki).

September 21 - Albacete
1. Morales (Yamaha); 2. Del Amor (Yamaha); 3. Cardoso (Suzuki); 4. B. Martinez (Yamaha); 5. K. Noyes (Suzuki); 6. Carrasco (Kawasaki); 7. Lozano (Honda); 8. Fores (Kawasaki); 9. Rocamora (Suzuki); 10. Mazuecos (Kawasaki).

The two last races (Valencia on November 9 and Jerez de la Frontera on the 16) took place after printing of "The Motorcycle Yearbook" had been completed. Result and final classification of the 2008 Spanish championship in the next issue.

FRENCH CHAMPIONSHIP
125

March 30 - Le Mans
1. Le Coquen (Honda); 2. Debise (KTM); 3. Carrillo (Honda); 4. Meco (Honda); 5. Deschamps (TVX); 6. Egea (Honda); 7. Ongaro (Honda); 8. Cousin (Honda); 9. Castillo (Honda); 10. Jacquet (KTM).

April 27- Nogaro
1. Debise (KTM); 2. J. Petit (Suzuki); 3. Major (Honda); 4. Ongaro (Honda); 5. Castillo (Honda); 6. Pagaud (Honda); 7. De Tournay (Honda); 8. Barbosa (Honda); 9. Meco (Honda); 10. Di Carlo (Honda).

May 25 - Le Vigeant
1. Le Coquen (Honda); 2. Meco (Honda); 3. Carrillo (Honda); 4. Egea (Honda); 5. Debise (KTM); 6. Castillo (Honda); 7. Ongaro (Honda); 8. A. Michel (Aprilia); 9. Marino (Honda); 10. Galiegue (Honda).

June 15 - Lédenon
1. Dunikowski (Honda); 2. Debise (KTM); 3. Le Coquen (Honda); 4. Ongaro (Honda); 5. Carrillo (Honda); 6. J. Petit (Honda); 7. Marino (Honda); 8. Castillo (Honda); 9. Jacquet (KTM); 10. Deschamps (TVX).

July 6 - Albi
1. Le Coquen (Honda); 2. Debise (KTM); 3. Dunikowski (Aprilia); 4. J. Petit (Honda); 5. Carrillo (Honda); 6. Pagaud (Honda); 7. Jaquet (KTM); 8. Deschamps (TVX); 9. Egea (Honda); 10. Di Carlo (Honda).

July 20 - Magny-Cours
1. Dunikowski (Honda); 2. Debise (KTM); 3. Le Coquen (Honda); 4. Carrillo (Honda); 5. Marino (Honda); 6. J. Petit (Honda); 7. Castillo (Honda); 8. Di Carlo (Honda); 9. De Tournay (Honda); 10. Egea (Honda).

September 7 - Lédenon
1. Dunokowski (Aprilia); 2. Major (Honda); 3. Debise (KTM); 4. Di Carlo (Honda); 5. Marino (Honda); 6. Ongaro (Honda); 7. Castillo (Honda); 8. Pagaud (Honda); 9. Deschamps (TVX); 10. Szalai (Honda).

FINAL CLASSIFICATION
1. Valentin Debise   KTM   132 points
2. Steven Le Coquen   Honda   107
3. Clément Dunikowski Aprilia 91
4. C. Carrillo (Honda), 67; 5. J. Castillo (Honda), 58; 6. O. Ongaro (Honda), 54; 7. J. Petit (Honda), 53; 8. F. Marino (Honda), 49; 9. K. Meco (Honda), 48; 10. S. Egea (Honda), 46. 29 finishers.

SUPERSPORT

March 30 - Le Mans
Race I: 1. Lagrive (Suzuki); 2. Gines (Yamaha); 3. Legrelle (B, Triumph); 4. Polesso (Yamaha); 5. Lefort (Yamaha); 6. Sohier (Triumph); 7. Brian (Honda); 8. Moreira (Yamaha); 9. Andrieu (Kawasaki); 10. Auger (Yamaha).
Race II: 1. Polesso (Yamaha); 2. J. Enjolras (Yamaha); 3. Lefort (Yamaha); 4. Gines (Yamaha); 5. Four (Suzuki); 6. Andrieu (Kawasaki); 7. Marsac (Triumph); 8. Brian (Honda); 9. Ruiz (Kawasaki); 10. Geers (Kawasaki).

April 27 - Nogaro
Race I: 1. Perret (Kawasaki); 2. Moreira (Yamaha); 3. Four (Suzuki); 4. Schier (Triumph); 5. Lefort (Yamaha); 6. Gines (Yamaha); 7. Enjolras (Yamaha); 8. Maurin (Kawasaki); 9. Andrieu (Yamaha); 10. Brian (Honda).
Race II: 1. Perret (Kawasaki); 2. Enjolras (Yamaha); 3. Gines (Yamaha); 4. Four (Suzuki); 5. Moreira (Yamaha); 6. Schier (Triumph); 7. Denis (Honda); 8. Marchand (Honda); 9. Auger (Yamaha); 10. Marsac (Triumph).

May 25- Le Vigeant
1. Denis (Honda); 2. Four (Suzuki); 3. Moreira (Yamaha); 4. Andrieu (Kawasaki); 5. Brian (Honda); 6. Gines (Yamaha); 7. Sohier (Yamaha); 8. Bouffier (Kawasaki); 9. Marsac (Triumph); 10. Castanet (Yamaha).

June 15 - Lédenon
Race I: 1. Enjolras (Yamaha); 2. Four (Suzuki); 3. Nivière (Yamaha); 4. Moreira (Yamaha); 5. Denis (Honda); 6. Andrieu (Kawasaki); 7. Marchand (Honda); 8. Gines (Yamaha); 9. Brian (Honda); 10. Polesso (Yamaha).
Race II: 1. Enjolras (Yamaha); 2. Four (Suzuki); 3. Nivière (Yamaha); 4. Gines (Yamaha); 5. Polesso (Yamaha); 6. Brian (Honda); 7. Marchand (Honda); 8. Denis (Honda); 9. Andrieu (Kawasaki); 10. Moreira (Yamaha).

July 6 - Albi
Race I: 1. Lagrive (Suzuki); 2. Andrieu (Kawasaki); 3. Gines (Yamaha); 4. Brian (Honda); 5. Four (Suzuki); 6. Enjolras (Yamaha); 7. Denis (Honda); 8. Sohier (Yamaha); 9. F. Millet (Honda); 10. Moreira (Yamaha).
Race II: 1. Lagrive (Suzuki); 2. Four (Suzuki); 3. Enjolras (Yamaha); 4. Gines (Yamaha); 5. Moreira (Yamaha); 6. Brian (Honda); 7. F. Millet (Honda); 8. Denis (Honda); 9. Sohier (Yamaha); 10. Polesso (Yamaha).

July 20 - Magny-Cours
Race I: 1. Four (Suzuki); 2. Enjolras (Yamaha); 3. Denis (Honda); 4. Gines (Yamaha); 5. Moreira (Yamaha); 6. Guittet (Triumph); 7. Auger (Yamaha); 8. Andrieu (Kawasaki); 9. Lefort (Yamaha); 10. Brian (Honda).
Race II: 1. Enjolras (Yamaha); 2. Four (Suzuki); 3. Guittet (Triumph); 4. Denis (Honda); 5. Gines (Yamaha); 6. Brian (Honda); 7. Moreira (Yamaha); 8. F. Millet (Honda); 9. Lefort (Yamaha); 10. Andrieu (Kawasaki).

September 7 - Lédenon
Race I: 1. Four (Suzuki); 2. Guittet (Triumph); 3. Nivière (Yamaha); 4. Gines (Yamaha); 5. Denis (Honda); 6. Polesso (Yamaha); 7. Moreira (Yamaha); 8. Brian (Honda); 9. Lefort (Yamaha); 10. Andrieu (Kawasaki).
Race II: 1. Four (Suzuki); 2. Gines (Yamaha); 3. Nivière (Yamaha); 4. Guittet (Triumph); 5. Denis (Honda); 6. Polesso (Yamaha); 7. Brian (Honda); 8. Moreira (Yamaha); 9. Ruiz (Kawasaki); 10. Bouffier (Yamaha).

FINAL CLASSIFICATION
1. Olivier Four   Suzuki   226 points
2. Mathieu Gines   Yamaha   176
3. Julien Enjolras   Yamaha   175
4. F. Moreira (Yamaha), 128; 5. K. Denis (Honda), 125; 6. L. Brian (Honda), 107; 7. M. Andrieu (Kawasaki), 97; 8. P. Polesso (Yamaha), 88; 9. B. Guittet (Triumph), 78; 10. M. Lagrive (Suzuki), 75. 32 finishers.

SUPERBIKE

March 30 - Le Mans

Race I: 1. Jonchière (Suzuki); 2. Piot (MV-Agusta); 3. Dietrich (Suzuki); 4. C. Michel (Suzuki); 5. Stey (Honda); 6. C. Tangre (Suzuki); 7. Brivet (Yamaha); 8. F. Foray (Suzuki); 9. Chapuis (Yamaha); 10. Ganfornina (Yamaha).

Race II: 1. C. Michel (Suzuki); 2. Giabbani (Kawasaki); 3. Dietrich (Suzuki); 4. Piot (MV-Agusta); 5. Metro (Ducati); 6. F. Foray (Suzuki); 7. Jonchière (Suzuki); 8. De Carolis (Suzuki); 9. J. Tangre (Suzuki); 10. Bouan (Yamaha).

April 27 - Nogaro

Race I: 1. De Carolis (Suzuki); 2. Dietrich (Suzuki); 3. Metro (Suzuki); 4. Nigon (Kawasaki); 5. C. Tangre (Suzuki); 6. Jonchière (Suzuki); 7. Brivet (Yamaha); 8. J. Millet (Yamaha); .9 Duterne (Yamaha); 10. Bouan (Yamaha).

Race II: 1. Dietrich (Suzuki); 2. De Carolis (Suzuki); 3. Nigon (Kawasaki); 4. C. Tangre (Suzuki); 5. J. Millet (Yamaha); 6. Bouan (Yamaha); 7. Jonchière (Suzuki); 8. J. Tangre (Suzuki); 9. Prulhière (Yamaha); 10. C. Michel (Suzuki).

May 25 - Le Vigeant

1. Metro (Suzuki); 2. Jonchière (Suzuki); 3. Nigon (Kawasaki); 4. Dietrich (Suzuki); 5. Tangre (Suzuki); 6. Duterne (Yamaha); 7. Giabbani (Honda); 8. J. Millet (Yamaha); 9. Dos Santos (Yamaha); 10. Piot (MV-Agusta).

June 15 - Lédenon

Race I: 1. De Carolis (Suzuki); 2. Dietrich (Suzuki); 3. Nigon (Kawasaki); 4. Da Costa (Suzuki); 5. J. Millet (Yamaha); 6. Metro (Suzuki); 7. C. Tangre (Suzuki); 8. Muscat (Honda); 9. Dos Santos (Yamaha); 10. J. Tangre (Suzuki).

Race II: 1. Da Costa (Suzuki); 2. Nigon (Kawasaki); 3. Dietrich (Suzuki); 4. De Carolis (Suzuki); 5. C. Tangre (Suzuki); 6. J. Millet (Yamaha); 7. Metro (Suzuki); 8. Giabbani (Honda); 9. Dos Santos (Yamaha); 10. Bouan (Yamaha).

July 6 - Albi

Race I: 1. Nigon (Kawasaki); 2. Dietrich (Suzuki); 3. C. Tangre (Suzuki); 4. Barrier (Yamaha); 5. C. Michel (Suzuki); 6. De Carolis (Suzuki); 7. Jonchière (Suzuki); 8. J. Millet (Yamaha); 9. Metro (Suzuki); 10. Mazuecos (Kawasaki).

Race II: 1. Nigon (Kawasaki); 2. Barrier (Yamaha); 3. De Carolis (Suzuki); 4. Dietrich (Suzuki); 5. Duterne (Yamaha); 6. C. Tangre (Suzuki); 7. Jonchière (Suzuki); 8. J. Tangre (Suzuki); 9. Bouan (Yamaha); 10. J. Millet (Yamaha).

July 20 - Magny-Cours

Race I: 1. Nigon (Kawasaki); 2. Giabbani (Kawasaki); 3. Dietrich (Suzuki); 4. Jonchière (Suzuki); 5. Metro (Suzuki); 6. C. Tangre (Suzuki); 7. J. Millet (Yamaha); 8. J. Tangre (Suzuki); 9. Mazuecos (Kawasaki); 10. Bouan (Yamaha).

Race II: 1. Dietrich (Suzuki); 2. Nigon (Kawasaki); 3. Giabbani (Kawasaki); 4. Jonchière (Suzuki); 5. Metro (Suzuki); 6. J. Tangre (Suzuki); 7. Bouan (Yamaha); 8. De Carolis (Suzuki); 9. Mazuecos (Kawasaki); 10. C. Michel (Suzuki).

September 7 - Lédenon

Race I: 1. Nigon (Kawasaki); 2. Dietrich (Suzuki); 3. Dos Santos (Yamaha); 4. C. Tangre (Suzuki); 5. Metro (Suzuki); 6. De Carolis (Suzuki); 7. Prulhière (MV-Agusta); 8. J. Tangre (Suzuki); 9. Bouan (Yamaha); 10. Muscat (Honda).

Race II: 1. Nigon (Kawasaki); 2. Dietrich (Suzuki); 3. J. Millet (Yamaha); 4. De Carolis (Suzuki); 5. Prulhière (MV-Agusta); 6. Metro (Suzuki); 7. Dos Santos (Yamaha); 8. Bouan (Yamaha); 9. C. Tangre (Suzuki); 10. J. Tangre (Suzuki).

FINAL CLASSIFICATION

1. Guillaume Dietrich	Suzuki	240 points
2. Erwan Nigon	Kawasaki	230
3. Lucas De Carolis	Suzuki	152

4. C. Tangre (Suzuki), 127; 5. T. Metro (Suzuki), 121; 6. E. Jonchière (Suzuki), 118; 7. J. Millet (Yamaha), 88; 8. C. Michel (Suzuki), 85; 9. D. Bouan (Yamaha), 77; 10. G. Giabbani (Kawasaki), 73. 34 finishers.

SIDE-CARS

March 30 - Le Mans

Race I: 1. Delannoy/Cluze (Suzuki); 2. Le Bail/Chaigneau (Auto Moto); 3. Ducouret/Herman (Suzuki); 4. F. Leblond/S. Leblond (Honda); 5. Bourch'is/Scellier (Honda); 6. Hergott/Moise (Suzuki); 7. Dernoncourt (Suzuki); 8. Marzelle/Lavidalie (Suzuki); 9. J.-C. Huet/J. Huet (LCR); 10. Bajus/Duhamel (Kawasaki).

Race II : 1. Delannoy/Cluze (Suzuki); 2. Le Bail/Chaigneau (Auto Moto); 3. Ducouret/Herman (Suzuki); 4. Bourch'is/Scellier (Honda); 5. Dernoncourt (Suzuki); 6. F. Leblond/S. Leblond (Honda); 7. Bajus/Duhamel (Kawasaki); 8. Marzelle/Lavidalie (Suzuki); 9. Le Lias/Le Ber (Yamaha); 10. Gallerne/Chesneau (Suzuki).

April 27 - Nogaro

Race I: 1. Delannoy/Cluze (Suzuki); 2. Le Bail/Chaigneau (Auto Moto); 3. Ducouret/Herman (Suzuki); 4. Beneteau/Chaussade (Suzuki); 5. Marzelle/Lavidalie (Suzuki); 6. S. Bessy/R. Bessy (Suzuki); 7. Bourch'is/Scellier (Honda); 8. Leguen/Minaret (Suzuki); 9. R. Poret/V. Poret (Suzuki); 10. F. Leblond/S. Leblond (Honda).

Race II: 1. Delannoy/Cluze (Suzuki); 2. Le Bail/Chaigneau (Auto Moto); 3. Ducouret/Herman (Suzuki); 4. S. Bessy/R. Bessy (Suzuki); 5. Beneteau/Chaussade (Suzuki); 6. Marzelle/Lavidalie (Suzuki); 7. Bourch'is/Scellier (Honda); 8. R. Poret/V. Poret (Suzuki); 9. Gallerne/Chesneau (Suzuki); 10. Leguen/Minaret (Suzuki).

May 25 - Le Vigeant

Race I: 1. Dernoncourt/Romand (Suzuki); 2. Ducouret/Herman (Suzuki); 3. Barbier/Chaperon (Suzuki); 4. R. Poret/V. Poret (Suzuki); 5. Marzelle/Lavidalie (Suzuki); 6. Beneteau/Chaussade (Suzuki); 7. Bourch'is/Scellier (Honda); 8. Guigue/Théveneau (Suzuki); 9. S. Bessy/R. Bessy (Suzuki); 10. Bajus/Duhamel (Kawasaki).

Race II: 1. Le Bail/Chaigneau (Auto Moto); 2. Dernoncourt/Romand (Suzuki); 3. Marzelle/Lavidalie (Suzuki); 4. Bourch'is/Scellier (Honda); 5. Hergott/Moise (Suzuki); 6. Le Lias/Debroise (Yamaha); 7. J.-C. Kestler/L. Kestler (Honda); 8. T. Le Neillon/P. Le Neillon (Windle); 9. S. Bessy/R. Bessy (Suzuki); 10. Gallerne/Chesneau (Suzuki).

June 15 - Lédenon

Race I: 1. Delannoy/Cluze (Suzuki); 2. Dernoncourt/Romand (Suzuki); 3. Le Bail/Chaigneau (Auto Moto); 4. Ducouret/Herman (Suzuki); 5. Barbier/Chaperon (Suzuki); 6. Marzelle/Lavidalie (Suzuki); 7. Beneteau/Vannier (Suzuki); 8. R. Poret/V. Poret (Suzuki); 9. Bourch'is/Scellier (Honda); 10. Gallerne/Chesneau (Suzuki).

Race II : 1. Delannoy/Cluze (Suzuki); 2. Dernoncourt/Romand (Suzuki); 3. Le Bail/Chaigneau (Auto Moto); 4. Ducouret/Herman (Suzuki); 5. Barbier/Chaperon (Suzuki); 6. Marzelle/Lavidalie (Suzuki); 7. R. Poret/V. Poret (Suzuki); 8. Beneteau/Vannier (Suzuki); 9. Gallerne/Chesneau (Suzuki); 10. Leguen/Minaret (Suzuki).

July 6 - Albi

Race I: 1. Dernoncourt/Romand (Suzuki); 2. Ducouret/Herman (Suzuki); 3. Le Bail/Chaigneau (Auto Moto); 4. S. Bessy/R. Bessy (Suzuki); 5. Marzelle/Lavidalie (Suzuki); 6. Barbier/Chaperon (Suzuki); 7. Beneteau/Leverdier (Suzuki); 8. Leguen/Minaret (Suzuki); 9. R. Poret/V. Poret (Suzuki); 10. Gallerne/Chesneau (Suzuki).

Race II: 1. Dernoncourt/Romand (Suzuki); 2. Ducouret/Herman (Suzuki); 3. Le Bail/Chaigneau (Auto Moto); 4. Barbier/Chaperon (Suzuki); 5. S. Bessy/R. Bessy (Suzuki); 6. Marzelle/Lavidalie (Suzuki); 7. Bourch'is/Scellier (Honda); 8. R. Poret/V. Poret (Suzuki); 9. Guigue/Théveneau (Suzuki); 10. Reynier/Deparier (Suzuki).

July 20 - Magny-Cours

Race I: 1. Delannoy/Cluze (Suzuki); 2. Ducouret/Herman (Suzuki); 3. Dernoncourt/Romand (Suzuki); 4. S. Bessy/R. Bessy (Suzuki); 5. R. Poret/V. Poret (Suzuki); 6. Beneteau/Bajus (Suzuki); 7. Gallerne/Chesneau (Suzuki); 8. Bourch'is/Scellier (Honda); 9. Leguen/Minaret (Suzuki); 10. Hergott/Moise (Suzuki).

Race II: 1. Delannoy/Cluze (Suzuki); 2. Dernoncourt/Romand (Suzuki); 3. S. Bessy/R. Bessy (Suzuki); 4. Barbier/Chaperon (Suzuki); 5. Beneteau/Bajus (Suzuki); 6. R. Poret/V. Poret (Suzuki); 7. Gallerne/Chesneau (Suzuki); 8. Bourch'is/Scellier (Honda); 9. Leguen/Minaret (Suzuki); 10. Hergott/Moise (Suzuki).

September 7 - Lédenon

Race I: 1. Delannoy/Cluze (Suzuki); 2. Dernoncourt/Romand (Suzuki); 3. Ducouret/Herman (Suzuki); 4. Beneteau/Bajus (Suzuki); 5. R. Poret/V. Poret (Suzuki); 6. Gallerne/Chesneau (Suzuki); 7. Bourch'is/Scellier (Honda); 8. Hergott/Moise (Suzuki); 9. Leguen/Minaret (Suzuki); 10. Guigue/Théveneau (Suzuki).

Race II: 1. Delannoy/Cluze (Suzuki); 2. Dernoncourt/Romand (Suzuki); 3. Ducouret/Herman (Suzuki); 4. Beneteau/Bajus (Suzuki); 5. R. Poret/V. Poret (Suzuki); 6. Gallerne/Chesneau (Suzuki); 7. Bourch'is/Scellier (Honda); 8. Guigue/Théveneau (Suzuki); 9. Hergott/Moise (Suzuki); 10. Leguen/Minaret (Suzuki).

FINAL CLASSIFICATION

1. Delannoy/Cluze	Suzuki	125 points
2. Dernoncourt/Romand	Suzuki	115
3. Ducouret/Herman	Suzuki	102

4. Le Bail/Chaigneau (Auto Moto), 84; 5. Bourch'is/Scellier (Honda), 62; 6. Beneteau/Chaussade/Bajus (Suzuki), 56; 7. Marzelle/Lavidalie (Suzuki), 52; 8. R. Poret/V. Poret (Suzuki), 51; 9. S. Bessy/R. Bessy (Suzuki), 45; 10. Gallerne/Chesneau (Suzuki), 44. 27 finishers.

Final classification Side F2:

1. Bourch'is/Scellier (Honda), 170; 2. Hergott/Moise (Suzuki), 106; 3. F. Leblond/S. Leblond (Honda), 84; 4. Bajus/Duhamel (Kawasaki), 78; 5. Le Lias/Le Ber (Yamaha), 63; 6. J.-C. Huet/J. Huet (LCR), 62. 15 finishers.

BRITISH CHAMPIONSHIP

125

April 6 - Brands Hatch GP

Race cancelled due to the snow.

April 20 - Thruxton

1. Jordan (Honda); 2. Wilcox (Honda); 3. Hoyle (Honda); 4. Ford (Honda); 5. Costello (Honda); 6. Finlay (Honda); 7. Hinton (Honda); 8. Hayward (Honda); 9. Mossey (Honda); 10. Glossop (Honda).

May 5 - Oulton Park

1. Hoyle (Honda); 2. Behan (Honda); 3. Costello (Honda); 4. East (Honda); 5. Hinton (Honda); 6. Hayward (Honda); 7. Hastings (Honda); 8. Ford (Honda); 9. Green (Honda); 10. Horsman (Honda).

May 11 - Brands Hatch GP

1. Hoyle (Honda); 2. Hinton (Honda); 3. Jordan (Honda); 4. Hastings (Honda); 5. Finlay (Honda); 6. Hayward (Honda); 7. Lewis (Honda); 8. Behan (Honda); 9. Lodge (Honda); 10. Horsman (Honda).

June 15 - Snetterton

1. Jordan (Honda); 2. Glossop (Honda); 3. Horsman (Honda); 4. Hayward (Honda); 5. Hastings (Honda); 6. Hinton (Honda); 7. Lodge (Honda); 8. Kewis (Honda); 9. Ford (Honda); 10. Costello (Honda).

June 29 - Mallory Park

Race I: 1. Costello (Honda); 2. Hayward (Honda); 3. Behan (Honda); 4. Hastings (Honda); 5. Jordan (Honda); 6. Hinton (Honda); 7. Thompson (Honda); 8. Malton (Honda); 9. Lodge (Honda); 10. East (Honda).

Race II: 1. Glossop (Honda); 2. Hastings (Honda); 3. Lewis (Honda); 4. Lodge (Honda); 5. Jordan (Honda); 6. Hayward (Honda); 7. Horsman (Honda); 8. Thompson (Honda); 9. Wilcox (Honda); 10. Malton (Honda).

July 20 - Oulton Park

1. Hoyle (Honda); 2. Hastings (Honda); 3. Glossop (Honda); 4. East (Honda); 5. Hayward (Honda); 6. Jordan (Honda); 7. Lodge (Honda); 8. Hinton (Honda); 9. Behan (Honda); 10. Wilcox (Honda).

August 10 - Knockhill

1. Hoyle (Honda); 2. Glossop (Honda); 3. Hastings (Honda); 4. East (Honda); 5. Lodge (Honda); 6. Waddell (Honda); 7. Hinton (Honda); 8. Jordan (Honda); 9. Horsman (Honda); 10. Behan (Honda).

August 25- Cadwell Park

1. Hoyle (Honda); 2. Glossop (Honda); 3. Hayward (Honda); 4. Hastings (Honda); 5. Jordan (Honda); 6. J. Lewis (Honda); 7. D. Brown (Honda); 8. East (Honda); 9. Horsman (Honda); 10. Behan (Honda).

September 14 - Croft

1. Hastings (Honda); 2. J. Lewis (Honda); 3. Behan (Honda); 4. Hayward (Honda); 5. Horsman (Honda); 6. D. Brown (Honda); 7. Lodge (Honda); 8. Thompson (Honda); 9. M. Hill (Honda); 10. Hinton (Honda).

September 28 - Silverstone

1. Hoyle (Honda); 2. Hastings (Honda); 3. Behan (Honda); 4. Lodge (Honda); 5. Hayward (Honda); 6. Jordan (Honda); 7. Horsman (Honda); 8. Thompson (Honda); 9. Green (Honda); 10. Blacklock (Honda).

October 12 - Brands Hatch Indy

1. Lodge (Honda); 2. Hoyle (Honda); 3. Behan (Honda); 4. East (Honda); 5. Horsman (Honda); 6. T. MacKenzie (Honda); 7. Hayward (Honda); 8. J. Lewis (Honda); 9. C. Lewis (Honda); 10. Thompson (Honda).

FINAL CLASSIFICATION

1. Matthew Hoyle	Honda	190 points
2. Tim Hastings	Honda	162
3. Paul Jordan	Honda	135

4. T. Hayward (Honda), 134; 5. C. Behan (Honda), 118; 6. J. Lodge (Honda), 109; 7. M. Glossop (Honda), 107; 8. L. Hinton (Honda), 91; 9. S. Horsman (Honda), 86; 10. J. Lewis (Honda), 71. 37 finishers.

SUPERSTOCK 600

April 6 - Brands Hatch GP

Race cancelled due to the snow.

April 20 - Thruxton

1. Jones (Yamaha); 2. Northover (Yamaha); 3. Hamilton (Kawasaki); 4. Morris (Suzuki); 5. Haire

(Yamaha); 6. Day (Yamaha); 7. Johnston (Yamaha); 8. R. Brown (Yamaha); 9. Gault (Kawasaki); 10. Stapleford (Kawasaki).

May 5 - Oulton Park
1. R. Brown (Yamaha); 2. Venter (Triumph); 3. Johnston (Yamaha); 4. J. Hill (Yamaha); 5. Iddon (Honda); 6. Haire (Yamaha); 7. Northover (Yamaha); 8. Hamilton (Kawasaki); 9. Dunn (Honda); 10. N. Coates (Honda).

May 11 - Brands Hatch GP
1. Jones (Yamaha); 2. Hunt (Yamaha); 3. Johnston (Yamaha); 4. Haire (Yamaha); 5. R. Brown (Yamaha); 6. Linsdell (Yamaha); 7. Gault (Kawasaki); 8. Stapleford (Kawasaki); 9. Hamilton (Kawasaki); 10. N. Coates (Honda).

May 26 - Donington
1. R. Brown (Yamaha); 2. Johnston (Yamaha); 3. Venter (Triumph); 4. Hamilton (Kawasaki); 5. Jones (Yamaha); 6. Burns (Yamaha); 7. Day (Yamaha); 8. Haire (Yamaha); 9. Northover (Yamaha); 10. Gault (Kawasaki).

June 15 - Snetterton
1. Jones (Yamaha); 2. Johnston (Yamaha); 3. Venter (Triumph); 4. R. Brown (Yamaha); 5. Stapleford (Kawasaki); 6. J. Hill (Yamaha); 7. Hunt (Yamaha); 8. Northover (Yamaha); 9. Day (Yamaha); 10. Hamilton (Kawasaki).

July 20 - Oulton Park
1. Venter (Triumph); 2. Stapleford (Kawasaki); 3. Day (Yamaha); 4. Johnston (Yamaha); 5. Hamilton (Kawasaki); 6. Gault (Kawasaki); 7. Hunt (Yamaha); 8. Morris (Suzuki); 9. J. Hill (Yamaha); 10. McLean (Yamaha).

August 10 - Knockhill
1. R. Brown (Yamaha); 2. Johnston (Yamaha); 3. Venter (Triumph); 4. J. Hill (Yamaha); 5. J. Burns (Yamaha); 6. Stapleford (Kawasaki); 7. Northover (Yamaha); 8. Kneen (Yamaha); 9. Neate (Kawasaki); 10. Railton (Yamaha).

August 25 - Cadwell Park
1. J. Hill (Yamaha); 2. Northover (Yamaha); 3. Johnston (Yamaha); 4. R. Brown (Yamaha); 5. Dickson (Yamaha); 6. Venter (Triumph); 7. Groves (Yamaha); 8. Neate (Kawasaki); 9. Hamilton (Kawasaki); 10. Linsdell (Yamaha).

September 14 - Croft
1. R. Brown (Yamaha); 2. Johnston (Yamaha); 3. N. Coates (Honda); 4. J. Burns (Yamaha); 5. Akroyd (Triumph); 6. Gault (Kawasaki); 7. Dickson (Yamaha); 8. L. Jones (Yamaha); 9. Venter (Triumph); 10. Stapleford (Kawasaki).

September 28 - Silverstone
1. L. Jones (Yamaha); 2. Johnston (Yamaha); 3. J. Hill (Yamaha); 4. Northover (Yamaha); 5. Venter (Triumph); 6. Gault (Kawasaki); 7. Stapleford (Kawasaki); 8. J. Burns (Yamaha); 9. Dickson (Yamaha); 10. Linsdell (Yamaha).

October 12 - Brands Hatch Indy
Race I: 1. J. Hill (Yamaha); 2. Northover (Yamaha); 3. Johnston (Yamaha); 4. Trayler (Kawasaki); 5. Bilton (Yamaha); 6. R. Brown (Yamaha); 7. Lyon (Yamaha); 8. Linsdell (Yamaha); 9. Haire (Yamaha); 10. Dickson (Yamaha).
Race II: 1. R. Brown (Yamaha); 2. Bilton (Yamaha); 3. Johnston (Yamaha); 4. Northover (Yamaha); 5. Trayler (Kawasaki); 6. Hunt (Yamaha); 7. Venter (Triumph); 8. Haire (Yamaha); 9. Linsdell (Yamaha); 10. Hamilton (Yamaha).

FINAL CLASSIFICATION
1. Lee Johnston   Yamaha   207 points
2. Robbie Brown   Yamaha   166
3. Chris Northover   Yamaha   135
4. A-J. Venter (Yamaha), 132; 5. L. Jones (Yamaha), 124; 6. J. Hill (Yamaha), 112; 7. L. Stapleford (Kawasaki), 81; 8. J. Hamilton (Yamaha), 77; 9. D. Haire (Yamaha), 62; 10. A. Gault (Kawasaki), 59. 41 finishers.

SUPERSTOCK 1000

April 6 - Brands Hatch GP
Race cancelled due to the snow.

April 20- Thruxton
1. Brogan (Honda); 2. Kirkham (Yamaha); 3. Donald (Suzuki); 4. Neill (Suzuki); 5. Hickman (Yamaha); 6. Cummins (Yamaha); 7. Seeley (Yamaha); 8. Johnson (Honda); 9. Mainwaring (Suzuki); 10. Cox (Yamaha).

May 5 - Oulton Park
1. Brogan (Honda); 2. Kirkham (Yamaha); 3. Cummins (Yamaha); 4. Seeley (Yamaha); 5. Wilson (Yamaha); 6. Neill (Suzuki); 7. Hickman (Yamaha); 8. Gilbertson (Kawasaki); 9. L. Jackson (Yamaha); 10. Cox (Yamaha).

May 11- Brands Hatch GP
1. Brogan (Honda); 2. Kirkham (Yamaha); 3. Neill (Suzuki); 4. Seeley (Yamaha); 5. Storrar (Suzuki); 6. L. Jackson (Yamaha); 7. A. Coates (Yamaha); 8. Cox (Yamaha); 9. Blair (Suzuki); 10. Hegarty (Yamaha).

May 26 - Donington
1. Neill (Suzuki); 2. Brogan (Honda); 3. A. Coates (Yamaha); 4. Seeley (Yamaha); 5. Storrar (Suzuki); 6. Cox (Yamaha); 7. Wilson (Yamaha); 8. Hickman (Yamaha); 9. Mainwaring (Suzuki); 10. L. Jackson (Yamaha).

June 15 - Snetterton
1. Brogan (Honda); 2. Kirkham (Yamaha); 3. Seeley (Yamaha); 4. A. Coates (Yamaha); 5. Neill (Suzuki); 6. Hickman (Yamaha); 7. Wilson (Yamaha); 8. Mainwaring (Suzuki); 9. L. Jackson (Yamaha); 10. Hegarty (Yamaha).

July 20 - Oulton Park
Race I: 1. Brogan (Honda); 2. Kirkham (Yamaha); 3. L. Jackson (Yamaha); 4. Coates (Yamaha); 5. Hickman (Yamaha); 6. Cox (Yamaha); 7. Donald (Suzuki); 8. Gilbertson (Kawasaki); 9. Cummins (Yamaha); 10. Stewart (Yamaha).
Race II: 1. Kirkham (Yamaha); 2. Brogan (Honda); 3. Coates (Yamaha); 4. L. Jackson (Yamaha); 5. Mainwaring (Suzuki); 6. Seeley (Yamaha); 7. Wilson (Yamaha); 8. Hickman (Yamaha); 9. Cox (Yamaha); 10. Donald (Suzuki).

August 10- Knockhill
1. Brogan (Honda); 2. Kirkham (Yamaha); 3. Gilbertson (Kawasaki); 4. Hegarty (Yamaha); 5. Storrar (Suzuki); 6. Warren (Yamaha); 7. Neill (Suzuki); 8. Donald (Suzuki); 9. Seeley (Yamaha); 10. Clarke (Honda).

August 25 - Cadwell Park
1. Brogan (Honda); 2. Kirkham (Yamaha); 3. Hickman (Yamaha); 4. A. Coates (Yamaha); 5. Wilson (Yamaha); 6. Gilbertson (Kawasaki); 7. Hegarty (Yamaha); 8. Hutchinson (Kawasaki); 9. L. Jackson (Yamaha); 10. Burrell (Yamaha).

September 14 - Croft
1. Kirkham (Yamaha); 2. Wilson (Yamaha); 3. Hickman (Yamaha); 4. Brogan (Honda); 5. Seeley (Yamaha); 6. A. Coates (Yamaha); 7. Storrar (Suzuki); 8. L. Jackson (Yamaha); 9. Cox (Yamaha); 10. Gilbertson (Kawasaki).

September 28 - Silverstone
1. Kirkham (Yamaha); 2. Brogan (Honda); 3. Wilson (Yamaha); 4. Hickman (Yamaha); 5. Cooper (Yamaha); 6. Cox (Yamaha); 7. Warren (Yamaha); 8. L. Jackson (Yamaha); 9. Cummins (Yamaha); 10. Mainwaring (Suzuki).

October 12 - Brands Hatch Indy
1. Brogan (Honda); 2. Hickman (Yamaha); 3. Seeley (Yamaha); 4. B. Wilson (Yamaha); 5. A. Coates (Yamaha); 6. R. Cooper (Yamaha); 7. Hegarty (Yamaha); 8. Cox (Yamaha); 9. Mercer (Yamaha); 10. L. Jackson (Yamaha).

FINAL CLASSIFICATION
1. Steve Brogan   Honda   273 points
2. Jon Kirkham   Yamaha   215
3. Peter Hickman   Yamaha   125
4. A. Seeley (Yamaha), 108; 5. B. Wilson (Yamaha), 103; 6. A. Coates (Yamaha), 102; 7. M. Neill (Suzuki), 93; 8. L. Jackson (Yamaha), 93; 9. V. Cox (Yamaha), 75; 10. J. Storrar (Suzuki), 56. 36 finishers.

SUPERSPORT

April 6 - Brands Hatch GP
Race cancelled due to the snow.

April 20 - Thruxton
1. Brogan (Honda); 2. Richards (AUS, Triumph); 3. C. Martin (Kawasaki); 4. Kennaugh (RSA, Yamaha); 5. Lowry (Suzuki); 6. Grant (Yamaha); 7. Nutt (Yamaha); 8. Hutchinson (Yamaha); 9. Young (Triumph); 10. Neate (Kawasaki).

May 5 - Oulton Park
1. Richards (AUS, Triumph); 2. Kennaugh (RSA, Yamaha); 3. Lowry (Suzuki); 4. C. Martin (Kawasaki); 5. Brogan (Honda); 6. Toal (Yamaha); 7. D. Cooper (Honda); 8. Fitzpatrick (Yamaha); 9. Hutchinson (Yamaha); 10. Neate (Kawasaki).

May 11 - Brands Hatch GP
1. Kennaugh (RSA, Yamaha); 2. Richards (AUS, Triumph); 3. Brogan (Honda); 4. Westmoreland (Honda); 5. Toal (Yamaha); 6. Fitzpatrick (Yamaha); 7. Hutchinson (Yamaha); 8. Nutt (Yamaha); 9. Weymouth (Yamaha); 10. Young (Triumph).

May 26 - Donington
1. Lowry (Suzuki); 2. Richards (AUS, Triumph); 3. Praia (POR, Honda); 4. Brogan (Honda); 5. C. Martin (Kawasaki); 6. J. Webb (Honda); 7. Frost (Triumph); 8. Fitzpatrick (Yamaha); 9. Young (Triumph); 10. Westmoreland (Honda).

15 June - Snetterton
1. Plater (Yamaha); 2. Richards (AUS, Triumph); 3. Westmoreland (Honda); 4. Kennaugh (RSA, Yamaha); 5. Lowry (Suzuki); 6. Brogan (Honda); 7. Beech (Yamaha); 8. C. Martin (Kawasaki); 9. Frost (Triumph); 10. Nutt (Yamaha).

June 29 - Mallory Park
1. Kennaugh (RSA, Yamaha); 2. Plater (Yamaha); 3. Lowry (Suzuki); 4. Hutchinson (Yamaha); 5. Richards (AUS, Triumph); 6. Westmoreland (Honda); 7. Toal (Yamaha); 8. J. Webb (Honda); 9. Cooper (Honda); 10. Nutt (Yamaha).

July 20 - Oulton Park
1. Richards (AUS, Triumph); 2. Kennaugh (RSA, Yamaha); 3. Lowry (Suzuki); 4. C. Martin (Kawasaki); 5. J. Webb (Honda); 6. Westmoreland (Honda); 7. Cooper (Honda); 8. Frost (Triumph); 9. Wylie (Yamaha); 10. Owens (Honda).

August 10 - Knockhill
1. Lowry (Suzuki); 2. Westmoreland (Honda); 3. Richards (AUS, Triumph); 4. J. Webb (Honda); 5. Kennaugh (RSA, Yamaha); 6. Kennedy (Yamaha); 7. Frost (Triumph); 8. C. Martin (Kawasaki); 9. Young (Triumph); 10. Neate (Kawasaki).

August 25 - Cadwell Park
1. Plater (Yamaha); 2. Richards (AUS, Triumph); 3. J. Webb (Honda); 4. Kennaugh (Yamaha); 5. Westmoreland (Honda); 6. Young (Triumph); 7. Frost (Triumph); 8. Lowry (Suzuki); 9. C. Martin (Kawasaki); 10. Bridewell (Honda).

September 14 - Croft
1. Richards (AUS, Triumph); 2. Westmoreland (Honda); 3. Kennaugh (Yamaha); 4. J. Webb (Honda); 5. Young (Triumph); 6. Nutt (Yamaha); 7. Spalding (Yamaha); 8. Dickinson (Yamaha); 9. C. Martin (Kawasaki); 10. Kennedy (Yamaha).

September 28 - Silverstone
1. Kennaugh (Yamaha); 2. Young (Triumph); 3. Plater (Yamaha); 4. Richards (AUS, Triumph); 5. Westmoreland (Honda); 6. Lowry (Suzuki); 7. C. Martin (Kawasaki); 8. D. Cooper (Honda); 9. Dickinson (Yamaha); 10. Kennedy (Yamaha).

October 12 - Brands Hatch Indy
1. Richards (AUS, Triumph); 2. Plater (Yamaha); 3. Brookes (AUS, Honda); 4. Westmoreland (Honda); 5. Frost (Triumph); 6. J. Webb (Honda); 7. D. Cooper (Honda); 8. Lowry (Suzuki); 9. C. Martin (Kawasaki); 10. Kennaugh (Yamaha).

FINAL CLASSIFICATION
1. Glen Richards (AUS)   Triumph   240 points
2. Hudson Kennaugh   Yamaha   187
3. Ian Lowry   Suzuki   146
4. J. Westmoreland (Honda), 136; 5. S. Plater (Yamaha), 106; 6. C. Martin (Kawasaki), 99; 7. J. Webb (Honda), 87; 8. S. Brogan (Honda), 95; 9. P. Young (Triumph), 68; 10. R. Frost (Triumph), 63. 35 finishers.

SUPERBIKE

April 6 - Brands Hatch GP
Race cancelled due to the snow.

April 20 - Thruxton
Race I: 1. Byrne (Ducati); 2. Crutchlow (Honda); 3. Rutter (Ducati); 4. L. Haslam (Honda); 5. Camier (Ducati); 6. Sykes (Suzuki); 7. J. Ellison (Honda); 8. Andrews (Yamaha); 9. Easton (Yamaha); 10. M. Laverty (Suzuki).
Race II: 1. Crutchlow (Honda); 2. Byrne (Ducati); 3. Rutter (Ducati); 4. Camier (Ducati); 5. M. Laverty (Suzuki); 6. Easton (Yamaha); 7. J. Ellison (Honda); 8. Sykes (Suzuki); 9. G. Martin (Honda); 10. McConnell (AUS, Kawasaki).

May 5 - Oulton Park
Race I: 1. Byrne (Ducati); 2. L. Haslam (Honda); 3. Camier (Ducati); 4. Rutter (Ducati); 5. Sykes (Suzuki); 6. Crutchlow (Honda); 7. M. Laverty (Suzuki); 8. J. Ellison (Honda); 9. Palmer (Honda); 10. Easton (Kawasaki).
Race II: 1. Byrne (Ducati); 2. J. Ellison (Honda); 3. Camier (Ducati); 4. L. Haslam (Honda); 5. M. Laverty (Suzuki); 6. Easton (Kawasaki); 7. Rutter (Ducati); 8. Andrews (Yamaha); 9. S. Smart (Kawasaki); 10. Watanabe (J, Suzuki).

May 11 - Brands Hatch GP
Race I: 1. Byrne (Ducati); 2. Sykes (Suzuki); 3. Crutchlow (Honda); 4. L. Haslam (Honda); 5. Camier (Ducati); 6. J. Ellison (Honda); 7. Easton (Kawasaki); 8. McConnell (AUS, Kawasaki); 9. Andrews (Yamaha); 10. Palmer (Honda).
Race II: 1. Crutchlow (Honda); 2. Byrne (Ducati); 3. Camier (Ducati); 4. M. Laverty (Suzuki); 5. Rutter (Ducati); 6. L. Haslam (Honda); 7. Easton (Kawasaki); 8. J. Ellison (Honda); 9. McConnell (AUS, Kawasaki); 10. S. Smart (Kawasaki).

May 26 - Donington
Race I: 1. Byrne (Ducati); 2. L. Haslam (Honda); 3. Sykes (Suzuki); 4. Ellison (Honda); 5. Camier (Ducati); 6. Crutchlow (Honda); 7. K. Harris (Yamaha); 8. Rutter (Ducati); 9. M. Laverty (Suzuki); 10. Andrews (Yamaha).
Race II: 1. Byrne (Ducati); 2. L. Haslam (Honda); 3. Crutchlow (Honda); 4. Camier (Ducati); 5. Ellison (Honda); 6. Sykes (Suzuki); 7. K. Harris (Yamaha); 8. Rutter (Ducati); 9. Andrews (Yamaha); 10. Mason (Honda).

June 15 - Snetterton
Race I: 1. Camier (Ducati); 2. Byrne (Ducati); 3. Sykes (Suzuki); 4. Crutchlow (Honda); 5. L. Haslam (Honda); 6. M. Laverty (Suzuki); 7. Ellison (Honda); 8. K. Harris (Yamaha); 9. Rutter (Ducati); 10. Andrews (Yamaha).
Race II: 1. Byrne (Ducati); 2. Camier (Ducati); 3. Crutchlow (Honda); 4. Rutter (Ducati); 5. L. Haslam (Honda); 6. M. Laverty (Suzuki); 7. Sykes (Suzuki); 8. Andrews (Yamaha); 9. Palmer (Honda); 10. Ellison (Honda).

June 29 - Mallory Park
Race I: 1. Byrne (Ducati); 2. L. Haslam (Honda); 3. Crutchlow (Honda); 4. Sykes (Suzuki); 5. Ellison (Honda); 6. McConnell (Kawasaki); 7. Andrews (Yamaha); 8. Palmer (Honda); 9. Watanabe (J, Suzuki); 10. J. Laverty (Ducati).
Race II: 1. Rutter (Ducati); 2. Byrne (Ducati); 3. Crutchlow (Honda); 4. Sykes (Suzuki); 5. K. Harris (Yamaha); 6. L. Haslam (Honda); 7. Andrews (Yamaha); 8. Camier (Ducati); 9. Palmer (Honda); 10. S. Smart (Kawasaki).

July 20 - Oulton Park
Race I: 1. Sykes (Suzuki); 2. Ellison (Honda); 3. Byrne (Ducati); 4. L. Haslam (Honda); 5. Andrews (Yamaha); 6. Crutchlow (Honda); 7. Rutter (Ducati); 8. McConnell (Kawasaki); 9. M. Laverty (Suzuki); 10. J. Laverty (Ducati).
Race II: 1. Sykes (Suzuki); 2. Crutchlow (Honda); 3. Byrne (Ducati); 4. L. Haslam (Honda); 5. Ellison (Honda); 6. Andrews (Yamaha); 7. M. Laverty (Suzuki); 8. S. Smart (Kawasaki); 9. K. Harris (Yamaha); 10. McConnell (Kawasaki).

August 10 - Knockhill
Race I: 1. Sykes (Suzuki); 2. Byrne (Ducati); 3. J. Ellison (Honda); 4. M. Rutter (Ducati); 5. Camier (Ducati); 6. M. Laverty (Suzuki); 7. K. Harris (Yamaha); 8. Andrews (Yamaha); 9. Palmer (Honda); 10. Mason (Honda).
Race II: 1. L. Haslam (Honda); 2. M. Rutter (Ducati); 3. K. Harris (Yamaha); 4. Sykes (Suzuki); 5. J. Ellison (Honda); 6. Andrews (Yamaha); 7. Crutchlow (Honda); 8. Camier (Ducati); 9. McConnell (AUS, Kawasaki); 10. C. Burns (MV-Agusta).

August 25 - Cadwell Park
Race I: 1. Haslam (Honda); 2. Sykes (Suzuki); 3. Byrne (Ducati); 4. Camier (Ducati); 5. Crutchlow (Honda); 6. Rutter (Ducati); 7. Andrews (Yamaha); 8. M. Laverty (Suzuki); 9. Watanabe (J, Suzuki); 10. Mason (Honda).
Race II: 1. Haslam (Honda); 2. Sykes (Suzuki); 3. Byrne (Ducati); 4. Camier (Ducati); 5. Rutter (Ducati); 6. Andrews (Yamaha); 7. Watanabe (J, Suzuki); 8. S. Smart (Kawasaki); 9. M. Laverty (Suzuki); 10. K. Harris (Yamaha).

September 14 - Croft
Race I: 1. Camier (Ducati); 2. Haslam (Honda); 3. Sykes (Suzuki); 4. Crutchlow (Honda); 5. Byrne (Ducati); 6. Rutter (Ducati); 7. M. Laverty (Suzuki); 8. K. Harris (Yamaha); 9. Ellison (Honda); 10. Andrews (Yamaha).
Race II: 1. Haslam (Honda); 2. Sykes (Suzuki); 3. Crutchlow (Honda); 4. Byrne (Ducati); 5. Camier (Ducati); 6. Rutter (Ducati); 7. Ellison (Honda); 8. K. Harris (Yamaha); 9. Andrews (Yamaha); 10. M. Laverty (Suzuki).

September 28 - Silverstone
Race I: 1. Camier (Ducati); 2. Crutchlow (Honda); 3. Byrne (Ducati); 4. Rutter (Ducati); 5. Andrews (Yamaha); 6. Palmer (Honda); 7. O'Halloran (AUS, Honda); 8. Easton (Kawasaki); 9. Watanabe (J, Suzuki); 10. McConnell (AUS, Kawasaki).
Race II: 1. Haslam (Honda); 2. Byrne (Ducati); 3. Sykes (Suzuki); 4. Camier (Ducati); 5. K. Harris (Yamaha); 6. Ellison (Honda); 7. Rutter (Ducati); 8. Andrews (Yamaha); 9. McConnell (AUS, Kawasaki); 10. O'Halloran (AUS, Honda).

October 12 - Brands Hatch Indy
Race I: 1. Byrne (Ducati); 2. Crutchlow (Honda); 3. Ellison (Honda); 4. L. Haslam (Honda); 5. Camier (Ducati); 6. Sykes (Suzuki); 7. Rutter (Ducati); 8. Andrews (Yamaha); 9. Kirkham (Yamaha); 10. Palmer (Honda).
Race II: 1. Byrne (Ducati); 2. L. Haslam (Honda); 3. Camier (Ducati); 4. Crutchlow (Honda); 5. Ellison (Honda); 6. Rutter (Ducati); 7. Andrews (Yamaha); 8. J. Laverty (Ducati); 9. Mason (Honda); 10. Kirkham (Yamaha).

FINAL CLASSIFICATION
1. Shane Byrne	Ducati	474 points
2. Leon Haslam	Honda	357
3. Cal Crutchlow	Honda	318

4. T. Sykes (Suzuki), 316; 5. L. Camier (Ducati), 306; 6. M. Rutter (Ducati), 256; 7. J. Ellison (Honda), 230; 8. S. Andrews (Yamaha), 176; 9. M. Laverty (Suzuki); 10. T. Palmer (Honda). 33 finishers.

ITALIAN CHAMPIONSHIP

125 GP

April 20 - Mugello
1. Savadori (Aprilia); 2. Folger (D, KTM); 3. Ferro (Honda); 4. Musco (Aprilia); 5. Ravaioli (Aprilia); 6. Moretti (Honda); 7. L. Vitali (Aprilia); 8. Marconi (Honda); 9. F. Biaggi (Honda); 10. Stirpe (Honda).

May 4 - Monza
1. Moretti (Honda); 2. Savadori (Aprilia); 3. Ravaioli (Aprilia); 4. Ferro (Honda); 5. L. Vitali (Aprilia); 6. Marconi (Honda); 7. Lamborghini (Aprilia); 8. Morciano (Aprilia); 9. Stirpe (Honda); 10. Sabatino (Aprilia).

May 25 - Vallelunga
1. Savadori (Aprilia); 2. Moretti (Honda); 3. Sabatino (Aprilia); 4. Morciano (Aprilia); 5. Capuano (Fibra); 6. Stirpe (Honda); 7. Farinelli (Aprilia); 8. Fratoni (Honda); 9. Lamborghini (Aprilia); 10. Amicucci (Honda).

July 27 - Misano
1. Moretti (Honda); 2. Savadori (Aprilia); 3. Tonucci (Aprilia); 4. Capuano (Friba); 5. Sabatino (Aprilia); 6. Ravaioli (Aprilia); 7. Lamborghini (Aprilia); 8. Marconi (Honda); 9. Stirpe (Honda); 10. Vargas (Aprilia).

September 28 - Misano
1. Savadori (Aprilia); 2. Moretti (Honda); 3. Lamborghini (Aprilia); 4. Sabatino (Aprilia); 5. Stirpe (Honda); 6. Morciano (Aprilia); 7. Marconi (Honda); 8. Sembera (CZ, Aprilia); 9. Farinelli (Aprilia); 10. Vargas (Aprilia).

October 19 - Mugello
1. Moretti (Honda); 2. Savadori (Aprilia); 3. Lamborghini (Aprilia); 4. Morciano (Aprilia); 5. Ferro (Honda); 6. Marconi (Honda); 7. Stirpe (Honda); 8. Della Biancia (Aprilia); 9. Farinelli (Aprilia); 10. Caraffini (Aprilia).

FINAL CLASSIFICATION
1. Lorenzo Savadori	Aprilia	135 points
2. Riccardo Moretti	Honda	126
3. Ferruccio Lamborghini	Aprilia	57

4. D. Stirpe (Honda), 51; 5. G. Sabatino (Aprilia), 46; 6. L. Marconi (Honda), 46; 7. L. Morciano (Aprilia), 45; 8. G. Ferro (Honda), 44; 9. M. Ravaioli (Aprilia), 39; 10. R. Farinelli (Aprilia), 33. 30 finishers.

SUPERSPORT

April 20 - Mugello
1. Roccoli (Yamaha); 2. Marrancone (Yamaha); 3. Battaini (Yamaha); 4. Migliorati (Kawasaki); 5. Ciavattini (Yamaha); 6. Corradi (Triumph); 7. Toti (Suzuki); 8. Lunadei (Honda); 9. Velini (Yamaha); 10. Iommi (Honda).

May 4 - Monza
1. Marrancone (Yamaha); 2. Roccoli (Yamaha); 3. C. Migliorati (Kawasaki); 4. Battaini (Yamaha); 5. Lunadei (Honda); 6. Corradi (Triumph); 7. Ciavattini (Honda); 8. Brannetti (Yamaha); 9. Ruggiero (Yamaha); 10. Dell'Omo (Honda).

May 25 - Vallelunga
1. Marrancone (Yamaha); 2. Brannetti (Yamaha); 3. C. Migliorati (Kawasaki); 4. Lunadei (Honda); 5. Toti (Suzuki); 6. Corradi (Triumph); 7. Giugovaz (Honda); 8. Pirro (Yamaha); 9. Velini (Yamaha); 10. Sassaro (Triumph).

July 27 - Misano
1. Roccoli (Yamaha); 2. Battaini (Yamaha); 3. Brannetti (Yamaha); 4. Palumbo (Kawasaki); 5. Lunadei (Honda); 6. Giugovaz (Honda); 7. Corradi (Triumph); 8. Velini (Yamaha); 9. Morelli (Yamaha); 10. C. Migliorati (Kawasaki).

September 28 - Misano
1. Roccoli (Yamaha); 2. Marrancone (Yamaha); 3. Brannetti (Yamaha); 4. C. Migliorati (Kawasaki); 5. Toti (Suzuki); 6. Palumbo (Kawasaki); 7. Ciavattini (Honda); 8. Corradi (Triumph); 9. Barone (Honda); 10. Lunadei (Honda).

October 19 - Mugello
1. Roccoli (Yamaha); 2. Battaini (Yamaha); 3. Marrancone (Yamaha); 4. Lacalendola (Triumph); 5. Brannetti (Yamaha); 6. Giansanti (Kawasaki); 7. Corradi (Triumph); 8. Sassaro (Yamaha); 9. Velini (Yamaha); 10. C. Migliorati (Kawasaki).

FINAL CLASSIFICATION
1. Massimo Roccoli	Yamaha	120 points
2. Danilo Marrancone	Yamaha	106
3. Alessandro Brannetti	Yamaha	71

4. C. Migliorati (Kawasaki), 70; 5. F. Battaini (Yamaha), 69; 6. A. Corradi (Triumph), 56; 7. R. Lunadei (Honda), 53; 8. T. Toti (Suzuki), 43; 9. A. Velini (Yamaha), 34; 10. A. Palumbo (Kawasaki), 33. 30 finishers.

SUPERSTOCK

April 20 - Mugello
1. Pirro (Yamaha); 2. Polita (Ducati); 3. Giugliano (Suzuki); 4. Pellizzon (Kawasaki); 5. Verdini (Yamaha); 6. Magnoni (Yamaha); 7. Cruciani (Ducati); 8. Baiocco (Kawasaki); 9. Saltarelli (Suzuki); 10. F. Gentile (Yamaha).

May 4 - Monza
1. Giugliano (Suzuki); 2. Pirro (Yamaha); 3. Magnoni (Yamaha); 4. Pellizzon (Kawasaki); 5. Polita (Ducati); 6. Saltarelli (Suzuki); 7. Goi (Yamaha); 8. Salvatore (Yamaha); 9. Laviola (Suzuki); 10. Cruciani (Ducati).

May 25 - Vallelunga
1. Pirro (Yamaha); 2. Giugliano (Suzuki); 3. Salvatore (Yamaha); 4. Cruciani (Ducati); 5. Polita (Ducati); 6. Magnoni (Yamaha); 7. Baiocco (Kawasaki); 8. Dionisi (MV-Agusta); 9. Seaton (AUS, Suzuki); 10. Caselli (Honda).

July 27 - Misano
1. Giugliano (Suzuki); 2. Pirro (Yamaha); 3. Cruciani (Ducati); 4. Polita (Ducati); 5. Magnoni (Yamaha); 6. Verdini (Yamaha); 7. Russo (Honda); 8. F. Gentile (Yamaha); 9. Saltarelli (Suzuki); 10. Sirch (Yamaha).

September 28- Misano
1. Pirro (Yamaha); 2. Cruciani (Ducati); 3. Giugliano (Suzuki); 4. Magnoni (Yamaha); 5. Verdini (Yamaha); 6. Russo (Honda); 7. F. Gentile (Yamaha); 8. Sirch (Yamaha); 9. Saltarelli (Suzuki); 10. Pellizzon (Kawasaki).

October 19 - Mugello
1. Cruciani (Ducati); 2. Giugliano (Suzuki); 3. Magnoni (Yamaha); 4. Pirro (Yamaha); 5. Pellizzon (Kawasaki); 6. Salvatore (Yamaha); 7. Russo (Honda); 8. Polita (Ducati); 9. Sirch (Yamaha); 10. Dionisi (MV-Agusta).

FINAL CLASSIFICATION
1. Michele Pirro	Yamaha	128 points
2. Davide Giugliano	Suzuki	122
3. Stefano Cruciani	Ducati	89

4. M. Magnoni (Yamaha), 76; 5. A. Polita (Ducati), 63; 6. F. Pellizzon (Kawasaki), 51; 7. G. Salvatore (Yamaha), 45; 8. S. Saltarelli (Suzuki), 38; 9. L. Verdini (Yamaha), 37; 10. E. Sirch (Yamaha), 31 points. 23 finishers.

SUPERBIKE

April 20 - Mugello
1. Corti (Yamaha); 2. Scassa (MV-Agusta); 3. Lucchiari (Ducati); 4. Prattichizzo (MV-Agusta); 5. Conforti

(Honda); 6. Mauri (Ducati); 7. Faccietti (Yamaha); 8. Blora (Ducati); 9. Di Maso (Suzuki); 10. Signorin (Honda).

May 4 - Monza

1. Corti (Yamaha); 2. Conforti (Honda); 3. Mauri (Ducati); 4. Prattichizzo (MV-Agusta); 5. Brignola (Honda); 6. Borciani (Ducati); 7. Pini (Yamaha); 8. Cipriani (Yamaha); 9. Faccietti (Yamaha); 10. Festa (Yamaha).

May 25 - Vallelunga

1. Brignola (Honda); 2. Scassa (MV-Agusta); 3. Conforti (Honda); 4. Corti (Yamaha); 5. Mauri (Ducati); 6. Prattichizzo (MV-Agusta); 7. Pini (Yamaha); 8. Borciani (Ducati); 9. Chiarello (Suzuki); 10. Festa (Yamaha).

July 27 - Misano

1. Brignola (Honda); 2. Scassa (MV-Agusta); 3. Mauri (Ducati); 4. Corti (Yamaha); 5. Conforti (Honda); 6. Borciani (Ducati); 7. Chiarello (Suzuki); 8. Bridewell (GB, Suzuki); 9. Di Maso (Suzuki); 10. Giannicola (Suzuki).

September 28 - Misano

1. Scassa (MV-Agusta); 2. Badovini (Kawasaki); 3. Brignola (Honda); 4. Bridewell (GB, Suzuki); 5. Conforti (Honda); 6. Chiarello (Suzuki); 7. Prattichizzo (MV-Agusta); 8. Pini (Yamaha); 9. Di Maso (Suzuki); 10. Grandi (Yamaha).

October 19 - Mugello

1. Scassa (MV-Agusta); 2. Chiarello (Suzuki); 3. Borciani (Ducati); 4. Gramigni (Yamaha); 5. Bridewell (GB, Suzuki); 6. Corti (Yamaha); 7. Conforti (Honda); 8. Mauri (Ducati); 9. Pini (Yamaha); 10. Mancuso (Ducati).

FINAL CLASSIFICATION

1. Luca Scassa	MV-Agusta	110 points
2. Claudio Corti	Yamaha	87
3. Luca Conforti	Honda	81

4. N. Brignola (Honda), 77; 5. L. Mauri (Ducati), 62; 6. R. Chiarello (Suzuki), 47; 7. M. Prattichizzo (MV-Agusta), 46; 8. M. Borciani (Ducati), 44; 9. L. Pini (Yamaha), 35; 10. F. Di Maso (Suzuki), 28. 36 finishers.

SWISS CHAMPIONSHIP

SUPERSTOCK 600

April 12-13- Hungaroring - Hungary

Race I: 1. Raschle (Kawasaki); 2. Leemann (Kawasaki); 3. Labarthe (Yamaha); 4. Rüegg (Honda); 5. Plüss (Kawasaki); 6. Dafflon (Suzuki); 7. Baumann (Suzuki); 8. Violland (Honda); 9. Nadalet (Kawasaki); 10. Girard (Yamaha).
Race II: 1. Raschle (Kawasaki); 2. Rüegg (Honda); 3. Labarthe (Yamaha); 4. Violland (Honda); 5. Dafflon (Suzuki); 6. Girard (Yamaha); 7. Baumann (Suzuki); 8. Nadalet (Kawasaki); 9. Y. Freymond (Honda); 10. Christen (Suzuki).

May 3-4 - Schleiz - Germany

Race I: 1. Raschle (Kawasaki); 2. Rüegg (Honda); 3. Labarthe (Yamaha); 4. Leemann (Kawasaki); 5. Violland (Honda); 6. Nadalet (Kawasaki); 7. Dafflon (Suzuki); 8. Wahr (Suzuki); 9. Pradier (F, Yamaha); 10. Y. Freymond (Honda).
Race II: 1. Raschle (Kawasaki); 2. Wahr (Suzuki); 3. Rüegg (Honda); 4. Leemann (Kawasaki); 5. Nadalet (Kawasaki); 6. Brandt (Honda); 7. Labarthe (Yamaha); 8. Violland (Honda); 9. Dafflon (Yamaha); 10. Pradier (F, Yamaha).

June 14-15 - Most - Czech Republic

Race I: 1. Rüegg (Honda); 2. Raschle (Kawasaki); 3. Volland (Honda); 4. Labarthe (Yamaha); 5. Leemann (Kawasaki); 6. Plüss (Kawasaki); 7. Y. Freymond (Honda); 8. Dafflon (Suzuki); 9. Gétaz (Yamaha); 10. Blatancic (CZ, Kawasaki).
Race II: 1. Raschle (Kawasaki); 2. Rüegg (Honda); 3. Plüss (Kawasaki); 4. Leemann (Kawasaki); 5. Nadalet (Kawasaki); 6. Y. Freymond (Honda); 7. Labarthe (Yamaha); 8. Gétaz (Yamaha); 9. Pradier (F, Yamaha); 10. Christen (Suzuki).

July 12-13 - Dijon - France

Race I: 1. Plüss (Kawasaki); 2. Raschle (Kawasaki); 3. Girard (Yamaha); 4. Leemann (Kawasaki); 5. Von Gunten (Suzuki); 6. Pradier (F, Yamaha); 7. Y. Freymond (Honda); 8. Nadalet (Kawasaki); 9. Violland (Honda); 10. Christen (Suzuki).
Race II: 1. Plüss (Kawasaki); 2. Raschle (Kawasaki); 3. Pradier (F, Yamaha); 4. Nadalet (Kawasaki); 5. Y. Freymond (Honda); 6. Girard (Yamaha); 7. Von Gunten (Suzuki); 8. Violland (Honda); 9. Labarthe (Yamaha); 10. Rüegg (Honda).

August 2-3 - Lausitz - Germany

Race I: 1. Rüegg (Honda); 2. Dafflon (Suzuki); 3. Labarthe (Yamaha); 4. Christen (Suzuki); 5. Violland (Honda); 6. Nadalet (Kawasaki); 7. Plüss (Kawasaki). 7 finishers.
Race II: 1. Girard (Yamaha); 2. Rüegg (Honda); 3. Labarthe (Yamaha); 4. Violland (Honda); 5. Plüss (Kawasaki); 6. Nadalet (Kawasaki); 7. Dafflon (Suzuki); 8. Christen (Suzuki); 9. Schwegler (Kawasaki). 9 finishers.

September 27-28 - Brno - Czech Republic

Race I: 1. Raschle (Kawasaki); 2. Rüegg (Honda); 3. Plüss (Kawasaki); 4. Violland (Honda); 5. Nadalet (Kawasaki); 6. Y. Freymond (Honda); 7. Labarthe (Yamaha); 8. Dafflon (Suzuki); 9. Gétaz (Yamaha); 10. Christen (Suzuki).
Race II: 1. Nadalet (Kawasaki); 2. Violland (Honda); 3. Plüss (Kawasaki); 4. Rüegg (Honda); 5. Y. Freymond (Honda); 6. Labarthe (Yamaha); 7. Gétaz (Yamaha); 8. Peter (Honda); 9. Dafflon (Suzuki); 10. K. Sutter (Honda).

FINAL CLASSIFICATION

1. Roman Raschle	Kawasaki	210 points
2. Christian Rüegg	Honda	198
3. Dominik Plüss	Kawasaki	139

4. B. Labarthe (Yamaha), 137; 5. A. Violland (Honda), 128; 6. P. Nadalet (Kawasaki), 124; 7. W. Dafflon (Suzuki), 90; 8. R. Leemann (Kawasaki), 83; 9. Y. Freymond (Honda), 83; 10. C. Girard (Yamaha), 67. 23 finishers.

SUPERSTOCK 1000

April 12-13 - Hungaroring - Hungary

Race I: 1. Sutter (Honda); 2. Muff (Suzuki); 3. Savary (Suzuki); 4. Wildisen (Suzuki); 5. Künzi (MV-Agusta); 6. Gantner (Honda); 7. Beglinger (Suzuki); 8. Sennhauser (Kawasaki); 9. Steinemann (Kawasaki); 10. K. Gisler (Suzuki).
Race II: 1. Muff (Suzuki); 2. Savary (Suzuki); 3. Sutter (Honda); 4. Wildisen (Suzuki); 5. Gantner (Honda); 6. Künzi (MV-Agusta); 7. Sennhauser (Kawasaki); 8. Beglinger (Suzuki); 9. Steinemann (Kawasaki); 10. J. Schmid (Yamaha).

May 3-4 - Schleiz - Germany

Race I: 1. Muff (Suzuki); 2. Wildisen (Suzuki); 3. Sutter (Honda); 4. Gantner (Honda); 5. Künzi (MV-Agusta); 6. Sennhauser (Kawasaki); 7. Savary (Suzuki); 8. Beglinger (Suzuki); 9. Pollheide (D, Suzuki); 10. Schmid (Yamaha).
Race II: 1. Muff (Suzuki); 2. Sutter (Honda); 3. Wildisen (Suzuki); 4. Gantner (Honda); 5. Savary (Suzuki); 6. Sennhauser (Kawasaki); 7. Beglinger (Suzuki); 8. Künzi (MV-Agusta); 9. Pollheide (D, Suzuki); 10. J. Schmid (Yamaha).

June 14-15 - Most - Czech Republic

Race I: 1. Muff (Suzuki); 2. Saiger (A, Suzuki); 3. Sutter (Honda); 4. Sennhauser (Kawasaki); 5. Gantner (Honda); 6. Künzi (MV-Agusta); 7. Wildisen (Suzuki); 8. Andenmatten (Suzuki); 9. Neumann (MV-Agusta); 10. Steinemann (Kawasaki).
Race II: 1. Saiger (A, Suzuki); 2. Muff (Suzuki); 3. Wildisen (Suzuki); 4. Gantner (Honda); 5. Künzi (MV-Agusta); 6. Sennhauser (Kawasaki); 7. Steinemann (Kawasaki); 8. Heimann (Honda); 9. Andenmatten (Suzuki); 10. Thierry (Honda).

July 12-13 - Dijon - France

Race I: 1. Saiger (A, Suzuki); 2. Gantner (Honda); 3. Wildisen (Suzuki); 4. Sutter (Honda); 5. Künzi (MV-Agusta); 6. Steinemann (Kawasaki); 7. Heimann (Honda); 8. Andenmatten (Suzuki); 9. J. Schmid (Yamaha); 10. Thierry (F, Honda).
Race II: 1. Muff (Suzuki); 2. Junod (Yamaha); 3. Wildisen (Suzuki); 4. Künzi (MV-Agusta); 5. Steinemann (Kawasaki); 6. J. Schmid (Yamaha); 7. Gantner (Honda); 8. Sutter (Honda); 9. Sennhauser (Kawasaki); 10. Thierry (F, Honda).

August 2-3 - Lausitz - Germany

Race I: 1. Muff (Suzuki); 2. Wildisen (Suzuki); 3. Gantner (Honda); 4. Thierry (Honda); 5. Steinemann (Kawasaki); 6. Malo (Suzuki); 7. Marti (Suzuki); 8. Heimann (Honda). 8 finishers.
Race II: 1. Muff (Suzuki); 2. Sutter (Honda); 3. Wildisen (Suzuki); 4. Gantner (Honda); 5. Andenmatten (Suzuki); 6. Sennhauser (Kawasaki); 7. Steinemann (Kawasaki); 8. Thierry (Honda); 9. Heimann (Honda); 10. Schmid (Yamaha).

September 27-28 - Brno - Czech Republic

Race I: 1. Gantner (Honda); 2. Sutter (Honda); 3. Steinemann (Kawasaki); 4. Andenmatten (Suzuki); 5. Thierry (F, Honda); 6. Malo (SF, Suzuki); 7. Wohlwend (FL, Suzuki); 8. Käppeli (Suzuki). 8 finishers.
Race II: 1. Schumacher (D, Honda); 2. Saiger (A, Suzuki); 3. Savary (Suzuki); 4. Gantner (Honda); 5. Wildisen (Suzuki); 6. Sutter (Honda); 7. Sennhauser (Kawasaki); 8. Andenmatten (Suzuki); 9. Steinemann (Kawasaki); 10. Thierry (F, Honda).

FINAL CLASSIFICATION

1. Patrick Muff	Suzuki	205 points
2. Daniel Sutter	Honda	165
3. Hervé Gantner	Honda	163,5

4. M. Wildisen (Suzuki), 160; 5. R. Steinemann (Kawasaki), 98,5; 6. . H. Saiger (A, Suzuki), 82,5; 7. L. Sennhauser (Kawasaki), 82; 8. C. Künzi (MV-Agusta), 79,5; 9. M. Savary (Suzuki), 76; 10. A. Andenmatten (Suzuki), 69,5. 24 finishers.

SUPERMOTARD

PRESTIGE 450 S2

June 1st - Hoch-Ybrig

Race I: 1. Götz (KTM); 2. Baumann (Suzuki); 3. D. Müller (Yamaha); 4. P. Dupasquier (KTM); 5. Meusburger (A, Yamaha); 6. Näpflin (Kawasaki); 7. Züger (KTM); 8. Herger (Suzuki); 9. S. Scheiwiller (Yamaha); 10. Reinhard (Honda).
Race II: 1. C. Scheiwiller (Yamaha); 2. Götz (KTM); 3. Meusburger (A, Yamaha); 4. Baumann (Suzuki); 5. Reinhard (Honda); 6. Näpflin (Kawasaki); 7. S. Scheiwiller (Yamaha); 8. A. Marti (Aprilia); 9. D. Müller (Yamaha); 10. Herger (Suzuki).

June 22 - St. Stephan

Race I: 1. P. Dupasquier (KTM); 2. D. Müller (Yamaha); 3. C. Scheiwiller (Yamaha); 4. Götz (KTM); 5. Gautschi (Aprilia); 6. Baumann (Suzuki); 7. S. Scheiwiller (Yamaha); 8. Tschupp (Husqvarna); 9. Reinhard (Honda); 10. Züger (KTM).
Race II : 1. P. Dupasquier (KTM); 2. C. Scheiwiller (Yamaha); 3. Baumann (Suzuki); 4. Götz (KTM); 5. D. Müller (Yamaha); 6. A. Marti (Aprilia); 7. S. Scheiwiller (Yamaha); 8. Reinhard (Honda); 9. Gautschi (Aprilia); 10. Tschupp (Husqvarna).

August 3 - Lignières

Race I: 1. P. Dupasquier (KTM); 2. Baumann (Suzuki); 3. C. Scheiwiller (Yamaha); 4. Volz (D, KTM); 5. Reinhard (Honda); 6. Herger (Suzuki); 7. Gautschi (Aprilia); 8. D. Müller (Yamaha); 9. A. Marti (Aprilia); 10. Züger (KTM).
Race II: 1. P. Dupasquier (KTM); 2. Baumann (Suzuki); 3. D. Müller (Yamaha); 4. Reinhard (Honda); 5. Volz (KTM); 6. C. Scheiwiller (Yamaha); 7. Gautschi (Aprilia); 8. Herger (Suzuki); 9. Züger (KTM); 10. Näpflin (Kawasaki).

August 31 - Sierre

Race I: 1. P. Dupasquier (KTM); 2. Baumann (Suzuki); 3. C. Scheiwiller (Yamaha); 4. Volz (D, KTM); 5. Näpflin (Kawasaki); 6. Meusburger (A, Yamaha); 7. Reinhard (Honda); 8. S. Scheiwiller (Yamaha); 9. Tschupp (Husqvarna); 10. Gautschi (Aprilia).
Race II: 1. P. Dupasquier (KTM); 2. C. Scheiwiller (Yamaha); 3. Baumann (Suzuki); 4. D. Müller (Yamaha); 5. Reinhard (Honda); 6. Näpflin (Kawasaki); 7. S. Scheiwiller (Yamaha); 8. Meusburger (A, Yamaha); 9. Tschupp (Husqvarna); 10. Möri (Yamaha).

October 5 - Frauenfeld

Race I: 1. P. Dupasquier (KTM); 2. Baumann (Suzuki); 3. Reinhard (Honda); 4. C. Scheiwiller (Yamaha); 5. S. Scheiwiller (Yamaha); 6. Volz (D, KTM); 7. Kammermann (KTM); 8. Herger (Suzuki); 9. Gautschi (Aprilia); 10. Waeber (Yamaha).
Race II: 1. Volz (D, KTM); 2. Baumann (Suzuki); 3. P. Dupasquier (KTM); 4. Reinhard (Honda); 5. C. Scheiwiller (Yamaha); 6. S. Scheiwiller (Yamaha); 7. D. Müller (Yamaha); 8. A. Marti (Aprilia); 9. Tschupp (Husqvarna); 10. Kammermann (KTM).

FINAL CLASSIFICATION

1. Philippe Dupasquier	KTM	266 points
2. Simon Baumann	Suzuki	231
3. Cyrill Scheiwiller	Yamaha	211

4. D. Müller (Yamaha), 176; 5. K. Reinhard (Honda), 170; 6. S. Scheiwiller (Yamaha), 153; 7. M. Volz (D, KTM9, 142; 8. M. Götz (KTM9, 123; 9. B. Gautschi (Aprilia), 120; 10. A. Marti (Aprilia), 115. 34 finishers.

CHALLENGER

June 1st - Hoch-Ybrig

Race I: 1. Scheidegger (Suzuki); 2. J. Minoggio (KTM); 3. R. Lanz (KTM); 4. Zimmermann (Suzuki); 5. Moor (Suzuki); 6. Nyffeler (Yamaha); 7. U. Müller (Yamaha); 8. Mettler (Kawasaki); 9. Sieber (Yamaha); 10. Spichtig (Kawasaki).
Race II: 1. Willimann (KTM); 2. Moor (Suzuki); 3. Zimmermann (Suzuki); 4. J. Minoggio (KTM); 5. U. Müller (Yamaha); 6. Mettler (Kawasaki); 7. Scheidegger (Suzuki); 8. Notari (KTM); 9. Nyffeler (Yamaha); 10. Rais (KTM).

June 22 - St. Stephan

Race I: 1. Wehrli (KTM); 2. Willimann (KTM); 3. R. Lanz (KTM); 4. Zimmermann (Suzuki); 5. Rais (KTM); 6. Moor (Suzuki); 7. Mettler (Kawasaki); 8. Barmettler (Kawasaki); 9. L. Minoggio (KTM); 10. Troxler (KTM).
Race II: 1. Willimann (KTM); 2. Wehrli (KTM); 3. J. Minoggio (KTM); 4. R. Lanz (KTM); 5. Zimmermann (Suzuki); 6. Rais (KTM); 7. Moor (Suzuki); 8. Troxler (KTM); 9. Rüdisüli (KTM); 10. Mettler (Kawasaki).

August 3 - Lignières
Race I: 1. Wehrli (KTM); 2. Singele (Yamaha); 3. Rais (KTM); 4. Lanz (KTM); 5. Moor (Suzuki); 6. Rüdisüli (KTM); 7. J. Minoggio (KTM); 8. Nyffeler (Yamaha); 9. Schärer (KTM); 10. Zimmermann (Suzuki).
Race II: 1. Wehrli (KTM); 2. Willimann (KTM); 3. Singele (Yamaha); 4. Rais (KTM); 5. Schärer (KTM); 6. Lanz (KTM); 7. Moor (Suzuki); 8. L. Minoggio (KTM); 9. Notari (KTM); 10. Zimmermann (Suzuki).

August 31 - Sierre
Race I: 1. Willimann (KTM); 2. Schärer (KTM); 3. Zimmermann (Yamaha); 4. Troxler (KTM); 5. Notari (KTM); 6. Sieber (Yamaha); 7. Rais (KTM); 8. Föhn (KTM); 9. L. Minoggio (KTM); 10. Spichtig (Kawasaki).
Race II: 1. Willimann (KTM); 2. Notari (KTM); 3. Moor (Suzuki); 4. Bürgler (KTM); 5. Schärer (KTM); 6. R. Lanz (KTM); 7. Sieber (Yamaha); 8. Rais (KTM); 9. Tanner (Suzuki); 10. Troxler (KTM).

October 5 - Frauenfeld
Race I: 1. R. Lanz (KTM); 2. Moor (Suzuki); 3. Schärer (KTM); 4. Notari (KTM); 5. Sieber (Yamaha); 6. Willimann (KTM); 7. L. Minoggio (KTM); 8. U. Müller (Yamaha); 9. Burch (Yamaha); 10. Haag (Yamaha).
Race II: 1. Rais (KTM); 2. Willimann (KTM); 3. Schärer (KTM); 4. R. Lanz (KTM); 5. Moor (Suzuki); 6. U. Müller (Yamaha); 7. Tanner (Suzuki); 8. Spichtig (Kawasaki); 9. Senn (Kawasaki); 10. Bürgler (KTM).

FINAL CLASSIFICATION
1. Reto Willimann   KTM   206 points
2. Marcel Moor   Suzuki   200
3. Roman Lanz   KTM   196
4. Y. Rais (KTM), 184; 5. H. Zimmermann (Suzuki), 135; 6. L. Minoggio (KTM), 114; 7. J. Minoggio (KTM), 112; 8. R. Schärer (KTM), 111; 9. P. Sieber (Yamaha), 109; 10. A. Notari (KTM), 105. 33 finishers.

ROOKIE

June 1st - Hoch-Ybrig
Race I: 1. Tellenbach (KTM); 2. Ehrenzeller (KTM); 3. Felder (Yamaha); 4. Inderbitzin (Kawasaki); 5. M. Weibel (Yamaha); 6. Loretter (KTM); 7. Fischer (Yamaha); 8. Jetzer (KTM); 9. Holzer (KTM); 10. Lienhard (KTM).
Race II: 1. Tellenbach (KTM); 2. Fischer (Yamaha); 3. Inderbitzin (Kawasaki); 4. Felder (Yamaha); 5. Holzer (KTM); 6. M. Weibel (Yamaha); 7. Jöri (Aprilia); 8. Jetzer (KTM); 9. Limacher (Yamaha); 10. Känel (Honda).

June 22 - St. Stephan
Race I: 1. Tellenbach (KTM); 2. Fischer (Yamaha); 3. Reynaud (Husqvarna); 4. Limacher (Yamaha); 5. Loretter (KTM); 6. Felder (Yamaha); 7. Ehrenzeller (KTM); 8. Holzer (KTM); 9. Inderbitzin (Kawasaki); 10. Jöri (Aprilia).
Race II: 1. Tellenbach (KTM); 2. Fischer (Yamaha); 3. Inderbitzin (Kawasaki); 4. Limacher (Yamaha); 5. M. Weibel (Yamaha); 6. Reynaud (Husqvarna); 7. Felder (Yamaha); 8. Loretter (KTM); 9. Ehrenzeller (KTM); 10. Jetzer (KTM).

August 3 - Lignières
Race I: 1. Tellenbach (KTM); 2. Jetzer (KTM); 3. Inderbitzin (Kawasaki); 4. Ehrenzeller (KTM); 5. Britschgi (Yamaha); 6. M. Weibel (Yamaha); 7. Loretter (KTM); 8. Felder (Yamaha); 9. Reynaud (Husqvarna); 10. Walder (KTM).
Race II: 1. Tellenbach (KTM); 2. Inderbitzin (Kawasaki); 3. Ehrenzeller (KTM); 4. Jetzer (KTM); 5. Felder (Yamaha); 6. Reynaud (Husqvarna); 7. M. Weibel (Yamaha); 8. Loretter (KTM); 9. Limacher (Yamaha); 10. Walder (KTM).

August 31- Sierre
Race I: 1. Tellenbach (KTM); 2. Inderbitzin (Kawasaki); 3. Ehrenzeller (KTM); 4. Joannidis (D, BMW); 5. Loretter (KTM); 6. M. Weibel (Yamaha); 7. Reynaud (Husqvarna); 8. Limacher (Yamaha); 9. Felder (Yamaha); 10. Jetzer (KTM).
Race II: 1. Tellenbach (KTM); 2. Inderbitzin (Kawasaki); 3. Joannidis (D, BMW); 4. Ehrenzeller (KTM); 5. Jetzer (KTM); 6. M. Weibel (Yamaha); 7. Felder (Yamaha); 8. Loretter (KTM); 9. Lienhard (KTM); 10. Tribelhorn (Honda).

October 5 - Frauenfeld
Race I: 1. Tellenbach (KTM); 2. Loretter (KTM); 3. Inderbitzin (Kawasaki); 4. Ehrenzeller (KTM); 5. Limacher (Yamaha); 6. M. Weibel (Yamaha); 7. Reynaud (Husqvarna); 8. Felder (Yamaha); 9. Tribelhorn (Honda); 10. Dörig (Honda).
Race II: 1. Tellenbach (KTM); 2. Felder (Yamaha); 3. Ehrenzeller (KTM); 4. Loretter (KTM); 5. Jetzer (KTM); 6. Reynaud (Husqvarna); 7. Dörig (Honda); 8. M. Weibel (Yamaha); 9. Tribelhorn (Honda); 10. Banzer (KTM).

FINAL CLASSIFICATION
1. Fabian Tellenbach   KTM   297 points
2. Philipp Inderbitzin   Kawasaki   200
3. Roman Ehrenzeller   KTM   188
4. E. Felder (Yamaha), 183; 5. D. Loretter (KTM), 181; 6. M. Jetzer (KTM), 174; 7. M. Weibel (Yamaha), 171; 8. L. Reynaud (Husqvarna), 141; 9. P. Limacher (Yamaha), 120; 10. P. Jöri (Aprilia), 117. 28 finishers.

PROMO

June 1st - Hoch-Ybrig
Race I: 1. Delacombaz (Husqvarna); 2. Wyer (Husqvarna); 3. Kisseleff (KTM); 4. Weiss (KTM); 5. Y. Gyger (Honda); 6. Abt (Yamaha); 7. Voser (KTM); 8. Ecker (D, Suzuki); 9. Blöchlinger (KTM); 10. Wüthrich (Yamaha).
Race II: 1. Delacombaz (Husqvarna); 2. Abt (Yamaha); 3. Weiss (KTM); 4. Wyer (Husqvarna); 5. Y. Gyger (Honda); 6. Kisseleff (KTM); 7. Blöchlinger (KTM); 8. Kalbermatter (KTM); 9. Wüthrich (Yamaha); 10. Büess (Husqvarna).

June 22 - St. Stephan
Race I: 1. Kisseleff (KTM); 2. T. Fuhrer (KTM); 3. Weiss (KTM); 4. Delacombaz (Husqvarna); 5. Wyer (Husqvarna); 6. E. Lüthi (Husqvarna); 7. R. Büss (Husqvarna); 8. Wicki (Kawasaki); 9. Ecker (D, Suzuki); 10. Bowee (KTM).
Race II: 1. Kisseleff (KTM); 2. Abt (Yamaha); 3. M. Büss (Husqvarna); 4. T. Fuhrer (KTM); 5. Y. Gyger (Honda); 6. R. Büss (Husqvarna); 7. Weiss (KTM); 8. Wicki (Kawasaki); 9. Ruchti (Husqvarna); 10. Kalbermatter (KTM).

August 3 - Lignières
Race I: 1. Borgeaud (KTM); 2. Bosshard (Yamaha); 3. Wyer (Husqvarna); 4. Weiss (KTM); 5. Altherr (KTM); 6. Y. Gyger (Honda); 7. Büess (Husqvarna); 8. Orlandini (Husaberg); 9. Koch (Honda); 10. Loner (KTM).
Race II: 1. Bosshard (Yamaha); 2. Weiss (KTM); 3. Borgeaud (KTM); 4. Y. Gyger (Honda); 5. Wyer (Husqvarna); 6. Kisseleff (KTM); 7. Ecker (Suzuki); 8. Vinzens (KTM); 9. Altherr (KTM); 10. Büess (Husqvarna).

August 31 - Sierre
Race I: 1. Kisseleff (KTM); 2. Wicki (Kawasaki); 3. Y. Gyger (Honda); 4. Orlandini (Husaberg); 5. Wyer (Husqvarna); 6. Ecker (D, Suzuki); 7. Heinrich (KTM); 8. M. Büss (Husqvarna); 9. R. Büss

(Husqvarna); 10. Perrin (KTM).
Race II: 1. R. Bosshard (Yamaha); 2. Y. Gyger (Honda); 3. Kisseleff (KTM); 4. Wyer (Husqvarna); 5. R. Büss (Husqvarna); 6. Orlandini (Husaberg); 7. Kalbermatter (Honda); 8. Ecker (D, Suzuki); 9. Robbiani (Husqvarna); 10. Heinrich (KTM).

October 5 - Frauenfeld
Race I: 1. Y. Gyger (Honda); 2. Wyer (Husqvarna); 3. Kisseleff (KTM); 4. U. Herzog (KTM); 5. Ulmann (Honda); 6. R. Bosshard (Yamaha); 7. Orlandini (Husaberg); 8. Ecker (D, Suzuki); 9. Grisoni (Kawasaki); 10. Manser (KTM).
Race II: 1. U. Herzog (KTM); 2. Weiss (KTM); 3. M. Herzog (KTM); 4. Ulmann (Honda); 5. Y. Gyger (Honda); 6. R. Bosshard (Yamaha); 7. Kisseleff (KTM); 8. M. Büss (Husqvarna); 9. Orlandini (Husaberg); 10. Koch (Honda).

FINAL CLASSIFICATION
1. Yann Gyger   Honda   206 points
2. Fabian Wyer   Husqvarna   189
3. Roland Büss   Husqvarna   122
4. M. Büss (Husqvarna), 116; 5. M. Abt (Yamaha), 106; 6. O. Delacombaz (Husqvarna), 103; 7. M. Orlandini (Husaberg), 94; 8. C. Koch (Honda), 93; 9. M. Wicki (Kawasaki), 90; 10. C. Kalbermatter (KTM), 61. 24 finishers.

YOUNGSTER 85

June 1st - Hoch-Ybrig
Race I: 1. C. Rossi (Honda); 2. M. Linssen (A, Suzuki); 3. Zimmermann (KTM); 4. Hug (Suzuki); 5. Moll (D, Kawasaki); 6. Huthmacher (D, Honda). 6 finishers.
Race II: 1. Zimmermann (KTM); 2. M. Linssen (A, Suzuki); 3. C. Rossi (Honda); 4. Hug (Suzuki); 5. Moll (D, Kawasaki); 6. Huthmacher (D, Honda). 6 finishers.

June 22 - St. Stephan
Race I: 1. Freidinger (KTM); 2. Raffin (Suzuki); 3. Zimmermann (KTM); 4. C. Rossi (Honda); 5. Hug (Suzuki); 6. Mollet (KTM); 7. Moll (D, Kawasaki); 8. M. Linssen (A, Suzuki). 9 finishers.
Race II: Annulée.

August 3 - Lignières
Race I: 1. Freidinger (KTM); 2. Raffin (Suzuki); 3. C. Rossi (Honda); 4. M. Linssen (A, Suzuki); 5. Zimmermann (KTM); 6. Hug (Suzuki); 7. Moll (D, Kawasaki). 7 finishers.
Race II: 1. Raffin (Suzuki); 2. Freidinger (KTM); 3. Zimmermann (KTM); 4. C. Rossi (Honda); 5. Hug (Suzuki); 6. Moll (D, Kawasaki); 7. M. Linssen (A, Suzuki). 7 finishers.

August 31 - Sierre
Race I: 1. Raffin (Suzuki); 2. Freidinger (KTM); 3. Zimmermann (KTM); 4. M. Linssen (A, Suzuki); 5. C. Rossi (Honda); 6. Hug (Suzuki); 7. Mollet (KTM). 7 finishers.
Race II: 1. Raffin (Suzuki); 2. Freidinger (KTM); 3. M. Linssen (A, Suzuki); 4. Zimmermann (KTM); 5. C. Rossi (Honda); 6. Hug (Suzuki); 7. Mollet (KTM). 7 finishers.

October 5 - Frauenfeld
Race I: 1. Raffin (Suzuki); 2. C. Rossi (Honda); 3. M. Linssen (A, Suzuki); 4. Zimmermann (KTM); 5. Hug (Suzuki); 6. Mollet (KTM); 7. Moll (D, Kawasaki). 7 finishers.
Race II: 1. Raffin (Suzuki); 2. M. Linssen (A, Suzuki); 3. Zimmermann (KTM); 4. C. Rossi (Honda); 5. Hug (Suzuki); 6. Moll (D, Kawasaki); 7. Mollet (KTM). 7 finishers.

FINAL CLASSIFICATION
1. Jesko Raffin   Suzuki   219 points
2. Markus Linssen (A)   Suzuki   205
3. Nicolai Hug   Suzuki   187
4. Y. Zimmermann (KTM), 177; 5. C. Rossi (Honda), 173; 6. P. Moll (D, Kawasaki), 135; 7. O. Mollet (KTM), 103; 8. L. Huthmacher (D, Honda), 72. 8 finishers.

YOUNGSTER 125-250

June 1st - Hoch-Ybrig
Race I: 1. K. Würterle (D, KTM); 2. Martignoni (Husqvarna); 3. Egger (Kawasaki); 4. Götzl (Kawasaki); 5. Peter (Kawasaki); 6. Kunz (Husqvarna); 7. Lindegger (Yamaha); 8. Stocker (Yamaha); 9. Übigau (KTM); 10. J. Würterle (D, KTM).
Race II: 1. K. Würterle (D, KTM); 2. Martignoni (Husqvarna); 3. Götzl (Kawasaki); 4. Egger (Kawasaki); 5. Kunz (Husqvarna); 6. Peter (Kawasaki); 7. Lindegger (Yamaha); 8. Baumgartner (KTM); 9. M.-R. Schmidt (Suzuki); 10. Portmann (Suzuki).

June 22 - St. Stephan
Race I: 1. Gosso (Yamaha); 2. Martignoni (Husqvarna); 3. Götzl (Kawasaki); 4. M.-R. Schmidt (Suzuki); 5. Egger (Kawasaki); 6. Zwisler (D, Kawasaki); 7. Portmann (Suzuki); 8. Gloggner (Yamaha); 9. Kunz (Husqvarna); 10. Baumgartner (KTM).
Race II: Annulée.

August 3 - Lignières
Race I: 1. Götzl (Kawasaki); 2. Martignoni (Husqvarna); 3. M.-R. Schmidt (Suzuki); 4. Kunz (Husqvarna); 5. Gosso (Yamaha); 6. Lindegger (Yamaha); 7. Stocker (Yamaha); 8. F. Chesaux (Yamaha); 9. Meier (KTM); 10. Portmann (Suzuki).
Race II: 1. M.-R. Schmidt (Suzuki); 2. Martignoni (Husqvarna); 3. Gosso (Yamaha); 4. Lindegger (Yamaha); 5. Stocker (Yamaha); 6. Kunz (Husqvarna); 7. Götzl (Kawasaki); 8. F. Chesaux (Yamaha); 9. Portmann (Suzuki); 10. Baumgartner (KTM).

August 31 - Sierre
Race I: 1. M.-R. Schmidt (Suzuki); 2. Martignoni (Husqvarna); 3. Kunz (Husqvarna); 4. Baumgartner (KTM); 5. Gosso (Yamaha); 6. Peter (Kawasaki); 7. Stocker (Yamaha); 8. Lindegger (Yamaha); 9. F. Chesaux (Yamaha); 10. A. Linssen (A, Suzuki).
Race II: 1. Götzl (Kawasaki); 2. Kunz (Husqvarna); 3. Gosso (Yamaha); 4. Baumgartner (KTM); 5. Portmann (Suzuki); 6. Martignoni (Husqvarna); 7. F. Chesaux (Yamaha); 8. Stocker (Yamaha); 9. M.-R. Schmidt (Suzuki); 10. A. Linssen (A, Suzuki).

October 5 - Frauenfeld
Race I: 1. Martignoni (Husqvarna); 2. M.-R. Schmidt (Suzuki); 3. Portmann (Suzuki); 4. Kunz (Husqvarna); 5. Baumgartner (KTM); 6. Stocker (Yamaha); 7. F. Chesaux (Yamaha); 8. Götzl (Kawasaki); 9. Gosso (Yamaha); 10. A. Linssen (A, Suzuki).
Race II: 1. Martignoni (Husqvarna); 2. Gosso (Yamaha); 3. Kunz (Husqvarna); 4. M.-R. Schmidt (Suzuki); 5. Lindegger (Yamaha); 6. Portmann (Suzuki); 7. Stocker (Yamaha); 8. Baumgartner (KTM); 9. Götzl (Kawasaki); 10. F. Chesaux (Yamaha).

FINAL CLASSIFICATION
1. Jonatan Martignoni   Husqvarna   247 points
2. Randy Götzl   Kawasaki   187
3. Simon Gosso   Yamaha   184
4. M.-R. Schmidt (Suzuki), 182; 5. M. Baumgartner (KTM), 158; 6. M. Kunz (Husqvarna), 156; 7. Y. Lindegger (Yamaha), 143; 8. K. Portmann (Suzuki), 134; 9. P. Stocker (Yamaha), 125; 10. F. Chesaux (Yamaha), 112. 27 finishers.

QUAD OPEN

June 1st- Hoch-Ybrig

Race I: 1. Lundbäck (S, KTM); 2. Wolber (D, KTM); 3. Farkas (H, KTM); 4. Herren (KTM); 5. Engel (KTM); 6. Helmer (S, KTM); 7. Gfeller (Vertemati); 8. U. Müller (Husqvarna); 9. Heidenreich (HPS); 10. R. Cuche (Kawasaki).
Race II: 1. Wolber (D, KTM); 2. Lundbäck (S, KTM); 3. Herren (KTM); 4. Farkas (H, KTM); 5. U. Müller (Husqvarna); 6. Helmer (S, KTM); 7. Engel (KTM); 8. Heidenreich (HPS); 9. Gfeller (Vertemati). 9 finishers.

June 22 - St. Stephan

Race I: 1. Bühler (RST); 2. Heidenreich (HPS); 3. Wolber (D, KTM); 4. Schwendimann (Vertemati); 5. Engel (KTM); 6. Herren (KTM); 7. U. Müller (Husqvarna); 8. Gfeller (Vertemati); 9. F. Zbaeren (ATV); 10. R. Zbaeren (ATV).
Race II: 1. Bühler (RST); 2. Schwendimann (Vertemati); 3. Wolber (D, KTM); 4. U. Müller (Husqvarna); 5. Engel (KTM); 6. Heidenreich (HPS); 7. Herren (KTM); 8. Gfeller (Vertemati); 9. F. Zbaeren (ATV); 10. R. Zbaeren (ATV).

August 3 - Lignières

Race I: 1. Donelly (IRL, KTM); 2. Sobczyk (POL, Aprilia); 3. Lundbäck (S, KTM); 4. Schwendimann (Vertemati); 5. Wolber (D, KTM); 6. Bühler (RST); 7. Herren (KTM); 8. Heidenreich (HPS); 9. Farkas (H, KTM); 10. Mc Dermott (IRL, Banshee).
Race II: 1. Donelly (IRL, KTM); 2. Sobczyk (POL, Aprilia); 3. Schwendimann (Vertemati); 4. Wolber (D, KTM); 5. Heidenreich (HPS); 6. Herren (KTM); 7. Mc Dermott (IRL, Banshee); 8. Lundbäck (S, KTM); 9. Zeller (Vertemati); 10. U. Müller (Husqvarna).

October 5 - Frauenfeld

Race I: 1. Wolber (D, KTM); 2. Schwendimann (Vertemati); 3. Sobczyk (POL, Aprilia); 4. Herren (KTM); 5. Engel (KTM); 6. Büchler (KTM); 7. U. Müller (Husqvarna); 8. Gfeller (Vertemati); 9. Marolf (Kawasaki); 10. Heidenreich (HPS).
Race II: 1. Sobczyk (POL, Aprilia); 2. Wolber (D, KTM); 3. Schwendimann (Vertemati); 4. Herren (KTM); 5. Heidenreich (HPS); 6. Engel (KTM); 7. Büchler (KTM); 8. Gfeller (Vertemati); 9. Marolf (Kawasaki); 10. U. Müller (Husqvarna).

FINAL CLASSIFICATION

1. Matthias Heidenreich	HPS	213 points
2. Hans-Rudolf Herren	KTM	212
3. Alfred Wolber (D)	KTM	209

4. J. Engel (KTM), 165; 5. U. Müller (Husqvarna), 160; 6. R. Schwendimann (Vertemati), 157; 7. D. Gfeller (Vertemati), 139; 8. N. Lundbäck (S, KTM), 114; 9. P. Sobczyk (POL, Aprilia), 100; 10. B. Zeller (Vertemati), 93. 18 finishers.

QUAD 450

1er June - Hoch-Ybrig

Race I: 1. C. Cuche (Vertemati); 2. Betschart (Yamaha); 3. Traber (Yamaha); 4. Kälin (KTM); 5. Dietiker (Yamaha); 6. Kanberg (S, Suzuki); 7. Ceccon (Yamaha); 8. Hofmann (S, HPS). 8 finishers.
Race II: 1. C. Cuche (Vertemati); 2. Hofmann (S, HPS); 3. Betschart (Yamaha); 4. Traber (Yamaha); 5. Kälin (KTM); 6. Dietiker (Yamaha); 7. Kanberg (S, Suzuki); 8. Ceccon (Yamaha). 8 finishers.

22 June - St. Stephan

Race I: 1. C. Cuche (Vertemati); 2. Hofmann (S, HPS); 3. Betschart (Yamaha); 4. Traber (Yamaha); 5. Dietiker (Yamaha); 6. Blanc (F, Vertemati); 7. Ceccon (Yamaha); 8. Laverrière (F, Suzuki). 8 finishers.
Race II: 1. C. Cuche (Vertemati); 2. Hofmann (S, HPS); 3. Betschart (Yamaha); 4. Traber (Yamaha); 5. Blanc (F, Vertemati); 6. Dietiker (Yamaha); 7. Laverrière (F, Suzuki); 8. Ceccon (Yamaha). 8 finishers.

3 August - Lignières

Race I: 1. Cicelet (F, Suzuki); 2. Hofmann (S, HPS); 3. Morin (F, Suzuki); 4. Vanpevenaege (B, Yamaha); 5. Betschart (Yamaha); 6. Traber (Yamaha); 7. Abfalter (F, Suzuki); 8. Schifferle (KTM); 9. Cornier (F, Suzuki); 10. Mazeron (F, Yamaha).
Race II: 1. Cicelet (F, Suzuki); 2. Morin (F, Suzuki); 3. C. Cuche (Vertemati); 4. Hofmann (S, HPS); 5. Cornier (F, Suzuki); 6. Vanpevenaege (B, Yamaha); 7. Betschart (Yamaha); 8. Traber (Yamaha); 9. Kälin (KTM); 10. Jacob (F, Yamaha).

5 October- Frauenfeld

Race I: 1. Betschart (Yamaha); 2. C. Cuche (Vertemati); 3. Sum (D, Yamaha); 4. Traber (Yamaha); 5. Blanc (F, Vertemati); 6. Laverrière (F, Suzuki); 7. Schifferle (KTM); 8. Ceccon (Yamaha); 9. Bürgler (BRP); 10. Zinczuk (POL, Yamaha).

FINAL CLASSIFICATION

1. Christophe Cuche	Vertemati	254 points
2. Adam Hofmann (S)	HPS	240
3. Nino Betschart	Yamaha	238

4. H. Traber (Yamaha), 195; 5. I. Dietiker (Yamaha), 137; 6. P. Ceccon (Yamaha), 132; 7. M. Blanc (F, Vertemati), 118; 8. L. Laverrière (F, Suzuki), 88; 9. Y. Cicelet (F, Suzuki), 50; 10. S. Morin (F, Suzuki), 42. 26 finishers.